The Neuroscience of The Shadow

Mapping the Obscure Psyche

Josiah Cornell

Copyright © 2025 Josiah Cornell
All rights reserved.

No part of this publication may be reproduced, distributed, or transmitted in any form or by any means, including photocopying, recording, or other electronic or mechanical methods, without the prior written permission of the author, except in the case of brief quotations used in reviews or scholarly analysis.

ISBN: 9798901486672

This book is intended for educational and informational purposes only. It is not a substitute for professional mental-health or medical advice. The author and publisher assume no responsibility for any actions taken based on the contents of this book.

Contents

The Architecture of You: A Guided Tour Through Your Brain	14
The Vault of the Disowned: Amygdala and Emotional Memory	38
The Chemical Orchestra: Neurotransmitters of the Dark	54
The Inner Critic and Self-Punisher	69
The Myth of Free Will: The Obscure Psyche's Control	84
Childhoods Blueprint: The Brain of the Wounded Child	96
The Echo of Trauma: When the Past Becomes the Present	112
The Shadow and the Fix: The Neuroscience of Substance Misuse	125
The Slip of the Tongue & The Faulty Action: Projection	144
The Shadow of Love: Attraction, Addiction and Attachment	163
The Trap of Success: The Biology of Self-Sabotage	177
The Dark Triad & The Social Shadow	193
The Body Knows: Somatic Practices and Stored Emotions	210
The Shadow of Health: The Placebo/Nocebo Effect	228
The Three Faces of Suffering: Brain, Mind, and Meaning	246
The Physiology of Forgiveness and Release	262
Rewiring the Complex: The Neuroscience of Integration	275
The Alchemy of Attention: Shadow Work in Action	292
The Inner Cinema: Dream Work and Active Imagination	311
Collective Shadows of the Future: Mortality and Wholeness	328
Wholeness: Becoming Fully Human	344
The Golden Shadow	363
The Secret Rooms of the Mind	382
Glossary	409
References	416
About the Author	420
Also By	422

Introduction

I want you to look up from the pages of this book for a moment, wherever you are. You may be on public transport, in a waiting room, or sitting at home looking at your other half. Take a good look at the people around you, really look at them. That person scrolling through their phone with furrowed brows, the one tapping their foot impatiently, the couple having a quiet conversation in the corner. Every single one of them is walking around with an entire universe inside their skull, a three-pound organ firing off electrical signals at lightning speed, processing thousands of thoughts they're barely aware of, making split-second decisions about where to look, what to say, whether to smile or stay silent. They're all going about their business, moving through the world with their own rhythms and patterns, each one convinced they're the main character in their own story, the conscious director of their own lives. But here's what's extraordinary, what's humbling really: despite all our differences, despite our unique histories and personal neuroses and the specific ways our mothers wounded us or our fathers disappointed us, we all share one fundamental thing in common. Every single human being you're looking at right now, including yourself, is operating on the same basic principle. We're all running on roughly five percent conscious awareness while ninety-five percent of what's actually driving us, the real machinery of thought, emotion, memory, and behaviour, is happening completely beneath the surface, in territories we can't access and don't even know exist. That stranger across from you who seems so different, so unknowable? They're just as much a stranger to themselves as you are to yourself. We're all walking around as mysteries, not just to each other, but to ourselves, and that's where our shared humanity truly begins.

In this book, I'm going to explain how we all work, from childhood up to adulthood, what makes us human and how we process things in our brains. We'll explore how trauma physically rewires the developing brain, altering the structure and function of regions responsible for emotion regulation, memory, and decision-making, leaving lasting effects that can limit our abilities throughout life.

Childhood trauma disrupts key brain networks responsible for emotional regulation and stress response, leading to difficulties that persist into adulthood. We'll look at how substance misuse works, like removing a mask, breaking down inhibitions and revealing parts of ourselves we usually keep hidden, as drugs and alcohol impair the brain's ability to control impulses and regulate behaviour. Those struggling with addiction often wear metaphorical masks to hide their vulnerability and shame, portraying a façade of functionality whilst the true self remains buried beneath layers of denial. And perhaps most surprisingly, we'll examine how we sabotage ourselves through unconscious patterns formed early in life, behaviours that once protected us but now keep us stuck, preventing us from becoming who we're truly capable of being. These patterns aren't conscious choices; they're adaptations that once saved our psychological health but now masquerade as obstacles blocking our path forward, keeping us strangers to our own potential, trapped in cycles we don't understand but somehow can't escape.

Have you ever found yourself in a situation where you blurt out something and immediately regret it, *wondering who even said that?*

You're mid argument with someone you actually care about, and suddenly you're firing off lines like you've been rehearsing those surgical digs. Precision strikes. You watch their face change, and even as you're speaking, you think, *This isn't me. I wouldn't do this.*

Except you did.

And the worst part is you knew exactly where to hit.

Then comes the crash. The guilt. The hangover of your own behaviour. That sick heavy feeling in your chest where your conscience pipes up like, "Mate... what was THAT?" But in the moment, something else was driving. Something you don't recognise. Something that clearly knows you better than you know yourself.

Sometimes it is not even an argument. It is 3 am, and you are doom scrolling like a zombie. Instagram. TikTok. Facebook. Back to Instagram. You do not care about any of it. Half of you is begging to sleep. The other half is acting like it is possessed. And you are thinking, "Why can't I stop? What is wrong with me?"

Or it is bigger. You sabotage a relationship that was actually going fine. You miss a deadline you have been building toward for months. You say yes when every cell in your body means to say no. Then you spend weeks resenting the entire thing.

That is not random chaos.

That is the part of you that lives underneath the part you think is you.

The bit you do not see, but you feel the consequences of.

The Obscure Psyche.

Here is the part no one likes hearing. You are only consciously aware of around five percent of what your mind is doing. Five. The other ninety five percent is running the show while your ego sits in the front seat pretending to steer like a toddler with a plastic steering wheel. For instance, have you ever found yourself reacting to a situation in a way that surprised you? That's your subconscious mind at work.

You act first.

Then you explain it.

Then you believe your own explanation because it makes you feel sane.

But most of the time, your explanation is a story you have made up to protect your image of yourself. Not maliciously. Just how the system works. Your conscious mind only sees the tip of the iceberg and assumes it is the whole thing.

It is like living with a roommate you have never met. Something moves in the kitchen. Something breaks in the bathroom. Food goes missing. The heating is on. The heating is off. You have never seen their face, but you know someone else is there. That is your mind. You share the same space with someone you have never actually spoken to. And it is running your life.

Your ego, the you you think you are, likes to keep things tidy. It filters out anything that does not match the version of yourself you want to believe in. If you think you are kind, you ignore the moments you are cruel. If you think you are logical, you pretend your emotional decisions were strategic. If you feel you are independent, you look everywhere except at your need for validation. The ego is not evil. It is just doing its job. It keeps a stable story going, so you do not feel like you are constantly falling apart. But the more it suppresses, the more the shadow grows. The more that 95% gets stuffed into the basement, the more power it has over your behaviour.

The ego is not evil. It is just doing its job. It keeps a stable story going, so you do not feel like you are constantly falling apart. But the more it suppresses, the more the shadow grows. The more that 95% gets stuffed into the basement, the more power it has over your behaviour.

Take a time you snapped over something tiny. Your partner's tone. A comment at work. Someone is not texting back fast enough. Your conscious mind rushed in with "They are being unreasonable. I am right to be annoyed." But the intensity, the emotional explosion, that was not about the situation at all. That was old shame. Old fear. Old rejection. The stuff you never asked for but still carry.

And because you do not see it, you blame the present instead of the past. So the pattern continues. You argue about the wrong thing with the wrong person for the wrong reason. Then you wonder why nothing changes.

You do this in dating. You do this at work. You do this with your fears, your habits, your temptations, your self-destruction. You think you are choosing consciously, but your brain is running on ancient wiring built long before you had adult logic.

You want love, but you chase what is familiar.

You want peace, but you repeat chaos.

You want growth, but you sabotage the very thing that would give it to you.

Your shadow, your Obscure Psyche, is not the villain. It is the collection of everything you have disowned because it did not match your self-image. The traits, the desires, the impulses, the memories, the wounds you pretend are not there. They do not disappear. They operate in the dark, shaping everything you do while you walk around, telling yourself you are making choices.

And here is the kicker. The more defensive you get when someone calls you out, the closer they are to naming your shadow. That is why criticism feels like a knife. They are poking a bruise you do not want to admit you have.

This work is uncomfortable. It has to be. Meeting the parts of yourself you have spent years avoiding will never feel like a lazy Sunday. But the alternative is worse. Living confused. Repeating patterns. Calling it bad luck or bad timing when really it is just unexamined wiring controlling you from behind the curtain.

This book is an introduction to the 95% of you who have never had a proper conversation with. The stranger inside. The part of you that has been making decisions while the ego waves its five percent, as if it were in control.

The goal is not to kill the ego or become some enlightened monk floating above your feelings. That is nonsense. The goal is simple. Close the gap between who you think you are and who you actually are. See your patterns instead of sleepwalking through them. Stop fighting yourself without realising it is yourself you are fighting.

Welcome to Neuroscience of the Shadow.

Your shadow is not your enemy.

It is the part of you you have ignored the longest.

It has been waiting.

Time to say hello.

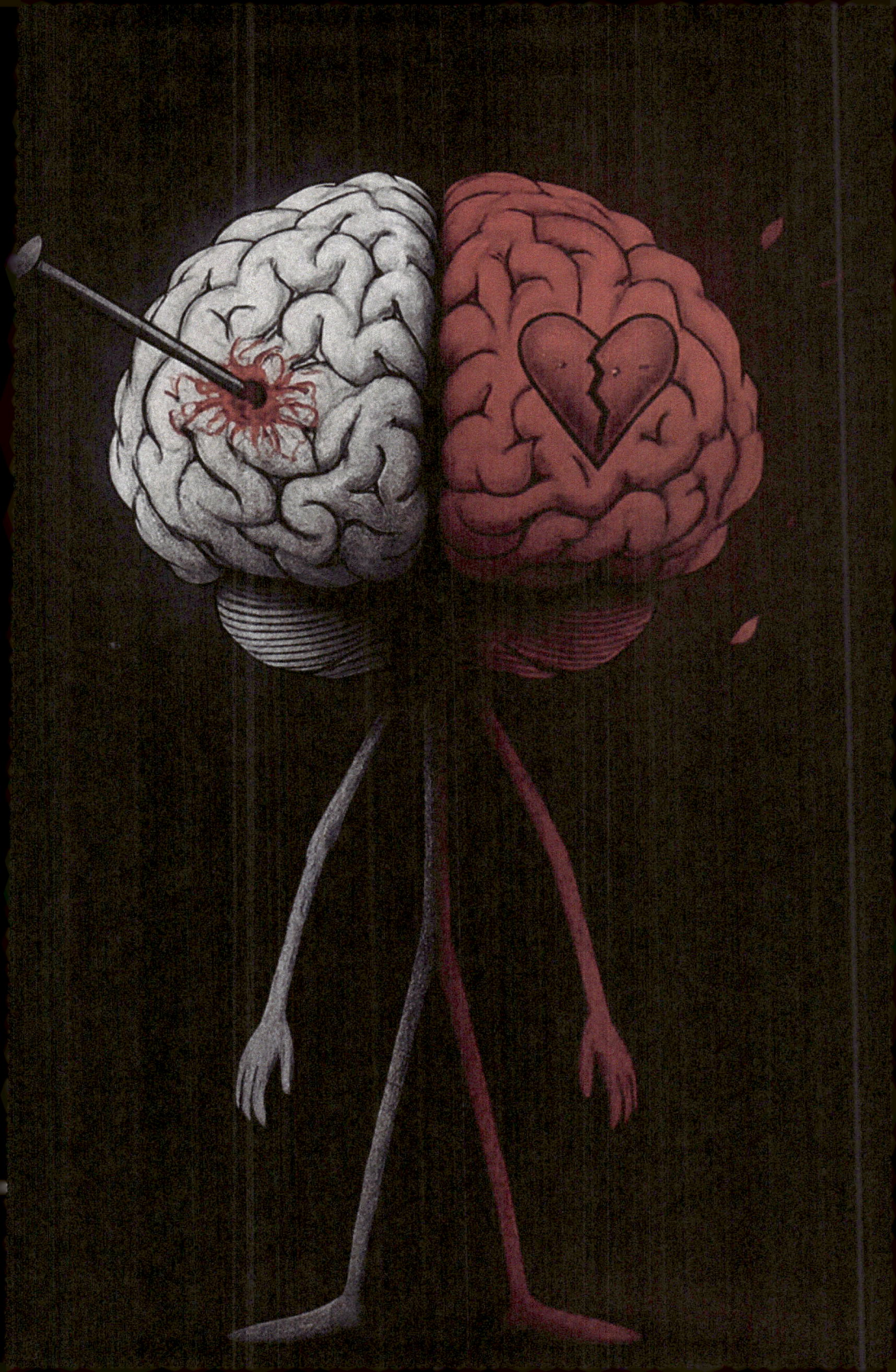

Chapter 1

The Architecture of You: A Guided Tour Through Your Brain

Before we dive deeper into the complex realms of the Obscure Psyche and explore how you may be a stranger to yourself, I need to discuss the physical structure where all of this occurs. It's essential to understand this: everything you've ever thought, every emotion you've felt, every memory you've stored, every decision you've made, and every sensation you've experienced is all happening in roughly three pounds of tissue located inside your skull. That's it. That's the entire operation.

I want you to consider this fact. It's both the most obvious concept in the world and something we tend to ignore for most of our lives. Now, let's explore the potential of your brain. Visualise this: within your skull, there's a wrinkled mass of tissue that has the consistency of firm jelly and resembles a walnut that has seen better days. This organ, your brain, is not a static entity. It has the remarkable ability to grow, change, and adapt. If you came across it lying on a table, you might be a bit put off, maybe even repulsed. But when you think about it, it's not exactly poetic, it's a symbol of hope and potential.

Yet, here's what never ceases to amaze me: this seemingly unimpressive blob is responsible for everything you're experiencing now. Every word you're reading in this chapter, every thought you're having, every emotion you're feeling, and every memory that suddenly comes to mind: your brain is not just a thinking machine, but also a master regulator, managing your heart rate, controlling your breathing, regulating your temperature, processing the visual information that allows you to read these words, and maintaining your balance in your chair all while you consciously focus on understanding what I'm saying. You are typically unaware of ninety-nine percent of what it's doing.

Consider the last time you completely lost your temper over something trivial, perhaps someone cut you off in traffic, your internet connection dropped just when you needed it, you were typing and suddenly you lost the whole lot because you forgot to press save, or someone said something that pushed you over the edge.

In that moment, you weren't thinking rationally; you weren't weighing consequences or considering alternative perspectives. You were consumed by pure fury, ready to fight, completely overwhelmed by emotion. Then afterwards, once you'd calmed down, you might have thought, "I don't know what came over me. That wasn't like me. I'm usually more controlled than that."

What actually happened wasn't some mysterious force taking over you. Instead, specific structures in your brain that handle threat detection and emotional response activated faster than the parts responsible for rational thought and impulse control could intervene. Your brain reacted to a perceived threat before it had time to assess whether that threat was serious, whether your response was appropriate, or if there were better ways to handle the situation. Different areas of your brain function at various speeds, and in that instance, the fast-acting emotional part triumphed before the slower, rational part could catch up.

This isn't a personal failing. It's not about you being hot-tempered or lacking self-control. This is related to the architecture of your brain and how different regions process information at varying speeds. The structures that evolved to keep you alive in immediate physical danger, running from predators or fighting rivals, are still active. They respond before the newer structures, which support nuanced reasoning and impulse control, can fully engage. Your brain is composed of multiple systems that don't always agree with one another. They process information differently and can pull you in contradictory directions while you experience it all as just being you having feelings and making choices.

We often think of the brain as a unified entity, a single organ with one purpose. However, this is not entirely accurate. Your brain is more like a team of specialists, each with its own area of expertise and distinct way of functioning. Imagine it as a bustling city, where each district has its own character and responsibilities. A fitting analogy might be Pixar's "Inside Out." Remember young Riley with her emotions, Joy, Sadness, Fear, Anger, and Disgust, all operating a control panel in her mind? Your brain isn't managed by tiny people at a control panel. Still, the film captures an essential truth about how different systems in your brain advocate for various behaviours, sometimes cooperating, often conflicting, and always influencing your next actions.

The wrinkled outer layer you would see if you could peek inside your skull is called the cerebral cortex, which is divided into four main sections known as lobes.

Each lobe has specialised functions and particular responsibilities, yet they are all interconnected and constantly communicate with one another. The frontal lobes act like a city hall, overseeing executive functions. The parietal lobes function as the sensory integration centre, managing all the information coming from your body. The occipital lobes serve as the visual processing district, making sense of everything your eyes take in. The temporal lobes handle sound and language but also contain structures critical to understanding your mind, which we will explore in detail.

Let's start with the frontal lobes, located right behind your forehead and extending back roughly to the middle of your skull. These are the largest of the four lobes, responsible for what we call executive functions: planning, decision-making, impulse control, personality, and social behaviour. This part of your brain is the management level, designed to run the show, make thoughtful decisions, and consider consequences before acting. The prefrontal cortex, the very front portion of these lobes, acts like the chief executive, trying to keep everything organised, make plans, and ensure you behave in socially appropriate ways rather than simply acting on every impulse that comes to mind.

Think of the frontal lobes as the traffic lights of your brain. They prevent you from voicing every thought that crosses your mind, much like a spam filter stops unwanted messages in your email. They stop you from acting on impulses such as hitting someone who annoys you, eating an entire cake despite knowing you'll regret it, or telling your boss exactly what you think of them and I think we have all been there at some point in our lives. They help you plan for tomorrow instead of just living in the moment, similar to how a calendar allows you to organise future events. Essentially, they serve as the adult supervision of your brain, ensuring that your actions are thoughtful and appropriate rather than merely reactive and impulsive.

There's compelling evidence of how essential the frontal lobes are for social functioning, particularly in the effects of damage to this part of the brain. Individuals who experience strokes, or injuries affecting their frontal lobes can undergo significant personality changes. For instance, a person known for their impeccable manners and thoughtful consideration of others might suddenly become blunt and inappropriate. They might, without malice, comment at a family gathering, "God, you've gotten fat," simply because the filtering system, a mechanism in the brain that usually evaluates and dismisses such thoughts before they are spoken, has been impaired. The thoughts that the frontal lobe would normally filter out are now being expressed uncensored.

It's important to understand that while the frontal lobes are powerful when functioning correctly, they are also the most recent evolutionary development in our brain's structure. The prefrontal cortex, the last part of the brain to mature, doesn't fully develop until a person reaches their mid-twenties. This helps explain many of the decisions people make in their teens and early twenties. Unfortunately, these executive functions are also the most susceptible to disruption. When you're stressed, exhausted, hungry, overwhelmed, or emotionally charged, the functioning of your frontal lobes diminishes, robbing you of the very abilities that contribute to feeling like a rational, controlled, and thoughtful person.

Consider how different you feel when well-rested, calm, and well-fed, compared to when you've had only four hours of sleep, are facing a crisis, and haven't eaten properly all day. It's not just a feeling; your brain is literally operating differently. The frontal lobes require large amounts of glucose and oxygen to function correctly. When these resources are depleted or diverted to respond to immediate threats, your capacity for rational thought, impulse control, and consideration of long-term consequences suffers first. This explains why you might snap at a loved one when stressed, or reach for a bag of chips when anxious, even though you know you'll regret it later. Essentially, your frontal lobes have shut downs while other parts of your brain continue to function.

Within the frontal lobes lies the motor cortex, a strip that runs from the top of your head down toward your ears. This region controls voluntary movement and transmits signals to your muscles. An intriguing insight into brain priorities is that different body parts occupy vastly different amounts of space on the motor cortex, depending on the level of fine control they require. For example, your hands and face have large representations because they demand extraordinary precision, considering the delicate movements you can make with your fingers or the varied expressions you can create with your facial muscles. In contrast, your torso, which doesn't require the same level of precision, occupies relatively little space on the motor cortex, reflecting the brain's efficient allocation of resources.

If you were to draw a human figure proportionate to how much motor cortex is assigned to each body part, it would look bizarre: a tiny body with enormous hands, oversized lips, and a massive tongue. This distorted representation is known as a motor homunculus and highlights a crucial point: the brain does not distribute its resources evenly across the body. Instead, it allocates substantial processing power to functions that are vital for human survival and social interaction, such as manipulating objects with your hands, speaking and eating with your mouth, and expressing and interpreting emotions with your face. These capabilities have been key to human success, enabling us to create tools, communicate complex ideas, and navigate intricate social hierarchies.

Located just behind the frontal lobes and separated by the central sulcus, the parietal lobes at the top and back of the brain have a unique function. They are responsible for sensory integration, a crucial process that involves synthesising information from all your body's senses to create your experience of your body in space. At the front of the parietal lobe is the somatosensory cortex, which processes touch sensations. This area has a distorted representation similar to that of the motor cortex; larger regions are dedicated to your lips and fingertips, which are incredibly sensitive, while smaller areas are reserved for your back and torso, which require less detailed resolution.

This intricate system of sensory processing in the parietal lobes is a testament to the awe-inspiring complexity of the human brain. It explains why you can feel a single hair being touched on your fingertip but might not notice light pressure against your back until it's fairly forceful. Your brain allocates much more processing power to your fingertips because they need detailed sensory information for manipulating objects, reading textures, and constantly engaging in the fine-level touch exploration that humans do. Your back, on the other hand, doesn't receive as much attention because there wasn't much evolutionary advantage to having hyper-detailed sensory feedback from that area.

In addition to processing touch, the parietal lobes play a critical role in spatial awareness, helping you understand where your body is in relation to the objects around you and co-ordinating movement through space. Whenever you reach for a cup without looking, navigate through a crowded room without bumping into people, or catch an object thrown to you, your parietal lobes perform extraordinarily complex calculations about positions, distances, and trajectories. What's truly impressive is that these calculations happen so quickly and automatically that you don't even realise it's occurring. This process allows your brain to create a constantly updated map of your body in space, predicting where things are and how you need to move to interact with them.

When the parietal lobes, especially on the right side, are damaged, something unusual can occur: hemispatial neglect. This condition causes individuals to ignore one side of their world entirely, usually the left side, despite having perfectly functioning eyes. They may eat food only from the right side of their plate, leaving the left untouched, or shave only the right side of their face. When drawing a clock, they might squish all the numbers onto the right side. For them, the left side of space appears to have ceased to exist, not because they can't see it, but because their brain is not processing information from that side or incorporating it into their spatial awareness. This condition is both heart-breaking and fascinating, as it demonstrates how much your perception of reality, what you perceive as simply "what's there", depends on the proper functioning of specific brain structures. The world they experience is radically different from yours, not due to issues with their eyes, but because the brain regions responsible for integrating visual information into spatial awareness have been compromised.

At the very back of your skull are the occipital lobes. Although they are the smallest of the four lobes, they play a crucial role in visual processing. When light hits your retinas, the information is transmitted through your optic nerves to the occipital lobes, where it is decoded and transformed into the rich, detailed, colourful visual world you experience. However, many people don't realise that it's somewhat unsettling when you fully understand it. You are not seeing reality directly. Instead, you see an interpretation of electrical signals constructed by your occipital lobes, essentially a simulation created by your brain based on the incoming information.

Your brain does not function like a camera that passively records what is outside. It continuously predicts what should be there based on past experiences, fills gaps, makes educated guesses, and creates a coherent picture from incomplete information. Each of your eyes has a blind spot where the optic nerve connects to the retina, which means there are no photoreceptors in that area to transmit information from your visual field. However, you never notice these blind spots because your brain fills them in, using information from the surrounding area and the other eye to create a seamless visual experience. This means that your brain is constantly 'editing' your visual field, filling in the gaps where your eyes cannot see, and creating a complete picture of the world around you.

The brain's visual perception is a masterful fiction, a best-guess reconstruction that it constantly creates. It does such an efficient job that you are usually unaware of the process. Different regions within the occipital lobes specialise in processing specific aspects of vision. Some neurons respond to horizontal lines, others to vertical lines, and still others to diagonal lines. Certain areas are dedicated to processing colour, while others focus on motion and faces. This specialised processing is then seamlessly integrated to create your unified visual experience, a truly impressive feat.

For instance, someone might lose the ability to perceive colour while everything else remains normal; they can still see shapes, movement, and faces, but the world around them appears in shades of grey. Alternatively, another person might lose the ability to perceive motion; moving objects seem like a series of static images, reminiscent of a slideshow rather than a continuous movement. This makes tasks, such as pouring a cup of tea, nearly impossible because they cannot see the liquid moving and track where it is; all they can see are still images frozen in different positions. Other deficits could include the inability to recognise shapes, leading to a condition known as visual agnosia, or the inability to recognise objects, known as object agnosia.

Some individuals even lose the specific ability to recognise faces while their other visual abilities remain intact. They can describe a face in detail, "This person has blue eyes, a straight nose, and is smiling", but they cannot recognise whose face it is, even if it is their spouses or their own reflection in a mirror. This condition, known as prosopagnosia, demonstrates that face recognition is not merely a general visual processing function; instead, it is a specific task handled by dedicated neural mechanisms that can be selectively impaired.

From an evolutionary perspective, this specialisation makes sense, given that recognising individuals and reading facial expressions have been vital for human survival and social interaction. Thus, the brain has evolved specialised systems specifically for processing faces. When these systems are damaged, individuals may experience the bizarre reality of seeing perfectly well while being unable to recognise the people they love, relying instead on voice, clothing, or context for identification rather than their faces.

The temporal lobes are located on the sides of your brain, roughly where your temples are. They are responsible for auditory processing, making sense of sounds, especially speech, but they also play a crucial role in memory formation and emotional processing. This is particularly important for understanding the concept of the Obscure Psyche, a term we will use to refer to the complex interplay of emotions, memories, and motivations that shape our behaviour. Deep within the temporal lobes, at the centre of your brain, lie structures central to everything we will explore in this book: the limbic system.

With its evolutionarily ancient roots, the limbic system is a part of our brain that connects us to our distant ancestors. Fish have limbic structures, reptiles have them, and all mammals possess them. These circuits were essential for the survival of your ancestors long before the massive frontal lobes that allow for abstract reasoning and long-term planning evolved. This is where emotional processing occurs, memories acquire their emotional weight, the brain evaluates threats and opportunities, and urgent, compelling responses are generated. Understanding the limbic system is vital for grasping human behaviour because it is where motivation, emotion, and memory intersect, and where the Obscure Psyche does some of its most powerful work.

At the heart of the limbic system is the amygdala, a small almond-shaped structure that is not to be underestimated. Its name, derived from the Greek word for almond, reflects its crucial role in processing emotions, particularly fear, anxiety, and anger. The amygdala is your threat-detection system, constantly scanning for danger. It operates with remarkable speed, capable of processing potential threats in about twelve milliseconds faster than conscious awareness can occur, faster than rational thought can engage, and quicker than your frontal lobes can assess whether a perceived threat is serious.

This speed is the main reason this system evolved. If your ancestor on the savannah saw something snake-shaped in the grass, it was vital that they didn't waste time debating whether it was a snake or just a stick that resembled one. They needed to jump back immediately and ask questions later because the cost of a false positive jumping back from a stick is negligible compared to the cost of a false negative not reacting to an actual snake. Therefore, the amygdala evolved to be fast and sensitive, erring on the side of caution by flagging potential threats before you consciously recognise what you're seeing. Your frontal lobes, which are responsible for higher-order thinking and decision-making, would then assess the situation and determine the appropriate response.

Remember the movie Inside Out? Think about the character Fear, who is always on high alert and constantly worried about potential dangers, trying to keep Riley safe. That represents your amygdala. It continually scans, evaluates everything for threats, and is ready to sound the alarm at the slightest provocation. When Fear takes control of Riley's console, she is not thinking rationally about whether something is genuinely dangerous; she is experiencing the full force of the threat response that Fear has initiated, heart racing, palms sweating, and an overwhelming urge to avoid or escape. This is the amygdala activating before your frontal lobes can put things into perspective.

The amygdala directly connects to your autonomic nervous system, which controls all your automatic bodily functions. When it detects danger, it can trigger an instant fight-or-flight response: your heart rate increases, blood pressure rises, stress hormones flood your system, your muscles tense, your attention narrows to the threat, and blood flow shifts from your digestive system to your muscles. All of this happens before you consciously realise why you're afraid, before you have had time to think about whether the threat is real, and before your rational brain has even registered what is occurring.

There is a significant issue with having threat-detection systems that are both incredibly fast and highly sensitive: they do not distinguish between physical threats and psychological ones. Your amygdala activates just as strongly in response to criticism, social rejection, or fear of poor performance as it does when facing physical danger. In fact, social rejection triggers the amygdala as much as physical threats do. When someone harshly criticises you, humiliates you in public, or makes you feel excluded, your amygdala reacts as if you were being chased by a predator. This explains why emotional pain can feel like physical pain; your brain processes it through the same threat-detection system.

As a result, your body may respond to an email from your boss with the same level of physiological activation that is typically reserved for life-threatening situations. The amygdala detects threats, such as potential criticism, job loss, or social evaluation. It triggers a complete threat response before your frontal lobes can assess the situation. Your rational brain recognises that while these situations are unpleasant, they are not actually dangerous. However, by the time your logical reasoning catches up, your emotional brain has already taken over, leading to anxiety, shaking hands, and difficulty thinking clearly, all because an ancient threat-detection system designed for facing sabre-toothed tigers is reacting to a simple email.

Furthermore, the amygdala is key in creating vivid and long-lasting memories. It responds to immediate threats and assigns emotional significance to experiences, effectively tagging them with labels that say, 'This matters, remember this.' This is why memories tied to strong emotions such as shame, joy, love, or grief are often vivid and hard to forget. You might not recall what you had for lunch last Tuesday. Still, you'll remember significant life events in striking detail, because your amygdala has marked those memories as crucial for your future survival.

When a significant emotional event occurs, especially if it's threatening or painful, your amygdala encodes that experience, creating a lasting record that flags that situation as dangerous and that feeling as important. These emotional memories are incredibly powerful and persistent, designed to ensure your survival by helping you quickly learn what is harmful and remember it for future reference. For example, if you once ate something that made you violently ill, you need to remember that particular food is dangerous and avoid it in the future. Similarly, if you were attacked in a specific location, it's crucial to remember that place as a threat to be avoided. The amygdala can create these associations through just one exposure, which can remain for a lifetime.

The issue at hand is that emotional memories, created by your amygdala, differ from the explicit, narrative memories you can consciously recall. Emotional memories are more like sensations, bodily states, and automatic responses triggered when you encounter situations reminiscent of the original experience. Even if you don't consciously remember the specific event responsible for the emotional learning, your amygdala retains that memory. It will activate a complete emotional and physiological response whenever similar cues arise.

For example, someone who has been in a serious car accident may experience overwhelming panic attacks years later when driving past the intersection where it occurred. Logically, they know they are safe. They can tell themselves that the accident is in the past and nothing is threatening them now, but this reasoning has no effect. The amygdala has encoded that location as dangerous, and when they approach it, it signals "danger," flooding their system with stress hormones before their rational frontal lobes can intervene. The panic is not a conscious choice; instead, their amygdala is hijacking their nervous system based on an emotional memory that is not accessible to their conscious mind.

This is why you might feel overwhelming anxiety in certain situations without understanding why, why specific individuals may trigger you for reasons that remain unclear, or why you have intense reactions that seem to arise from nowhere. These feelings are not without origin; they stem from your amygdala, which has stored emotional associations throughout your life, especially from childhood, and activates those associations in response to cues in your current environment that match the original experience. Your conscious mind cannot access this process; you can't directly introspect on your amygdala's stored associations or observe when they're being triggered. Instead, you simply feel the emotional response and then create narratives to explain it based on your current situation, often missing the actual source entirely.

Situated right next to the amygdala is the hippocampus, which is shaped like a seahorse and whose name is derived from the Greek word for seahorse. These two structures function like dance partners, performing very different roles. While the amygdala serves as the emotional stamp that signifies "this matters," the hippocampus acts as the filing system that organises how and where those memories are stored. It also plays a role in forming emotional memories, particularly in the context of explicit memory. When an emotional event occurs, the hippocampus helps encode the details of the event, such as where it happened and what was happening at the time, contributing to the formation of a complete memory.

The hippocampus is crucial for forming new explicit memories that you can consciously access. When you learn someone's name, remember what happened yesterday, or store information about where you parked your car, your hippocampus encodes that information and files it for later retrieval.

Also the hippocampus is essential for episodic memories, specific events that occurred at particular times and places. These memories form the narrative memories that create your autobiographical history. These memories make up your life story, detailing experiences you can describe and events you can contextualise in time. They are akin to the memory orbs depicted in the film Inside Out, specific experiences and moments that can be recalled and replayed.

An intriguing fact about the hippocampus is that it is one of the few regions in the adult brain where new neurons are continuously generated throughout life. This process, known as neurogenesis, indicates that your brain is not fixed or static; it constantly creates new cells, particularly in this memory-forming structure. These new neurons play a role in memory formation and can be influenced by your experiences. For example, chronic stress tends to reduce neurogenesis in the hippocampus, while activities like exercise, learning new things, and living in enriched environments tend to increase it. In essence, your brain is being actively shaped by how you live, what you do, and the experiences you encounter, which can directly impact your memory formation and recall.

Understanding your obscure psyche involves grasping how childhood experiences, even those you don't consciously remember, can profoundly affect your adult behaviour. This is due to the different types of memories created by the hippocampus and the amygdala.

The hippocampus is responsible for forming contextual memories, which include details such as when the event happened, where you were, and what occurred before and after it. In contrast, the amygdala creates memories lacking this context; it focuses solely on the emotional significance of an experience and its bodily state. Importantly, the hippocampus doesn't fully develop until around three years of age, while the amygdala is functional from birth.

As a result, experiences from very early childhood, before the hippocampus matured enough to encode detailed narrative memories, can still be stored as potent emotional memories by the amygdala. Although not consciously remembered and lacking a narrative to explain them, these memories profoundly impact your emotional responses and relationship patterns. This is a powerful demonstration of how childhood experiences can significantly influence your adult behaviour.

When adult situations trigger these early amygdala-encoded associations, you may experience strong emotional reactions such as anxiety, fear, shame, or rage without understanding their origins. This happens because the hippocampus didn't encode those memories; thus, there's no narrative memory to access or a story to explain your feelings. This lack of narrative can lead to a sense of confusion as your conscious mind scrambles for explanations that often miss the real source of the feelings.

Stress can exacerbate these issues and significantly impact the hippocampus. Chronic stress from unresolved trauma or ongoing threats can shrink the hippocampus, impair neurogenesis, and damage memory formation and retrieval. This underlines the urgency of managing stress, as prolonged trauma often leads to memory issues, creating gaps in your autobiographical narrative while emotional memories in the amygdala remain intact.

This situation can be particularly challenging: you may have intense emotional reactions to situations that trigger old, amygdala-encoded associations without the hippocampus's narrative memories to provide context. This lack of context makes it difficult to recognise that these reactions stem from past experiences, not the present moment. As a result, you can feel overwhelmed by emotions that seem to arise from nowhere and don't match current circumstances, leading to a sense of confusion and distress as you struggle to explain your reactions.

The good news is that the hippocampus is remarkably resilient. It can recover through the growth of new neurons, a process known as neurogenesis, and the repair of its memory filing system. Although this process isn't quick or easy, it is possible. This resilience explains why therapy can be effective, why spending time in nature is beneficial, and why positive experiences are crucial for emotional healing. You're not just feeling better psychologically but also supporting neurogenesis in your hippocampus, creating the biological conditions that enhance memory formation and retrieval. This can fill in some gaps in your narrative while improving your capacity to contextualise the emotional memories stored in your amygdala.

All of these brain structures we've discussed, your frontal lobes, which handle executive control; your parietal lobes, which manage sensation and spatial processing; your occipital lobes, which create your visual world; your temporal lobes, which process sound and language; and your limbic system, which generates emotional responses and encodes memories, are supposed to work together. They coordinate, communicate, and create a unified experience that leads to coherent behaviour. For instance, when you're driving a car, your occipital lobes are processing the visual information of the road, your parietal lobes are managing the sensation of the steering wheel, and your frontal lobes are making executive decisions about when to turn or stop. However, they operate at different speeds and through various mechanisms, sometimes drawing different conclusions about what you should do.

This is where the metaphor from the movie "Inside Out" becomes particularly useful. Remember how Riley's emotions constantly compete for console control, pushing different buttons to create various responses? Your neurotransmitter systems, the chemicals that enable neurons to communicate with each other, are similarly in constant flux. They influence, compete, and cooperate to shape your moment-to-moment experiences. These chemicals form the language through which neurons communicate, and different neurotransmitters create profoundly different effects, much like the emotional characters in the film pressing distinct buttons.

A command centre also orchestrates much of this chemical release: the pituitary gland. This tiny structure, about the size of a pea, is located at the base of your brain and is often called the master gland due to its significant role in regulating various bodily functions. It releases hormones that control growth, reproduction, stress responses, and metabolism. Working closely with the hypothalamus, which is located just above it, they form what's known as the hypothalamic-pituitary axis, a central control system for maintaining balance and responding to challenges. The hypothalamus, a small but crucial part of the brain, plays a key role in this axis. It regulates body temperature, hunger, thirst, and other homeostatic systems and is also involved in controlling the pituitary gland. Think of the pituitary gland as headquarters or mission control, constantly monitoring what's happening in your body and brain, receiving signals about what's needed, and releasing chemical messengers to address those needs.

Let's delve into the fascinating world of dopamine, a neurotransmitter that plays a pivotal role in our anticipation and motivation. You might remember Joy from the movie Inside Out-she's the one who's always upbeat and ready for action. Much like Joy, dopamine is released when something positive happens, like achieving a goal, receiving a reward, or experiencing pleasure. But here's the twist: dopamine isn't the pleasure itself; it's the anticipation of pleasure. The 'more, please!' chemical drives us to pursue what we desire, making it a key player in our daily motivations.

Dopamine, a key player in our neurochemical system, travels along the mesolimbic system, often referred to as the reward pathway. This pathway, extending from deep brain structures to the prefrontal cortex, is where dopamine surges when we achieve something positive, receive recognition, or have a pleasurable experience. This surge creates a sense of satisfaction and motivation, highlighting the crucial role of dopamine in our reward system.

However, dopamine is complex, much like the character Joy in the film. Low levels of dopamine can lead to anhedonia, the inability to feel pleasure, which is common in depression. When this occurs, the world can seem dull and unrewarding, making it feel like nothing is worth doing. People with Parkinson's disease, characterised by the loss of dopamine-producing neurons, often experience low motivation and mood issues alongside their motor symptoms. On the other hand, excessive dopamine activity in specific pathways is linked to psychosis, which can result in hallucinations and delusions. This is why antipsychotic medications work by blocking dopamine receptors.

Drugs of abuse can hijack the dopamine system, causing surges in dopamine that far exceed what natural rewards can produce. The brain is not designed to handle these extreme spikes, and with repeated exposure, the dopamine system becomes less sensitive. As a result, individuals may require more of the drug to achieve the same effect. This is akin to turning the volume on your radio up to maximum and then turning it back down; normal sounds seem inaudible afterwards. In essence, this is what we call dopamine dysregulation- the 'joy button' has been pressed so long that it stops functioning correctly, leading to a diminished response to natural rewards.

Serotonin, often called the 'feel-good' neurotransmitter, serves as a stabiliser in your neurochemical system. Its role extends beyond creating positive feelings; it also regulates mood, appetite, sleep, pain perception, and even gut function. Remarkably, about ninety percent of your body's serotonin is found in the digestive system, highlighting the intriguing connection between gut health and mental health. When serotonin levels are optimal, you experience emotional stability, not necessarily exuberance, but a sense of balance. This balance allows you to feel a full range of emotions without becoming stuck in any of them, underscoring the crucial role of serotonin in maintaining emotional equilibrium.

When serotonin levels are low, particularly in pathways linking the raphe nuclei in your brainstem to various regions of the brain, you become more vulnerable to depression and anxiety. Negative thoughts can linger, making it challenging to shift your emotional state. This explains why selective serotonin reuptake inhibitors (SSRIs) like Prozac, Zoloft, and Lexapro are commonly prescribed for depression. These medications increase the availability of serotonin in the synapse, helping to stabilise mood over time. They do not create artificial happiness; they facilitate access to your full emotional range, making it easier to move out of negative emotional states and respond to positive experiences. This process effectively reduces the volume of negative thoughts without eliminating appropriate sadness or the ability to process difficult emotions.

Fear in Inside Out represents the norepinephrine and adrenaline systems' interplay with your amygdala. When the amygdala detects a threat, it triggers a cascade of chemical releases. Norepinephrine floods the brain, while adrenaline is pumped into the bloodstream from your adrenal glands. This initiates the fight-or-flight response, characterised by a spike in heart rate, increased blood pressure, dilated pupils, a shift in blood flow from digestion to muscles, and the liver releasing glucose for energy. During this rapid transformation, your attention becomes laser-focused on the perceived threat, preparing you to fight or flee.

This system is highly beneficial during genuine emergencies. For example, if a car is about to hit you, you want this response to kick in; you need that sudden burst of energy and focus. However, it's important to remember that the amygdala does not distinguish between physical and psychological threats. Work deadlines, tough conversations, and social evaluations can all trigger this fight-or-flight response. Individuals with anxiety disorders often have an overactive norepinephrine system, experiencing fear as if they are constantly hitting the panic button, even when there's no actual danger present. Their sympathetic nervous system remains in overdrive, leaving them in a perpetual state of fight-or-flight, which can be exhausting and debilitating.

However, fear is not inherently the enemy. We need a healthy amount of it; a lack of fear can lead to reckless behaviour, an inability to learn from danger, and poor risk assessment. People with damaged amygdalae often display dramatically reduced fear responses, which might sound appealing. Still, in reality, they tend to take dangerous risks, fail to recognise social threats, and struggle to learn from negative consequences. The goal is not to eradicate fear but to refine it, allowing us to distinguish between genuine threats and false alarms. We need a reliable alarm system that alerts us to real danger without going off every time a leaf rustles.

Anger, as depicted in Inside Out, is characterised as aggressive, reactive, and hot-tempered. Neurochemically, anger involves norepinephrine and dopamine, with low serotonin playing a significant role. When your goals are blocked, someone violates your boundaries, or you confront injustice, your brain releases norepinephrine for arousal and dopamine to stimulate action. However, serotonin is crucial for regulating the anger response. Low serotonin levels can diminish impulse control and the ability to manage anger appropriately. This is why selective serotonin reuptake inhibitors (SSRIs) can sometimes aid anger management by boosting serotonin to help mitigate impulsive aggression.

The connection between anger and violence is influenced by the regulation of the prefrontal cortex. You can feel angry without acting aggressively if your prefrontal cortex manages your response effectively. However, aggressive behaviour can arise when regulation falters and the neurochemistry of anger becomes overwhelming. Brain injuries that compromise the prefrontal cortex can transform someone who previously did not exhibit violent behaviour into a person who explodes over minor frustrations. While the neurochemistry of anger remains unchanged, the crucial braking system needed to control it is lost. This is not a failure of character but rather an impairment of brain function.

Disgust in Inside Out acts as a protective shield for Riley against poison, social contamination, and potential harm. Primary disgust, our revulsion towards spoiled food, faeces, and vomit, is mediated by the insula, a brain region responsible for processing visceral sensations and emotions. This form of disgust defends against disease: you instinctively recoil from potentially harmful substances without consciously thinking, "That might contain pathogens." Humans also experience moral disgust, which involves revulsion toward unethical behaviours or violations of social norms like lying, cheating, exploitation, or betrayal. This response also activates the insula, indicating that our moral intuitions are rooted in ancient disease-avoidance mechanisms. In this way, we literally find immoral behaviour disgusting, employing the same neural systems that protect us from contamination.

However, many neurotransmitters are beyond those simplified in "Inside Out" for children. Oxytocin, often referred to as the bonding chemical, is released during close physical contact, breastfeeding, orgasm, and meaningful social connections. It promotes trust, reduces fear, and facilitates social bonding, which is why hugs feel good and spending time with loved ones is restorative. The pituitary gland releases oxytocin in response to social and physical warmth, creating a chemical basis for connection.

Endorphins act as natural painkillers and are released during exercise, laughter, and even certain types of pain, producing a "runner's high." They bind to the same receptors as opioid drugs, which explains why morphine and heroin effectively relieve pain; they hijack your endorphin system.

Glutamate is the main excitatory neurotransmitter, essential for learning and memory. When neurons fire together and form connections, glutamate facilitates this process. However, excessive glutamate can be toxic, leading to neuron damage due to over-excitation. For example, strokes can trigger a massive release of glutamate due to oxygen deprivation, potentially killing neurons.

On the other hand, GABA (gamma-aminobutyric acid) is the primary inhibitory neurotransmitter. It calms neural activity, prevents over-excitation, and helps you relax and sleep. Medications like benzodiazepines enhance GABA activity, which makes them effective for anxiety, albeit with a sedative effect. Alcohol also enhances GABA, producing relaxation at low doses but depressing the nervous system at high doses. The balance between glutamate and GABA is crucial; excessive glutamate without sufficient GABA can lead to anxiety, seizures, and difficulty sleeping, while too much GABA with too little glutamate can result in sedation, cognitive slowing, and learning difficulties.

Acetylcholine is linked to attention and learning and is essential for sensory processing and executive functions. It helps you focus, process sensory information, and form memories. People with Alzheimer's disease often have depleted acetylcholine, particularly in the pathways connecting the basal forebrain to the hippocampus and cortex, which explains their difficulties with attention and memory. Many Alzheimer's medications aim to boost acetylcholine function.

Returning to the film "Inside Out": the emotions continually vie for control of the console, pressing different buttons to create various responses. Similarly, your neurotransmitter systems are in constant flux, influencing, competing, and cooperating to shape your moment-to-moment experiences. When something positive occurs, dopamine surges, serotonin stabilises, and oxytocin may be released, especially in social situations. This creates a sense of well-being, motivation, and connection. Conversely, when a threatening situation arises, norepinephrine and adrenaline spike, cortisol floods from the adrenal glands, and GABA decreases, triggering the fight-or-flight response. Chronic stress keeps cortisol levels elevated, suppressing serotonin and dopamine function. As a result, feelings of joy and stability can be chemically suppressed while fear and stress chemicals dominate.

Just as Riley needs all her emotions working together, sadness is as vital as Joy, Fear keeps her safe, and Anger helps her stand up for herself, you need all your neurotransmitter systems functioning in balance. The goal isn't to maximise dopamine, serotonin, or any single chemical; it's about achieving balance, flexibility, and appropriate responses to different situations.

Mental health conditions often reflect neurochemical patterns operating outside of optimal ranges. For example, depression typically features low serotonin and dopamine levels, combined with high cortisol levels resulting from chronic stress. This can damage the hippocampus and hinder neurogenesis. In such cases, the pituitary-adrenal axis becomes overactive, flooding the body with stress hormones. Anxiety often arises from overactive norepinephrine levels combined with low GABA; this means Fear manifests as persistent panic without sufficient calming mechanisms to counterbalance it. ADHD likely involves dysregulation of dopamine and norepinephrine in the prefrontal cortex, affecting attention, motivation, and impulse control. Medications like Ritalin and Adderall aim to increase dopamine and norepinephrine in these circuits.

Understanding the neurochemical basis of mental health issues helps remove stigma and fosters empathy. Mental health problems are not signs of weakness or a lack of willpower. They are the result of neurochemistry operating differently. Depression isn't someone's fault, anxiety isn't a choice to worry excessively, and ADHD isn't laziness. This understanding encourages compassion towards those facing mental health challenges.

The encouraging aspect is that your brain is adaptable. Your neurochemical systems can readjust over time through repeated experiences. You influence your neurochemistry when you engage in activities that challenge habitual patterns. For instance, exercising despite lacking motivation can boost dopamine, teaching your brain that action leads to reward. Confronting anxiety rather than avoiding feared situations helps your norepinephrine system recognise that the threat isn't real, which in turn strengthens your GABA system's inhibitory response. Practising gratitude can activate the dopamine and serotonin pathways associated with positive emotions. Spending time with loved ones releases oxytocin, which strengthens social bonds at a chemical level. Getting proper sleep allows your pituitary gland to optimise hormone release, supporting repair and growth.

Therapy can also be a catalyst for neurochemical shifts. Cognitive-behavioural therapy has been shown to alter brain chemistry as effectively as medications for many conditions. Through psychological work, you're literally retraining your neurotransmitter systems. A key insight from "Inside Out" is that all emotions are necessary. Just as Riley needed both Sadness and Joy, you need your full range of neurochemicals. The goal is not to eliminate Fear, sadness, or Anger but to ensure they respond appropriately, proportionately, and flexibly.

When Fear responds to genuine danger, it is adaptive. However, it becomes problematic when Fear reacts to imagined catastrophes that are statistically unlikely to occur. Anger that motivates you to confront injustice is valuable, while Anger that erupts disproportionately over minor frustrations indicates a regulation problem. The control panel operated by various neurotransmitter systems and coordinated by the pituitary gland is complex, but it can malfunction, get stuck in patterns, or respond improperly.

While you cannot directly control your neurochemistry, such as forcing yourself to have more serotonin or less norepinephrine, you can create conditions that influence these systems. Regular exercise, a healthy diet, mindfulness practice, and social support work in harmony with your brain's chemistry rather than against it. Understanding how everything works allows you to engage more skillfully, effectively, and compassionately.

Think of your brain as headquarters, your neurotransmitters as control panel operators, memories as stored experiences, and habits as programmed responses. As a conscious, aware individual who makes choices, you are learning to work with all of this. You can influence and gradually shape it into something that serves you better. This is the incredible power of neuroplasticity; its psychological growth occurs at a biological level, giving you the potential to change and grow.

Your amygdala processes threats in just twelve milliseconds, while your frontal lobes take several hundred milliseconds to evaluate rationally. During that gap, your emotional brain can initiate responses that your rational brain would have vetoed if consulted. By the time your frontal lobes catch up, you have already responded, acting on emotional evaluation rather than reasoned consideration. This creates a conflict between different parts of yourself: the you that responds emotionally and the reasons, the struggle between immediate gratification and long-term goals, and the contradiction between who your conscious mind believes you are and who your behaviour reveals you to be.

These challenges aren't moral failings or psychological weaknesses. They are features of how your brain is built, how different systems process information at various speeds and through other mechanisms, and how coordination between brain regions requires active maintenance that can fail under stress. Understanding this architecture won't give you perfect control; you still can't consciously override your amygdala's responses or think your way out of emotional reactions. However, it changes how you relate to yourself, understand your behaviour, and work with your brain instead of against it, giving you greater control over your responses.

When you recognise that losing your temper isn't a character failure but a predictable result of the amygdala activating faster than frontal lobe regulation, you can stop berating yourself for feeling inadequate. Instead, you can create conditions that support the brain function you need, such as better sleep, effective stress management, and recognising when your capacity for self-regulation is depleted. Understanding that disproportionate reactions often stem from amygdala-encoded associations from your past, rather than solely from present circumstances, allows you to become curious about your responses, rather than immediately making excuses for them.

Realising that different brain regions process information in distinct ways and can be in conflict helps you see internal conflict not as evidence of being damaged, but as a regular part of being human, with multiple systems that don't always agree. The part of you that wants to eat healthily and the part that craves chocolate cake aren't engaged in a moral debate; they are different neural networks with other priorities. The long-term health goals maintained by your frontal regions clash with immediate reward-seeking driven by your limbic areas. Whichever network is more activated at any moment influences your behaviour, which is a regular part of the human experience.

This is the architecture of you, the machinery that creates everything you experience as being yourself. The Obscure Psyche doesn't exist in mystical realms; it consists of patterns of activation in specific brain structures, emotional associations encoded in your amygdala that you can't consciously access, and processing that occurs in limbic regions faster than your frontal lobes can engage. Coordination failures between brain areas create the experience of being divided against yourself.

Your frontal lobes maintain executive control, your amygdala detects threats and encodes emotional associations, your hippocampus files explicit memories, your parietal lobes create your sense of body in space, and your occipital lobes construct your visual world. All these regions coordinate or fail to coordinate, processing at different speeds and sometimes working together, while other times pulling in various directions. This is true, not the narrative your conscious mind tells about who you are, not the carefully constructed ego identity you present, and not the person you think you should be. This is the neurobiological reality that creates your experiences and determines your behaviour.

Once you begin to see yourself this way, recognising that you are not a unified person making free choices through pure rationality, but rather a collection of brain systems that evolved at different times for different purposes, everything about your experience starts to make more sense. Your internal conflicts are not moral failures but different brain systems advocating for various behaviours. Emotional hijacking, a term that describes the overwhelming emotional response that can override rational thinking, is not a sign of weakness; your amygdala reacts more quickly than your frontal lobes can regulate. The patterns you struggle to change despite your conscious intentions are encoded in neural circuitry that cannot be altered by conscious thought alone, requiring different approaches for modification.

This is the architecture of you. These structures are responsible for everything you think, feel, remember, desire, fear, love, and hate. Engaging with your 'Obscure Psyche', a term used to describe the less understood aspects of your mind, and developing a relationship with the stranger residing in your mind begins with understanding this machinery. It involves recognising which parts of your brain do what and developing the ability to notice when different systems are in conflict instead of feeling as though you're going mad because you can't control yourself. Your brain's hardware determines what is possible, sets the constraints within which you operate, and creates mechanisms for change.

Welcome to your brain, the physical reality behind your mental life. This architecture has been shaping you since before you were born, influenced by your experiences while also shaping how you process those experiences. Although the basic structure cannot be changed, it is remarkably flexible in other ways. How those structures activate, connect, and function can change throughout your life based on what you practice, expose yourself to, and repeatedly do. Your brain's remarkable flexibility facilitates this journey of self-discovery and growth.

This is where it all happens. This is the stage on which the drama of your conscious life unfolds. This is the machinery of the Obscure Psyche, the neural substrate where everything we will explore in the coming chapters takes place. Understanding this foundation and how your brain is built and functions is not just theoretical knowledge. It's practical. It allows you to see yourself more clearly, to recognise patterns operating beneath your awareness, and to develop the capacity to engage with your entire psychological reality rather than just the small portion you can consciously access.

Now, we can properly explore what happens when things don't work as they should: when trauma shapes development, when detrimental patterns such as addiction or negative self-talk get encoded, and when your Obscure Psyche operates in ways that confuse your conscious awareness because you only see the results without understanding the machinery producing them. The architecture is mapped, and the machinery is revealed. Now we can delve into how to work with it,e when different systems are active, create conditions that support the brain functions you need, and gradually reshape patterns through the remarkable flexibility your brain maintains throughout life.

Your brain is real. The patterns are neurological. The work ahead engages actual structures operating through real mechanisms. That grounding in reality and understanding the physical substrate makes change possible, rather than just talking about problems endlessly without a framework for addressing them. Welcome to your architecture. Now, let's explore what it creates and how to work with it consciously, instead of being controlled unconsciously by machinery you don't understand

VAULT OF THE DISOWNED

Chapter 2
The Vault of the Disowned: Amygdala and Emotional Memory

I want you to think back to an experience you've likely encountered more times than you'd want to admit. You're going about your day, feeling fine and managing life reasonably well, when suddenly, something triggers an intense emotional reaction. It could be a comment someone makes, a specific scent, a particular tone of voice, or even finding yourself in a particular situation. At that moment, you're overwhelmed by emotion, rage, terror, shame, or grief so powerful that it feels like you might drown in it. Your rational mind shuts down, and you become purely emotional, completely hijacked by what you're feeling.

It is even more frustrating that you often have no idea why you're reacting this way. You can't identify a specific memory that explains the intensity of your feelings. Your conscious mind tries to concoct reasons: "I'm just stressed," "They were being unreasonable," or "I'm overtired", but none of these explanations truly match the depth of what you're experiencing. The emotion seems ancient and feels larger than the present moment, stemming from a deep part of yourself that you can't understand or control.

Sometimes, the emotional overflow isn't dramatic but instead more subtle and insidious. You might notice patterns in your behaviour that are hard to explain. Perhaps you sabotage relationships just as they begin to become intimate. You might consistently avoid certain situations, even if you logically know they're not dangerous. You experience unexplained anxiety about specific things like crowded spaces, authority figures, being seen, being ignored, success, or failure. While you can create narratives to justify your avoidance of these situations, those stories fail to capture the genuine feelings behind your reactions.

This is what it feels like to live with what I'll call "the vault." You're carrying something significant that actively shapes your behaviour and emotional responses, but is locked away in a place that your conscious awareness cannot reach. This isn't a case of forgetting; forgetting implies you once knew something and then lost access to it. This is different. It's material that was never consciously processed, experiences encoded in your brain in a way that bypasses conscious memory entirely. Instead, they're stored in neural structures that your conscious mind isn't equipped to access directly.

This phenomenon isn't just a rare condition affecting people with severe trauma; it's something that happens to all of us constantly throughout our lives. Every day, your brain encodes experiences, forms associations, and stores information across various memory systems. Only some of these systems yield memories you can consciously recall. The rest, the vast majority, are stored in ways that influence your behaviour while remaining completely outside of your awareness. You are guided by memories you're oblivious to, responding to associations you cannot identify, and living according to learning that occurred even before you had the language to articulate it.

Consider the last time you met someone and instantly disliked them without being able to explain why. Or perhaps you immediately trusted someone despite having no rational basis for that trust. Your conscious mind creates stories like, "They remind me of someone," "They seem untrustworthy," or "They have a trustworthy face." However, these are post-hoc rationalisations narratives your consciousness constructs to explain reactions originating in brain structures operating below your awareness. Something about that person, such as their facial structure, vocal tone, posture, or energy-matched patterns, is stored in your emotional memory. These patterns are linked with feelings of safety or danger, comfort or threat, leading your amygdala to react before your conscious mind even registers what it is responding to. Emotional memory's power is fascinating, influencing our behaviour in ways we may not even realise.

Now, think about a recent social situation where you behaved in ways that surprised even you. Perhaps you became small and quiet when you usually feel confident or aggressive and defensive when you are normally measured. You might have felt overwhelming shame about something trivial or found yourself unable to speak up when you had something important to say. Afterwards, you probably thought, "Why did I act that way? That's not like me. What came over me?" But nothing came over you; rather, something in that situation triggered material stored in your emotional memory vault from earlier experiences when those behaviours were protective or necessary. Understanding the role of emotional memory in shaping our behaviour can help us become more self-aware and in control of our actions.

The issue is that this material doesn't come with timestamps. It doesn't arrive with a note saying, "This response is from when you were six years old and learned that speaking up resulted in punishment." Instead, it activates, floods your system, influences your behaviour, and then retreats back into the vault while your conscious mind is left bewildered about why you just acted in a way that seems so unlike yourself. In fact, it wasn't unlike yourself; it was a version of you formed in response to earlier circumstances, a version encoded in emotional memory that remains active and influential even though you are entirely unaware of it. Recognising the influence of past experiences on our present behaviour can foster empathy and understanding towards ourselves and others.

This is the vault of the disowned, the repository for everything your conscious mind couldn't process, integrate, or acknowledge. It stores experiences in forms that ensure they continue influencing you while remaining invisible to conscious introspection. To understand how this works and why you carry material that you can't access but that actively shapes your life, we must explore how your brain creates different types of memory. We must examine how specific experiences bypass conscious processing entirely and how the very mechanisms designed to protect you in childhood may imprison you in adulthood.

The human brain doesn't have just one memory system; it has multiple systems that encode information differently, store it in distinct neural structures, and retrieve it through various mechanisms. This isn't a design flaw but rather an evolutionary solution to how different types of learning require different types of storage. Some memories need to be conscious and accessible for deliberate recall, complete with context about when and where they occurred. Other memories need to trigger automatic responses quickly, without the delay of conscious processing, as speed is often more critical than accuracy when dealing with potential threats.

The hippocampus, which has a seahorse-like shape, is responsible for creating what are known as explicit or declarative memories. These are the memories that you can consciously recall and describe. They come with context, such as when they happened, where you were, what led up to them, and what occurred afterwards. These memories form your autobiographical narrative; the story you tell about your life. For instance, when you remember your first day at school, your wedding, what you had for breakfast this morning, or a conversation from last week, you are accessing memories stored in the hippocampus. Similarly, the amygdala creates memories of emotional experiences, such as the fear you felt when you encountered a snake, the joy you experienced at a surprise party, or the anger you felt during an argument. These memories are not consciously recalled, but they influence your emotional responses in similar situations in the future.

Explicit memories, created by the hippocampus, are remarkably adaptable. They can be updated with new information and combined with other memories to form new understandings. This flexibility reassures us that our memory is not a static entity, but a dynamic process that can evolve with our experiences. However, this adaptability comes with a cost. These memories take time to form, and encoding them requires attention, processing, and collaboration between the hippocampus and the cortex to store the information correctly. Additionally, they are susceptible to disruption. Stress, trauma, or anything that impairs hippocampal function can prevent these memories from being formed accurately or can hinder your ability to retrieve them later.

The amygdala, on the other hand, creates a different type of memory known as implicit or non-declarative memories, particularly emotional memories or conditioned fear responses. These memories are not like the explicit memories of the hippocampus. They are not stories that can be recounted. Instead, they are encoded as associations indicating that a particular situation is dangerous, a specific person is threatening, or a certain feeling is overwhelming, without the contextual details that accompany hippocampal memories. What's striking about these memories is their speed of formation. Sometimes, they can be formed with just a single exposure, and once formed, they are extraordinarily persistent, often lasting a lifetime without significant decline. This emphasises the power of our emotional responses, which can be triggered by these memories in an instant.

It's important to understand that you cannot consciously recall these amygdala-encoded memories in the same way you can reach into your hippocampal memories. You cannot simply sit down and think, "Let me remember that association created by my amygdala when I was three." These memories exist as patterns of neural connections, associations between stimuli and responses, and as bodily states that automatically get triggered by specific cues. You do not remember them; you feel them, enact them, and experience them as immediate reactions rather than as memories from the past. This underlines the automatic nature of these memories, which can trigger our emotional responses without any conscious effort on our part.

This explains why someone who has experienced trauma may have overwhelming emotional and physiological responses to reminders of that trauma, even without any conscious recollection of the event itself. The hippocampus may have been overwhelmed during the traumatic incident, stress hormones impairing its function, and attention too fragmented to form a coherent narrative, resulting in no explicit memory being created. However, the amygdala would have adequately functioned, encoding every detail of the situation as dangerous and forming associations between the sensory elements of the trauma and the terror felt. This implicit memory would trigger automatically whenever similar cues arise.

Years later, decades later, certain cues, such as a specific smell, a particular tone of voice, or a specific type of situation, can trigger responses. The amygdala, a key player in this process, recognises these patterns, activating stored associations and triggering a complete fear response before conscious awareness even registers what's happening. This can lead a person to experience overwhelming anxiety or even a panic attack without understanding why. The memory that creates this response isn't accessible to their conscious awareness; there's no narrative to retrieve and no story connecting the present trigger to past trauma. Instead, there is just a raw emotional and physiological response that seems to come from nowhere, leaving them confused and out of control.

This illustrates how the emotional memory vault operates. Experiences are stored in formats that continue to influence behaviour while remaining inaccessible to conscious thought. While trauma is the most obvious example, this mechanism operates all the time for everyone, creating a repository of emotional learning that shapes our behaviour without our awareness. This continuous influence of emotional memory on our behaviour, whether we realise it or not, is a fascinating aspect of our brain's functioning. Whenever something overwhelming occurs in childhood, when a reaction must be suppressed to maintain safety or connection, or when something happens before one can cognitively process it, this material is encoded in emotional memory and stored in the vault, remaining active despite a lack of conscious access.

Let's explore why this occurs. Why does the brain create a split between conscious narrative memory and unconscious emotional memory? The answer lies in brain development, a complex and fascinating process. Specifically, it lies in how the hippocampus and amygdala handle different situations, and how the nervous system responds to experiences that exceed our capacity to process them consciously.

The amygdala is functional from birth. Even newborn infants have amygdalae that are busy encoding emotional associations, learning what's safe and what's threatening. This creates an implicit memory store that guides behaviour before any conscious thought can take place. This makes evolutionary sense; babies need to quickly learn which situations and people are safe versus dangerous. They must encode this learning in ways that produce automatic responses, without waiting for the slower, more deliberate hippocampal memory system to mature.

However, the hippocampus doesn't fully mature until around three years of age. During the first three years of life, the brain encodes experiences and creates emotional associations, storing vast amounts of information about how the world works and how relationships function. But none of this is stored in the hippocampal system that facilitates later conscious recall. This is why we don't have conscious memories from infancy and early toddlerhood, not because the memories were lost, but because they were never encoded in a way that allows for conscious recall. They exist only as emotional memories encoded by the amygdala, which implicitly learns about safety and danger, creating felt associations that continue to influence behaviour while being completely outside conscious awareness.

This leads to what is often termed "infantile amnesia," the inability to consciously recall experiences from roughly the first three years of life. However, it's not truly amnesia in the sense of having lost memories; instead, those experiences were never encoded in a format that supports conscious recall. They exist within the implicit memory system, shaping attachment patterns, influencing the sense of safety in relationships, and affecting automatic stress responses as well as baseline levels of anxiety or trust, all while being absent from one's conscious autobiographical narrative.

Consider what this means: The most formative period of your life, when your brain is learning fundamental lessons about relationships and whether the world is safe or dangerous, about whether your needs will be met or ignored, and about the consequences of expressing certain feelings, was occurring before your hippocampus could encode explicit memories. These experiences shaped your nervous system, created your attachment patterns, and established your baseline expectations for how relationships function, all through the amygdala-based emotional memory system that doesn't produce conscious recall.

You carry a significant amount of learning from earlier periods in your life, and this learning actively shapes how you behave in relationships, react to stress, and perceive safety in the world. However, the mystery lies in the fact that you cannot consciously remember the experiences that led to this learning. For example, you can't sit down and think, "Ah, yes, when I was eighteen months old, my caregiver responded to my distress with irritation instead of comfort. That's why I learned that expressing vulnerability leads to rejection, and why I automatically shut down emotionally when I feel needy in adult relationships." This explicit narrative simply doesn't exist. Instead, you just have the automatic response when you feel needy, shutting down without access to the underlying learning that created this pattern.

Even after your brain's memory centre matures and you start forming memories you can recall, some experiences continue to bypass this system and are mainly or only stored in the part of your brain that handles emotional memory. This bypass happens when experiences are too much for you to process consciously, especially when your threat response is so strong that it impairs your brain's ability to form memories you can recall. In these moments, you might need to disconnect or shut down to cope. Under these conditions, while creating memories that you might remember may not work, forming emotional memories continues to work well.

This explains how trauma can create gaps in conscious memory while leaving powerful emotional memories intact. When you are overwhelmed by a sense of threat, and your stress response is at its peak, the massive release of stress hormones can impair your hippocampus's function. The hippocampus, which requires optimal conditions to encode memories effectively, begins to malfunction when flooded with stress hormones. It fails to create the coherent narrative memories that would allow you to recall the events, their timing, and the context surrounding those experiences.

In contrast, the amygdala thrives under these circumstances. High levels of stress hormones actually enhance their function, strengthening emotional memory formation and ensuring that every detail of the threatening situation is encoded as dangerous. The amygdala does precisely what it evolved to do: it learns rapidly from life-threatening conditions, creating associations that help you avoid similar threats in the future. It encodes information to produce quick, automatic responses without the delay of conscious processing, ensuring you react to similar situations before your conscious mind can question whether the threat is real. This resilience of the amygdala is a reassuring aspect of our brain's functioning.

The problem arises later, sometimes much later, when the associations encoded by the amygdala are triggered in situations that aren't genuinely dangerous but resemble the original trauma in some way. Your amygdala detects a pattern that matches a similar situation, a specific type of person, a particular emotional tone, or specific sensory details. It activates the full threat response before you can consciously understand what's happening. You might experience overwhelming fear, rage, shame, or the urge to flee, fight, or freeze, all while your conscious mind struggles to understand why you are reacting in this way. The memory driving the response isn't stored in a format you can easily access.

As a result, your consciousness tries to create explanations for your reactions. It examines the present situation and generates a narrative about why you are feeling this way, attributing your reactions to current circumstances rather than recognising that it's old material being triggered. This disconnect is why people often lack insight into their patterns, even though those patterns may be glaringly obvious to others. However, understanding the role of implicit memories can empower you to gain insight into your own behaviour. The patterns are rooted in implicit memories that cannot be accessed by consciousness. The stories created to explain behaviour are based only on what is consciously available, which often misses the trustworthy source entirely.

This phenomenon operates at a neurological level, specifically through a type of repression. It's important to clarify that this is not repression in the Freudian sense, where unacceptable thoughts are consciously pushed out of awareness. Instead, it involves experiences being encoded in neural structures that do not support conscious recall. The material isn't actively suppressed by some psychological defence mechanism; rather, it exists in a format that consciousness cannot directly access. This is not a matter of effort but rather the result of how different memory systems are structured.

Another layer complicating this process is that experiences can end up in this "vault" even when they could be consciously processed. Sometimes, experiences are too threatening, not to the body, but to the ego, to one's sense of self, or to the need to maintain certain beliefs about oneself and one's caregivers. Acknowledging certain truths, such as recognising that one's parents caused harm, can feel psychologically unbearable. Accepting these realities could shatter a carefully constructed identity or force recognition of qualities that one deems unacceptable. In such cases, the experience may be relegated to implicit memory, even when hippocampal encoding is possible.

This is where psychological defence mechanisms intersect with neurological memory systems. When something feels too threatening to acknowledge consciously, attention is diverted during the encoding process, preventing the hippocampus, a key structure for conscious recall, from fully processing it. As a result, the experience might be encoded in emotional memory, but not in the narrative memory system that allows for later conscious recall. You may emotionally and behaviourally respond to an experience without forming a conscious memory that you can later reflect upon and integrate.

Children often do this instinctively, as a means of survival. When recognising that a caregiver is frightening, threatens the attachment bond that is essential for survival, or when feeling anger toward that caregiver feels too dangerous, conscious processing can become disrupted. This diversion teaches the child what they need to know to survive, such as when to be quiet, when to hide, and which emotions are dangerous to express. However, this learning occurs through amygdala-based conditioning rather than conscious understanding.

This is how the psychological 'shadow' forms neurologically. Every quality you possess that contradicts your conscious self-image, every unacceptable desire, and every threatening emotion gets pushed into emotional memory. These aspects of experience, which you cannot consciously acknowledge, become encoded in the vault of implicit memory. They continue to influence your behaviour while remaining hidden from conscious awareness. The amygdala, a key player in this process, forms associations that connect these disowned qualities with feelings of threat, ensuring that when circumstances may trigger their expression, you automatically experience anxiety or shame and engage in defences that prevent these memories from surfacing.

For example, you may feel inexplicable anxiety in situations that could lead to expressing anger. This happens because your amygdala has learned that expressing anger is dangerous, forming an association between anger and threat. Consequently, defensive responses trigger before you can consciously recognise the anger. Similarly, you may feel an overwhelming sense of shame when you succeed because your amygdala has encoded a link between success and danger. This could stem from caregivers who needed you to fail or from experiences where excellence attracted harmful attention. These feelings arise before conscious thought; physiological responses occur before you are fully aware, and your behaviour is often dictated by implicit memory while your consciousness conjures narratives that overlook the actual dynamics at play.

Jung's work on the shadow is profoundly important because it aligns with what neuroscience has discovered about implicit memory systems. These systems, which are not consciously accessible, store information from past experiences that continue to influence behaviour. Jung intuitively understood, and neuroscience has now confirmed, that the psyche contains vast areas inaccessible to consciousness. These areas form from experiences that couldn't be consciously integrated. The material relegated to these territories continues to influence behaviour while remaining invisible, creating a split between the conscious and unconscious mind. This split is often the source of the suffering and self-sabotage that brings individuals to therapy.

Jung described the shadow as encompassing everything the ego cannot accept about itself, everything excluded from the persona, and anything incompatible with the ideals and self-image that consciousness maintains. Neuroscience reveals that this exclusion happens through specific neurological mechanisms: the amygdala, a part of the brain responsible for emotional processing, encodes experiences in emotional memory rather than the hippocampus, which is responsible for narrative memory. Implicit learning, a process that shapes behaviour without creating conscious recall, forms associations that consciousness cannot directly perceive.

Whenever an experience occurred that you couldn't consciously acknowledge, such as feeling rage toward a loved one or having unacceptable desires, these experiences were encoded in your emotional memory vault, the amygdala. The amygdala created associations, stored the learning, and prepared you to avoid similar situations in the future by triggering defensive responses before the unacceptable material could become conscious. This underscores the power of the amygdala in shaping our responses based on past experiences.

Over time, as thousands of experiences were processed this way, you developed a vast repository of emotional memories that shape your behaviour without your awareness. Patterns encoded in childhood continue influencing your actions in adulthood, and associations formed under past circumstances trigger responses as if those situations were still present. Learning that was protective in one context may continue operating harmfully in entirely different situations where it is no longer necessary.

This is why people often find themselves repeating patterns they consciously want to change. The maintenance of these patterns isn't a result of conscious choice; it's encoded in implicit memory and is triggered automatically by situational cues. These responses are often enacted before you can consciously intervene, highlighting the lack of control over these automatic responses.

You may not remember the original learning that established the pattern because it was encoded implicitly. You might not recognise when the pattern is triggered, as it happens too quickly for conscious awareness to catch. You may not understand why you continue behaviours you claim to want to change, as these actions are driven by neural structures you cannot introspect, by memories you cannot consciously recall, or learning that occurred before you had the language to describe it or under conditions that prevented conscious encoding.

This phenomenon is not a container but a function, resulting from how your brain creates different types of memory. The experiences themselves may have occurred decades ago and may be resolved entirely, yet the learning from those experiences, encoded in your amygdala and stored as implicit associations, remains timeless. This learning does not recognise that circumstances have changed and continues to operate as if the original threat, danger, or necessity for suppression still exists.

Your conscious mind believes it is free, making choices, and understanding why you act as you do. However, your amygdala runs programs established decades ago, triggering responses based on obsolete circumstances, and determining behaviour through inaccessible associations. This complex dynamic represents the Obscure Psyche, operating through neurological mechanisms that ensure vast portions of your learning remain permanently obscure to conscious introspection.

While the influence of early programming suggests complete determinism, it's important to remember that change is always possible. Understanding these mechanisms doesn't eliminate the potential for change; it simply explains why change can be challenging when approached solely through conscious insight and willpower. More importantly, it points to methods that can effectively modify implicit memory by creating new experiences rather than simply rethinking old ones, offering hope for transformation.

It's crucial to understand that the amygdala, the seat of your emotional memory, cannot be reasoned with. Conscious thought and rational argument are ineffective in altering the associations it stores. When these stored associations are triggered, you cannot simply think your way into feeling differently. The amygdala does not process language, respond to logic, or heed your conscious intentions. It responds to experience, to repeated exposure that leads to new learning, and to situations where predicted threats do not materialise, allowing these associations to gradually update.

Exposure therapy is effective for phobias and trauma responses, not because you consciously decide to feel differently, but because it allows your amygdala to learn something new through experience. Repeatedly experiencing the feared situation without the predicted disaster enables your amygdala to update its understanding: that the problem isn't actually dangerous, that the threat response is unnecessary, and that you can tolerate the experience without being overwhelmed. This reassures us that the implicit memory can be updated through new implicit learning, which relies on experience rather than thought.

Implicit memories are not primarily cognitive; they are bodily and felt, encoded in neural structures that process sensation and emotion rather than language and narrative. To access this material, you need to work with your body, with sensations, and with the felt sense of what is stored implicitly. This is where somatic approaches to therapy, which focus on bodily experiences, often succeed where purely cognitive methods fall short.

Your body holds memories that your mind cannot access, and your nervous system carries patterns that your consciousness cannot directly perceive. The sensations you experience when triggered, such as the tightness in your chest, the knot in your stomach, the tension in your shoulders, and the shakiness in your legs, are not just reactions to current circumstances. They are manifestations of implicit memories activating, of amygdala-encoded associations being triggered, and of material stored within you finding expression through the only means available when conscious recall isn't possible.

When you learn to pay attention to these bodily sensations rather than immediately creating stories about them, when you develop the ability to feel what arises without needing to explain it or make it stop, and when you create space for implicit memories to surface through sensation and emotion rather than through narrative, you begin accessing that stored material. This process empowers you to gradually make what has been stored implicitly available to conscious awareness through a different route than verbal memory, putting you in control of your own healing journey.

This is part of what makes shadow work challenging and why it requires more than just intellectual understanding. You are not trying to remember experiences you've forgotten; you are trying to access learning that was never encoded in a format that supports conscious recall. You aim to bring awareness to material that exists as bodily felt associations, automatic responses, and patterns encoded in neural structures, which do not produce the kind of conscious experience we typically associate with remembering.

The process of integration is not about recovering buried memories, although that may sometimes occur as a side effect. Instead, it focuses on the crucial task of recognising when implicit memories are active. This understanding helps you become more self-aware, recognise when your responses are driven by stored associations rather than current circumstances, and develop the ability to feel what arises without being completely overwhelmed by it. This process also involves gradually creating new experiences that help update old associations.

It's about working directly with the nervous system, fostering a sense of safety that allows repressed material to surface, and practising patience with a process that cannot be rushed. The brain learns slowly, through repeated experience rather than sudden insights. This emphasis on patience should reassure you and alleviate any anxiety about the pace of your healing journey.

Whenever you have a disproportionate emotional response, it is likely due to material from your past being triggered. When you find yourself in unexplainable patterns, implicit memory may be influencing your behaviour. Experiencing bodily sensations that don't align with your current circumstances, such as feeling terror when there is no real threat, feeling shame without having done anything wrong, or feeling rage over minor frustrations, can indicate that your amygdala, a part of the brain responsible for processing emotions, is activating stored associations. This is a manifestation of implicit memory, which expresses itself through any available channels when conscious recall is not possible.

The vault of implicit memories is not your enemy; it serves as a survival mechanism. It allows you to cope when experiences are too overwhelming to process consciously. It protects you from confronting things that would be psychologically unbearable and ensures you learn necessary lessons to stay safe, even if that learning doesn't occur through conscious understanding. The issue is not with the existence of the vault, but with living your life unaware of its contents. When you are unconsciously led by these implicit memories, believing you are making free choices, you become a stranger to the learning that shapes your behaviour, as this learning exists in formats your consciousness cannot directly perceive.

Meeting your obscure psyche involves developing a relationship with your vault: recognising when implicit memories are active, creating practices that allow bodily sensations to surface without overwhelming you, and gradually updating old associations through new experiences. It's important to understand that you cannot force this process through willpower or insight alone. The material in your vault will continue to influence you, regardless of whether you acknowledge it. The real question is whether you will develop the ability to work with it consciously or continue to be unconsciously controlled by implicit memories while believing you understand yourself.

Your amygdala operates with programs that were installed decades ago. Your implicit memory system influences your behaviour more than your conscious mind may acknowledge. This 'vault', a metaphor for the subconscious mind, has been full since childhood and continues to fill with every experience you cannot consciously process, every emotion you cannot acknowledge, and every aspect of yourself that contradicts your conscious self-image. This isn't a pathology; it's simply part of being human. We have a brain with multiple memory systems that encode information differently, and we must live with the consequences of experiences that occurred before we had the capacity to integrate them consciously.

Welcome to the vault. This is the realm of implicit memory, amygdala-encoded associations, and learning that shapes behaviour while remaining invisible to conscious awareness. The work ahead involves accessing this material not by trying to remember it, but by learning to feel it. You, as the key player, must recognise its activation in your body and create experiences that allow old associations to update. Your Obscure Psyche resides here, within these neural structures operating beneath awareness, in the patterns encoded before language, and in the associations stored in formats that consciousness cannot directly perceive.

To meet that stranger within you and develop a relationship with what has been vaulted, you must first understand the mechanisms that create the split between what you consciously remember and what is actually stored in the various memory systems that shape your experiences and influence your behaviour. This journey of self-discovery is both fascinating and enlightening.

Chapter 3
The Chemical Orchestra: Neurotransmitters of the Dark

I want you to reflect on a time when you felt overtaken entirely by your own body. Not just anxious or upset, but genuinely hijacked, as if someone else had seized the controls, leaving you a mere passenger watching yourself spiral out of control. Maybe it was a panic attack that struck without warning, your heart racing so violently you thought it might burst from your chest, your hands trembling, and your mind racing with catastrophic thoughts that you couldn't quell. Or perhaps it was a surge of rage so overwhelming that you found yourself saying things you would never usually say, doing things you would never normally do, while a small part of you watched in horror, thinking, "Stop, stop, what are you doing?" But you couldn't stop, couldn't pause, couldn't think clearly enough to choose differently.

Or it might have been that relentless, exhausting anxiety that lingered for weeks or months, leaving you to wake each day with a clenched stomach, a tight jaw, and a mind spinning with worries you couldn't silence. You tried everything you were told to try: deep breathing, positive thinking, and reminding yourself that most of what you worried about probably wouldn't happen, but nothing made the slightest difference. Your body stayed in a state of high alert, your nervous system remained activated, your thoughts continued to spiral, and you felt utterly powerless to change it because your experience wasn't stemming from your thoughts or your conscious mind; it came from a deeper place, one you couldn't reach with willpower or rational thinking.

Here's what makes this particularly frustrating: you know it's unreasonable. You understand that your reaction is disproportionate. You are aware that you shouldn't be feeling this way. But knowing changes absolutely nothing because the chemicals driving your experience are indifferent to your knowledge; they don't respond to logic and don't consult your conscious preferences before overwhelming your system and determining your state. However, understanding your conscious preferences and learning to manage them can influence the intensity and duration of these chemical responses.

Consider how utterly bizarre this is when you really sit with it. Your conscious awareness, your sense of self, and your ability to make choices are essentially along for the ride while chemical systems in your body decide whether you feel calm or panicked, focused or scattered, capable or overwhelmed. You don't choose to have adrenaline surge through your system. You don't consciously flood yourself with cortisol. You don't regulate the complex cascade of stress hormones that can transform you from functioning reasonably to barely holding it together in mere minutes.

These systems operate beyond conscious control, reacting to perceived threats such as a sudden loud noise, a confrontation, or a looming deadline, faster than your conscious awareness can engage. They create bodily states that, in turn, generate the thoughts and feelings you experience as 'being anxious,' 'being angry,' or 'being depressed.' However, it's not entirely accurate to say that you're 'being' those things. It's more precise to say that chemical cascades create physiological states, which your consciousness then experiences and interprets, constructing narratives to explain sensations originating from systems you cannot directly control.

Understanding these processes can be profoundly unsettling when you first grasp them. You think of yourself as being in charge, as the author of your experiences, and as someone who can manage emotions through thoughts and choices. Then you find yourself completely hijacked by your stress response system, having chemicals flood your body that transform your experiences regardless of your conscious desires. This leads you to realise just how limited your conscious control truly is. However, there are strategies you can learn to manage these chemical responses, such as mindfulness, deep breathing, and cognitive restructuring. You're not driving; you're sitting in the passenger seat while ancient survival systems, which evolved millions of years before conscious thought even existed, determine your physiological state. This, in turn, shapes your psychological state, which you then interpret as just being you.

Before this begins to sound like a form of biological determinism, where you might feel like a helpless victim of your neurochemistry, let me clarify: understanding these systems does not eliminate your agency. Instead, it empowers you by shifting where your agency operates. You cannot directly control your stress hormones through willpower. You cannot simply think your way into having different neurochemistry, nor can you decide to feel calm when your body is flooded with adrenaline and cortisol. However, you can learn to understand what is happening, recognise when these systems are activated, create conditions that influence them over time, and develop practices that gradually reshape your stress response.

The issue is that most people do not understand these systems. They do not recognise when they are being chemically hijacked, nor do they fully grasp what is happening in their bodies when they feel out of control. Instead, they experience overwhelming feelings and create narratives about why they think this way. These stories often blame their current circumstances or personal inadequacies, without realising they are experiencing the downstream effects of a stress response system doing precisely what it was evolved to do, still, in situations it wasn't designed for. By understanding these systems, you are enlightened and can avoid falling into these common misconceptions.

So let's explore what happens when you feel chemically out of control, when your stress response takes over, and when hormones flood your system, altering your experience in ways your conscious mind cannot regulate. We will look into the mechanisms behind these experiences, understand why these systems activate when they do, and grasp how this ancient survival apparatus that kept your ancestors alive can make modern life feel utterly unbearable.

Your body has an extraordinarily sophisticated system for responding to threats, maintaining internal balance, and mobilising resources when action is needed. This system, known as the HPA axis (hypothalamic-pituitary-adrenal axis), is essentially your body's primary stress response mechanism. It involves a cascade of chemical signals that starts in your brain and results in hormones flooding your bloodstream. When activated, the HPA axis transforms every system in your body in a matter of seconds to minutes.

Here's how it works: the hypothalamus, a small region at the base of your brain that acts as your body's central regulatory centre, constantly monitors both your internal state and your environment for any signs of threat or imbalance. When it detects a need for a stress response, whether from physical danger, psychological threats, or internal disruptions to homeostasis, it releases a hormone called CRH (corticotropin-releasing hormone). This is the first trigger in a cascade that will transform your entire physiology.

CRH travels a short distance to the pituitary gland, a pea-sized master gland located just below the hypothalamus. The pituitary responds to CRH by releasing its own hormone, ACTH (adrenocorticotropic hormone), into your bloodstream. ACTH then travels through your blood to your adrenal glands, which sit atop your kidneys like little hats. Upon receiving the ACTH signal, the adrenal glands release cortisol and adrenaline, the stress hormones that flood your system, creating the experience of being stressed, anxious, and activated, whether you consciously want to be or not.

This entire process, from the initial detection of a threat to cortisol flooding your system, takes mere seconds for the adrenaline response and several minutes for full cortisol mobilisation. Your conscious mind often barely registers that something is happening before your body has already responded and activated the stress response, initiating changes throughout your physiology that will affect your experience for at least the next several hours. Understanding the rapidity of this response is crucial in managing stress effectively.

Let's start with adrenaline, also known as epinephrine, as this is the chemical responsible for that immediate, overwhelming sense of panic or activation that feels so out of control. Your adrenal glands can release adrenaline within seconds of detecting a threat. Once it enters your bloodstream, it triggers a series of changes throughout your body more quickly than you can consciously track.

Your heart rate can spike dramatically, transitioning from a resting pace to racing in moments. Your blood pressure rises as blood vessels constrict in some areas while dilating in others. Blood flow is redirected away from your digestive system and skin, anything non-essential, and shunted toward your large muscles, your legs for running, your arms for fighting, preparing you for intense physical action. Your pupils dilate to allow more light in, sharpening your visual focus on potential threats. As your breathing rate increases, more oxygen is pumped into your system. Your liver releases glucose into your bloodstream, providing immediate fuel for the fight-or-flight response you are about to engage in.

Your entire body transforms into a system designed for emergency action, fully optimised for dealing with immediate physical threats through fighting or fleeing. All of this occurs automatically, outside of conscious control, triggered by adrenaline binding to receptors throughout your body. You do not consciously recognise this as "my adrenaline levels have increased." Instead, you experience it as terror, panic, and overwhelming activation; your body screams at you that something is desperately wrong and that you need to act NOW.

However, this creates a significant problem in modern life: this system evolved to handle physical threats that required physical responses. Our ancestors, when facing a predator or a hostile rival, needed exactly this response: the immediate surge of energy, sharpened focus, and physical capacity for intense action. Those threats were external, physical, and could be resolved through fighting or fleeing. Once the threat was dealt with, the stress response would decrease.

Modern threats, however, are different. You aren't facing predators or physical attackers; instead, you encounter psychological threats, social evaluations, potential rejections, work deadlines, relationship conflicts, financial worries, and existential anxieties about the future. None of these threats requires physical action or can be resolved through fighting or fleeing, and they don't end neatly, making it difficult for your stress response to stand down. They are ongoing and persistent, and your stress response system has no way of differentiating between "there's a tiger about to eat you" and "your boss sent a tersely worded email."

As a result, you experience the complete physical stress response: a racing heart, shallow, rapid breathing, muscle tension, and a surge of energy, yet you cannot act on it. You might be sitting at your desk, lying in bed, or standing in a social situation. Your body prepares you to run or fight, but your circumstances require you to remain still and socially appropriate. The energy mobilised by the stress response has nowhere to go, leading to increased tension and distress.

Since these psychological threats cannot be resolved through action and do not conclude swiftly, your stress response does not shut off. It keeps running, activating the system and flooding it with adrenaline every time your brain detects a threat cue, something that occurs constantly in modern life. An email notification, a social interaction, worries about the future, or memories of past failures can all trigger your threat detection system. It interprets all of this as danger, initiates the stress response, floods your system with adrenaline, and you experience it as anxiety, panic, or an overwhelming sense of losing control. At the same time, your conscious mind struggles to understand what's wrong and what to do about it. To manage this chronic stress, it's important to develop coping strategies such as mindfulness, exercise, and social support, which can help regulate the stress response and reduce its negative effects on your health and well-being.

Anxiety can often feel very physical, appearing more like a physiological issue than a psychological one. Many people assume that anxiety stems from worried thoughts or catastrophic thinking, essentially, that the mind creates problems. However, the reality is quite the opposite. The body's threat response activates first: the amygdala detects what it perceives as danger, triggering the HPA axis to release adrenaline throughout the system. It is only after this physiological response occurs that the conscious mind attempts to rationalise the feelings associated with anxiety, generating thoughts that align with this state. The worries and catastrophic scenarios that arise feel like the cause of anxiety, but they are actually responses to a bodily state initiated by an automatic reaction beyond conscious control.

This is why using cognitive strategies to manage anxiety often falls short. You're trying to think your way out of a physiological state that originated in non-cognitive systems and is sustained by chemical processes operating outside of your awareness. While the conscious mind can create narratives to explain the anxiety and reassure itself that the threats aren't real, these thoughts do not directly influence the adrenaline flooding the system or the activation of the sympathetic nervous system. The cascade of physiological changes responsible for the sensations perceived as anxiety remains unchanged.

Now, let's discuss cortisol. While adrenaline generates immediate panic and activation, cortisol is what maintains the stress response, leading to the exhausting, chronic sense of stress prevalent in modern life. Cortisol, the body's primary stress hormone, is released more slowly than adrenaline but lasts much longer. It brings about changes throughout the body that can persist for hours, days, or even weeks if stress is chronic.

When cortisol enters the bloodstream, it prepares the body for sustained threats, allowing for ongoing vigilance and resource mobilisation. It raises blood sugar levels, ensuring a steady energy supply. It suppresses the immune system because fighting infections requires resources better allocated to immediate threats. It impairs digestive function because digestion is not a priority when facing danger. It disrupts memory formation and retrieval; as cognitive resources are focused on managing threats instead of detailed memory processing. It also interferes with sleep because staying alert takes precedence over resting in threatening situations.

These changes were critical for our ancestors, who faced real, sustained physical threats like famine, ongoing conflicts, or dangerous environments. They needed enhanced energy and alertness while decreasing long-term functions like immunity and digestion to survive immediate dangers. Once the crisis passed, cortisol levels would return to normal, and regular bodily functions would resume.

However, modern stress is different. We face ongoing psychological stressors that never fully resolve. Our brains continuously interpret these stressors as threats, leading to the HPA axis being activated day after day, week after week, month after month. As a result, the stress response never completely shuts off; it continuously produces cortisol in reaction to a constant stream of perceived threats generated by modern life.

Chronic elevation of cortisol results in severe consequences for both the body and brain. The immune system remains suppressed, increasing vulnerability to illness. The digestive system becomes impaired, leading to gut issues that can, in turn, exacerbate stress through the gut-brain connection. Sleep disruptions create exhaustion, affecting the ability to manage stress, which spirals into an ongoing cycle of increasing anxiety and further sleep disturbance. Additionally, elevated cortisol damages the hippocampus, a crucial structure for memory formation, causing it to shrink, killing neurons, and impairing its overall function.

Chronic stress often leads to memory problems, difficulty concentrating, and a general feeling of cognitive dysfunction. This is not a figment of your imagination; it's a direct result of cortisol, a stress hormone, damaging the brain structures crucial for optimal cognitive function. Prolonged high levels of cortisol are neurotoxic, particularly affecting the hippocampus. This leads to the death of brain cells and impairs the regions necessary for making sense of experiences and forming memories that provide context and perspective.

Moreover, cortisol plays a significant role in understanding the impact of stress on the psyche. While it impairs the function of the hippocampus, hindering the formation of explicit and conscious memories, it also enhances the function of the amygdala. The amygdala is responsible for creating implicit emotional memories, storing associations between situations and threats, and encoding the learning that shapes automatic responses. Under stress, when cortisol levels rise, the ability to form conscious narrative memories decreases, while the ability to create emotional, implicit memories increases.

As a result, stressful experiences are more likely to be encoded as implicit memories rather than explicit ones. This leads to the creation of automatic emotional responses instead of consciously retrievable narratives. Consequently, traumatic experiences are often stored in a way that remains inaccessible to conscious thought, ending up in a "vault" of disowned experiences rather than in accessible autobiographical memory. The stress response system activated by perceived threats ensures that these experiences are encoded in formats that cannot be consciously accessed, solidifying automatic responses while preventing the conscious processing necessary for integration.

This is why trauma tends to be stored implicitly: the intense stress of traumatic events floods the body with cortisol, which impairs hippocampal function and inhibits explicit memory formation, all while enhancing amygdala function. This ensures that every detail of the trauma is encoded as implicit emotional memory. Clinically, we observe that people often exhibit strong emotional and physiological reactions to trauma reminders, even though they may not have clear narrative memories of the trauma itself. They can struggle to recall what happened in a way that allows for the processing and integration of the experience.

This exact mechanism is also present in less extreme stressful situations. When stress is activated, experiences are more likely to create implicit memories and automatic response patterns. This results in associations being stored in a less accessible format rather than as conscious memories that can be examined and worked with. The stress response triggered by perceived threats simultaneously ensures that related material is stored in formats inaccessible to consciousness, leading to patterns that operate automatically in future situations but remain hidden from awareness.

This creates a damaging cycle: stress impairs the ability to process difficult experiences consciously, which leads to implicit encoding. These implicit memories, in turn, generate automatic responses that activate the stress response in similar future situations. The cycle continues as the stress response impairs conscious processing, leading to increased implicit encoding and further automatic stress responses. As a result, stress breeds more stress while conscious understanding becomes increasingly elusive.

It's essential to recognise that chronic stress can significantly impact cognitive function. Individuals under chronic stress often feel as though they are losing their mental capacity, becoming less capable, and struggling to manage their lives. This is not a mere perception; their stress response system produces physiological changes that impair cognitive function, harm memory structures, prevent conscious processing, and create automatic responses that are difficult to understand or control. All the while, they may be trying harder to think their way out of the problem, unaware that their stress-impaired brains are the least capable of practical thinking during such times.

You might be thinking that this situation feels utterly hopeless, as if you are trapped in your stress response without any way out or any ability to influence systems that operate beneath your conscious control. However, understanding how these systems work is actually the first step toward working with them, rather than being unconsciously controlled by them. Once you recognise what's happening and understand that feeling out of control is often the predictable result of chemical cascades doing what they evolved to do, you can stop blaming yourself for responses you cannot directly control. Instead, you can start to create conditions that indirectly influence these systems, knowing that they follow a predictable pattern.

While you can't directly think your way to lower cortisol levels or consciously decide to reduce the adrenaline flooding your system, these systems can respond to certain types of intervention. They are not entirely beyond influence; they are just beyond direct conscious control. They react to experiences, repeated input, changes in how you relate to stress, and practices that work with your physiology rather than trying to override it through sheer mental effort. This means that with consistent effort, you can indirectly influence your stress responses.

Your stress response system is constantly scanning for threats and assessing whether you are safe or in danger. When it determines you are in danger, it activates: the hypothalamus releases CRH, the pituitary gland releases ACTH, the adrenal glands release cortisol and adrenaline, and you experience a cascade of physiological changes. Conversely, when it identifies safety, meaning threat cues are absent and safety signals are present, it can deactivate: HPA axis activity decreases, cortisol levels drop, and adrenaline levels normalise, allowing you to shift from a state of activation to calm. Safety signals could be anything from a supportive friend's voice to a peaceful environment.

The challenge is that your stress response system evolved in a very different environment compared to modern life. It interprets safety and danger based on cues that made sense in our ancestral environment but may not apply to contemporary realities. For example, it tends to see fast, unpredictable, and uncontrollable situations as dangerous. Being alone, being evaluated, or being uncertain about outcomes is interpreted as threatening. Additionally, a lack of physical movement, social connection, or contact with nature signals to your body that something is wrong. Although none of these conditions are actual physical threats, your stress response system doesn't recognise that. It simply responds to these conditions based on patterns associated with danger throughout our evolutionary history.

This is why many modern lifestyle factors contribute to chronic stress activation. For instance, sitting still all day leads your body to interpret a lack of movement as a sign of being trapped or injured. Constant exposure to screens creates ongoing vigilance demands on your nervous system, as it is constantly processing information and responding to stimuli. Similarly, the social evaluations inherent in social media may be interpreted as ongoing threats to your social standing. Lastly, being isolated from nature, the community, and the natural rhythms of day and night results in your regulatory systems losing the external cues they evolved to use for determining when to activate and when to rest.

Your stress response system is constantly activated because modern life consistently triggers it, yet it rarely provides the necessary cues to reassure you that you're actually safe. Most people fail to recognise that their chronic stress isn't a personal failing or a weakness of character; rather, it is a predictable reaction to environmental conditions that frequently activate systems designed to handle short-term physical threats. These systems are not equipped to manage ongoing psychological stressors in an environment that never signals, "All clear, you can rest now."

Consider the last time you felt genuinely calm, safe, and relaxed, not just distracted from stress or numbed out, but actually in a state where your nervous system was at ease. When was the last time you could simply be present, without vigilance or worry? For many, it has been so long that they can barely remember what that feels like. They've been in a constant state of activation, experiencing chronic elevation of stress hormones, persistent vigilance, and perpetual preparation for threats that often do not materialise, resulting in a loss of their baseline.

When you experience chronic stress and your body's stress response system, the HPA axis (hypothalamic-pituitary-adrenal axis), is activated for extended periods, it does more than create immediate experiences of anxiety and overwhelm. It alters your baseline, your set point, and even what your body considers normal. Your hypothalamus, a part of your brain, becomes increasingly sensitive to perceived threats, causing the stress response to be triggered more easily and frequently. Additionally, your cortisol rhythm can become disrupted; instead of following the typical pattern of being high in the morning and low at night, it may remain elevated or become erratic. This impairment affects your ability to down-regulate, meaning you struggle to shut off the stress response even when no real threats are present.

This phenomenon is known as allostatic load, which can be understood as the cumulative burden of chronic stress on your body and brain. Continuous activation of your stress response and persistent flooding of stress hormones cause your body to wear out and lose flexibility. As a result, it faces challenges in responding appropriately to actual threats because it is already maximally activated from constantly responding to perceived threats. This leaves you less capable of handling genuine emergencies since your stress response system has been overtaxed by psychological stressors.

The effects of chronic stress manifest in various ways. You might find yourself reacting disproportionately to minor stressors, losing your temper over trivial frustrations, or experiencing panic attacks in situations that previously wouldn't have bothered you. Tasks that should be manageable can feel completely overwhelming. Physical symptoms may arise, such as headaches, muscle pain, digestive issues, and frequent illness, as your immune system struggles to function. Cognitive symptoms can include poor concentration, memory problems, difficulty making decisions, and a sensation of mental fog. Mood changes may also occur, leading to irritability, depression, anhedonia (inability to feel pleasure), and emotional numbness that alternates with overwhelming emotional reactivity.

Chronic stress response activation manifests in many ways, resulting from consistently elevated cortisol levels and frequent adrenaline surges. When your HPA (hypothalamic-pituitary-adrenal) axis remains in an "on" position, your brain detects threats without recognising sufficient safety cues, which prevents the system from fully relaxing. Most people don't recognise these gradual changes as stress-related; instead, they simply feel more anxious, depressed, unwell, or cognitively impaired, without connecting these changes to the chronic activation of their stress response systems, systems that are fundamentally altering their physiology.

It's important to realise that while these changes are neurobiological and chemical, and operate beyond conscious control, they are not permanent. Your stress response system can recalibrate. The HPA axis can return to healthier patterns, cortisol levels can normalise, and your nervous system can learn to differentiate between actual threats and false alarms. This potential for change should give you hope and motivate you to create conditions that allow your stress response to deactivate. It provides your system with the safety cues necessary to determine that constant vigilance is unnecessary.

This isn't merely about positive thinking or convincing yourself that you're not stressed. Remember, your stress response does not respond to conscious narratives; it reacts to genuine physiological signals and experiences that demonstrate safety rather than just thoughts about it. You need to offer your body experiences that interrupt the stress cycle, signal that you are safe, and create physiological conditions incompatible with chronic stress activation.

Physical movement, especially rhythmic activities like walking or dancing, is a powerful tool for metabolising stress hormones, channelling the energy mobilised by the stress response, and signalling to your body that you took action against a threat. This is why exercise is effective for anxiety, not simply because it distracts you from worrying thoughts, but because it allows your body to discharge energy, creating physiological changes that counteract stress activation. Understanding this can empower you to take control of your stress levels.

Social connection, specifically safe and attuned interactions with others, is one of the most potent signals of safety your nervous system can receive. When you are in the presence of someone calm and non-threatening, your nervous system can align with theirs and begin to regulate toward calmness. This explains why isolation exacerbates stress, while genuine connection alleviates it not just psychologically but physiologically, through actual changes in nervous system activation that occur during social engagement. This underscores the value of human interaction in managing stress.

Contact with nature, natural rhythms, and environments that resemble those in which your stress response system evolved provides multiple safety cues. These cues include the unpredictability of natural sounds (unlike the threatening unpredictability in human environments) and the soft fascination that allows your attention to rest (as opposed to the demanding attention required in built environments). Engaging with nature fosters a connection to something larger than immediate concerns, countering the narrowed focus that threat responses create.

Practices that directly affect your physiology, such as breath work, progressive muscle relaxation, or anything that activates your parasympathetic nervous system, can interrupt the stress cascade, signalling to your body that you are safe. These practices work not by changing your thoughts but by creating physiological states that are incompatible with stress activation, giving your HPA axis the permission to stand down, allowing cortisol levels to drop, and enabling your system to reset.

Recognition is essential. When you feel chemically out of control, remember that you are not failing, weak, or broken. You are experiencing the predictable effects of stress response systems acting as they evolved to do, reacting to modern psychological stressors as if they were life-threatening dangers. These reactions create chemical cascades that transform your entire experience while operating beyond conscious control.

The goal isn't to gain conscious control over these systems; this is impossible since they are designed to operate faster than our conscious minds can engage. Instead, the aim is to understand how they function, recognise when they are activated, create conditions that indirectly influence them, and develop the ability to work with your physiology rather than against it. This involves gradually retraining your threat detection system to differentiate between actual danger and the constant stream of perceived threats that modern life generates.

Your hypothalamus is constantly monitoring your body. Your pituitary gland responds to signals, and your adrenal glands release hormones. This cascade operates whether you are aware of it or not, shaping your moment-to-moment experience through chemical signals that determine your physiological state. This, in turn, influences your psychological state, allowing you to simply be yourself, feeling what you feel, while remaining largely unconscious of the machinery generating these feelings.

Welcome to your chemical orchestra, the systems that create the music to which you are dancing, whether you recognise the tune or not. The stress response apparatus can make you feel utterly out of control because, consciously, you do not control cortisol release, decide when adrenaline floods your system, or regulate the HPA axis that affects so much of your experience. However, you can seek to understand this system, recognise its workings, create conditions that influence it, and build a relationship with your stress response instead of being unconsciously controlled by it while insisting that you are fine, in control, and that nothing is wrong with you that positive thinking won't fix.

The chemical orchestra continues to play. The question is whether you will learn its rhythms, understand its patterns, and work with its nature, or if you will persist in believing that you should be able to conduct it with willpower alone, remaining baffled about why you often feel so out of control. Your Obscure Psyche also resides within these chemical cascades operating below awareness, within the stress responses triggered by implicit memories, in the machinery that has shaped your experience since before you were born and will continue to do so until you die, whether you ever come to fully understand it or not.

Chapter 4
The Inner Critic and Self-Punisher

Before we delve into this chapter, let's acknowledge something that's likely been a constant in your life, yet often overlooked. There's a voice in your head that speaks to you in ways you'd never tolerate from another person. It tells you that you're worthless, inadequate, and deeply flawed. It meticulously catalogues your failures while conveniently forgetting your successes. It compares you unfavorably to everyone around you, finding you lacking in every regard. It predicts your future failures with absolute certainty, reminds you of past mistakes with cruel accuracy, and interprets present circumstances through the lens of your inadequacy. You're not alone in this experience.

The truly remarkable and troubling thing is that you believe it. Not just intellectually, but in the moment when that voice is speaking, when it's telling you that you're a fraud, that you'll fail, that everyone can see how inadequate you are, you don't question it. You don't examine the evidence. You don't consider alternative perspectives. You simply accept it as truth, as an accurate assessment, as the harsh reality you need to confront about yourself.

Think about the last time you made a mistake. Not even a significant mistake, just a minor error, something trivial. You forgot something, said something awkward in a social situation, or made a slight error at work. What happened in your mind immediately afterwards? That voice probably started up instantly: "You idiot. Why did you do that? Everyone thinks you're incompetent now. You always do this. You're never going to get it right. What's wrong with you?"

Now imagine a friend made the same mistake. Would you speak to them that way? Would you tell them they're an idiot, that they always mess up, that there's something fundamentally wrong with them? Of course not. You should offer reassurance, remind them that everyone makes mistakes, and help them move past it. But when it's you who erred, that kindness disappears entirely. The voice becomes vicious, relentless, and merciless in its assessment of your failures and flaws.

This isn't just negative self-talk that you could eliminate through positive affirmations or cognitive restructuring. This is something much more fundamental, more entrenched, and deeply connected to how you've learned to relate to yourself. This is your inner critic, and it's not just being mean; it's serving a function. It attempts to protect you through punishment and keep you in line through shame, operating according to a logic that made sense during your development, even though it creates misery now. But the good news is, it's possible to change this pattern.

However, there's something even more important to understand about this voice that most people never recognise: the inner critic isn't actually criticising your behaviour. It's attacking your being. It doesn't say, "You did something wrong," which would refer to specific actions that could be changed. Instead, it says, "You are wrong, fundamentally, at your core, in your essence." This distinction between shame and guilt is crucial for understanding why the inner critic is so devastating and why it resists the usual techniques people try for managing negative thoughts.

Remember, guilt says, "I did something bad." Shame says, "I am bad." Guilt focuses on behaviour: "I made a mistake, I hurt someone, I failed to do what I should have done." Shame focuses on identity: "I'm a mistake, I'm a bad person, I'm fundamentally flawed." But here's the truth: you are not your mistakes. You are not fundamentally flawed. Guilt creates discomfort about specific actions and motivates changes in behaviour. Shame, on the other hand, creates a global negative self-assessment and motivates hiding, withdrawal, and giving up entirely. But you are not your shame. You are worthy of love, acceptance, and change.

When you feel guilty about lying to someone, you're acknowledging a specific action that violated your values. This discomfort can serve as a powerful motivator, prompting you to apologise, repair the harm, and commit to being more honest in the future. Guilt, while uncomfortable, is also empowering; it guides you toward specific behaviour changes, encourages you to make amends, and helps align your actions with your values. Guilt essentially says, "I can do better," creating a sense of control and motivation to actually improve.

On the other hand, when you feel shame about lying, it's not just about the action; it's about your entire self. It's about saying "I'm a liar" instead of "I lied," and "I'm dishonest" rather than "I was dishonest in that situation." Shame generalises from specific behaviour to your entire identity, shifting from "I did something wrong" to "I am wrong." When you believe you are fundamentally flawed, the problem feels like it's about who you are rather than what you did, making change seem urgent and necessary. You might change your actions, but you can't change your core self. Therefore, shame leads to a sense of urgency for change, hiding, and feeling beyond redemption.

Now, consider your inner critic. Listen to how it speaks: "You're so stupid," not "that was an unwise decision." "You're pathetic," not "you're struggling with this situation." "You're a failure," not "you failed at this specific thing." "There's something wrong with you," not "you made an error." The critic uses the language of shame, attacking your identity instead of your behaviour, which creates a global negative self-assessment rather than providing specific feedback on actions that could be changed. This damaging self-talk underscores the need for self-compassion and understanding.

What's particularly insidious about this is that shame doesn't motivate positive change as its proponents often claim. People with harsh inner critics are not necessarily more successful, disciplined, or likely to achieve their goals. Instead, they are more likely to avoid challenges, give up easily, engage in self-sabotage, and remain stuck in patterns they consciously want to change. If you believe you are fundamentally flawed if your identity is based on being inadequate or damaged, then success feels threatening. Achieving success would require you to update your core beliefs about who you are, which can feel impossible or even dangerous to the parts of you that have formed around a shame-based identity.

Your inner critic isn't trying to help you improve; it aims to keep you small and safe through containment, preventing you from taking risks that might lead to rejection or failure, the very things that would confirm what it already believes about you. It operates under a disturbing logic: if I criticise myself first, pre-emptively, before others can, then I maintain control over the condemnation. If I keep myself small and hide my inadequacies, I won't be exposed or rejected. If I punish myself enough for my flaws, I can prevent the catastrophic rejection that would happen if others saw my true self.

This is why the inner critic is so persistent and why it doesn't respond to rational counterarguments. Positive affirmations often worsen the situation rather than improve it. The inner critic is not making logical claims that can be disputed through evidence; it expresses a core belief about identity that formed long before you had the capacity for rational thought. This belief is encoded in implicit memory and tied to survival needs from development, the need to maintain attachment, even when caregivers were critical or rejecting, and the need to make sense of painful experiences by locating the problem within yourself rather than recognising flaws in those you depended on.

Consider a child whose parent is consistently critical, harsh, and impossible to please. That child has two options for understanding this experience: "My parent is the problem, they're mean, damaged, or failing to meet my needs," or "I'm the problem, I'm not good enough; if I could just be better, they would love me properly." The first option is more accurate, but it's psychologically unbearable for a child dependent on that parent for survival. Believing that your caregiver is fundamentally flawed, unreliable, and incapable of meeting your needs can be terrifying when you are entirely dependent on them.

The second option is painful, but it's safer because it preserves hope and maintains the illusion of control. If I am the problem, then theoretically, I could fix it; I could become good enough to earn the love and acceptance I need. However, if the parent is the problem, I am completely helpless and at the mercy of someone damaged and unreliable, with no possibility of changing the situation. As a result, the child internalises the criticism, decides they are the problem, and develops a shame-based identity as a protective mechanism, even though this creates lifelong suffering.

The inner critic is the internalised voice of critical caregivers, harsh authorities, or a culture that conveys messages about your inadequacy or wrongness. It is the voice you learned to use when speaking to yourself because that was how you were spoken to, or because it prevented even harsher criticism from external sources. Sometimes, attacking yourself first meant you had some control over when and how you would be condemned. This inner critic formed as a way to protect yourself, helping you maintain attachment and hope in unbearable circumstances.

However, you are no longer a dependent child. The circumstances that necessitated a shame-based identity no longer exist. Yet, the inner critic lingers, operating automatically and determining your self-assessment. It constrains your behaviour according to rules that made sense decades ago but are now actively harmful. This inner critic is persistent, not just psychologically but neurologically, as actual brain structures have been shaped by repeated activation of shame and self-criticism throughout your development.

A critical region in your brain is the anterior cingulate cortex (ACC), which sits roughly in the middle of your frontal lobes, where the two hemispheres meet. This structure has multiple functions, but one of its primary roles is error detection and conflict monitoring. It constantly scans for discrepancies between your intended and actual actions, your expectations and reality, your values and behaviour, and between who you think you should be and who you actually are.

When the ACC detects a discrepancy, it creates a signal, essentially an alarm, saying, "Attention needed here, something's wrong, mismatch detected." This is adaptive in appropriate doses. You need some capacity to notice errors, recognise when your behaviour doesn't match your intentions, and detect conflicts between competing goals or values. This part of you is essential for learning, self-correction, and navigating a complex social reality where you need to monitor your progress and adjust accordingly.

However, the ACC doesn't just detect errors; it can get stuck on them. When the same type of error or conflict is detected repeatedly, and attention is consistently drawn back to the same discrepancies, the ACC can enter a state of perseverative activation. This essentially means that the alarm won't shut off, constantly signalling "error, error, error" even when you're not making mistakes or when there's no current discrepancy to address. This is the neural basis of rumination, the experience of getting stuck in repetitive negative thoughts, and the inner critic's relentless focus on your flaws and failures.

Your ACC activates when you make a mistake, act contrary to your values, or fail to meet your own standards. This activation creates discomfort, a signal that something needs attention and correction. In a healthy system, you notice the error, make adjustments, and the ACC activity returns to baseline. But with a harsh inner critic, when shame is your baseline rather than occasional appropriate guilt, your ACC doesn't just signal errors, it gets stuck on them. It keeps firing, creating the subjective experience of "something's wrong, something's wrong, something's wrong" long after any actual error has passed and long after any functional correction could be made.

This phenomenon creates rumination, which refers to repetitive and persistent thinking about your failures, flaws, and mistakes. You find yourself repeatedly going over these thoughts without finding resolution, making progress, or arriving at any valid conclusions. Your mind gets stuck in loops: "I shouldn't have said that. Why did I say that? Everyone thinks I'm an idiot now. I always do this; there's something wrong with me. I need to figure out what's wrong so I can fix it, but I can't fix what I am..." These thoughts cycle endlessly while your anterior cingulate cortex (ACC) continues to signal error and generate the uncomfortable urge to solve a problem that can't be resolved through thought alone. The real issue isn't necessarily your actions; it's how you've come to see yourself.

People often describe rumination as a way of thinking through their problems or working through difficulties. However, if you pay close attention to the content of this ruminative thinking, you'll see that it is not productive problem-solving. It's repetitive and circular, focusing on questions without answers or past events that can't be changed. Questions like, "Why did I do that? What's wrong with me? Why can't I ever get it right?" are not genuine inquiries seeking information. Instead, they are shame-based attacks disguised as self-inquiry, where your inner critic uses questioning to deliver condemnation. Meanwhile, your ACC continues to activate, perpetuating the illusion that if you just think about it enough, you'll eventually figure it out and resolve the perceived error or fix the fundamental flaw causing all your problems.

However, you can't think your way out of a shame-based identity, nor can you resolve rumination merely through more thinking. The discomfort caused by ACC activation, which drives rumination, does not cease when you reach a logical conclusion. Instead, it shuts off when it no longer detects an error, when the discrepancy signal resolves. If the discrepancy lies between who you are and who you believe you should be, and if the error is your very existence rather than your behaviour, then no amount of thinking can resolve that discrepancy. The only potential resolution would be to become a different person, which is impossible. Thus, the ACC continues firing, driving rumination and perpetuating the subjective experience of needing to solve a problem that cannot be resolved through cognitive effort alone.

The link between ACC activity and the inner critic becomes particularly evident when discussing moral rumination, which involves repetitive negative thinking about your moral failures, times you've violated your values, or ways you've harmed others or failed to meet your ethical standards. This is not a healthy moral reflection that encourages growth and making amends; instead, it's a fixation on past moral failures, using them as proof of your fundamental badness, allowing previous mistakes to define your identity rather than inform your future behaviour.

This is what Jung would refer to as the moral shadow, the disowned parts of yourself that contradict your ego ideal. These parts reveal your capability for actions that you've decided good people don't perform, highlighting the gap between who you claim to be and who you actually are during your worst moments. Everyone has a moral shadow and is capable of selfishness, cruelty, cowardice, or betraying their values under pressure. Everyone has done things they are ashamed of, actions that contradict their moral self-image and reveal they aren't as ethical, noble, or consistent as they prefer to believe.

The question isn't whether you have a moral shadow; you do; everyone does. The real question is how you choose to handle it. Do you acknowledge your capacity for behaviour that you condemn? Do you recognise that being capable of cruelty doesn't mean you are cruel, that having selfish impulses doesn't make you a selfish person, and that doing something shameful in a single moment doesn't define your entire character? Or do you entirely disown these aspects, insist that you aren't capable of such behaviours, and project them onto others whom you then judge harshly for possessing the very qualities you refuse to acknowledge in yourself?

The harsh inner critic often emerges from this divide between your moral ego ideal and your moral shadow. You may have decided that good people, those deserving of love and belonging, don't possess certain qualities, such as getting angry, feeling envy or hatred, or failing to live up to their values. These disowned qualities are relegated to the shadow and excluded from your self-concept. However, they don't disappear; they continue to exist, express themselves, and influence your behaviour when stress or circumstance overwhelms your ability to maintain the idealised version of yourself.

When the shadow aspects of our personality come to the surface, such as feelings of anger, selfish actions, or failing to uphold our values, the inner critic responds with harshness. This reaction occurs because these behaviours threaten our self-concept. If we see ourselves as good people who never act this way, then behaving contrary to that belief can make us question our identity. It can shatter the ego ideal we've constructed and lead us to feel fundamentally flawed. The criticism we experience is often disproportionate to the behaviour itself; it's less about the actions and more about the threat they pose to our identity and the uncomfortable truths about ourselves that they reveal.

This situation creates a challenge. The stricter your moral standards, the larger your moral shadow becomes. Your moral shadow is the collection of qualities and behaviours that you disown or suppress because they don't align with your moral self-concept. As more qualities and behaviours get pushed into the "unacceptable" category, this moral shadow grows larger. The more likely you are to express the qualities you've disowned, whether you acknowledge them or not. Each time you express these qualities, the inner critic becomes more aggressive in its response, as these expressions challenge your moral self-concept. As the inner critic attacks more, your ethical standards often become even more rigid, as you try to prevent further manifestations of your shadow.

This leads to ongoing internal conflict: one part of you strives to maintain an impossible standard of moral perfection. In contrast, another part inevitably fails, since humans cannot consistently embody idealised values. This failure triggers even harsher self-criticism, which can lead another part of you to retreat or shut down due to the overwhelming nature of the attacks. Your Anterior Cingulate Cortex (ACC) is constantly identifying discrepancies between your moral ideals and actual behaviour, resulting in a cycle of rumination focused on your moral failures with no resolution in sight. The only true resolution lies in accepting your humanity, which involves dismantling the shame-based identity you've built.

Consider the amount of energy this internal struggle consumes. How much mental space is occupied by self-criticism, rumination, and attempts to uncover what is wrong with you and how to fix it? How much of your behaviour is constrained by a desire to avoid triggering the inner critic, leading you to play it small and safe and to steer clear of risks that might expose your inadequacies? How much suffering arises from viewing yourself through a lens of shame, rather than recognising your full humanity, including the aspects that contradict your ideal self-image?

What's particularly tragic is that the inner critic claims to be protecting you, insisting that its role is to keep you moral and acceptable. In reality, it does the opposite. A shame-based identity, which might manifest as constantly seeking approval, avoiding risks, or feeling unworthy, doesn't enhance your ethics; it makes you more defensive and rigid, increasing the likelihood of denying responsibility for harm. Acknowledging wrongdoing would destabilise your fragile sense of self. Those with harsh inner critics often struggle to engage in genuine moral reflection because they cannot bear to see themselves clearly. They can't recognise their failures without spiralling into self-condemnation and are unable to differentiate between "I did something harmful" and "I am harmful."

In contrast, guilt allows for repair because it fosters the belief that you are a capable person who has made a mistake. For instance, feeling guilty for not meeting a deadline can motivate you to work harder and meet the next one. This belief enables you to make amends, learn from your errors, and strive to do better. Shame, however, obstructs repair by insisting that you are fundamentally flawed. For example, feeling ashamed for not being as successful as your peers can lead to self-doubt and inaction. Consequently, any harmful action merely affirms this belief, solidifying the notion that you are beyond redemption and validating the inner critic's assessment of your worthlessness. This is why people trapped in shame often find it hard to apologise sincerely, take responsibility clearly, or make adequate amends. The acknowledgement required for genuine repair feels too threatening to their already fragile sense of self.

The inner critic, while it may seem to block access to your moral shadow, can be understood and managed. When certain qualities become completely unacceptable, and expressing them leads to harsh self-attack, you lose the ability to examine, understand, or consciously work with these qualities. However, with the proper knowledge and tools, you can regain control. They remain split off from your awareness and find expression through projection or sudden eruptions, especially when your defences are overwhelmed. As a result, you become more controlled by shadow material rather than less, because the harsh inner critic prevents the acknowledgement and integration needed for conscious choice about how these aspects can be expressed.

Consider someone who insists they are never angry and attacks themselves viciously whenever they feel angry. This person learns that anger is entirely unacceptable. What happens to their anger? It doesn't disappear. Instead, it manifests through passive aggression, sudden outbursts, choosing partners who express the anger they've disowned, or depression, which is often anger turned inward. Their anger runs their life from the shadow side, creating suffering and damaging relationships, all while remaining unacknowledged because the inner critic makes a conscious relationship with anger impossible.

Now, think about someone who believes they are always selfless and punishes themselves for having needs. This person has learned that wanting anything for themselves is shameful. Their disowned neediness does not vanish; it finds expression through manipulation, by creating situations where others are compelled to care for them while maintaining the facade of selflessness. They may choose relationships where they continually feel frustrated because they cannot directly ask for what they need. This leads to resentment that builds as they give without recognising their own desire for something in return. Their neediness shapes their life from the shadow side, while the inner critic upholds rigid standards of selflessness, preventing the conscious acknowledgement and direct expression of actual needs.

This is the fundamental dysfunction of the inner critic: it claims to be improving you while actually hindering the self-awareness and self-acceptance necessary for genuine growth. Recognising and accepting your shadow is a crucial step towards personal growth. It keeps you trapped in a shame-based identity, drives rumination through relentless activation of the anterior cingulate cortex (ACC), and maintains rigid moral standards that ensure your shadow remains large and split off. It prevents integration by making the acknowledgement of disowned material too threatening to bear.

You might wonder why some people experience persistent ACC activation while others do not, or why some have relatively quiet inner critics while others endure harsh and relentless internal voices. The answer partly lies in genetics; some individuals have more reactive patterns of ACC activation and more sensitive error detection systems, with brains that signal discrepancies quickly but return to baseline more slowly. However, it also stems from early development, specifically what you learned about yourself based on how you were treated and the conclusions you drew about your worth and acceptability from your caregivers and culture.

If you grew up with consistent criticism, impossible standards, and love that felt conditional on perfect behaviour, your brain became hypervigilant for errors. You learned to see mistakes as catastrophic threats rather than normal aspects of learning. You also learned that discrepancies between your ideal self and your actual self-signal danger rather than just areas for growth. Your ACC was developed in an environment where error detection had to be highly sensitive. Errors truly threatened your sense of attachment, resulting in rejection or punishment, proving that you were the problem that needed fixing.

This sensitivity persists even when circumstances change, such as when you are no longer dependent on critical caregivers or when mistakes no longer lead to the same catastrophic consequences they did in childhood. Your anterior cingulate cortex (ACC) continues to activate with the same intensity, creating a sense of urgent alarm and driving rumination as if your survival still depends on being perfect, never making mistakes, and upholding impossible standards. The inner critic echoes the voices of early critics, internalises messages you received about your worth, and continues to enforce conformity through shame long after those original critics are gone.

However, it's essential to understand that recognising this mechanism isn't about pathologising usual guilt or suggesting you should never feel bad about your behaviour. Appropriate guilt is healthy, helpful, and necessary for moral functioning. The ability to feel bad about harm you have caused, to experience discomfort when you violate your values, and to have the motivation for repair and growth are integral to being a functional ethical person. The problem lies not in guilt but in shame, the tendency to globalise behaviour with identity, and the inner critic that attacks your very being instead of addressing your actions.

The goal isn't to eliminate your capacity for self-reflection or moral evaluation. Instead, the aim is to shift from shame to guilt, from identity-based attacks to behaviour-based feedback, and from unproductive rumination to constructive reflection. This involves moving away from rigid moral perfectionism, which creates a large split-off shadow, toward more flexible moral standards that allow for the acknowledgement of your full humanity. The work entails developing the ability to say, "I did something harmful," without spiralling into, "I am harmful," to recognise failures and flaws without generalising them into total self-condemnation, and to embrace both your capacity for good and your capacity for harm without needing to disown either.

This requires engaging with your ACC not by trying to suppress its activity, which often backfires by creating increased activation due to the pressure of suppression, but by recognising when you are ruminating instead of reflecting productively. Pay attention to when your inner critic attacks your identity rather than addressing your behaviour, and when shame is at play instead of healthy guilt. Rumination has specific characteristics you can learn to identify: it is repetitive, circular, focused on unanswerable questions or an unchangeable past, increases distress without producing resolution or insight, and pulls you away from present reality into abstract negative thinking.

When you find yourself ruminating, the solution isn't to try to think more positively or convince yourself the critic is wrong. Remember, the critic doesn't make logical claims that can be easily disputed. Instead, you should shift from abstract thinking to present-moment sensory awareness—feel your body, notice your breath, and engage with the immediate physical reality. This literal change in focus alters which brain regions are most active, shifting from ACC-driven perseverative thinking to present-moment sensory processing. It interrupts the rumination loop not by addressing the content of your thoughts but by changing the mode of processing.

You can also learn to differentiate the inner critic's voice from more helpful forms of self-reflection by observing the quality of the voice. The critic speaks in absolutes using terms like always, never, totally, and completely. It generalises from specific incidents, believing that one mistake makes you a total failure. It attacks character rather than addressing behaviour, saying you are stupid instead of you made an unwise choice. It offers condemnation without constructive guidance, labelling you as pathetic without suggesting how things might be different. It cultivates shame that fosters hiding rather than guilt that encourages repair.

Contrast this with how you might speak to yourself from a place of genuine care, often referred to as the "inner compassionate observer." This voice acknowledges difficulties without generalising it's more about saying, "That situation was really hard," rather than "You're weak." It focuses on specific behaviours instead of attacking your character by saying "You handled that poorly," rather than "You're a terrible person." It offers understanding while maintaining accountability with statements like, "You were exhausted and overwhelmed, which explains but doesn't excuse what you said. So, what repair is needed now?" This approach fosters motivation for growth rather than paralysis.

The shift from shame to guilt, from critic to compassionate observer, brings a sense of relief. It's not about being lenient with yourself or avoiding responsibility. It's about being effective rather than destructive, about creating conditions that actually allow for change, rather than conditions that prevent it. It's about relating to yourself in ways that support integration rather than creating fragmentation. When you're trapped in shame, when your inner critic is relentlessly attacking, you cannot access your moral shadow or acknowledge your full humanity. You struggle to engage with the aspects of yourself that need integration rather than condemnation.

However, when you recognise both your capacity for harm and your capacity for good, acknowledge failures without generalising them into total self-condemnation, and work with guilt that points toward specific behavioural changes rather than shame that insists you are fundamentally flawed, then integration becomes possible. You can examine your moral shadow, the selfishness, cruelty, cowardice, and instances where you've violated your values, without being devastated by what you see. You can recognise these aspects as part of your human psychology, rather than as proof of your fundamental badness. You can learn from them, make amends where possible, and commit to different behaviours, while also understanding that being capable of harm does not define your entire character.

This is the space where the Obscure Psyche operates: through the inner critic, a shame-based identity, rumination driven by perseverative activation in the anterior cingulate cortex (ACC), and a moral shadow that remains split off because acknowledging it feels too threatening. Understanding these dynamics can free you from their grip. Your inner critic doesn't just make you feel bad; it maintains your fragmentation, ensuring that material contradicting your ideal self stays locked away, preventing the very integration that could help you become more whole.

The work ahead involves recognising the inner critic's voice, understanding its origins, and developing the capacity to relate to yourself in a different way. This shift doesn't come from positive affirmations like "I'm wonderful and perfect," which often prompt the critic to attack more vigorously by listing all the evidence against that statement. Instead, it requires acknowledging your full humanity. This means shifting from shame to guilt, recognising that having a moral shadow doesn't make you immoral, and developing a compassionate observer who can see clearly without globally condemning yourself. Remember, this is a gradual process, and each step brings you closer to a more empathetic relationship with yourself.

Your Anterior Cingulate Cortex (ACC) will continue to detect errors; it's its job, and it adapts in appropriate doses. Your inner critic will persist, as these speaking patterns have been encoded over decades and don't disappear overnight. Your moral shadow will also remain; you are human, not perfect, and capable of both good and harm. The real question is whether you will remain unconscious of these dynamics, trapped in rumination and shame while believing you're simply being realistic about your flaws. Or will you cultivate a conscious relationship with these patterns, learning to work with them rather than being controlled by them, while your obscure psyche operates through mechanisms you don't understand and cannot see? The power is in your hands, through self-awareness and conscious effort, to shape your relationship with your inner critic and moral shadow.

Welcome to the realm of the critic and the punisher, of shame versus guilt, and of the moral shadow split off due to standards that are too rigid to allow for the acknowledgement of full humanity. Welcome to the understanding of how your ACC drives rumination, how your brain can get stuck on errors, and how neural mechanisms interact with psychological patterns to create persistent suffering that feels like truth but is actually just familiar pain. The inner critic has been in control, maintaining your fragmentation through shame. It's time to meet it, understand it, and learn to distinguish its voice from more helpful forms of self-reflection. Gradually, you can develop the capacity to relate to yourself with the clarity and compassion that enable integration, rather than the condemnation that ensures continued division.

Chapter 5

The Myth of Free Will: The Obscure Psyche's Control

I need you to do something for me, something that seems simple. Right now, make the decision to lift your right hand. Go on, do it. Lift your hand.

Did you do it? Good. Now here's a question that might unsettle you more than you expect: Did you actually decide to lift your hand, or did your brain decide for you and then create the experience of you making that choice? This paradox of conscious decision-making is a fascinating concept to ponder. Did you consciously initiate that action, or did you merely become aware of an action that was already in progress before your consciousness knew anything about it? Was that feeling of making a choice, that sense of deciding and then acting on it, a genuine instance of causation, or merely a story your consciousness constructed about processes that were already underway?

You likely felt as though you made the decision. There was a moment when you thought, "I'll lift my hand now," and then your hand lifted. The timing seemed right, decision first, action second, just as it should be if you're consciously controlling your behaviour. But what if that sense of timing is an illusion? What if your brain had already initiated the action before you were consciously aware of deciding to act? What if the feeling of choosing is simply something your consciousness generates afterwards to create the illusion of control, while the actual control is happening through neural processes that you cannot consciously access?

This is not just philosophical speculation; it's a concept that neuroscience is increasingly shedding light on. Research supports the idea that your sense of being the author of your actions, the feeling that you consciously decide what to do and then do it, is at least partially an illusion. It's a narrative your brain constructs after the neural processes determining your behaviour have already commenced. This intersection of philosophy and neuroscience is a rich field for exploration and can be genuinely disturbing once you fully grasp its implications.

Consider the last significant decision you made. You may have chosen to accept a new job, end a relationship, or move to a different city. You likely experienced that process as conscious deliberation, weighing options, considering consequences, and making a choice. But what if much of that decision was already made before your conscious mind began to deliberate? What if your unconscious brain, a powerful and often overlooked force, had already processed the relevant information, determined the outcome, and your conscious reasoning was just a post-hoc rationalisation, creating plausible-sounding explanations for a decision that was actually made through processes operating entirely beneath your awareness?

This feels wrong, doesn't it? It contradicts your direct experience of being a conscious agent making choices. You feel like you're deciding what to have for breakfast, what to say in conversations, and how to respond to situations. The sense of authorship, the feeling of steering your life through conscious decisions, is immediate and compelling. The idea that this might be illusory seems absurd. However, your subjective experience of deciding doesn't prove that you are genuinely making the decisions, rather than simply becoming aware of choices made by processes you cannot introspect.

Let me introduce you to an experiment that has fundamentally altered the landscape of neuroscience and our understanding of conscious will. This experiment, conducted by the pioneering neuroscientist Benjamin Libet in the 1980s, is a simple yet profoundly unsettling study that has sparked heated debate for decades. Libet's approach was unique; he didn't just measure when participants acted, but also when they reported consciously choosing to act, when their muscles actually moved, and when their brain showed electrical activity indicating preparation for movement.

If conscious will functions the way it feels it should, we'd expect a specific sequence: conscious decision, then brain preparation, and finally muscle movement. That's how it feels, how we generally think about voluntary behaviour, and how it should happen if consciousness truly initiates actions instead of merely observing them. However, Libet's findings challenged this expectation. He discovered that brain activity, known as the readiness potential, which is a specific pattern of electrical activity in the brain that precedes voluntary movement, indicating preparation for movement, began several hundred milliseconds before participants reported consciously deciding to act.

Let's delve deeper into what this means: your brain was preparing to act before you consciously experienced deciding to act. The neural processes that initiated the movement were already underway while your consciousness still thought it was deliberating about whether to act. By the time you felt you were making a choice, your brain had already made that choice. The conscious experience of deciding followed the neural activity that initiated the action, instead of preceding it. The feeling of authorship, the sense that you chose and then acted, was temporally reversed from what actually occurred neurologically, a revelation that can be pretty unsettling.

This is genuinely disturbing. It suggests that the conscious experience of willing an action is an add-on and an after-the-fact construction created by your brain to provide the illusion of control. The consciousness that feels like it is steering and making decisions acts more like a narrator, coming in after the fact and creating stories about why you did what neural processes had already determined. This challenges the traditional concept of free will, suggesting that our conscious decisions may not be as free as we believe them to be.

Before we succumb to the idea that free will is entirely illusory, it's crucial to acknowledge some essential nuances. Libet's experiment involved simple, arbitrary actions like flexing a wrist or pressing a button, not complex decisions involving values or long-term planning. The readiness potential initiated before conscious awareness is indeed less than a second. Libet himself argued that while consciousness might not initiate actions, it could still veto them. You can consciously stop an action that has been initiated, even if you didn't consciously start it. Thus, consciousness can be seen as a veto rather than the author, acting as an editor instead of the original writer, offering a sense of control in the face of these unsettling revelations.

Even with these nuances, the fundamental finding remains deeply unsettling for our perception of being conscious agents. Subsequent research has only made this situation more disturbing. Neuroscientists using brain-scanning technology have discovered that they can predict simple decisions people will make several seconds before those individuals consciously experience making a decision. This prediction is based solely on patterns of brain activity occurring before conscious awareness. Your brain processes information, draws conclusions, and initiates actions while your consciousness remains unaware; only afterwards does consciousness create the narrative of having made a decision.

This aligns with what we've been exploring about the Obscure Psyche: vast areas of mental processing occur outside of awareness, with behaviour driven by implicit memories, automatic responses, and neural processes that cannot be introspected. However, it goes further. It's not just that some of your behaviour is unconscious; even the behaviour you perceive as consciously chosen or as the result of deliberate decision-making may be primarily determined by unconscious processes, with consciousness constructing the sense of authorship after the fact.

Consider what happens during a conversation. Words flow from your mouth, forming grammatically correct sentences that express coherent thoughts. Did you consciously construct each sentence before speaking it? Did you deliberately choose each word, plan the grammatical structure, and decide on the syntax before articulating your speech? Of course not. The words just come out. You have a general intention, "I want to express this idea", but the actual construction of sentences, the selection of specific words, and the coordination of the motor movements required for speech all happen automatically, beneath conscious awareness. While you're aware of speaking, you're not consciously crafting what you're saying; an unconscious process generates the speech, and your consciousness observes, feeling as if it's in control.

Now think about walking. If you're sitting right now, you could stand up and walk across the room. It feels like a conscious decision to walk, and then you walk. But are you consciously controlling the thousands of muscle movements required for walking? Are you deciding which muscles to contract in which sequence, how to shift your weight, or how to maintain balance? No, you have the intention to walk, and then unconscious motor control systems execute that intention through processes you have no conscious access to. The control is automatic, but your consciousness experiences it as a willed action because the movement aligns with your intention.

To extrapolate this to more complex behaviours. How many of your actions, responses, and decisions are actually determined by unconscious processes while consciousness constructs post-hoc narratives about having chosen? When you snap at someone in anger, did you consciously decide to be cruel, or did the cruelty emerge automatically while consciousness scrambled to justify it afterwards? When you avoid a difficult conversation, did you consciously choose to evade it, or did your nervous system automatically seek safety? At the same time, consciousness created reasons why now wasn't a good time. When you chose your romantic partner, were you consciously evaluating compatibility, or were you unconsciously responding to attachment patterns while consciousness fabricated stories about why this person seemed right?

The research on predictive coding plays a crucial role in understanding how consciousness relates to behaviour. Your brain doesn't passively wait for sensory information to then decide how to respond. Instead, it is constantly making predictions about what will happen next, generating models of reality based on past experiences, and checking whether incoming sensory information matches these predictions. Most of the time, the predictions are accurate enough, so your conscious experience is based on these predicted experiences rather than the actual sensory input.

This means that your conscious experience is always slightly behind reality; it is a construction based on predictions rather than a direct perception of what is actually happening. Your brain predicts what you'll see, hear, feel, and do, compares these predictions to the actual input, and adjusts the model when the predictions are incorrect. Essentially, your consciousness experiences the predicted reality, the model your brain has constructed, rather than the actual sensory information coming in.

For example, when you reach for a cup, your brain predicts its weight, texture, and temperature based on past experiences with cups. Your conscious experience of picking up the cup is shaped by this prediction, which is adjusted in real-time if the actual sensory input differs significantly from your expectations. Similarly, when you're having a conversation, your brain predicts what the other person will say, how they will respond, and what you will say next. Consequently, your conscious experience is of these predictions rather than of directly perceiving and responding to raw sensory data.

This predictive processing is remarkably efficient; it is much faster to rely on predictions than to process all incoming sensory information from scratch every moment. However, this also means that your consciousness is constantly experiencing a constructed reality, a model generated by prediction rather than direct perception. If your brain is predicting your subsequent actions and generating responses based on those predictions before you consciously experience the decision to act, then what feels like conscious choice is your awareness of predictions your unconscious brain has already made.

This is the concept of the 'Obscure Psyche' at its most fundamental level. The 'Obscure Psyche' refers to the vast, unconscious processes that determine your behaviour. Your brain is constantly processing information, making predictions, and initiating actions, while your consciousness observes only a fraction of this process and constructs narratives about being in control. The vast majority of what determines your behaviour, such as pattern recognition, implicit memory retrieval, emotional evaluations, and automatic responses, occurs beneath your awareness. All the while, consciousness maintains the illusion of steering your actions.

Consider decisions you have made and later regretted, where you thought, "Why did I do that? That wasn't what I really wanted." Perhaps you agreed to something you did not want to do, said yes when you meant no, or chose short-term pleasure over long-term goals. In those moments, it may have felt like you were making a conscious choice. However, upon reflection, you recognise that something else was driving the choice—something beneath your conscious control, influencing your behaviour while your consciousness created justifications that felt compelling at the time but don't make sense in hindsight.

What happened? Your 'Obscure Psyche' was at work. Implicit memories were triggered, emotional responses were generated, and automatic patterns were engaged. These unconscious processes initiated behaviours before your consciousness could intervene. You may have experienced the act of deciding. Still, the actual decision had already been made by neural processes operating faster than your conscious awareness processes, driven by implicit learning and automatic responses rather than deliberate reasoning. Your consciousness arrived afterwards, creating a narrative that justified the action: 'I want to do this; it's fine; it makes sense.' However, this narrative was merely a post-hoc rationalisation, not the actual cause of your behaviour.

This is why willpower often fails. You may consciously decide to change a behaviour, create plans, intentions, and commitments, but when the moment arrives, you find yourself reverting to old habits. Why does this happen? Because the behaviour is not generated by your conscious intentions, it is driven by implicit memories, automatic responses, and neural patterns activated by situational cues before your consciousness can engage. Your conscious mind may have decided one thing. Still, your unconscious brain acted on another path, leaving your consciousness only aware of what you were doing either as it occurred or after it had already happened.

People often interpret certain behaviours as signs of weakness, lack of discipline, or evidence that someone doesn't honestly want to change. However, such behaviours actually show that conscious intention alone is insufficient for changing actions driven by unconscious processes. You can make conscious decisions, but if your behaviour is initiated by implicit memory, triggered by environmental cues, and governed by automatic response patterns, then your conscious decision will have limited influence over your actions in the moment.

This situation can be deeply unsettling for our sense of agency. We want to believe that we are in control, that our conscious choices dictate our behaviour, and that we are the authors of our actions through our conscious will. The alternative that we are essentially passengers in bodies driven by unconscious processes beyond our direct control strips away our sense of agency. It suggests that we are deterministic machines with no absolute freedom, which can eliminate moral responsibility. If we are not genuinely choosing our actions, how can we be held accountable for them?

Yet this conclusion overlooks something vital. Understanding that conscious will has its limits does not eliminate agency; it relocates it. When you know how your brain operates, recognise that most behaviours are generated by unconscious processes, and realise that consciousness acts more as an observer and narrator than an author, you can start to work with your brain's natural mechanisms instead of struggling against them with willpower that is often insufficient.

You can't directly control unconscious processes through conscious intention. However, you can influence them through experience, practice, and by changing the conditions that prompt automatic responses. While you cannot consciously override implicit memories, you can create new experiences that update those memories. Though you can't prevent automatic responses, you can recognise when they occur and decide whether to continue with them or interrupt the pattern. You may not be able to author complex behaviour consciously, but you can set intentions and create conditions that increase the likelihood of certain behaviours.

This presents a different kind of agency than what we usually envision. It is not the agency of a conscious will commanding the body to obey, but rather the agency of understanding systems and working with them instead of against them. It is not simply about deciding and then acting; it is about recognising what drives behaviour and creating circumstances that gradually reshape those drivers. It is not the agency of control but the agency of influence, aligning with your brain's actual mechanisms rather than assuming it will function the way it feels it should.

Consider learning any complex skill. At first, performing each movement requires conscious attention; you must deliberately think about each component, control every action, and monitor everything carefully. This process can be exhausting and may not yield great results. However, with practice, the skill becomes automatic. You no longer have to consciously control your movements; instead, your intention to perform the skill leads unconscious processes to execute it flawlessly while your consciousness observes. This transition from conscious control to automatic execution signifies learning, as the skill becomes encoded in unconscious processes that run without conscious oversight.

Now, apply this understanding to changing behaviour patterns. While you cannot directly control automatic responses through conscious means, you can practice new responses repeatedly in situations where old automatic patterns would typically activate. Eventually, with enough repetition, the latest response becomes automatic, encoded in unconscious processes, and becomes the default reaction before consciousness even registers what is happening. You didn't change the behaviour through conscious control in the moment; you changed it by creating new implicit learning that updated the automatic responses influencing your behaviour.

This is why exposure therapy works, why habit formation is effective, and why practices like meditation can create real change. It's not because you gain direct conscious control over unconscious processes, but because repeated experiences lead to new implicit learning, which updates automatic responses and gradually reshapes the unconscious processes that determine behaviour. This change occurs beneath our awareness, through mechanisms that we can't directly observe, but we can intentionally create conditions that enable those mechanisms to learn something new.

This is also why understanding your Obscure Psyche is so essential. If you believe that you are consciously authoring all of your behaviour, or if you think that willpower and conscious intention are enough for change, you will likely keep attempting strategies that are ineffective because they target the wrong level. You may continue making conscious decisions to change while unconscious processes are still generating the same automatic responses. As a result, you might interpret inevitable failures as personal inadequacy, rather than recognising that you were trying to change unconscious patterns with conscious efforts alone, which was never going to be sufficient.

When you acknowledge that most behaviour is generated unconsciously, and that consciousness acts more as a narrator than an author, you can begin to work with the actual machinery of your mind. This understanding allows you to recognise when automatic responses are activated before consciousness has even registered what is happening. You can create conditions that interrupt these automatic patterns before they fully engage. You can practice new responses in situations similar to those where old responses typically activate. Instead of trying to override unconscious processes through conscious will, which will never be strong enough, you can work in harmony with your nervous system, implicit memory, and automatic responses.

The philosophical implications of this research continue to be hotly debated. Some argue that it completely abolishes free will; if our actions are determined by neural processes before consciousness becomes involved, then consciousness is neither free nor capable of choosing or authoring, rendering the sense of free will an illusion. Others advocate for compatibilism, suggesting that free will can coexist with determinism. They argue that even if our actions are caused by prior neural processes we didn't consciously control, we remain free as long as those processes are ours, representing our values and goals even if they are unconscious.

Some philosophers argue that Libet's experiments do not threaten free will because they focus only on when we become conscious of our decisions, not on the moment the decisions themselves occur. Perhaps the decision happens earlier than our conscious awareness, but it is still our decision, part of our mental processes, even if it is not consciously accessible. By 'neural processes', we mean the complex series of electrical and chemical signals that occur in the brain, leading to a decision or action. The fact that consciousness is not involved in initiating an action doesn't mean the action isn't free; it simply means that freedom resides in unconscious processes rather than in conscious awareness.

Regardless of your philosophical stance, the practical reality remains: the feeling of consciously authoring your actions is at least partially illusory. The sensation of deciding and then acting, where conscious will appears to cause behaviour, doesn't accurately reflect the actual timing of neural events. Consciousness often arrives after processes have already begun, crafting the narrative of choice, constructing the sense of authorship, and making it feel as though you made a decision, when in fact your brain had already initiated the action before you were consciously aware of it.

This illustrates the fundamental level of the Obscure Psyche's influence. It's not just that some of your behaviour is unconscious while other behaviour is conscious; even the actions you perceive as clearly, obviously chosen are largely determined by unconscious processes, with consciousness creating narratives after the fact to give the impression of control. The obscurity lies not only in hidden aspects like repressed memories or disowned qualities but also in the fundamental structure of how consciousness relates to behaviour. There is a gap between the feeling of being a conscious agent and how your brain actually generates action.

Every moment, your brain processes information you're not aware of, makes predictions you don't consciously form, initiates actions before you decide, and creates your experience of reality from constructed predictions rather than direct perception. Most of what happens is not directly authored by you. Instead, you become aware of what has already been determined, observe actions that have already been initiated, and narrate processes that are already underway. This gives you the compelling illusion that your consciousness is in control.

However, this doesn't mean you're powerless. It doesn't mean change is impossible, nor does it mean you're not responsible for your behaviour. It simply indicates that conscious intention alone is not enough; willpower alone cannot override automatic processes. Understanding how your brain works is essential for working with it effectively. The agency you have is not the same as having a conscious will commanding obedience. Instead, it involves understanding systems and creating conditions that reshape these systems over time through new learning.

You are not as free as you feel, but you're also not as trapped as this might initially suggest. The critical question is whether you will continue to insist on a model of conscious control that your brain does not actually implement. Will you keep trying to change through willpower alone, wondering why your efforts keep failing? Will you keep blaming yourself for not having enough conscious control over processes that were never under conscious control to begin with? Or will you accept the actual architecture of your brain, recognise the limits of conscious will, and begin to work with your unconscious processes rather than trying to override them through mental effort that was never going to be sufficient?

Your "Obscure Psyche" not only contains hidden material but also drives most of your behaviour through processes operating beneath your awareness. At the same time, your consciousness observes and constructs narratives about being in control. The myth of free will is not that you have no agency; it's that the agency you possess works differently than it feels. It operates through different mechanisms than you might imagine and requires you to work with unconscious processes rather than attempting to command them through conscious intention alone.

Welcome to understanding the fundamental obscurity, the deepest level at which you are a stranger to yourself. This goes beyond not knowing what you contain; it involves not understanding who is really steering, deciding, and controlling your actions while your consciousness maintains a compelling but ultimately inaccurate narrative about being the author of your experiences.

The work ahead involves recognising these limits, working within them rather than denying them, and developing agency through understanding rather than insisting on impossible levels of conscious control. Your brain runs programs you didn't write, makes decisions you don't consciously author, and generates behaviour through processes you cannot directly perceive. The question is whether you will continue pretending otherwise or whether you will start working with the actual machinery that creates your experience and determines your behaviour, even though much of that machinery will always remain obscure to your conscious awareness.

Chapter 6

Childhoods Blueprint: The Brain of the Wounded Child

You should consider something in a way you may not have thought of before. Every adult relationship you've had, whether it be friendships, romances, or working partnerships, has been influenced by experiences and patterns formed before you turned three years old. The dynamics you engage in with intimate partners, your reactions to closeness, and the defensive strategies you employ when connection feels threatening or insufficient are not conscious choices. They stem from templates or programming that were established so early in your life that you have no conscious memory of learning them. These patterns run automatically beneath your awareness while you believe you're making free choices about how to connect with others.

Think about the last relationship you sabotaged or the recurring pattern you've noticed despite your intentions to change. You may consistently choose emotionally unavailable partners, which keeps you at a distance and leaves you feeling insecure about your place in the relationship. Or maybe you withdraw just when things start to get genuinely intimate, creating excuses to leave at crucial moments, unable to handle the vulnerability that comes with being truly seen. Alternatively, you might oscillate between desperate clinging and harsh rejection, struggling to find a stable middle ground while grappling with anxiety about abandonment, yet simultaneously pushing people away.

Each time, you likely think, "This time will be different. I've learned from my past mistakes. I know what I want now. I'm going to make better choices." But then, you find yourself repeating the same patterns, facing the same outcomes, and wondering how you ended up in this situation again despite your determination to change. You consciously wanted to do things differently and meant to choose wisely. However, when the moment came, something unrelated to your conscious intentions took over, rooted in programming installed decades ago when you lacked the awareness or ability to comprehend it.

This repetition is not a moral failing. It isn't about being foolish, self-destructive, or unconsciously seeking suffering. It's simply your brain operating as it does, using past experiences to predict future situations and responding according to lessons learned about relationships before you could articulate them. You learned these lessons without explicit memory or the ability to assess whether they would serve you positively as you grew older or trap you in patterns that made sense during childhood but lead to suffering in adulthood.

In the last chapter, we explored the limitations of conscious will and how most behaviours are generated by unconscious processes before our conscious mind is even aware of them. Now, we need to understand why our unconscious processes develop specific patterns, why we are attracted to certain types of people while feeling repelled by others, why we respond to intimacy in particular ways, and why we can't simply decide to change our relationship patterns even when we consciously recognise that our current ones aren't working.

The answer to these questions lies in childhood, particularly in how our brains developed within the context of early relationships. It's crucial to understand that our early experiences play a significant role in shaping our brain's blueprint for connection, even before we can consciously think about it. This foundational understanding, established so early in our lives, empowers us to recognise and change our relationship patterns.

At birth, the human brain is extraordinarily undeveloped compared to other mammals. This underscores the immense role of caregivers in our lives. While a foal can stand and walk within hours, a human infant is completely helpless and entirely dependent on caregivers for survival, remaining dependent for years. This extended dependency means that human brain development occurs largely after birth, shaped by the specific environment and caregiving an infant receives. Our brains are not fully developed at birth; they begin to develop, and their completion depends significantly on our early experiences.

The most critical period for brain development is roughly the first three years of life, before the hippocampus matures and we start forming conscious narrative memories. During this time, our brains learn fundamental lessons about relationships: whether the world is safe or dangerous, whether our needs will be met or ignored, how others respond when we are distressed and need comfort, whether people are reliable or unpredictable, and whether we matter or are invisible. These lessons are not stored as explicit memories that we can later recall; instead, they are stored as implicit learning, neural patterns, and automatic responses that feel normal and expected rather than as specific remembered experiences.

This early learning primarily occurs through our relationships with our primary caregivers, creating what attachment researchers refer to as our attachment style. This internal working model of relationships influences how we connect with others throughout our lives. This concept is not just abstract psychology; it's neurobiology. Actual patterns of brain development are shaped by relational experiences, with neural pathways being strengthened or weakened based on how our environment responds to our needs.

Let's discuss what happens neurologically when a baby's needs are consistently and responsively met. When a baby experiences distress due to hunger, discomfort, fear, or loneliness, they signal this distress by crying. If a caregiver responds promptly and appropriately to feeding when the baby is hungry, providing comfort when they are scared, or offering connection when they are lonely, the baby's distress is alleviated. This sequence occurs hundreds or even thousands of times during infancy and early childhood.

What happens in the baby's brain during these interactions? It's a fascinating process. When distress is experienced, the amygdala, a key player in emotional processing, is activated, stress hormones are released, and the nervous system enters a state of activation. When relief comes, when the caregiver provides what is needed, another set of neural responses occurs. The ventral striatum, a region deep within the brain involved in reward processing and motivation, releases dopamine. This dopamine release creates a positive association, essentially teaching the brain that "seeking help leads to relief, connection brings reward, and other people are sources of comfort and safety."

The ventral striatum is a crucial part of the brain's reward circuitry, which helps us learn which actions and situations lead to positive outcomes. When we experience pleasure, achieve a goal, or receive something we desire, dopamine is released through pathways connecting the ventral striatum to other areas of the brain. This flood of dopamine generates the subjective experience of reward and encodes the learning associated with what led to that reward. This process is how our brains learn what to pursue and what to avoid, what is valuable and what is dangerous, and which behaviours to repeat or eliminate.

For an infant whose needs are consistently met, whose distress is regularly alleviated through attentive caregiving, the ventral striatum learns that other people are rewarding and that connection is valuable. When the infant expresses needs or seeks proximity, they experience positive outcomes. Over time, this pattern of distress, signalling, caregiver response, relief, and dopamine reward wires the infant's brain to expect that relationships function in a trustworthy manner. The infant learns that people can generally be relied upon for comfort, that they can depend on others during tough times. That connection is safe and rewarding rather than dangerous or disappointing.

This nurturing environment fosters what attachment researchers refer to as secure attachment. This doesn't imply that caregiving is perfect; it's never flawless. Instead, it means it is good enough, consistent, and responsive enough for the baby's brain to learn that people are generally reliable. It leads the baby to understand that expressing needs usually results in those needs being met and that the world is fundamentally safe, even if bad things occasionally happen. As a result, the infant develops a nervous system capable of tolerating distress, anticipating relief, maintaining connections under stress, and approaching relationships with an inherent assumption of safety instead of danger.

However, what happens when an infant's needs aren't consistently met? When the baby cries and sometimes receives comfort, but at other times is ignored, or when the comfort provided fails to meet their needs, what should be done? If a caregiver is overwhelmed or unable to respond appropriately, what occurs neurologically when the sequence of distress, signal, response, and relief is disrupted? When relief doesn't come, and the expected reward fails to materialise?

In these situations, the distress remains unresolved. Stress hormones continue to rise, causing the amygdala to associate distress with emergencies, while learning that help may not be forthcoming. As a result, the ventral striatum does not receive the dopamine reward that would encode the lesson "seeking help works." Instead, it encounters continued distress, an absence of the expected sequence, and a lack of reward where one should have been. This teaches a very different lesson: that people are unreliable, that expressing needs does not ensure they will be met, and that one cannot rely on others to provide necessary support.

If these circumstances persist, not out of neglect, but perhaps because the caregiver is struggling with their own issues like depression, trauma, or addiction, the baby's brain adapts. It must be true, as the infant cannot leave or change their caregivers. The only choice is to adjust to the available conditions, develop strategies for coping with inconsistent or inadequate care, and establish patterns that maximise survival, even if those patterns lead to suffering later in life.

One adaptation identified by attachment researchers is known as anxious or preoccupied attachment. In this pattern, a baby learns that their needs might be met by intensifying their signals, such as crying louder and for longer, or by demanding attention more forcefully. The ventral striatum, a key area of the brain, becomes wired to understand that the connection is intensely desirable; when it occurs, it is desperately needed, but also unpredictable. This leads to a brain that remains hyper-vigilant for signs of potential abandonment, constantly anxious about relationship security, and in need of frequent reassurance. The individual may feel overwhelmed by their own desire for connection while simultaneously fearing that such needs will drive others away.

Another adaptation is known as avoidant attachment. In this case, the baby learns that expressing needs does not reliably bring comfort. Seeking connection often results in disappointment or rejection, leading the child to manage their distress alone rather than through relationships. The ventral striatum in these individuals learns that a connection can be either unfulfilling or painful, associated with disappointment rather than relief and safety. This results in a brain that minimises emotional expression, feels uncomfortable with intimacy, and values independence, not out of genuine strength, but as a protective response to the unavailability of consistent connection.

The most devastating pattern is referred to as disorganised attachment, which develops when the caregiver is not only unavailable but also frightening. In this scenario, the baby experiences a difficult bind: when distressed, their instinct is to seek comfort from the caregiver, yet that very caregiver is a source of distress. Approaching them brings danger, while avoidance can lead to abandonment. No strategy works, and there is no coherent pattern to maximise safety. The ventral striatum receives profoundly contradictory signals; a connection is desperately needed, but it is also terrifying; proximity brings both reward and threat simultaneously.

This results in a brain that cannot develop a coherent strategy for relationships, swinging chaotically between desperate clinging and harsh rejection. Individuals with disorganised attachment crave and fear intimacy at the same time. They often describe feeling as though they are constantly walking on eggshells, as if relationships are minefields where any misstep might trigger disaster. They want closeness but are unable to tolerate it when it is actually available.

This sounds like determinism, suggesting that whatever attachment pattern was established in infancy is permanent, and that you are doomed to repeat these patterns forever because they were formed before you could influence them. However, this view is not entirely accurate. While these patterns are powerful, persistent, and influential, they are not absolutely fixed. The brain retains plasticity throughout life, allowing for the capacity to learn from new experiences and to update old patterns through repeated exposure to different relationship dynamics. It is crucial to understand, however, that changing these patterns cannot be achieved through conscious decision alone. It requires more than simply choosing to relate differently or relying solely on willpower or insight.

Remember from the chapter on free will: you can't consciously override unconscious programming. Attachment patterns are encoded in your ventral striatum, amygdala, and implicit memory systems that operate beneath conscious awareness. These patterns run automatically, activating before you are even aware of what's happening, and they determine your behaviour through processes that you cannot directly control. For instance, you don't consciously decide to feel anxious when a partner is distant, nor do you deliberately choose to shut down emotionally when someone gets close. These responses are automatic, triggered by situational cues that your brain interprets based on templates formed in childhood.

Consider what happens in adult relationships when your attachment system activates. When your partner doesn't text back immediately, you may suddenly feel flooded with anxiety, convinced they're pulling away, all while imagining worst-case scenarios and needing reassurance even though you rationally know that you're overreacting. What has happened here? Your brain detected a cue, such as an absence of an expected response or a change in your partner's behaviour, and it interpreted this through your attachment template. Suppose that the template learned that inconsistent responses indicate impending abandonment. In that case, your ventral striatum signals a threat rather than a reward, your amygdala activates, stress hormones flood your system, and you experience overwhelming anxiety before your conscious mind can regain perspective.

On the flip side, when your partner expresses a desire for more closeness, vulnerability, or emotional intimacy, you might find yourself shutting down, pulling away, and suddenly fixating on their flaws, even inventing reasons why the relationship isn't right. Again, what happened? Your brain detected a cue pressure for intimacy and interpreted it through your attachment template. Suppose that the template learned that closeness leads to disappointment or suffocation. In that case, your ventral striatum signals danger instead of reward, activating your defences and prompting you to create distance before your conscious mind can question whether this response aligns with your actual goals.

These are not conscious choices; they are automatic responses generated by neural patterns established decades ago, functioning based on programming that was installed before you had any say in the matter. Because they're automatic and activate so quickly, your conscious mind often only becomes aware of them once you're already anxious, shutting down, and responding according to the old template. Your conscious mind, which is responsible for rational thinking and decision-making, struggles to regain control over these automatic responses. Meanwhile, your consciousness scrambles to create explanations that feel logical but miss the actual source entirely.

This is why you can know intellectually that your partner is reliable yet still feel constant anxiety about abandonment. It explains why you can consciously desire intimacy but automatically pull away when it's offered. You might clearly recognise your patterns, understand their origins, and see that they're not serving you, yet still find yourself repeating them. The knowledge is conscious, but the patterns are unconscious. Understanding the pattern doesn't grant you conscious control over it because it operates at the level of implicit memory, automatic responses, and neural pathways reinforced through numerous repetitions in childhood. These patterns now run automatically whenever relevant cues appear.

The situation becomes even more complicated and insidious when we consider that your attachment template not only triggers automatic responses in relationship situations but also influences your attractions. This creates a self-fulfilling dynamic that perpetuates the original pattern. Your ventral striatum learns what relationships look like, what connection feels like, and what is considered normal in intimacy. While you may consciously desire secure, stable, and consistent love, your ventral striatum is drawn to what feels familiar and matches your template. This means it activates the neural pathways that have been reinforced through repeated experiences.

For instance, if you have an anxious attachment style and your ventral striatum has learned that a connection is highly desirable but unpredictable, requiring constant effort to maintain, you might find secure, stable, and consistently available partners to be boring. These partners may not trigger the same feelings of attraction and chemistry as someone who mirrors your original dynamic. A reliable partner doesn't provoke the dopamine surge that someone who is inconsistently available might, as your reward system has been conditioned to associate connection with uncertainty and effort, not with ease and reliability.

On the other hand, if your attachment template is avoidant, and your ventral striatum has learned that closeness is uncomfortable. At the same time, independence feels safe, but partners who desire intimacy can feel threatened. Consequently, those who maintain distance may feel more comfortable, even if that familiarity leads to loneliness. When someone pursues you, it activates your defences. At the same time, a partner who remains equally distant does not trigger your reward system either, because connection is not particularly rewarding in your template. This may result in relationships that are distant and unsatisfying, or in prolonged solitude. You convince yourself that you prefer independence, yet, unconsciously, your avoidance continues to recreate the emotional isolation you adapted to in childhood.

This creates a terrible bind: you are unconsciously attracted to dynamics that match your template, even when those familiar dynamics are painful. You find yourself recreating the original attachment circumstances because your reward system has been conditioned to recognise these unhealthy connections as relationships. While engaging in these dynamics, you enact the patterns you developed to manage them, such as anxiety, avoidance, or disorganisation, which often elicit the exact responses your template expects. This reinforces the original learning and strengthens the pattern even further.

For example, someone with an anxious attachment style may choose an inconsistently available partner, leading to anxiety about that inconsistency. They might demand reassurance from their partner, which could push that partner away, confirming the belief that people are unreliable and that abandonment is always a threat. This, in turn, strengthens the anxious attachment pattern. Conversely, someone with an avoidant attachment style might choose a partner who respects their boundaries or may push away anyone who doesn't. They maintain emotional distance to feel safe, might experience loneliness, but convince themselves they are okay. This confirms their belief that independence is necessary and that closeness is threatening, thereby strengthening the avoidant pattern.

The cycle continues: the attachment template creates attraction, which leads to dynamics that match the template. These dynamics further validate your original learning, perpetuating the pattern across decades and multiple relationships. All the while, your conscious mind remains convinced it's making free choices about whom to connect with and how to relate. However, in reality, you're not freely choosing; you're enacting programming that was installed before you were able to think, responding through patterns laid down before you could articulate them, and attracted to dynamics that match templates formed by circumstances beyond your control.

Let's delve into the profound and lasting effects of developmental trauma, which occurs when early experiences are not just insufficient but actively harmful. When childhood involves trauma, abuse, or neglect that overwhelms a child's ability to cope, we refer to this as developmental trauma. Its effects extend beyond merely forming attachment patterns; it shapes the entire nervous system and wires the brain in ways that can lead to lifelong suffering, often remaining largely unconscious.

When a child is faced with chronic threats, whether from abuse, witnessing violence, living with an addicted or severely mentally ill caregiver, or enduring neglect that poses real danger, the developing nervous system shows remarkable resilience in adapting to survive in a hostile environment. The amygdala becomes hyper-reactive, constantly detecting threats because they are prevalent. The stress response system remains chronically activated because this ongoing activation is essential for survival. As a result, the ventral striatum learns to perceive the world as fundamentally dangerous, viewing people as potential threats instead of sources of safety, leading to the understanding that connection often brings pain rather than comfort.

This doesn't merely create attachment patterns; it fundamentally alters how the nervous system operates. Children with developmental trauma frequently develop brains that are perpetually in some degree of stress response. They struggle to access states of calm and safety, misinterpret ambiguous situations such as a caregiver's neutral expression or a sudden change in routine as threatening, and have difficulty regulating emotions because the necessary regulatory circuits never developed adequately amidst chaotic or unsafe caregiving.

Additionally, the ventral striatum in these children experiences severely disrupted reward processing, which is the brain's way of recognising and responding to pleasurable experiences. Everyday experiences that should be rewarding, such as connection, achievement, or pleasure, often fail to activate appropriate dopamine responses. Their systems are so focused on threat detection and survival that the processing of rewards becomes suppressed. This leads to adulthood marked by difficulty experiencing joy, challenges with motivation due to an abnormal reward system, and potentially engaging in increasingly extreme behaviours in an attempt to activate reward pathways that have been dampened by chronic stress.

This is one reason why individuals with childhood trauma are more susceptible to addiction. Their ventral striatum doesn't respond normally to natural rewards; relationships, achievements, and everyday pleasures do not release sufficient dopamine to induce motivation and satisfaction. However, drugs can hijack this system, forcing the release of dopamine far beyond what natural rewards provide. This can temporarily allow individuals to feel something other than the baseline activation and emptiness that characterises their usual state. Addiction is not a sign of weakness or moral failing; it is an attempt to compensate for a reward system that was damaged by childhood circumstances beyond the person's control.

Developmental trauma significantly impacts the prefrontal cortex, the area of the brain responsible for executive functions such as emotional regulation, planning, and impulse control. When a child's stress response system is chronically activated, and cortisol levels remain elevated for extended periods, the developing prefrontal cortex suffers. Resources intended for creating sophisticated regulatory circuits are instead diverted to survival, managing immediate threats, and preventing the overactive stress response from overwhelming the system.

This leads to adults who struggle with self-regulation, have difficulty managing emotions, act impulsively, and face challenges in effective planning. These difficulties are not chosen but result from the brain regions crucial for these functions not developing correctly. They are trying to navigate adult life with regulatory systems compromised during their development due to circumstances that required a survival focus rather than optimal growth.

Additionally, much of this occurs beneath conscious awareness and is encoded in implicit memory. It influences behaviour through automatic processes, while the conscious mind creates narratives that overlook the real sources of the issues. An adult with developmental trauma doesn't think, "My ventral striatum is dysregulated and my prefrontal cortex is underdeveloped due to chronic childhood stress." Instead, they might think, "I'm broken; I can't manage normal life; there's something fundamentally wrong with me." They face the consequences of their experiences, relationship problems, emotional dysregulation, and struggles with motivation and pleasure without understanding their neurobiological origins. They fail to recognise that their behaviours are adaptations to impossible situations rather than personal failings.

This is where shame often enters. The inner critic, discussed in earlier chapters, can become particularly harsh. Without awareness of how their struggles stem from brain development influenced by childhood circumstances, without recognising that their attachment patterns and stress response systems were formed before they had any choice, they may interpret their difficulties as evidence of their fundamental inadequacy. They compare themselves to others who seem to navigate relationships effortlessly, regulate their emotions smoothly, and experience pleasure and motivation naturally, leading to feelings of defectiveness, damage, and flaws.

However, they are not defective; they are adapted. Their brains developed in specific circumstances and adjusted to those environments in ways that maximised their chances of survival. Even if these adaptations result in suffering in different circumstances, that doesn't render them wrong or indicate inadequacy. They were necessary and sensible at the time; they kept the individual alive when no other options were available. The tragedy lies not in the development of these patterns but in the fact that they're still operating on programming designed for circumstances that no longer exist. Individuals react to current situations using templates created for past dangers, becoming trapped in necessary patterns, and thus creating suffering now.

Understanding this reality doesn't immediately change the patterns. It's important to remember that these patterns are not conscious programs that can simply be rewritten through insight. They are implicit, automatic, and encoded in neural structures that do not respond to rational argument or conscious intention. However, understanding does change how one relates to oneself, reduces the shame that exacerbates the original difficulties, and opens the door to different kinds of interventions than those previously attempted.

Understanding that your anxious attachment is rooted in a ventral striatum that learned an unreliable connection can bring a sense of relief. It's not your fault that you feel anxious. Instead, you can see it as an activation of old programming. Similarly, knowing that your emotional dysregulation is a result of childhood stress and compromised prefrontal cortex development can alleviate self-blame. You're not weak; you're working with your actual neurobiology, not against it.

Realising that your challenges with pleasure and motivation stem from a reward circuitry shaped by early deprivation or threat can be empowering. You're not like others whose reward systems developed differently, and that's okay. Instead of comparing, you can explore approaches that are more suitable for your own nervous system, putting you in control of your healing journey.

Changing these patterns is not simply about consciously deciding to relate differently, relying on willpower or positive thinking, or understanding why you are this way and then choosing to be different. The patterns are deeply ingrained, automatic, and fundamentally wired into your nervous system architecture. The real work involves creating new experiences, repeated over time, that allow your implicit memory to update. It provides your ventral striatum with new associations to encode, demonstrating to your amygdala that different responses are indeed possible.

Relationship-focused therapy, which creates experiences of reliable connection, can be a beacon of hope for addressing attachment difficulties. The ventral striatum doesn't update through understanding alone; it updates through experience. As you repeatedly experience someone being reliable, consistently available, and responding appropriately to your needs, your reward system gradually learns new associations. This process is slow and requires extensive repetition, but it is possible because your brain retains plasticity and the capacity to encode new implicit learning even in adulthood.

Approaches that work directly with your nervous system, such as somatic therapies, practices that create feelings of safety in your body, and techniques that help your stress response system learn to down-regulate, can be effective for healing developmental trauma in ways that merely talking about trauma cannot. Your nervous system does not change through discussion; it changes through repeated experiences that demonstrate safety. These experiences allow your amygdala to learn that threat responses are not always necessary, providing your prefrontal cortex with opportunities to practice regulation in manageable conditions instead of being constantly overwhelmed.

Understanding attachment and developmental trauma is crucial for the work of exploring your deeper self. The patterns operating beneath your awareness, shaping your behaviour, are influenced by your conscious mind, which tells stories that overlook the actual sources. They were not generated randomly, nor do they signify fundamental flaws. Instead, they are learned adaptations to specific circumstances, encoded in your developing brain before you could question whether those circumstances were normal or healthy, before you could envision different possibilities, and before you had any choice about how your brain was wired.

Your attachment template operates automatically, influencing who you are attracted to and how you respond to intimacy. Your reward circuitry functions based on lessons learned in childhood about what is safe and dangerous, what is rewarding and what is threatening. Your stress response system activates according to patterns established when you were too young to remember learning them. Your ability to regulate emotions is constrained by the development that occurred under specific circumstances. All of this happens beneath your conscious awareness, through implicit memory and automatic processes, while your conscious mind maintains a narrative of freely choosing and being in control.

However, you weren't in control when these patterns were formed. You had no choice in the circumstances of your upbringing, no ability to select different caregivers, and no capacity to shape how your brain was wired. These patterns were created as adaptations to situations beyond your control. Now, they operate automatically, beneath your awareness, determining behaviour through processes that your conscious mind cannot directly access or override. This illustrates why free will is so limited, not just because unconscious processes operate faster than conscious thought, or because explicit memory comprises a small fraction of all learning, but because the foundational architecture was established during childhood, shaped by circumstances you could not influence. These templates continue to run automatically even decades later.

The blueprint was drawn before you could hold the pen. The wiring was installed before you knew there was a system. The patterns were encoded before you had words to describe them. Now, you live according to a programming you didn't write, responding through templates you didn't create, and constrained by the neural architecture shaped by circumstances that no longer exist, yet whose influence persists through implicit memory operating beneath awareness. Meanwhile, your conscious mind insists that you are free, that you are choosing, that you are in control. In reality, you are enacting patterns laid down so early that they feel like intrinsic parts of who you are, rather than recognising them as learned adaptations to specific circumstances.

Welcome to the understanding of why you are the way you are, why you keep recreating dynamics you consciously want to change, and why certain people attract you. In contrast, others repel you. Why intimacy triggers specific responses, and why you struggle with regulation, motivation, or pleasure in ways that others do not. Welcome to recognising that your Obscure Psyche isn't merely containing hidden material; it is functioning on fundamental architecture installed in childhood, operating through patterns encoded before you could begin to question whether what you were learning would serve you throughout life.

Childhood wounds are not just memories; they are the architects of our neural structure. They create patterns in our reward circuitry and calibrate our stress responses. These experiences shape our attachment styles, influencing who we perceive as safe and who we see as threatening. They inform our implicit understanding of how relationships function and dictate our automatic reactions to situations reminiscent of our past. These early experiences serve as blueprints that influence much of our adult lives, often remaining largely hidden from our conscious awareness. This is because they were established before we could consciously observe or remember them, before we could choose differently. Understanding this can bring a new level of self-awareness and enlightenment.

This foundational aspect underlies what can be described as the 'Obscure Psyche.' It represents early development that creates patterns, which may play out in the shadows of our lives, leading us to feel like strangers to ourselves while believing we can understand ourselves solely through introspection. Our brains were moulded by our childhood experiences, and this shaping continues to affect our current realities, creating a bridge that connects our past and present selves.

Recognition is the key to initiating change. Once we acknowledge that genuine change involves working with our implicit memories and unconscious processes, we can begin to break free from the patterns established before we had the capacity to question them. We often find ourselves trapped in dynamics learned in our early years, adhering to blueprints created under circumstances beyond our control. However, with recognition, we can start to dismantle these patterns and regain a sense of freedom, choice, and control over our behaviours.

Chapter 7

The Echo of Trauma: When the Past Becomes the Present

Let's reflect on a time when you had an overwhelming emotional reaction to something that was relatively minor. We're not talking about just feeling a bit annoyed or slightly upset; instead, think of moments when your emotions became overwhelming, experiencing terror, rage, or despair that was completely disproportionate to the situation at hand. For example, perhaps your partner forgot to call you back, leading you to spiral into panic, convinced they were leaving you. You felt a sense of abandonment that was so intense it felt like you were dying. Or maybe someone criticised your work, and you were consumed by a crushing shame that made you want to disappear entirely, as if you had been exposed as fundamentally fraudulent. You couldn't breathe properly for hours afterwards.

Another instance might be when you found yourself in a crowded area and suddenly felt an overwhelming sense of dread, prompting an urgent need to escape. Your heart was racing, your palms sweating, and your mind was filled with danger signals, despite knowing on a rational level that you were perfectly safe.

What makes these experiences so confusing is that, deep down, you know you're overreacting. Your rational mind might be telling you, "This isn't that serious. It doesn't warrant this level of response. Why am I feeling this way?" However, that awareness doesn't change how you feel. Your emotional response remains unaffected by your attempts to calm yourself with logic or perspective. It continues to overwhelm you, creating sensations and feelings that don't align with present reality and are instead tied to something from the past that you may not even be able to identify.

This is what living with unprocessed trauma feels like. It's not the dramatic flashbacks often portrayed in films where a person suddenly relives vivid memories of past events, being clearly transported to another time and place. While this can happen, it is pretty rare. More commonly, and more insidiously, individuals experience what's known as an emotional flashback. In such cases, you may feel the emotional weight of past trauma without having any conscious memory of it; you don't realise you're reacting to past events instead of the current situation, and you may not understand that you're being triggered by implicit memories from experiences that might have occurred decades ago.

Consider what happens to your body during these disproportionate reactions. Your heart rate likely spikes dramatically. Your breathing may become rapid and shallow, or you might even hold your breath entirely. Your muscles tense up, preparing for action, your stomach clenches, and your vision narrows as you fixate on the perceived threat. Your thinking tends to become rigid, losing its flexibility; you can only see catastrophe instead of considering other options. This entire physiological shift is your body's way of preparing for immediate danger, responding as if you were in a life-threatening situation, even when the reality is that you are not in danger at all.

Your nervous system is reacting to past experiences rather than the present moment. It activates threat responses learned in childhood or encoded during traumatic incidents, treating current situations as if they pose the same dangers as those from the past. Your conscious mind may not recognise these, but your implicit memory does. The resemblance may be obvious, such as someone raising their voice, triggering memories of being shouted at as a child, or it could be more subtle, like a specific tone of voice, a particular facial expression, a feeling of being trapped, or an emotional atmosphere that resonates with something from your past, even if the actual circumstances are not overtly similar.

Remember that your amygdala stores associations without timestamps. It records "this situation is dangerous" without marking when that danger occurred, without recognising that circumstances have changed, and without distinguishing between past and present. When something in your current environment resembles a pattern it learned to recognise as dangerous, it triggers the complete threat response before your conscious mind even has a chance to assess whether a threat actually exists. So, you're responding to historical danger as if it is present danger, enacting defensive patterns that made sense at the time but are misaligned with current reality. As a result, you find yourself controlled by a past that has merged with the present, all through mechanisms that operate beneath your conscious awareness.

It gets even more complicated. Trauma not only triggers reactions to situations that resemble past dangers; it can create a compulsion to recreate that trauma. You may unconsciously seek out circumstances that will trigger those old patterns, replaying the original dynamics. This phenomenon is known as repetition compulsion. While Freud's explanations for why this occurs were sometimes questionable, the reality of the phenomenon itself is very real and utterly baffling when you find yourself caught in it.

You don't consciously decide, "I think I'll recreate my childhood trauma in this relationship." You don't deliberately choose partners who will treat you the way your caregivers did. You don't intentionally place yourself in situations where you'll be rejected, abandoned, controlled, or harmed. Yet somehow, you keep ending up in these scenarios, repeatedly finding yourself in dynamics that feel painfully familiar, experiencing the same hurt you vowed you'd never endure again. With each instance, you are genuinely surprised, confused about how you ended up back here, and convinced that this time is supposed to be different.

Consider the person who grew up with an angry, unpredictable parent and now finds themselves in relationships with angry, unpredictable partners. Or the individual who experienced neglect and abandonment and continues to choose emotionally unavailable people, recreating that sense of abandonment. Or the person who was controlled and dominated, repeatedly finding themselves in relationships where their autonomy is systematically undermined. These patterns are so consistent that they seem almost deliberate, yet they are not conscious choices. The person genuinely tries to choose differently and wants something better, but something beneath their awareness drives them back to the familiar dynamics of their childhood, activating old implicit memories.

Why would your brain compel you to recreate experiences that caused you suffering? This seems maladaptive, as if it contradicts what a survival-oriented system should do. If something was traumatic, shouldn't you be wired to avoid it at all costs rather than unconsciously seeking it out? However, the repetition compulsion is not about seeking suffering; it's about seeking resolution. It's an unconscious attempt to master what couldn't be controlled initially and to achieve a different outcome by recreating similar circumstances.

The child who couldn't manage an unpredictable parent lives in constant anxiety about when the subsequent explosion will occur. They develop an unconscious belief that if they can just figure out the pattern, behave correctly, or be good enough, they can prevent the anger and create safety through perfect performance. This belief does not disappear in adulthood, even though it is inaccurate; the parent's anger is unrelated to the child's behaviour. The adult unconsciously seeks out situations that resemble their original trauma, believing, "This time I'll get it right; this time I'll figure out how to make them love me; this time I'll master what I couldn't master before."

Yet it never works. You cannot resolve childhood trauma by recreating it with different people. You cannot heal abandonment wounds by choosing someone who abandons you and trying to make them stay. You cannot master being controlled by finding someone controlling and attempting to maintain autonomy. The situations may resemble the original trauma, but they are not the same, and resolving them wouldn't heal the original wound, even if you could. Yet the compulsion persists, driving you toward what feels familiar, toward dynamics that feel like home, even when that home was painful. This leads to activating all the old implicit learning while you consciously insist that you are making free choices, trying something different, and believing that this time will be better.

This is the trauma loop where unprocessed trauma creates patterns. These patterns drive you toward situations that recreate the trauma, which in turn activate more trauma responses. This strengthens the patterns, making you more likely to recreate the trauma again. It becomes a cycle, with the past becoming present. Current circumstances trigger past responses, while those past responses influence your present choices, often without your awareness. You may believe you are responding to what is happening now rather than recognising that you are reacting to echoes from decades ago.

Running beneath our experiences of feeling trapped in trauma is a brain network designed to help us understand ourselves and our experiences. However, in the context of trauma, this network can become stuck, turning into a generator of suffering instead of facilitating sense-making. This network is known as the Default Mode Network (DMN), and understanding its functioning and dysfunction is crucial for grasping why trauma continues to feel present even when it is in the past. It explains why moving on can seem impossible, even when we consciously desire to, and why thinking about trauma often worsens our emotional state rather than alleviating it. However, this understanding also reveals the potential for the DMN to aid in trauma treatment, inspiring optimism and motivation in mental health professionals and trauma survivors alike.

The Default Mode Network comprises a collection of brain regions that activate when we are not focused on external tasks. It engages when our attention turns inward, fostering self-referential thinking, reflecting on ourselves, our lives, our past, our future, our relationships, and our identities. This network includes the medial prefrontal cortex, the posterior cingulate cortex, the precuneus, and parts of the temporal lobes. These areas work together when we are mind-wandering, daydreaming, reminiscing about the past, planning for the future, contemplating how others perceive us, or constructing narratives about who we are and what our lives mean. In this way, the DMN's role is a universal aspect of the human experience, connecting us all in our shared capacity for introspection and self-reflection.

In healthy functioning, the DMN enables helpful self-reflection, facilitates learning from past experiences, plans for the future based on past patterns, maintains a continuous sense of identity over time, and derives meaning from our experiences. When we are not engaged with immediate external tasks, the DMN activates, allowing us to think about our lives, process recent events, evaluate our situations, and update our understanding of ourselves and our relationships. This ability is both adaptive and essential to being human.

However, in the case of trauma, the DMN can become problematic. Instead of enabling productive self-reflection, it leads to repetitive, circular thinking about traumatic experiences, what is wrong with us, the threats we face, and negative interpretations of ourselves and our lives. The network that should aid in making sense of our experiences instead gets stuck on traumatic content, continuously reactivating the neural patterns linked to trauma. This keeps emotional and physiological responses active long after the actual danger has passed.

Research indicates that individuals with post-traumatic stress disorder, depression, or anxiety disorders exhibit overactive DMNs. When their brains are not engaged in external tasks, they default to patterns of negative self-referential thinking. They ruminate on past trauma, worry about potential future threats, and engage in harsh self-criticism while constructing narratives that emphasise their fundamental inadequacy or the dangers in the world. Since the DMN includes areas connected to emotional processing, memory retrieval, and bodily sensations, this rumination does not just involve abstract thoughts; it activates the whole emotional and physiological experience of trauma.

When your default mode network (DMN) activates and begins processing traumatic content, several things happen simultaneously. The medial prefrontal cortex, which is involved in self-referential processing, activates patterns associated with your identity as traumatised, damaged, or under threat. This self-referential thinking is a process where you relate everything back to your trauma, interpreting events and situations through the lens of your past experiences. The posterior cingulate cortex, which is involved in memory retrieval and emotional processing, brings up implicit memories related to trauma. The precuneus, responsible for our sense of self and mental imagery, creates vivid imagined scenarios of past traumas or potential future harms. These regions work together to create the subjective experience of trauma as if it were present, even when it is not.

This situation is particularly distressing because you are not consciously choosing to activate these patterns. You may be sitting quietly, trying to relax, and yet your DMN activates in its usual way when you are not focused externally. Instead of engaging in pleasant mind-wandering or productive reflection, you suddenly find yourself immersed in traumatic content, experiencing emotional flashbacks and overwhelming anxiety, depression, or shame without any external trigger. This occurs simply because your resting-state brain network has defaulted to trauma processing rather than neutral or positive content.

As a result, individuals with trauma often find it challenging to tolerate quiet or to be alone with their thoughts, requiring constant distraction or stimulation to prevent their minds from veering into dark places. When external focus ceases and attention turns inward, the DMN activates and immediately defaults to trauma content. This happens because the strongest neural pathways are tied to trauma; that is, what has been rehearsed most often, and trauma has essentially hijacked the system meant for self-reflection, turning it into a trauma-replay mechanism.

Consider what occurs when you try to relax, meditate, or simply be present without distraction. If you have unprocessed trauma, these attempts can often make things worse rather than better. Your DMN activates and defaults to trauma processing, flooding you with overwhelming emotions, disturbing thoughts, and physical sensations of danger, even when you are in a perfectly safe environment doing something that should be calming. This isn't a case of you doing something wrong; it's your DMN operating according to what it has been conditioned to do: defaulting to danger processing and negative self-referential thinking whenever it is not engaged in external tasks.

This also explains why therapy focused purely on discussing trauma can sometimes exacerbate the situation. When you talk about trauma and deliberately focus on traumatic memories, you activate your DMN while simultaneously invoking the emotional and physiological responses associated with trauma. Suppose you are not in a position to process this activation, unable to metabolise the emotional content and integrate the experience. In that case, you can end up merely rehearsing the trauma patterns, strengthening the neural pathways, and training your DMN to default even more strongly to trauma content. You are not processing; you are re-traumatising yourself.

This is why approaches like Eye Movement Desensitisation and Reprocessing (EMDR), somatic experiencing, and sensorimotor psychotherapy can be more effective. These methods address trauma through pathways other than mere discussion, focusing on the body's responses rather than just cognitive content. They help you metabolise and discharge the physiological activation rather than simply rehearsing the narrative of what happened.

To understand emotional flashbacks, it's essential to differentiate them from explicit memory flashbacks, which are what most people think of when they hear the term. An explicit memory flashback occurs when you suddenly and vividly recall a traumatic event; you might see images, hear sounds, or smell familiar scents from the trauma as if you're transported back to that time. These dramatic flashbacks are often depicted in media and typically occur in individuals with PTSD resulting from adult-onset trauma, where they have a clear memory of the event.

In contrast, emotional flashbacks are different and much more common, especially for those who have experienced childhood trauma or developmental trauma that took place before explicit memory formation. During an emotional flashback, you experience the emotional and physiological reality of past trauma without any conscious recollection of the event, no images, no narrative, and you may not even realise you're reacting to something from the past. Instead, you might suddenly feel overwhelming terror, crushing shame, intense rage, or desperate loneliness, without understanding why these feelings have arisen, as you are not consciously recalling any specific trauma.

This is due to the way traumatic experiences are processed in the brain. The hippocampus, responsible for forming narrative memories, is often compromised by stress hormones, making it difficult to encode explicit memories of the trauma. However, the amygdala, which encodes implicit emotional memory, is not affected in the same way. It stores the complete physiological and emotional state associated with the trauma. When something triggers these implicit memories, the entire emotional state is activated, often without any conscious awareness of the trigger.

You might feel as if you're five years old again, small, powerless, and terrified, yet you have no conscious memory of being that age, no images from that time, and no narrative about what occurred. You simply feel it in your body, in your nervous system, with an overwhelming emotional reality that doesn't correspond with anything happening in the present but perfectly aligns with something that took place decades ago, stored as implicit memory without timestamps, context, or conscious access. Your Default Mode Network (DMN) might attempt to rationalise your feelings, generating thoughts that seem to explain your emotions, such as "my partner is going to leave me," "I'm going to fail at work," or "everyone sees how inadequate I am." However, these thoughts completely miss the mark, as they fail to account for the activation of implicit memories that are responsible for your emotional response.

This leads to profound confusion. You might have intense emotional reactions that appear to come from nowhere, which don't match present reality and which you cannot explain or understand. Your conscious mind tries to make sense of the situation by looking at current circumstances and finding plausible explanations. Still, these interpretations are often entirely incorrect because they don't recognise the influence of implicit memory on your response. This is your Obscure Psyche operating at full capacity, shaping your experience through processes you cannot consciously access. It creates your present reality from past material you don't remember and hijacks your nervous system through implicit learning while your consciousness fabricates false narratives about what is happening.

Recognising emotional flashbacks involves noticing the disproportion between your emotional response and the current situation. When your reaction is dramatically larger than what the situation warrants, such as feeling crushing shame from a minor criticism, overwhelming rage from a small conflict, or intense abandonment terror from a brief separation, this intensity serves as a clue that you are not responding to the present moment but to past experiences that have been activated through implicit memory.

However, identifying an emotional flashback while you're in one is extremely challenging. Part of what makes trauma overwhelming is that it disrupts your ability to gain perspective and recognise that "this is a response, not reality." When your nervous system is highly activated and implicit memories hijack your physiology, the parts of your brain responsible for perspective, particularly the prefrontal cortex, go offline. At these moments, you cannot think clearly, recall your patterns, or understand that you are being triggered rather than responding appropriately to a current threat.

This is why having external support during flashbacks is so crucial. Therapy that focuses on creating a sense of safety and developing your capacity to tolerate activation, rather than merely exploring traumatic content, can be particularly effective. When you're overwhelmed, you cannot simply think your way out of a flashback because the necessary cognitive functions are unavailable. Instead, you need strategies that engage with your physiology and sensations, helping to bring your nervous system out of maximum activation through methods that do not rely on the cognitive functions that are currently offline.

Consider what helps when you feel overwhelmed. It is often not rational thoughts or logical arguments but rather physical activities such as feeling your feet on the ground, noticing your breath, moving your body, experiencing temperature or texture, or connecting with someone who is calm and present. These practices work because they directly engage your nervous system, providing input that counters the threat response and helping your body recognise, "I'm here now, in present reality," instead of being trapped in past memories that have intruded upon the present.

Patterns like repetition compulsion, emotional flashbacks, and an overactive Default Mode Network (DMN) that fixates on trauma content are mechanisms that keep the past alive in the present. These processes, which operate primarily beneath conscious awareness, stem from implicit memory and automatic responses. Meanwhile, our consciousness creates narratives that misinterpret the dynamics at play, often blaming current circumstances or personal inadequacies without acknowledging the impact of the past on our present experiences.

Breaking the trauma loop requires acknowledging its existence, understanding that present reactions might be rooted in historical responses, and recognising that overwhelming emotions may be flashbacks rather than appropriate reactions to current situations. However, recognition alone is insufficient because these patterns are deeply ingrained and too automatic to disrupt through conscious awareness. Therefore, approaches that work with implicit memory, nervous system activation, and the body's responses are essential, not just cognitive understanding.

You need repeated experiences of facing activation without feeling overwhelmed, addressing trauma-related material while staying grounded in the present, and feeling your emotions without being consumed by them. Updating implicit memory involves not only talking about trauma but also experiencing something different, such as cultivating relationships that do not replicate past trauma, being in situations where anticipated catastrophes do not occur, or feeling distress while receiving appropriate support, which reinforces the understanding that you are not alone in confronting unbearable experiences.

To address your DMN, it's essential to develop the ability to notice when you're ruminating or stuck in trauma processing, gently redirecting your focus to present-moment sensory experiences instead of engaging in abstract negative thinking that reinforces trauma patterns. This approach is not about positive thinking or denial; it is about recognising when you're rehearsing trauma and consciously choosing to engage with the present reality, gradually retraining your DMN to adopt different defaults beyond trauma processing.

You need to learn to recognise emotional flashbacks, not while you are experiencing them, this is often impossible when you're overwhelmed, but afterwards, in reflection. Notice moments when your response seems disproportionate or the intensity doesn't match the situation; you might have been triggered by the past rather than responding to the present. This recognition, accumulated over many instances, helps you gradually develop the ability to catch flashbacks earlier. You can learn to recognise your activation while your cognitive functions are still online, allowing you to interrupt patterns before they entirely hijack your system.

This is a slow process. The patterns are deeply ingrained, created through repeated traumatic experiences and strengthened by countless activations. These patterns operate through implicit memory systems that change slowly with new experiences rather than quickly through insights. However, it is possible to change because your brain retains plasticity, the capacity to encode new learning, update old patterns, and create new defaults through sufficient repetition of different experiences. The past doesn't have to remain in the present. The trauma loop can be broken, and the echo can fade, allowing it to be recognised as an echo rather than felt as current reality.

This requires understanding what's happening, recognising the mechanisms, and working with your actual neurobiology rather than trying to think your way out of patterns that don't operate on a cognitive level. Your Default Mode Network (DMN) will continue to activate when you're not focused externally. Your implicit memories will continue to store experiences without timestamps. Your amygdala will continue to respond to patterns that match the present with those of the past. These are features of how your brain functions, not flaws to be eliminated. The question is whether you will remain unaware of these dynamics or develop the capacity to recognise when the past becomes the present, when trauma is replaying, and when you're stuck in a loop instead of responding to current reality.

Welcome to understanding the echo: how trauma reverberates through time, influencing the present with patterns encoded in formats beyond conscious access, creating loops that feel endless. At the same time, you're unaware of being in them. Recognise that your Obscure Psyche isn't just containing hidden material; it actively recreates the past as present through repetition compulsion, emotional flashbacks, DMN patterns stuck on trauma, and implicit memory activation without your awareness or consent, while your conscious mind crafts narratives that miss the actual sources entirely.

The trauma occurred then, but it's also happening now. This happens through mechanisms you didn't choose, through patterns formed before you could protest, and through neural pathways reinforced by circumstances you had no control over. Until you recognise these mechanisms, understand the distinction between past and present, and develop the capacity to work with implicit memory and nervous system activation rather than trying to think your way out of patterns that operate below consciousness, you will remain trapped in this loop, recreating scenarios that you cannot remember, responding to shadows while insisting you're responding to reality. You will live in the past disguised as the present. At the same time, your consciousness perpetuates a fiction of being here now, even as you're partly stuck in the past every day, driven by the mechanisms of the Obscure Psyche that ensure trauma remains unprocessed and unintegrated until it is fully acknowledged rather than simply survived or suppressed.

Chapter 8

The Shadow and the Fix: The Neuroscience of Substance Misuse

I need you to be honest with yourself about something you might not like admitting. There may be a substance, whether it's alcohol, cannabis, prescription medication, something more substantial, or even something socially acceptable like caffeine or sugar, that you use not because you genuinely enjoy it but because you need it to feel normal. You might rely on it to manage states that feel unbearable without it, turning down the volume on internal experiences that seem too loud, too intense, or too overwhelming to tolerate. Deep down, beneath all the justifications and rationalisations, you know that you're not using this substance recreationally. You're self-medicating, trying to chemically fix something inside yourself that feels fundamentally broken.

However, here's what most people miss, and it's crucial for understanding substance misuse and your obscure psyche: the substance is not creating new experiences. It's not inserting foreign thoughts or emotions into your mind. Instead, it reveals what was already there, amplifying existing patterns and unlocking doors to rooms that have always been part of the house. The substance acts as a mirror, not a magic wand. What you see in that mirror, whether it's euphoria or terror, confidence or paranoia, peace or rage, that's you. Those aspects of yourself were always there; you just couldn't access them, didn't know they existed, or had been desperately trying to keep them hidden.

Perhaps alcohol allows you to relax after days of feeling tense, helps you sleep when your mind won't stop racing, or makes social situations tolerable that might otherwise trigger crippling anxiety. When you're drunk, you might feel funny, confident, and charming attributes you don't access when sober. Maybe stimulants help you focus and feel capable and productive, rather than scattered and inadequate, revealing a competence and brilliance you believe is your "true self" finally emerging. Or perhaps sedatives turn off the constant vigilance, the ongoing threat-scanning, and the exhausting high alert your nervous system defaults to without chemical intervention. Maybe opioids create a warm cocoon of safety and comfort that you've never felt without them, finally dulling the emotional pain that has been your constant companion for as long as you can remember.

What makes this particularly difficult to acknowledge is that it works. At least initially, the substance does precisely what you need it to do. It genuinely provides relief from states that feel intolerable. It effectively reduces the amygdala's threat responses and floods your nucleus accumbens with dopamine that your natural reward system cannot produce sufficiently. It temporarily reveals aspects of yourself, the confidence, the calm, the creativity, the peace that feel impossible to access any other way. This isn't a matter of you being weak, making poor decisions, or lacking willpower. It's a realisation that chemistry can achieve what psychology, willpower, and conscious effort cannot. It can fundamentally alter your neurological state, creating experiences of calm, energy, pleasure, or connection that your brain doesn't generate naturally, providing relief from suffering that nothing else has touched.

Yet, the cruel irony is this: while the substance reveals genuine aspects of yourself, qualities that are authentically part of your psychological potential, it does so through means that will ultimately make accessing those aspects even more difficult than before. The confidence you found through alcohol, the focus you discovered through stimulants, and the peace you experienced through opioids are real capacities you possess. However, by accessing them chemically, you're training your brain to believe these states are only available through substances. You're creating neurobiological dependence that impairs the natural pathways to these states, trapping yourself in a situation where the solution becomes the problem, even though it feels like the only option available.

Consider what happens when you use substances to manage unbearable states. You're not just getting high, drunk, or sedated. You're discovering what your consciousness feels like without the constant anxiety, crushing depression, overwhelming activation, or gnawing emptiness that have been your normal experience for so long that you thought that's just how life feels. Someone who's dealt with chronic anxiety since childhood might take a benzodiazepine and suddenly realise, "I didn't even know I was tense. I thought everyone felt this way. I thought this constant vigilance was just how consciousness works." Someone who has never felt safe in their own body might take an opioid and discover, "This is what peace feels like. This is what other people mean when they say they feel comfortable. I've never had this without chemicals."

These are genuine revelations about what your consciousness can experience. The tragedy lies not in the discoveries being false, but that they are true. The real tragedy is the dependence on substances that prevent you from accessing these states naturally. Instead, you are using mechanisms that hijack your brain's reward system, leading you to depend on the substance not to feel good, but merely to feel normal; not for pleasure, but to prevent the pain that the substance use itself creates and intensifies.

Let's delve into the neurological processes that occur when you use substances, and why they are initially so effective. The nucleus accumbens, a key part of the ventral striatum deep in your brain, plays a central role in reward processing and motivation. When you engage in activities vital for survival, such as eating when hungry, having sex, achieving a goal, or forming social bonds, your nucleus accumbens releases dopamine. This release creates the subjective experience of pleasure while also encoding the learning that 'this behaviour is valuable; repeat it.' This is how your brain motivates adaptive behaviour, learns what to seek and avoid, and creates the drives that keep you pursuing activities necessary for survival and well-being.

The increase in dopamine from natural rewards is significant but limited to roughly two to three times your baseline levels. This release occurs in patterns that correspond to the reward and declines fairly quickly once the rewarding stimulus ends. Your brain is designed to handle these natural fluctuations, with regulatory mechanisms that maintain homeostasis, allowing it to return to baseline relatively quickly after dopamine surges from natural sources. This system is calibrated for the types of rewards available in the environment in which humans evolved, such as food, sex, social connection, and achievement. It responds to these with dopamine increases sufficient to motivate pursuit without overwhelming the system.

However, substances bypass all of these natural constraints. They either directly activate dopamine release or prevent dopamine reuptake, creating surges that surpass what natural rewards produce. Stimulants like cocaine and amphetamines can increase dopamine levels ten times above baseline or more. It's crucial to understand that the subjective experience of this dopamine surge is entirely shaped by what is already present in your psyche, your existing drives, desires, and psychological patterns. The substance doesn't create the experience; it reveals and amplifies what was already there.

For example, someone driven by professional ambition who uses cocaine may feel like a genius capable of superhuman productivity. Someone seeking social status might feel charismatic and superior to others. Another individual motivated by creative expression may experience themselves as an artistic visionary with unparalleled insights. The dopamine surge is the same for all of them, but what that surge amplifies, making it conscious and intense, is determined entirely by each person's psychological landscape. The substance is consistent; what varies is what it uncovers when it enters your mind, illuminating aspects of yourself, your drives, desires, and capacities that are typically suppressed or unavailable.

Consider alcohol, which enhances GABA, your brain's primary inhibitory neurotransmitter, while interfering with glutamate, the main excitatory neurotransmitter. This creates a systematic dismantling of inhibition, removing the filters and controls that typically keep certain aspects of ourselves in check. The ancient Romans understood this with the phrase "in vino veritas," in wine, truth. It's not that alcohol makes people truthful; instead, it removes the social conditioning, the self-censorship, and the regulatory mechanisms that usually prevent certain aspects of ourselves from being expressed.

A person who becomes cruel when drunk isn't being made cruel by alcohol; they're expressing anger, resentment, or cruelty that has always been there, but has been suppressed by empathy and social awareness when sober. This hidden anger erupts when those regulatory mechanisms are chemically disabled. Similarly, someone who becomes weepy and vulnerable when drunk isn't being made sad by alcohol; they're releasing grief, loneliness, or emotional pain that they constantly carry but never express, finally able to feel it when inhibitions are lowered. Likewise, a person who becomes confident and charming isn't gaining confidence from alcohol; they're accessing natural charisma that is usually constrained by anxiety and self-consciousness, finally able to express aspects of themselves that typically remain inaccessible.

This is why the same person can have wildly different experiences with the same substance depending on their psychological state. Cannabis provides a clear example. The same dose of cannabis can produce euphoric laughter in someone feeling secure and relaxed, or overwhelming paranoia in someone carrying unexpressed anxiety. The THC binds to the same endocannabinoid receptors in both cases, creating the same neurological effects. What differs is the emotional and psychological content being amplified.

When you feel paranoid while using cannabis, you're not experiencing something created by the cannabis; you're experiencing anxiety and mistrust that you carry with you but usually manage to suppress. Cannabis removes that suppression, amplifying what has always been there, bringing into conscious awareness the threat-scanning and vigilance that have been operating beneath the surface. Conversely, when you feel profound peace using cannabis, you're not encountering something foreign; you're accessing a capacity for calm that exists within you but is usually unavailable due to constant stress activation. The substance reveals what your consciousness can experience when specific filters are removed and regulatory systems are altered.

This understanding changes our perspective on substance use and misuse. You're not seeking an escape from yourself; you're seeking access to aspects of yourself that feel unreachable otherwise. You're not running away from who you are; you're running toward parts of yourself that require chemical assistance to access. The confidence, creativity, calm, peace, and freedom from constant vigilance are genuine aspects of your psychological potential. The tragedy is that you are accessing these aspects through means that will ultimately make them less accessible, creating dependence while promising liberation.

Now, let's talk about the effects of repeated use and how the neurobiological trap snaps shut, making it difficult to escape. Your brain is designed to maintain homeostasis, keeping neurochemical systems within specific ranges. When you repeatedly flood your nucleus accumbens with dopamine, creating massive surges far beyond natural levels, your brain must adapt. It can't maintain responsiveness to such enormous inputs, so it down-regulates, reducing the number of dopamine receptors, decreasing the sensitivity of existing receptors, and increasing the activity of enzymes that break down dopamine. This is tolerance: needing more of the substance to achieve the same effect because your brain has adapted to the previous dose by becoming less responsive.

But here's where it becomes truly devastating: as your reward system becomes less responsive to a substance, and you derive less pleasure from its use, your motivation to consume it actually increases. This phenomenon, known as incentive sensitisation, is a key aspect of addiction. It creates a vicious cycle. You become more driven to seek the substance; it dominates your thoughts, triggers intense cravings, and feels absolutely essential even as you experience diminishing pleasure from using it. The desire intensifies while the enjoyment diminishes. You feel an urgent need to use, even though you are gaining less satisfaction, trapping yourself in a loop where the substance becomes increasingly important, even as it offers less pleasure.

Meanwhile, your amygdala, a key player in the brain's emotional processing, is forming associations between the substance and relief from distress. It encodes the idea that this substance is necessary for managing unbearable emotional states. As we've discussed in earlier chapters, your amygdala creates implicit memories without timestamps, stores associations in formats that you cannot consciously access, and triggers responses before you are even aware of what is happening. Each time you use a substance to alleviate anxiety, pain, or emotional activation, your amygdala learns: "This chemical is essential for survival; this substance provides relief from unbearable states; I need this to function."

These associations become extraordinarily powerful and persistent because they are encoded through the exact mechanisms your brain uses to learn what is necessary for survival. The amygdala cannot distinguish between "this helps me feel better" and "this is crucial for my continued existence." It simply recognises that this substance reliably provides relief from perceived threats, and it encodes that learning as strongly as it would encode the lessons learned for escaping predators or finding food when starving. The associations are stored in implicit memory and are automatically triggered by contextual cues, activating before your conscious awareness can evaluate whether they are still accurate or helpful.

Consider the implications for someone trying to quit using a substance through willpower alone. The confidence they derived from alcohol is a genuine capacity they possess, but they have trained their brain to believe that this confidence is only available through chemical means. The calm they experienced with benzodiazepines is a real state their nervous system can achieve, but their implicit memories have encoded this calm as something that requires chemical intervention. The focus they discovered through stimulants is an authentic capability. However, they have altered their reward system to believe that natural efforts to achieve focus are insufficient and lack the worth needed to produce a dopamine surge signalling genuine achievement.

They are attempting to consciously override learning encoded in implicit memory, trying to rationally control behaviour driven by nucleus accumbens activation, and resisting cravings generated by dopamine surges in response to cues. At the same time, their prefrontal cortex, the area of the brain responsible for decision-making and impulse control, has been weakened due to chronic substance use. This weakening of the prefrontal cortex makes it even more challenging for individuals to resist their cravings and make rational decisions. They are struggling with the wrong tools against the wrong target, trying to use conscious intention to override unconscious drives and thinking their way out of a neurobiological trap that does not respond to conscious thought.

There is another layer that connects substance misuse directly to shadow work, trauma, and the Obscure Psyche we've been exploring throughout this book. Substances offer more than just neurochemical relief; they provide access to disowned aspects of ourselves, allowing for a temporary dissolution of the defences that usually keep our shadow material suppressed. They can create brief experiences of wholeness that feel impossible without chemical assistance.

When someone is intoxicated, they are not just experiencing altered neurochemistry; they are temporarily freed from the need to maintain their carefully constructed persona. This liberation allows emotions that feel too threatening to be expressed, as well as aspects of themselves they've relegated to the shadow to surface.

For instance, the anxious person who becomes articulate and charming when drinking is tapping into a genuine part of themselves that is usually inaccessible due to anxiety. Similarly, the controlled person who becomes spontaneous and playful when using cannabis is revealing an authentic playfulness, which is typically defended against because it feels too vulnerable. Even the individual who struggles to express their needs may become weepy and demanding when drunk, those needs are real but typically suppressed because expressing them feels too risky.

In this way, substances create space for shadow material to emerge and for disowned aspects to find expression. However, this isn't genuine integration. It does not create a conscious relationship with shadow material. Instead, it leads to a chaotic eruption of these aspects rather than a deliberate engagement with them. Because this shadow material is only accessible while intoxicated, individuals do not develop the capacity to work with these aspects when sober. As a result, the underlying split persists. People remain fragmented, with parts of themselves that only emerge under the influence of substances. This means that the only way they know to access their shadow material is through chemical assistance, which fosters an artificial sense of wholeness that ultimately deepens their fragmentation instead of healing it.

Consider the person who feels confident only when drinking, relying on alcohol to access qualities like assertiveness, playfulness, or sexuality. When sober, these qualities remain suppressed and unavailable. The act of drinking can bring these traits to the surface, allowing for their expression and creating a sense of completeness. However, because these qualities can only be accessed chemically, they are never truly integrated. They remain split off, reliant on substance use for expression. This reinforces the belief that "I can only be like this when I'm drinking," making sobriety feel like a return to a diminished, incomplete version of oneself. While substances reveal these aspects, the revelation occurs through means that prevent actual integration.

Now, let's specifically discuss opioids, as they uncover something particularly devastating about the human experience of suffering. When someone uses opioids and describes the experience as "finally feeling like myself," they may be expressing relief from a lifelong sense of dysphoria, discomfort, or disconnection that has been their normal experience since childhood. Opioids create a state of warmth, comfort, contentment, and safety in one's own body, feelings that they may have never experienced naturally.

Opioids bind to receptors in the brain and body that are usually activated by endorphins, which are the body's natural pain-relieving chemicals. When opioids flood these receptors, they not only mask physical pain but also create an artificial state of profound well-being. This can reveal the extent of psychological pain that a person may have been carrying without even realising it. For someone using opioids for the first time, the experience may highlight what life can feel like without the burdens of constant anxiety, depression, or emotional numbness. It's important to understand that the drug isn't creating these feelings; instead, the individual is discovering a sense of peace that their consciousness can attain when freed from the chronic psychological pain they've resigned themselves to as just "how life feels."

This is why opioid dependence is so devastating and why treating it requires more than simply addressing the physical addiction. A person struggling with opioid addiction often isn't merely choosing pleasure over responsibility; they're seeking a state of consciousness where their chronic psychological pain feels manageable. They want to feel normal and experience a sense of well-being that seems natural to others. By temporarily easing their stress response systems, often chronically activated since childhood, opioids reveal what peace can feel like. Once they have experienced that feeling, returning to their previous state becomes intolerable.

This is closely connected to trauma, attachment issues, and the developmental damage explored in earlier chapters. People who have secure attachments, whose childhoods fostered well-regulated nervous systems, and who possess standard reward circuitry, can often use substances casually without developing a dependence. This is because their baseline state is tolerable, natural rewards are sufficient for them, and they have internal resources to manage discomfort. Conversely, individuals with insecure attachments, developmental trauma, and chronically dysregulated nervous systems are particularly vulnerable to substance dependence, as these substances provide what their neurobiology cannot generate on its own.

This vulnerability is not a matter of moral character or willpower; it involves neurobiological and psychological conditions that substances can temporarily alleviate. For example, someone with a hyperactive amygdala may desperately need the calming effect that alcohol provides, as it genuinely reduces their sense of threat. A person with compromised reward circuitry may need the motivation and energy boost from stimulants, as their depleted system cannot produce it naturally. Similarly, someone with unprocessed trauma may seek the relief that opioids offer, acting as a chemical barrier between their consciousness and the unbearable implicit memories that are constantly threatening to surface.

The crucial question to consider is this: If substance use is often a way to cope with unprocessed trauma, to regulate dysregulated nervous systems, or to access psychological states that feel unattainable naturally, does this imply that treating the underlying trauma and nervous system issues can resolve substance dependence? Understanding the research on this topic is nuanced and significant because it offers hope, influencing our approach to both prevention and treatment.

The evidence strongly indicates that addressing underlying trauma significantly enhances addiction treatment outcomes. Studies consistently demonstrate that integrated treatment, where both substance use and underlying psychological issues are addressed simultaneously, is more effective than treating addiction alone. Integrated treatment typically involves a combination of trauma-focused therapy, addiction counselling, and possibly medication management. Individuals with a history of childhood trauma who receive trauma-focused therapy alongside addiction treatment exhibit lower relapse rates, improved psychological functioning, and more sustained recovery compared to those who only receive addiction treatment without trauma work. The link between unresolved trauma and substance dependence is real, powerful, and therapeutically important.

However, it is essential to note that treating trauma does not simply 'cure' addiction, and here's why: The neurobiological changes caused by chronic substance use persist even after the trauma has been processed. This is what we refer to as 'neurobiological dependence'. The brain's nucleus accumbens has learned, through many repetitions, that the substance is highly valuable. Additionally, dopamine receptors may have been down-regulated, and the stress response system has been disrupted not only by trauma but also by the rebound effects of repeatedly using substances to manage it. These changes do not instantly reverse when trauma treatment begins. The brain requires time to recalibrate, benefits from repeated experiences of managing emotional states without chemical intervention, and needs to gradually rebuild natural reward responses and stress regulation abilities.

Moreover, while trauma is a significant factor in many cases of substance dependence, it is not the only factor. Genetic vulnerabilities, which can predispose individuals to addiction, social and environmental influences, the specific neurochemical effects of certain substances, the age at which use began, and the duration and pattern of use all contribute to the development and maintenance of dependence. For instance, someone might have minimal trauma but significant genetic vulnerability to addiction. In contrast, another individual might have substantial trauma but develop dependence partly due to the ready availability of substances and cultural normalisation of their use. The situation is complex and multifactorial, not simply reducible to a 'trauma causes addiction' model.

Research indicates that untreated trauma makes recovery from substance dependence extremely difficult. When someone is asked to give up their method of managing overwhelming states without offering alternative coping strategies, it sets them up for failure. It's akin to asking someone to put down crutches without first healing a broken leg; they cannot walk without the crutches because the underlying injury has yet to be addressed. Similarly, asking someone to stop using substances while their nervous system remains chronically dysregulated, while unprocessed trauma continues to create unbearable distress, and while they lack alternative methods for achieving the calm, confidence, or peace that substances provided, this approach is likely to lead to failure.

Effective treatment, therefore, requires addressing multiple levels simultaneously: the neurobiological dependence by allowing time for recalibration, possibly using medications to support this process; the underlying trauma through approaches that engage with implicit memory and nervous system regulation; the psychological dependence on substances as a means to access disowned aspects of themselves by developing alternative strategies for reaching those aspects; and the social and environmental factors that may contribute to ongoing substance use. This comprehensive, long-term approach is reassuring, as it acknowledges the complexity of the issue and provides a roadmap for effective treatment.

Recognising the role of trauma significantly changes our approach to recovery in essential ways. It involves understanding that substance use often begins as a means of adaptation, a solution to real problems, and an attempt to manage genuine suffering, even though it ultimately leads to additional suffering through neurobiological mechanisms. The person isn't broken or weak; they simply found a tool that worked for them until it stopped working. This tool initially provided real relief but eventually became a source of suffering. It served as a solution before turning into a problem, all while still feeling like the only available option.

Recovery, therefore, focuses on developing alternative methods for managing the substances used, accessing what they provided, and tolerating the states from which these substances allowed escape. This process is slow, much slower than the immediate relief that substances offer. It requires processing trauma through methods that engage implicit memory, a type of long-term memory that doesn't require conscious thought to recall. Examples of such methods include somatic therapies and EMDR approaches, which help your nervous system update old learnings encoded before you had conscious awareness. It also demands learning to regulate your nervous system through non-chemical means, practices that create feelings of safety in your body, help your stress response system learn to down-regulate, and gradually build the capacity to tolerate activation without becoming overwhelmed.

Moreover, it requires recognising that the aspects of yourself accessed through substances, such as confidence, creativity, calmness, and freedom from vigilance, are genuine capacities you possess, not mere illusions created by chemicals. The work involves learning to access these capacities without chemical assistance and developing the neurological and psychological frameworks that enable you to experience these states naturally. This shifts the focus from 'stop using substances' to 'develop alternative pathways to the states that substances provided,' and from 'resist temptation through willpower' to 'gradually build the capacity for experiencing what substances allowed you to experience.'

Consider the practical implications of this. Someone who discovered their capacity for social confidence through alcohol needs to cultivate that confidence through repeated experiences of successful social interactions while sober. This process gradually updates their implicit memory, reshaping social situations from being perceived as threatening to rewarding. It takes time and numerous repetitions to counteract decades of contrasting learning encoded in implicit memory. However, it is achievable because neuroplasticity, the brain's ability to reorganise itself by forming new neural connections, is real. This allows your brain to create new associations even in adulthood. The capacities revealed through substances can be accessed through other means, albeit with more time and effort required to develop them.

A person who uses cannabis to tap into their creative and philosophical side must create circumstances where these aspects can emerge without chemical assistance. This might involve setting aside dedicated time for reflection, being in environments that foster contemplation, or engaging in practices like journaling or meditation that facilitate different modes of consciousness. This creativity and philosophical inclination are genuinely theirs; they didn't only surface while using cannabis, they were always present, just suppressed by the demands and distractions of daily life, as well as by defences that cannabis temporarily dissolved but can now be worked through consciously.

Someone who relies on opioids to escape the constant background noise of trauma activation needs to process that trauma directly. They must help their nervous system recognise that the threat is historical rather than current, gradually building their capacity to feel safe in their own body without chemical intervention. This is not a quick process; trauma processing is slow, careful work that cannot be rushed because overwhelming the system can recreate rather than resolve trauma. However, as implicit memories are updated through new experiences of safety, as the nervous system learns to down-regulate, and as the individual develops the ability to tolerate distress without being overwhelmed, the need for chemical escape lessens because the states they were trying to escape become less unbearable.

Let's specifically discuss the amygdala in relation to substances, as this understanding sheds light on why certain substances initially provide relief and then lead to rebound effects that exacerbate problems. Many substances, particularly alcohol and benzodiazepines, genuinely decrease amygdala activity. They enhance GABA, the inhibitory neurotransmitter that calms neural activation, creating a state where the amygdala is less reactive, where threat signals are diminished, and where constant vigilance finally subsides. For someone whose amygdala has been signalling danger for years, perhaps due to trauma, anxious attachment, or chronic stress, this relief is profound, revelatory, and life-changing.

They discover that they can exist without feeling constantly on edge, interact socially without crippling anxiety, sleep without their minds racing with threats, and feel something approximating peace. Of course, they use it again. The substance provides what their own nervous system cannot, creating a state of calm and safety they have been desperately seeking. It reveals what consciousness feels like when threat detection isn't constantly activated. This isn't about seeking pleasure or escaping responsibility; it's about realising that life doesn't have to feel like a constant emergency. Their nervous system can experience states other than being on high alert, and consciousness without hypervigilance is indeed possible.

However, when substances are repeatedly used to suppress amygdala activity, a key part of the brain's limbic system responsible for processing emotions, and when threat responses are continually dampened through chemical means, the brain adapts by hyperactivating the very systems that are being suppressed. The amygdala becomes even more reactive during periods without the substance, resulting in rebound anxiety that is worse than the baseline. The stress response system becomes more sensitive and easily triggered, making it more challenging to down-regulate. The withdrawal state periods between uses become characterised by heightened threat detection, increased stress hormone release, and exaggerated fear responses that are worse than what initially drove the person to use substances.

This creates a vicious cycle: people use substances to reduce an overactive amygdala, the substance works temporarily, the brain compensates by making the amygdala even more reactive when the substance wears off, which leads to worse anxiety than they started with. This increases the urgency to use the substance, further dysregulating their stress response, trapping them in a loop where what provided relief is now worsening their condition, even as it remains the only solution they know.

This is why recovery requires directly addressing amygdala function and stress response regulation, rather than merely abstaining from substances and hoping the nervous system will recalibrate on its own. Approaches such as somatic experiencing, which help the body complete defensive responses that were frozen during trauma; EMDR, which assists in updating implicit memories stored in the amygdala; and practices that gradually build resilience to activate these, address the actual neurobiological issues that made substances so reinforcing in the first place. The goal isn't just to remove the substance; it's to understand why the amygdala was so hyperreactive that turning it off felt like a revelation, and why the nervous system was so dysregulated that chemical calm seemed like an authentic experience of consciousness.

Now, it might seem like this perspective implies a sense of biological determinism, suggesting that you are trapped by neurochemistry and trauma with no real capacity for change. However, understanding these mechanisms does not eliminate agency; it actually relocates where agency operates. It shows how to work with your natural systems rather than fighting against them through sheer willpower, which is often insufficient. The confidence alcohol provided, the focus stimulants delivered, the peace opioids created, and the calm benzodiazepines produced. These are genuine capacities that exist within you independently of chemicals, even though chemicals initially revealed them.

The work involves developing sustainable, non-chemical methods for accessing these states and building the neurological infrastructure necessary to achieve the capacities that substances artificially revealed. This means that a person who found confidence through alcohol will develop it through repeated experiences of successful social engagement while sober, through therapy that addresses underlying social anxiety, and by gradually updating implicit memories regarding social situations. Someone who discovered focus through stimulants will work on underlying attention difficulties, create environmental conditions that support concentration, and learn to manage the restlessness or distractibility that the stimulants temporarily suppressed. Other non-chemical methods include mindfulness practices, physical exercise, and cognitive-behavioural therapy.

A person who found peace through opioids will engage in trauma processing that addresses underlying activation, implement practices that help their nervous system learn to regulate, and gradually build their capacity to feel safe in their own body. None of this process is quick. All of it requires time, effort, repeated practice, and patience in a journey that moves more slowly than chemical interventions. However, it is sustainable and builds rather than depletes natural capacities; it fosters genuine integration rather than a chemical bypass, a temporary and often harmful shortcut, that ultimately leads to fragmentation.

This understanding also alters our approach to prevention. Suppose substance dependence often arises in individuals with dysregulated nervous systems, unprocessed trauma, dysfunctional reward systems, and chronic states of distress. In that case, prevention should focus on creating conditions that reduce these vulnerabilities. This includes addressing childhood trauma before it becomes ingrained in implicit memory and shapes development, supporting healthy attachment to promote well-regulated nervous systems, effectively treating anxiety and depression before individuals turn to substances for relief, and fostering societies where people's basic needs are met, making life feel worth living rather than something to escape.

Your Obscure Psyche plays a significant role in substance dependence. Implicit memories trigger cravings, shadow material has been accessed through substances without genuine integration, trauma is encoded in ways you can't consciously access, and attachment patterns drive you toward chemical solutions for relational and regulatory challenges. The developmental damage contributes to neurobiological vulnerabilities. Substances are not merely hijacking your reward system; they maintain your fragmentation, preventing you from doing the integration work you need. They offer an escape from the consciousness that should be expanding, defend against shadow material that needs acknowledgement rather than suppression, and reveal aspects of yourself in ways that hinder proper integration.

These substances act as mirrors, reflecting parts of yourself that exist but remain inaccessible due to trauma, developmental damage, nervous system dysregulation, and split-off shadow material. The confidence, calm, creativity, peace, and freedom from constant vigilance are genuinely part of your psychological potential. The tragedy is that you are accessing these aspects through means that hinder natural access, creating dependence while promising liberation, and deepening the split they temporarily bridge.

Recovery involves more than just stopping substance use; it requires engaging with your Obscure Psyche, developing the capacity to confront what you've been chemically avoiding, processing what substances enabled you to leave unaddressed, and integrating what remained fragmented. At the same time, you relied on chemicals for management and accessed naturally occurring substances through artificial means. The substances have allowed you to remain estranged from parts of yourself, keeping you dependent on chemicals to access your genuine attributes, while avoiding the developmental and integrative work necessary for sustainable access.

The work required for recovery is immense; it involves addressing neurobiological dependence, processing underlying trauma, developing alternative methods for accessing revealed capacities, working through shadow material, building regulatory capacity, and transforming environmental conditions. The discomfort is real, the timeline is lengthy, and the suffering is significant. However, transformation is achievable because neuroplasticity exists. Trauma can be processed even when encoded in implicit memory, and nervous systems can learn to regulate despite long-standing dysregulation. Capacities revealed through substances can also be accessed through other, more patient and sustained methods.

Welcome to the understanding of the shadow and the fixation in your substance use, the way it intersects with your Obscure Psyche. This involves recognising the neurobiological trap that begins as revelation but becomes a prison, with chemicals serving as mirrors that expose aspects of yourself that remain inaccessible due to unwelcome wounds and ingrained patterns. Your nucleus accumbens has been hijacked, your amygdala dysregulated, your reward system has learned the wrong lessons, your shadow material has found chemical access instead of conscious integration, and your trauma has sought chemical escape instead of genuine processing.

Recovery is a courageous journey that goes beyond just abstaining from substance use. It necessitates confronting the issues that those substances were masking. It's about managing the issues they helped you avoid, processing the emotions they allowed you to escape, and integrating the parts of yourself that remained disconnected while chemical defences kept you fragmented. This work is challenging, often harder than continued substance use, but it's a testament to your strength and resilience. It demands facing the issues that substances allowed you to sidestep. However, continuing to use ultimately leads to greater suffering, deepening the fragmentation that substances seemed to resolve. It also makes it increasingly difficult to access your full psychological potential, as dependence on chemicals prevents you from living without that assistance.

The substances you used acted as a mirror, reflecting not only who you were during moments of intoxication but also who you could become if you learned to access your full psychological potential through sustainable and integrated methods. The confidence, creativity, peace, and calm you seek have always been within you. Still, they have become inaccessible due to conditions you didn't create, wounds you didn't choose, and patterns in your nervous system established before you had awareness or agency. The substances revealed the potential that was always there. Now, the task is to learn how to access it naturally, integrating what was once available only through chemicals, and becoming whole rather than relying on substances to bypass fragmentation ultimately worsening it in ways you might not fully understand. This journey is a path of hope and optimism, leading to your true potential.

You are more than you realise. The substances merely uncovered what was hidden, what trauma suppressed, what your development damaged, and what shadow work could help integrate. This requires a commitment to the gradual and challenging process of genuine transformation, rather than settling for the temporary revelations provided by drugs that can become a prison. Your obscure psyche contains both the potential highlighted by substances and the wounds that made that potential inaccessible in natural ways. The journey ahead involves confronting and integrating both aspects, while developing sustainable access to your full psychological potential, rather than remaining chained to the chemical keys that initially promised freedom. This journey is about self-discovery and personal growth, inspiring you to reach your full potential.

Chapter 9

The Slip of the Tongue & The Faulty Action: Projection

Consider a time when you had a strong, seemingly disproportionate reaction to someone else's behaviour. This wasn't just a mild annoyance or reasonable disagreement; it was a reaction that triggered intense emotions such as rage, contempt, disgust, or moral outrage. These feelings felt justified at the moment, but later seemed excessive given the actual situation. Perhaps a coworker took credit for your work, igniting a fury that lingered for days, even though you knew it wasn't that serious. Or maybe you encountered someone whose confidence struck you as arrogance, whose assertiveness felt aggressive, whose self-promotion seemed intolerably narcissistic. Your reactions were so intense that you couldn't stop thinking about them, cataloguing their flaws, and sharing your feelings with anyone willing to listen.

Now, consider this unsettling question: Why did you react this way to that specific individual? Why this behaviour? Why this quality? Why does your colleague's self-promotion infuriate you while another colleague's similar behaviour passes unnoticed? Why does this person's confidence register as intolerable arrogance, while someone else's confidence seems admirable? Why is your response so overwhelming, so consuming, and so hard to let go of, even when you recognise, on some level, that your reaction is overblown?

The uncomfortable truth is that you're not actually reacting to them but to yourself. You're seeing in them something you possess but cannot acknowledge, something you've repressed and relegated to your shadow self. This quality threatens your carefully constructed self-image. The intensity of your reaction isn't about them; it's about you and the internal conflict between acknowledging a personal trait and disowning it. This conflict often gets resolved through projection, where you externalise the trait to judge and attack it in others while remaining convinced it belongs solely to them. But once you recognise this, you can start to peel back the layers of your own psyche, gaining a deeper understanding of your true self.

This concept, known as projection, is a powerful, pervasive, and often invisible mechanism through which your internal psyche shapes your experiences without your awareness. You perceive yourself in others, responding to your own disowned qualities reflected back at you. You create enemies from your rejected aspects, all while your consciousness insists that you are accurately perceiving them and responding to their actual flaws.

Reflect on how much of your emotional life is consumed by reactions to other people. Consider how much time you spend ruminating over someone who annoyed you, analysing their faults, justifying your feelings of anger or contempt, or feeling morally superior. Notice how much mental space is occupied by their actions rather than your own, how much energy goes into critiquing their behaviour instead of focusing on your own experiences.

What makes this particularly insidious is that projection often feels like accurate perception. It doesn't feel like you are disowning your own qualities by recognising them in others; it feels like you're simply observing reality. You believe you're seeing what is genuinely there, and your reactions appear justified by their actual behaviour. The person seems genuinely arrogant, selfish, or whatever quality is triggering your feelings. You have evidence to support your case, and it feels entirely convincing.

However, the intensity of your reaction is the clue. The disproportionate nature of your response, the consuming preoccupation, the difficulty in letting go, and the way your reaction greatly exceeds what the situation warrants are signals that projection is at play. You aren't just reacting to them; you are responding to your own disowned traits reflected in them. The external trigger has activated an internal conflict that you're not consciously aware of. Because this conflict remains unconscious, and because the disowned quality operates in the shadows, you may have no awareness of the actual dynamics at work. You only experience intense reactions to others' flaws while being blind to the fact that you possess those same flaws yourself. But once you understand this, you can start to reclaim those disowned traits, relieving the burden of projection and gaining a deeper understanding of yourself. This understanding empowers you to take control of your reactions and your life, confident in your ability to navigate your internal conflicts.

Let me provide a concrete example. Imagine someone who prides themselves on being humble, on never seeking attention, and on always putting others first. They have built their identity around not being self-centred, narcissistic, or someone who craves validation or recognition. Now, they encounter a person who confidently promotes their achievements, openly speaks about their successes, and clearly enjoys recognition without hesitation. This encounter elicits feelings of rage, contempt, and moral disgust in the humble individual. They can't stop thinking about how awful this person is and how narcissistic and desperately needy for attention they seem. They discuss their disdain with friends, create elaborate critiques, and feel completely justified in their judgment because, after all, isn't this behaviour objectively terrible?

However, what's actually happening is that the "humble" person has disowned their own desire for recognition. They share the same need for validation and the same longing to be seen and appreciated that every human being has. At some point, probably during childhood, they learned that expressing this need was unacceptable and shameful, something that could lead to punishment or withdrawal of love. As a result, they suppressed their desire and constructed an identity focused on its opposite, making humility and self-effacement central to their sense of being a good person. Their need for recognition didn't disappear; it simply went into the shadows, continuing to exist but now entirely denied and disowned.

When they encounter someone expressing this need openly, something happens beneath their conscious awareness. The disowned need is triggered, threatening to surface and create enormous anxiety. Acknowledging it would shatter their identity as humble and selfless. Accepting that they possess the very quality they define themselves against would be unbearable. Therefore, the psychological defence mechanism of projection activates automatically, unconsciously, and instantaneously.

Instead of thinking "I want recognition but cannot admit it," their perception shifts to "They desperately want recognition, and it's pathological." The internal conflict between possessing and disowning resolves through externalisation. Now, they can see the quality in the other person, respond to it, judge it harshly, and feel morally superior, all while remaining completely unaware that they are responding to their own reflection. Everything they condemn in the other person exists in themselves, and the intensity of their judgment correlates with how desperately they need to disown what they are criticising.

This is projection in full force: seeing in others what you cannot recognise in yourself, responding to your own disowned qualities as if they are external flaws, and creating enemies from your own rejected aspects. All the while, your consciousness maintains the illusion that you are accurately perceiving reality and that your reaction is solely about them and their behaviour, rather than your inability to acknowledge the same behaviour in yourself.

You might be thinking, "But sometimes people actually are arrogant or selfish or possess the quality I'm reacting to. How do I differentiate between genuine observation and projection?" This is a fair question, and the answer lies in the intensity and quality of your reaction. Accurate perception of someone else's flaws doesn't lead to a consuming preoccupation. It doesn't generate a disproportionate emotional response or make you unable to let go or stop thinking about them.

When you accurately perceive someone else's flaws without projecting your own, your reaction is proportionate. For instance, you might notice, "This person is quite self-centred," without that observation triggering rage. You might recognise, "They seem to need a lot of validation," without feeling contempt. You can clearly observe their behaviour and perhaps even feel compassion for the insecurity underlying it, without becoming emotionally hijacked, obsessing over it, or needing to condemn them to others. Other disowned qualities could include arrogance, neediness, or even positive traits like intelligence or creativity.

In contrast, when projection is at play, and you see your own disowned qualities reflected in another, your reaction is different. The intensity of your feelings becomes disproportionate. The preoccupation is consuming, and the judgment is harsh, unforgiving, and morally charged. You cannot let it go because you are not merely responding to their behaviour; you are reacting to the threat it poses to your identity, the anxiety triggered by their expression of disowned qualities, and the internal conflict between possessing and disowning that their presence activates.

Introducing the Disproportionate Reaction Test, a valuable self-diagnostic tool that puts the power in your hands to recognize when projection is at play. When you find yourself reacting more intensely than the situation warrants, when your emotional response seems excessive for the actual event, or when you can't stop focusing on someone else's flaws or behaviour, it's a signal that projection may be active. This means you're seeing aspects of yourself in them, and the quality triggering you is one you possess but cannot acknowledge.

The test is composed of three crucial components: intensity, duration, and compulsion. Understanding these elements is key to using the test effectively.

First, intensity: Is your emotional reaction disproportionately strong compared to what actually occurred? Suppose someone's minor self-promotion triggers intense rage. In that case, if their normal confidence feels like unbearable arrogance, or if their reasonable boundary-setting seems to you like cruel rejection, this suggests that projection rather than accurate perception is at work.

Second, duration: Can you move on from the incident, or does it linger in your thoughts for hours, days, or even weeks? Suppose you find yourself still fuming days later about something relatively minor, cataloguing someone's flaws long after the interaction has ended, or constantly explaining to yourself or others why they are terrible. In that case, it indicates that you are grappling with something internal rather than just reacting to an external event.

Third, compulsion: Do you feel compelled to talk about it, to explain why the other person is wrong, to build a case against their behaviour, or to convince others to see them as you do? This compulsive need to justify your reaction and to recruit others to your viewpoint suggests projection. When you are accurately perceiving someone's flaws without personal investment, you don't feel the need for validation from others; you can simply observe and move on.

When all three elements are present, disproportionate intensity, extended duration, and compulsive preoccupation, it is almost certain that projection is occurring. You are projecting something within yourself onto others while insisting that you are perceiving their reality. This results in internal conflict that gets projected outward, while your consciousness remains blind to the actual dynamics at play.

Let's also explore the neuroscience behind projection, as understanding this process makes it less mystical and more recognisable. Projection is not merely a psychological defence; it is rooted in how your brain processes information about other people, understands their internal states, and simulates their experiences to make sense of their behaviour. The key neural structure involved is known as mirror neurons, which form the basis for empathy, but can also contribute to projection when combined with your own unconscious material.

The discovery of mirror neurons was a fascinating accident by Italian researchers studying motor control in monkeys. They stumbled upon specific neurons that fired both when a monkey performed an action and when it observed another monkey performing the same action. This unique phenomenon, where the same neurons are activated whether the monkey is doing something or watching someone else do it, led to the name 'mirror' neurons, as they reflect observed actions as if being performed by the observer.

Humans possess a remarkably advanced mirror neuron system compared to other primates. These neurons are spread throughout the brain in motor regions, areas that process sensation, and regions involved in emotion. When you observe someone else's actions, your mirror neurons simulate performing those actions yourself. If you witness someone experiencing an emotion, your mirror neurons activate the same emotional circuits that you would use if you were experiencing that emotion yourself. This neural process is the foundation of empathy, allowing you to intuitively understand others' internal states and sense what they are feeling without them needing to explicitly tell you.

For example, if you watch someone stub their toe and wince, your mirror neurons activate the pain circuits in your brain, creating a diminished version of the experience they're having. Alternatively, when you see someone smile genuinely, you'll feel a subtle positive shift as your mirror neurons activate your neural circuitry for happiness, allowing you to share in their joy. This automatic, unconscious simulation of others' experiences occurs constantly, without your awareness, enabling you to navigate social situations with an intuitive understanding of what others are thinking and feeling.

However, the role of mirror neurons in projection is a significant aspect to consider. When your mirror neurons simulate someone else's internal state, they don't have direct access to that person's actual experience. Instead, they create a simulation based on observed behaviour, but the content of that simulation is drawn from your own psychological material, including your own experiences and associations. In essence, you're using yourself to understand them, projecting your own internal expertise onto them to form your perception of what they might be feeling.

Most of the time, this process works reasonably well because humans share enough common psychological traits, allowing your experience to serve as a decent approximation of theirs. For instance, if you see someone crying, your mirror neurons activate your sadness circuits, giving you a sense of their sadness, which is likely accurate. However, when the behaviour you observe connects with aspects of your own shadow, such as disowned qualities, suppressed emotions, or unacknowledged desires, the simulation created by your mirror neurons can become tainted by your own unconscious material. In this case, you're no longer simply empathetically sensing what they are experiencing; instead, you're projecting your own disowned content onto them and responding to that projection as though it were an accurate perception.

Consider what happens when someone who has disowned their anger encounters another person expressing anger. Their mirror neurons simulate the experience of expressing anger. Still, because that anger is in their shadow, linked to feelings of anxiety and shame, the simulation includes all of that shadow material. They aren't just sensing the other person's anger; they are also experiencing their own relationship with anger, including their suppressed rage and anxiety about anger being dangerous or unacceptable. Consequently, the simulation becomes overwhelmed with its own material, and its perception of the other person becomes dominated by projection.

People may perceive others as terrifyingly rageful or dangerously out of control, threatening violence, when in fact the person is merely expressing usual frustration in an appropriate manner. Conversely, they might misinterpret righteous anger about injustice as abusive aggression because their own anger has never been allowed a righteous expression; it has always been associated with badness and danger. This perception occurs because their mirror neurons simulate the expression of anger based on psychological associations, leading to a view more influenced by their own unresolved issues than by the reality of the other person's feelings.

This explains why the same behaviour from different individuals can trigger very different reactions. Someone who is comfortable with their own anger can observe another person's anger without becoming overwhelmed because their mirror neuron simulation is not clouded by unresolved issues. They can accurately assess whether the anger is proportionate, appropriately expressed, and whether it poses a genuine threat or is simply a normal human emotion. However, someone who has disowned their own anger will interpret the same behaviour differently, influenced by their own unresolved feelings about anger.

Your mirror neurons are constantly active, simulating others' internal states and creating an intuitive sense of what others are thinking and feeling. However, when you notice behaviour that connects with your unresolved issues, what is often referred to as your "shadow material", the simulation shifts from empathy to projection. Instead of sensing the other person's emotions, you are responding to your own psychological state, seeing your reflection instead of perceiving their reality. This 'shadow material' could be your own unacknowledged anger, fear, or other emotions that you have disowned or suppressed.

Another important neural system involved in understanding projection is your threat detection network, notably your amygdala and insula, which work together to identify potential dangers in your social environment. Your amygdala, a key player in this network, continuously scans for threats, detecting potential dangers faster than conscious awareness and triggering defensive responses before you are even aware of your reactions. It does this by releasing stress hormones and narrowing your focus to the perceived threat. This scanning involves not only physical threats but also social threats, interpersonal dangers that may jeopardise your sense of self, social standing, or safety in relationships.

When you encounter someone displaying qualities you have disowned, your threat detection system is activated because these qualities pose an internal danger. By 'disowned qualities', we mean traits or emotions that you have suppressed or denied in yourself. This is not an external threat but a threat to your identity, the risk that your own disowned qualities might come to light. For example, if someone displays confidence, it may trigger a defensive response in someone who has disowned their desire for recognition. This confidence could highlight their own need for recognition and threaten their identity as humble and selfless. Similarly, when someone sets boundaries, it might trigger a defensive response in those who have disowned their own needs, as this could expose their inability to set boundaries and threaten their self-image as accommodating and selfless.

Your amygdala does not distinguish between external physical threats and internal psychological threats. When someone's behaviour brings your shadow material to the surface or threatens to make those qualities conscious, your amygdala reacts as if you are facing a danger. Stress hormones are released, narrowing your focus to the perceived threat. Consequently, your perception becomes biased toward viewing the other person as dangerous, wrong, or problematic. Since all of this occurs beneath conscious awareness without you recognising that your threat detection is responding to internal rather than external danger, you may experience it as an accurate assessment of real threat posed by the other person.

The interaction of mirror neurons, a fundamental part of our brain's functioning, plays a key role in the projection process. These neurons create a simulation that can be influenced by your shadow material, while threat detection responds to internal dangers. This combination results in a powerful projection that feels undeniably true. Instead of simply recognising your disowned qualities in others, you perceive them as threats, dangerous and needing to be defended against, attacked, or condemned. This projection is moralised; it becomes about viewing others as wrong, bad, or problematic. Your threat detection system reinforces this by signalling genuine danger, even though the actual threat is internal and relates to your own disowned material that feels like it might become conscious.

A clear example of this projection and threat detection working together is homophobia. Research consistently shows that individuals with strong anti-gay attitudes often exhibit higher physiological arousal when viewing same-sex erotic images compared to those who are comfortable with homosexuality. These individuals experience an automatic sexual response, a response that threatens their identity as heterosexual and activates their disowned same-sex attraction. Their threat detection system categorises gay people as threatening, wrong, and in need of condemnation. The interplay of disowned sexuality and threat detection leads to moral condemnation that feels entirely justified and comes with a solid conviction that the other person is wrong. They fail to recognise that the actual dynamics at play are internal rather than external.

This mechanism of projection is not unique to a few individuals, but rather operates in many contexts. For instance, a person may condemn others for being selfish while remaining blind to their own selfishness. Another might be outraged by others' dishonesty while continually lying to themselves. Additionally, someone may feel disgusted by others' neediness while having significant unacknowledged needs themselves. There are those who display contempt for others' weaknesses while desperately defending against their vulnerabilities. In each case, mirror neurons create simulations influenced by shadow material. The threat detection system responds to internal dangers, creating a projection that feels like an accurate perception and absolute conviction, without realising they are actually seeing themselves while insisting they are observing others. This is a common human experience, and understanding it can help us all grow and develop.

Now, let's discuss how to handle this. We can use our reactions as diagnostic information rather than being unconsciously controlled by projection while insisting that we are accurately perceiving reality. The Disproportionate Reaction Test I mentioned earlier is your primary tool. Its purpose is to help you recognise when your reactions are disproportionate to the situation, which can be a sign of projection. Whenever you notice an intense, prolonged, or compulsive reaction to someone else, stop. Do not continue to build your case for why they are terrible. Avoid explaining to yourself or others what is wrong with them. Instead, pause and consider: What if this is a projection? What if I possess the quality I'm judging in them? What would I need to acknowledge in myself to stop requiring them to be this way?

Recognising projection is a significant step in self-awareness. It's a challenging task because projection convinces you that you're accurately perceiving external reality. When you're in its grip, the idea that you might possess the quality you're judging feels absurd, offensive, obviously wrong. 'I'm not arrogant like they are. I'm not selfish like them. I'm not needy the way they are.' The denial is immediate, absolute, and completely convincing to your conscious mind. This is how projection protects itself, by making the disowned quality feel so foreign, so unlike you, that even considering the possibility you possess it seems ridiculous.

But the intensity of your denial is often proportional to how accurate the interpretation of the projection is. When someone suggests you possess a quality you've genuinely integrated, when they point out something that's not in shadow, you can usually consider it without immediate defensive reaction. "Maybe I am being a bit impatient today, yes, I can see that." But when they're touching shadow material, when they're pointing to something you've deeply disowned, the reaction is different. The denial is vehement. The defence is immediate. The rejection of the possibility is absolute. The very suggestion feels like an attack, a misunderstanding, or that they're completely wrong about you.

When you find yourself in a disproportionate reaction, and the Disproportionate Reaction Test indicates projection might be at play, it's essential to create space. Don't immediately accept or reject the possibility that you possess the quality you're judging. Just hold it as a possibility. This space allows for self-reflection, for noticing your resistance to considering it, and for understanding how threatening it feels to entertain that you might be selfish, arrogant, needy, or whatever quality you're condemning in the other person.

When you're judging someone as arrogant, it's crucial to look for the core quality underneath. You're not looking for the exact same behaviour the other person is displaying because your expression of the disowned quality will be different. You're looking for the core quality underneath, expressed in ways that might be unique to you, hidden in shadows they cannot see because they're looking for the obvious version. This approach helps in understanding the root of the issue.

If you're judging someone as arrogant, don't look for whether you're arrogant in the same way, whether you boast about achievements or demand recognition. Look for whether you have a hidden sense of superiority, whether you quietly judge others as less intelligent or capable, or whether you have fantasies of being special or exceptional that you never express. Look for subtle arrogance, internal arrogance, arrogance that manifests as contempt for others' limitations rather than as overt self-promotion.

If you're condemning someone as selfish, don't look for whether you're obviously selfish in ways they are. Look for whether you have hidden resentment about giving, whether you keep score secretly about who does more, whether you have unexpressed needs you're bitter about not having met. Look for covert selfishness, selfishness that manifests as secret resentment rather than as open self-interest. It's selfishness that's been driven so deep into shadow that it can only be detected by its effects: the bitterness, the keeping score, the feeling of being taken advantage of.

If you're disgusted by someone's neediness, don't look to see if you're obviously needy. Look for whether you have needs you never express, whether you've built relationships around being needed because being needed is the only way you allow yourself proximity to getting needs met, whether you have a profound longing for care and attention that's completely disowned, that can only express itself through making yourself indispensable to others who have obvious needs.

The quality is there. If the reaction is disproportionate and projection is operating, the quality you're judging exists within you. It must. That's how projection works. But it won't look like you expect it to look because if it were apparent to you, it wouldn't be in shadow, wouldn't be disowned, and wouldn't need to be projected onto others. You're looking for the hidden version, the underground version, the version that's been so thoroughly suppressed and disguised that only its effects are visible. The intensity of this can be incredibly challenging because projection thrives on a strong belief that you're accurately perceiving external reality. When you're caught in projection, the idea that you might have the very quality you're criticising feels absurd, offensive, and obviously wrong. You might think, "I'm not arrogant like they are. I'm not selfish like them. I'm not needy the way they are." The denial is immediate, absolute, and convincing to your conscious mind. This is how projection protects itself: by making the disowned quality seem so foreign, so unlike you, that even considering the possibility that you possess it feels ridiculous.

However, the intensity of your denial is often proportional to the accuracy of the projection. If someone suggests that you possess a trait you have genuinely integrated, you can usually consider it without an immediate defensive reaction. For example, you might think, "Maybe I am being a bit impatient today; yes, I can see that." But when someone touches on shadow material, when they point out something you've deeply disowned, your reaction is different. The denial is vehement, the defence immediate, and the rejection of the possibility absolute. The very suggestion feels like an attack, a misunderstanding, or a complete misjudgement of you.

So, when you find yourself reacting disproportionately, when your Disproportionate Reaction Test indicates that projection might be in play, try this: don't immediately accept or reject the idea that you possess the quality you're judging. Instead, simply hold it as a possibility. Create space between the suggestion and your automatic denial. Observe your resistance to considering it. Notice how threatening it feels to contemplate that you might be selfish, arrogant, needy, or possess any other quality you are condemning in someone else.

Next, look for the quality within yourself, but remember: don't search for an identical expression. This is crucial. You're not looking for the exact same behaviour the other person displays because your expression of the disowned quality will be different. Instead, look for the core quality underneath, expressed in ways that may be unique to you and hidden in your shadows, while others seek an obvious version.

For instance, if you are judging someone as arrogant, don't check if you are arrogant in the same way, such as boasting about achievements or demanding recognition. Instead, look for a hidden sense of superiority, quietly judging others as less intelligent or capable, or fantasising about being special or exceptional without expressing it. Seek out subtle arrogance, internal arrogance, or arrogance that manifests as contempt for others' limitations rather than overt self-promotion.

If you think someone is selfish, don't act like you are obviously selfish, too. Look for hidden resentment about giving, keeping score secretly about who does more, or unexpressed needs that you feel bitter about not having met. Seek covert selfishness that manifests as secret resentment instead of open self-interest; selfishness that has been pushed deep into the shadow, detectable only by its effects, the bitterness, the scorekeeping, and the feeling of being taken advantage of.

If you feel disgusted by someone's neediness, don't look for apparent neediness in yourself. Instead, check for needs you never express, whether you've built relationships around being needed because that's the only way you allow yourself to get your own needs met, or if you have a profound longing for care and attention that is completely disowned and can only express itself through making yourself indispensable to those who have obvious needs.

The quality is there. If your reaction is disproportionate, if projection is indeed operating, then the quality you're judging exists within you. It must. That's how projection works. But it may not look like what you expect because if it were obvious to you, it wouldn't be in shadow, wouldn't be disowned, and wouldn't need to be projected onto others. You're looking for the hidden version, the underground version, one that has been so thoroughly suppressed and disguised that only its effects are visible, with your intense judgment being the primary effect.

When you start to recognise certain qualities within yourself and realise, "Actually, I do possess this, just expressed differently," a profound sense of relief washes over you. The intensity of your judgment lessens. The preoccupation fades, and the urge to condemn others diminishes. This change doesn't occur because you are becoming less moral or discerning; instead, you are no longer engaging in an internal struggle through external condemnation. By acknowledging these qualities in yourself, you bridge the divide between what you possess and what you disown. This makes projection unnecessary because you are integrating what was once hidden in your shadow.

This doesn't mean that the other person is without flaws; they may indeed be arrogant, selfish, or needy in ways that cause issues. However, your relationship with their flaws transforms completely when you're no longer responding to your own disowned versions of those flaws. You can see them more clearly, respond more appropriately, and have compassion for the wounds that contribute to their problematic behaviour instead of needing to condemn them as a way to defend against your own inner conflicts. This newfound clarity brings a deeper understanding and empathy for the other person's struggles.

The other person becomes human rather than monstrous. They turn into someone with their own struggles rather than a personification of everything that's wrong. You relate to them with perspective and proportion, rather than allowing them to disrupt your emotional stability through unconscious projection. True freedom lies not in changing the other person, escaping from them, or convincing others that your judgment is correct, but in recognising these qualities within yourself, integrating them, and eliminating the need for projection. This process empowers you with a sense of control and self-mastery over your own internal dynamics.

There is a deeper layer to projection that is even more subtle and pervasive. You're not merely projecting individual traits like arrogance or selfishness; you're projecting your entire relationship with yourself onto others. You see different aspects of your internal dynamics reflected in those around you, creating external dramas that replay your internal conflicts. Every relationship, every interaction that triggers strong emotions, and every significant person in your psychological life serves as a screen onto which you project aspects of yourself, creating external representations of internal dynamics that you can then work through.

For instance, consider a boss who triggers intense anxiety and a sense of never being good enough. That boss may genuinely be critical and demanding, but the intensity of your reaction and the way they occupy your thoughts, as if you can never meet their standards, is not solely about them. This is tied to your relationship with your inner critic, the part of you that is never satisfied, constantly finds fault, and maintains impossible standards. The boss activates this internal critic, projecting your internal dynamics onto them and allowing you to see externally what is happening within.

Similarly, think about a partner whom you feel compelled to please, who makes you anxious about disappointing them. You may constantly modify your behaviour to meet their needs, revealing your relationship with yourself. This highlights how you abandon your own needs for the sake of connection and how you learned, perhaps in childhood, that love is contingent upon being what others need. While this partner may truly be demanding or challenging, the intensity of your need to please them, your anxiety about potential disappointment, and your willingness to betray yourself for their approval reflect internal patterns established long before this relationship began.

Every person who evokes intense emotions, occupies a significant space in your psychological life, or triggers patterns you keep repeating, is revealing something about yourself. They reflect some aspect of your internal world and manifest externally what is happening inside you. This occurs not because these individuals lack their own psychology; they certainly have one, but because your brain often uses others as mirrors to better understand yourself. It creates simulations of their internal states using your own psychological material, projecting your internal dynamics onto relationships where they can be observed, experienced, and potentially worked through.

Therapy that focuses solely on external problems, such as "My boss is terrible," "My partner is difficult," or "My parent was abusive", is limited in its effectiveness. While it's true that external realities matter and that others' behaviours affect you, until you recognise what you are projecting onto these situations, and until you see how much of your reaction stems from your own psychology rather than solely from their behaviour, you will continue to recreate the same dynamics with different people. You will attract bosses who never approve, partners who provoke desperate attempts to please, and relationships that repeat the same patterns, because these patterns are yours. They are projections of your internal experiences rather than simply reflections of the specific individuals you encounter. However, once you understand this, you gain the power to change these patterns.

You might worry that recognising projection means you can never trust your perceptions; that every reaction could be projection rather than an accurate observation; and that you're trapped in a solipsistic bubble where everything is just your psychology, rendering external reality non-existent. However, that's not the case. Recognising projection doesn't mean denying external reality. It means understanding that your internal dynamics also play a significant role in your perceptions and reactions. External reality is real, and other people have their own psychological experiences. Their behaviour matters. At times, your reactions may accurately assess problematic behaviour rather than merely project your own issues onto them.

The key lies in the quality of your reaction and your ability to recognise when projection is at work. When you accurately perceive someone's flaws without projecting your own issues, you can maintain perspective. This allows you to see their behaviour in context, to feel compassion while acknowledging their problems, and to let go and move on. In contrast, when projection operates, your reaction is often disproportionate, consuming, and hard to release, with an intensity that far exceeds the situation at hand. Understanding projection can bring a sense of relief, as it helps you understand the source of these intense reactions.

Importantly, recognising your projection doesn't make the other person's behaviour irrelevant; it simply adds another layer of understanding. They might genuinely exhibit arrogance while you project your own disowned arrogance onto them; both realities can coexist. Understanding your projection does not excuse their behaviour or deny its impact. Instead, it means you see the full situation, recognising both what the other person is actually doing and what you're contributing through projection. This awareness allows for a more effective response based on accurate information rather than being overwhelmed by unconscious dynamics.

The process of recognising projection is lifelong, as shadow material persists, seeks expression, and finds screens to project onto. You will never reach a point where projection ceases entirely, as it is too fundamental to how humans perceive social reality, driven by mirror neuron function and the simulation of others' internal states. However, you can develop the ability to recognise it more quickly, catching it before it completely takes over your emotional life. Utilise your reactions as insights about yourself rather than merely judgments about others.

Every intense reaction is a potential doorway to self-knowledge. Every disproportionate response signals that shadow material is active. Each person who triggers your overwhelming preoccupation reflects disowned qualities and manifests your internal dynamics externally, where they can be recognised and integrated. The question is whether you will use these reactions as diagnostic tools, as insights into your own psychology and opportunities for integration, or whether you will remain convinced that you are accurately perceiving reality. At the same time, your obscure psyche shapes your experiences through unrecognised projection.

Welcome to the journey of understanding projection. This involves recognising that you see aspects of yourself in everyone else. It means using your reactions as mirrors reflecting your shadow back to you. The goal is to develop the ability to catch projection at work before it shapes your relationships, even if you believe you are simply responding accurately to others' flaws. Your mirror neurons create simulations, and your threat detection reacts to internal dangers. Meanwhile, your shadow material is projected onto external surfaces where you can see, judge, and condemn it, remaining blind to the fact that you possess it yourself. Remember, self-awareness is the key to healthier relationships.

The work involves building the capacity to recognise this. You can apply the transformative Disproportionate Reaction Test to identify disowned qualities in yourself when you find yourself consumed by judgment of others. The aim is to integrate what has been split, rather than only seeing it when it's projected outward. The people who trigger you most intensely can be your greatest teachers, not because they are terrible, but because they reflect your own shadow and bring forth your disowned material in ways that can be acknowledged if you are willing to look into the mirror, rather than insisting you are merely looking through a window at someone fundamentally different from yourself.

The differences you perceive often disguise your disowned qualities when they are projected outward. This is how shadow material appears when seen in others rather than being acknowledged within yourself.

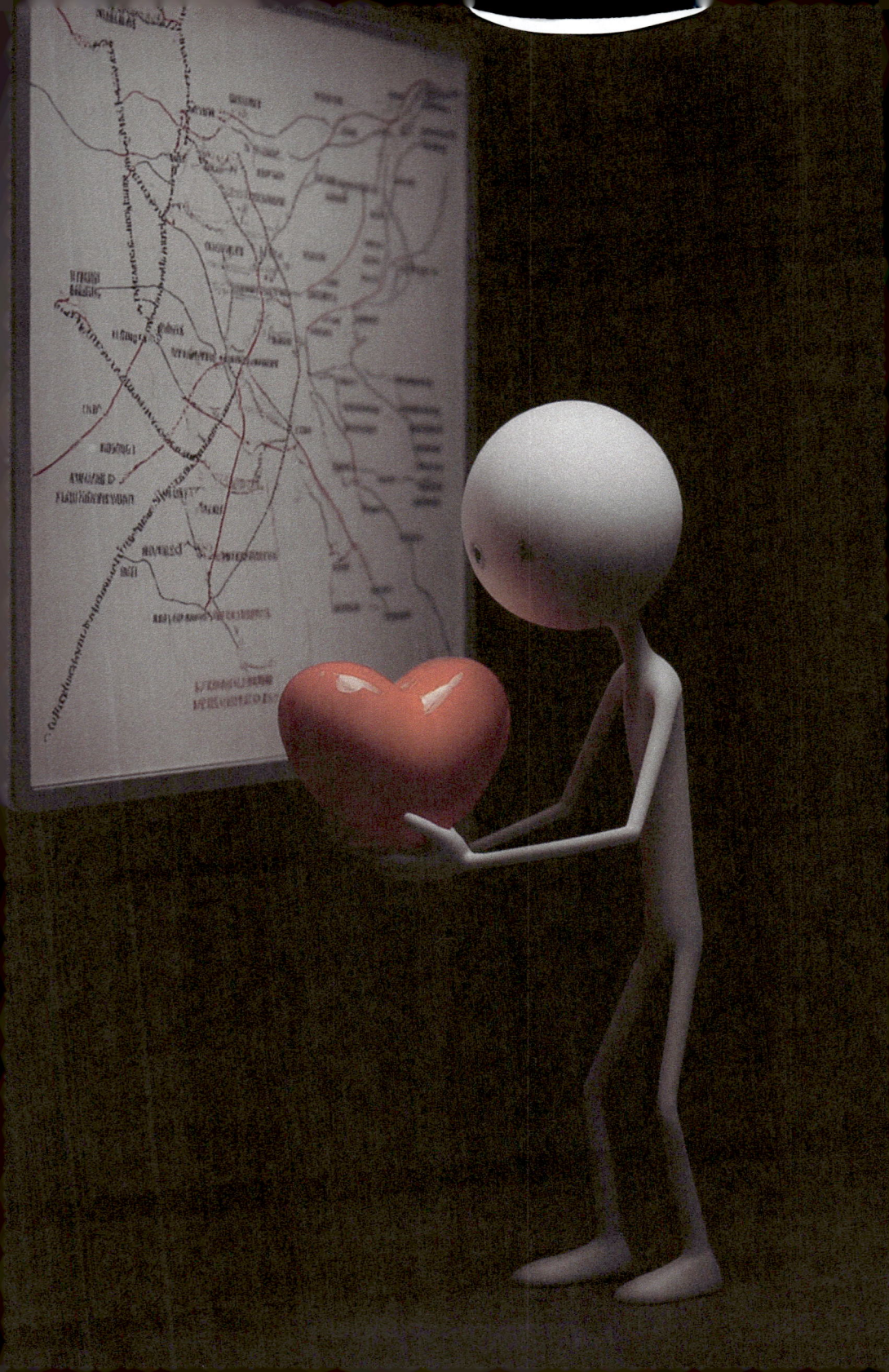

Chapter 10
The Shadow of Love: Attraction, Addiction and Attachment

When was the last time you felt that overwhelming, consuming attraction to someone, not just finding them attractive or enjoying their company, but experiencing a visceral pull that made you unable to stop thinking about them. Every text message sent your heart racing; the mere possibility of seeing them created an electric tension in your body, with rational thought fading in favour of obsessive preoccupation. It was a feeling where every love song suddenly made sense, a time when you found yourself acting in ways completely unlike your usual behaviour. You were willing to overlook obvious red flags because the attraction felt so powerful, so destined, so undeniably right, despite all evidence suggesting it might be wrong.

Now, here's a question that may deeply unsettle you: why that person? What was it about this individual, with their specific qualities, behaviours, and way of being, that triggered such an intense response while other equally wonderful people left you feeling... nothing? Why does chemistry ignite with someone who is emotionally unavailable, critical in ways that remind you of your father, or who needs rescuing in ways that mirror your mother's helplessness? Why do you find yourself drawn to charismatic yet unreliable individuals whose patterns feel painfully familiar?

Often, the people who trigger the strongest attraction turn out to be those who recreate your earliest wounds, revisit childhood dynamics, and present another chance to win the love you needed but never truly received. But why do the people who would genuinely be good for you, those who are consistent, available, and kind, seem boring? Why is there no chemistry, no thrill, no intense pull? Why does stability feel like settling? Why does security appear unexciting? Why does someone who treats you well somehow feel wrong or incomplete, even though you can't quite articulate what's missing?

The uncomfortable truth, one that challenges everything you believe about romantic love, soulmates, and finding "the one," is this: that overwhelming chemistry, that sense of rightness, that feeling of coming home, isn't recognising your perfect match. It's recognising your original wound. That electricity you feel isn't love, it's your attachment system detecting familiar patterns, your reward circuitry activating in response to cues aligned with your childhood experiences, and your unconscious mind sensing an opportunity to replay old dynamics in the hope of achieving a different outcome. You're not falling in love with who this person is; you're falling in love with the chance they represent to finally master what couldn't be mastered before. It's about finally getting the unavailable parent to choose you, earning the love that was always conditional, and trying to prove your worth to someone who demands you prove it over and over without ever confirming it.

Consider your last few significant relationships, not casual dating, but the ones that gripped you, where you felt that powerful pull and couldn't let go even when you should have. Now, look for patterns among these people. Notice the similarities, not in the obvious ways they might have looked entirely different, held different careers, and come from various backgrounds, but in how they made you feel, the roles they needed you to play, the dynamics that emerged, the wounds that were activated, and the things you did to maintain the connection.

Perhaps you're always attracted to emotionally unavailable people, leaving you anxious about where you stand. Maybe you're drawn to those who need fixing, struggling with addiction, mental health issues, or challenging life circumstances, who seek your help and support. It's also possible that you repeatedly find yourself with people who are critical, making you feel like you're constantly falling short when trying to earn their approval. Or, you might be attracted to chaotic and unpredictable individuals, creating drama and intensity, who swing between idealising you and devaluing you, keeping you perpetually off-balance.

These are not random patterns or unfortunate coincidences. They reflect your attachment system recognising what's familiar, your reward circuitry responding to cues that match your earliest relationship templates, and your unconscious mind recreating dynamics it knows, even if those dynamics caused pain, even when they never worked, and even after you've consciously vowed never to get involved with that type again. These responses are driven by programming established before you could think, instinctual reactions formed before you had words, and an attraction fuelled by mechanisms operating entirely beneath your awareness. All this occurs while your conscious mind constructs stories about soulmates, destiny, and finally finding someone who truly understands you.

Let's begin with neuroscience, as understanding what happens in your brain during attraction and attachment can make these patterns less mysterious and more identifiable. The ventral tegmental area (VTA) is a small region in your midbrain that plays a crucial role in motivation, reward, and romantic attachment. The VTA contains neurons that produce dopamine and send it to several brain regions, particularly to your nucleus accumbens, the reward centre we've discussed in earlier chapters and to your prefrontal cortex. When the VTA is activated and floods these areas with dopamine, you experience intense motivation, substantial reward, and an overwhelming drive to pursue whatever caused this activation.

The VTA-dopamine system is key to assigning significance, creating a sense that something matters greatly, and generating the drive to pursue goals and rewards with focused determination. This system activates when you achieve something significant, experience intense pleasure, or form powerful attachments. It goes into overdrive during the early stages of romantic love, leading to obsessive preoccupation, an overwhelming desire for proximity, and the feeling that nothing else matters except being with that person.

Brain imaging studies of individuals in the early stages of romantic love reveal VTA activation patterns that closely resemble those seen in addiction. The same neural circuits light up, resulting in dopamine surges and intense motivation and craving. People in love exhibit reduced activity in regions related to negative emotions and increased activity in areas involved in reward and motivation. They become less capable of evaluating their partner objectively, less responsive to negative information about them, and more focused on their partner's positive qualities while ignoring potential red flags. This is not just a poetic metaphor; romantic love literally hijacks your reward system in ways similar to drug addiction, creating a powerful motivation to be with that person while impairing your ability to assess whether the relationship is good for you.

What's essential to understand is that the VTA does not activate randomly. It doesn't create attraction to just anyone. Instead, it responds to specific cues, recognising particular patterns and activating in response to traits that your brain has learned to associate with reward or importance. And what has your brain learned to associate with love, attachment, and relationships? Your earliest experiences with caregivers, the patterns encoded before explicit memory, the template formed through countless interactions, before you could consciously reflect on what you were learning. These early experiences have a profound impact on your brain's reward system and how you perceive love and attachment.

If your early attachment involved an inconsistently available caregiver, sometimes responding to your needs and sometimes ignoring them, your VTA would learn to associate uncertainty with attachment. The dopamine system particularly responds to unpredictable rewards, which sometimes come and sometimes don't, generating a stronger motivational response than predictable rewards. This is why gambling can be addictive. The unpredictability of winning creates a more intense dopamine response than guaranteed rewards. Your VTA learned this pattern with attachment: love is uncertain, connection is unpredictable, and you never know if your needs will be met. This uncertainty makes the occasional connections feel exceptionally rewarding.

As an adult, when you meet someone who is emotionally available, consistent, and reliably responsive to your needs, your VTA barely responds. There's no spike in dopamine. There's no overwhelming attraction. They may feel friendly and pleasant, but not exciting or compelling, the person you can't stop thinking about. This is because your reward system wasn't calibrated for consistent availability; it was calibrated for uncertainty and intermittent reinforcement, which brings the dopamine spike that occurs when an unpredictable reward finally arrives.

Then, you encounter someone emotionally unavailable, inconsistent in their attention, sometimes showing interest and sometimes being distant, leaving you unsure about where you stand. Suddenly, your VTA lights up. Dopamine floods your system. You can't stop thinking about them. Every small sign of interest feels like a monumental reward because your system is tuned to this very pattern. When they text you after days of silence, show affection after being distant, or pay attention after ignoring you, the dopamine surge is intense because this is the pattern your reward system has learned to recognise as love. The chemistry you feel isn't about finding your soul mate; it's your VTA responding to familiar patterns of intermittent reinforcement, with uncertainty activating reward circuitry shaped by inconsistent early caregiving.

Or perhaps your early attachment was with a caregiver who relied on you for emotional support, needing you to manage their feelings and meet needs that should have been fulfilled by adults. As a result, your Ventral Tegmental Area (VTA) learned to associate love with being needed, being useful, and having a specific role to play. Connection meant being indispensable, managing someone else's emotional state, and tying your self-worth to how well you could meet another person's needs.

Now that you're an adult, if you encounter someone who is emotionally healthy and has their own support system and doesn't rely on you to rescue them or manage their feelings, they may not activate your reward system. You might respect them and intellectually acknowledge that they are a good person, but there's no intense attraction or overwhelming pull.

However, when you meet someone who is struggling and seems to need help with problems you feel you can solve, your VTA activates powerfully. For instance, if you're a problem-solver and they're facing a challenge you're adept at, or if they're in emotional distress and you're good at comforting, your VTA will light up. The attraction feels overwhelming, not because you consciously want to repeat old patterns, but because your reward system recognises this familiar dynamic, associating it with attachment and love. Being needed feels like love, simply because that's what your earliest experiences taught you.

It's crucial to recognise that the person who triggers this response might not necessarily be a good match; they could be using you, incapable of reciprocating, or need more than you can sustainably provide. Your reward system isn't concerned with sustainability or a healthy relationship. It responds to cues that match your attachment template, flooding you with dopamine whenever you encounter patterns reminiscent of your early relationship experiences. This motivates you to pursue people who will recreate the familiar dynamics, even if they initially caused you pain. This attraction feels right, like coming home, as if it's what you've been searching for because it is, on some unconscious level. But with self-awareness and the right tools, you can break free from these patterns and form healthier attachments.

Now, let's discuss Jung's concept of anima and animus, which adds another layer to understanding romantic attraction, particularly how we project idealised images onto partners and fall in love with our own projections rather than with who the other person truly is. Jung observed that men carry an unconscious feminine aspect called the anima, essentially a template of feminine qualities developed mainly through relationships with mothers and other early female figures. Conversely, women have an unconscious masculine aspect called the animus, an internalised template of masculine qualities primarily derived from fathers and early male figures.

These concepts do not promote gender stereotypes or biological essentialism; instead, they concern internalised images of the 'other.' These templates for relating to people perceived as different from yourself are formed from your earliest intimate relationship experiences. The anima or animus contains qualities you experienced in your opposite-sex parent, encompassing aspects you admired, feared, or needed, all of which became intertwined with your notions of intimacy, love, and relationships. These internalised images can significantly influence how we perceive and interact with potential partners, often leading us to fall in love with our own projections rather than with who the other person truly is.

In romantic attraction, we tend to project this internal image onto potential partners, falling in love not with who they truly are but with how well they correspond to or activate our internalised templates.

Consider what happens in the early stages of romantic attraction. You meet someone and quickly start filling in the gaps in your knowledge about them, constructing elaborate ideas based on minimal actual information. You notice a few qualities that match your template and assume a whole range of other attributes must also be true. If they seem slightly mysterious, you may imagine them as deep. If they appear confident, you might assume they are capable and strong. If they are creative, you could project that they are also sensitive and understanding. In reality, you are not responding to who they actually are; instead, you are reacting to your projection, to your anima or animus being activated, and to your internal template finding external form in this new person.

The early stages of romantic love often involve a significant amount of idealisation. During this time, you're not truly seeing the person as they are; instead, you're projecting your internalised image of an ideal partner onto them. This image is shaped by qualities from your opposite-sex parent and attributes you've disowned in yourself. Essentially, the person becomes a canvas onto which you project your own psyche, and you fall in love with what you're projecting while believing you're in love with who they really are.

As time passes, the person you're in a relationship with starts to reveal qualities that don't align with your projection. They may not be as deep as you imagined, or perhaps they are sensitive in ways you didn't expect, or they may excel in certain areas while struggling in others. This is not a betrayal or a change in the person; it's the natural progression of a relationship. You're starting to see them more clearly rather than through the lens of your projection. The person you initially fell in love with never existed; it was your anima or animus at play, your internal template of an ideal partner projected onto someone who matched it sufficiently at first.

Understanding the role of projection in romantic attraction can be enlightening. It explains why relationships that begin with intense chemistry and idealisation often end in disappointment and disillusionment. You weren't engaging with a real person; you were relating to your projection. When that projection collapses, and you finally perceive who's actually there, feelings of betrayal can arise. But the person was merely being themselves all along. You were the one projecting an elaborate fantasy based on your internal template. When that fantasy crumbled, you mistakenly attributed the loss to the other person's failure rather than recognising your own projection.

Moreover, this is connected to childhood wounds and trauma patterns. Your anima or animus not only embodies idealised qualities but also reflects problematic patterns from your opposite-sex parent, the wounds they created, and the ways they fell short in meeting your needs. This understanding can help you become more self-aware and make conscious choices in your relationships.

Someone whose father was critical and complex to please might find themselves attracted to partners who are similarly critical and whose approval is difficult to attain. This attraction isn't a conscious desire for criticism but arises because their animus contains criticism as part of the masculine intimacy template. Their reward system has learned to associate criticism with paternal attention. Consequently, seeking the approval of critical partners may feel familiar, despite being painful.

Similarly, a person whose mother was emotionally unstable and required constant management might be drawn to partners who also exhibit instability and create drama. This attraction isn't about enjoying drama; rather, it stems from their anima containing instability as part of the feminine intimacy template. Their reward system has associated caretaking with maternal connection, so managing someone else's emotional state feels like a familiar form of love, even if it is exhausting.

This highlights a challenging aspect of romantic attraction: the people who activate your reward system most powerfully are often those who resonate with your wounds. They tend to recreate your earliest traumas and offer opportunities to replay unresolved dynamics from your past. Your unconscious psyche maintains hope that this time will be different, that ultimately you'll find the love, attention, or approval that was previously withheld. Understand that the intense chemistry experienced is not love; it's merely a recognition of familiar pain your reward system is responding to cues that align with your attachment template, along with the projection of your anima or animus onto a partner who triggers this powerful response.

People who could genuinely be good for you often don't activate the same emotional responses as those who match your past wounds. They may feel pleasant, but they aren't as exciting. While you can recognise, on an intellectual level, that they are wonderful, there often isn't an overwhelming attraction or a strong pull, a sense of destiny or coming home. This is because they don't fit your established patterns or triggers; they don't stimulate the reward centres in your brain in the same way your childhood experiences did.

This dilemma is a common one, causing many to feel torn between their desires and their needs, between chemistry and compatibility. The person who sparks that intense feeling often does so by activating your reward circuitry through familiar yet unhealthy patterns, patterns tied to past wounds that may lead to suffering. They feel right because they are familiar, rather than because they are healthy. On the other hand, the person who would actually be good for you doesn't activate those circuits, feels different, and thus can seem wrong or unappealing to your unconscious mind.

Reflect on how this pattern has influenced your romantic history. Recall those moments of intense chemistry. What childhood wounds were being triggered at those times? For instance, with the emotionally distant partner who kept you on edge, what does that anxiety remind you of from your youth? If you were involved with a critical partner, who were you truly seeking approval from? And if you felt the need to rescue a partner, what family role were you playing?

When you walked away from someone who was genuinely good for you because there wasn't enough chemistry, what were you leaving behind? What unfamiliar patterns made you uncomfortable? For instance, did the steady, available partner feel boring compared to your usual experiences with unavailability? Did a partner who didn't require fixing seem wrong because of the role you were accustomed to? Did a partner who wasn't critical feel like they didn't care, based on previous experiences where love was equated with criticism?

You might be thinking this all sounds deterministic, suggesting you're doomed to keep choosing partners who recreate your childhood wounds. However, understanding these mechanisms isn't about accepting fate; it's about recognising what influences your attraction so you can consciously navigate it rather than being unconsciously controlled while believing you're following your heart. It's about taking back control and making conscious, informed decisions about your relationships.

The process begins with acknowledging that intense chemistry often signals pattern recognition rather than true compatibility. When you feel an overwhelming attraction to someone and can't stop thinking about them, take a moment to pause. Don't just follow the feeling. Instead, ask yourself: What aspects of this person or dynamic feel familiar? What childhood experiences are being triggered? What role are you being offered in this familiar drama? What unresolved issues are you hoping to master this time around?

This doesn't mean you should avoid pursuing relationships that involve chemistry. Instead, it means approaching them with awareness and recognising what emotions and patterns are being activated. It's essential to consciously understand these dynamics, rather than repeating unconscious patterns, such as always being attracted to emotionally unavailable partners or seeking validation from others while believing you are finally finding true love.

For instance, you might recognise, "My ventral tegmental area (VTA) is activating because this person's unavailability mirrors my mother's inconsistent attention." With this awareness, you can make a conscious decision about whether to engage with that dynamic and assess whether it's likely to lead to a healthy relationship. Consider whether the temporary dopamine rush is worth the inevitable suffering that often arises from familiar patterns.

You may also catch yourself projecting your idealised self onto someone new, filling in gaps in your knowledge about them with fantasies based on your internal template. This is what we call 'projection' in psychology, a defence mechanism that involves attributing our own unacceptable qualities or feelings to others. It's crucial to slow down in such moments, gather real information about the person in question, and check if the qualities you assume they possess genuinely exist or are merely products of your imagination. You can identify when you are idealising someone you barely know and remind yourself, "This is projection; my unconscious template is seeking external form. This isn't about who they really are."

Additionally, you might notice that there's no intense chemistry with a person who is actually available, consistent, and kind. Instead of jumping to the conclusion that they aren't right for you, consider asking yourself: "What if my sense of chemistry is calibrated to dysfunction? What if I need to recalibrate my reward system? What if I should give this enough time for new patterns to become familiar before my VTA learns to respond to them?" This realisation opens up a world of possibilities, where conscious choices can lead to a recalibrated reward system and healthier relationships.

Choosing to pursue relationships with people who don't immediately activate your reward system can be beneficial. Recognise that your reward system has been shaped by past patterns that caused suffering, so the lack of immediate intense attraction is a good sign rather than a reason to keep looking.

This is exceptionally challenging because VTA activation feels like the truth. Chemistry can feel like a recognition of rightness, and overwhelming attraction may seem like finally discovering what you've been seeking. In these moments, your entire body may scream, "This is it! This is the one!" Your dopamine-flooded brain becomes less capable of objective evaluation as your unconscious psyche seeks familiar dynamics. Choosing to pursue someone who doesn't ignite that intensity can feel like settling or betraying yourself, creating internal conflict that's difficult to overcome. For instance, you might feel intense chemistry with someone who shares your past traumas, or you might feel a strong connection with someone who reminds you of a parent figure.

Consider this: What if everything you've learned to associate with love, chemistry, and rightness in relationships is simply a recognition of familiar dysfunction? Realising this can be liberating, freeing you from the patterns that have caused you pain. What if your reward system, shaped by past wounds, is an unreliable guide for choosing healthy partners? What if you need to consciously make different choices than those driven by your unconscious patterns, allowing your VTA to gradually learn to respond to new experiences that update old associations?

This is the essential work recognising that attraction reflects your internal template, your wounds, and your unconscious patterns, rather than providing reliable information about whether someone is good for you. Use intense chemistry as a signal to explore what's being activated rather than as a green light to pursue a relationship despite warning signs. Be mindful of when projection occurs and when you are relating to your anima or animus instead of the real person in front of you. Consciously choose to allow opportunities with people who do not immediately activate your reward circuitry, which is calibrated to dysfunction. Understand that familiarity does not equate to rightness, intensity does not equal love, and chemistry often signifies familiar pain.

Your ventral tegmental area (VTA) will continue to activate in response to cues that align with your attachment template. Similarly, your anima or animus will be projected onto potential partners, and your unconscious mind will seek opportunities to replay old dynamics. These mechanisms do not vanish through insight alone; they are driven by neural pathways shaped over decades, formed by patterns ingrained before conscious memory, and by reward associations that your system has learned are essential even when they lead to suffering.

However, you can develop the capacity to recognise when these systems are active. By observing them in operation rather than being unconsciously controlled by them, you can make conscious choices instead of being driven by programming you didn't choose. You can also gradually update your reward circuitry through new experiences. By allowing relationships with available partners to continue long enough, you can start to feel that availability is normal, that consistency isn't boring, and that security is associated with reward rather than settling.

Your VTA can learn new associations, but this requires you to repeatedly choose differently from your immediate attractions. It involves staying in situations that do not yield immediate, intense chemistry while your reward system gradually learns that these situations can lead to absolute satisfaction and connection. It also means tolerating the discomfort of unfamiliar patterns while new neural pathways slowly form that associate these patterns with rewards.

This process takes time. The patterns are deeply ingrained, encoded through thousands of early experiences, and change slowly through the repetition of new experiences rather than quickly through insight. Yet it is possible because neuroplasticity is fundamental. Reward systems can recalibrate, and you can gradually learn to feel attracted to patterns that don't enhance your wounds to people who offer different dynamics than those you experienced in childhood and to relationships that feel unfamiliar precisely because they are healthy rather than merely replaying familiar dysfunction.

The people you find most intensely attractive often reflect your wounds rather than your potential future. The chemistry that feels like destiny is usually just a recognition of familiar pain. The strong pull toward someone emotionally unavailable, critical, or unstable isn't true love; it's your attachment system recognising patterns that match your earliest relationship template. Your VTA floods you with dopamine in response to cues resembling what you learned the connection feels like, while your unconscious mind senses an opportunity to master what you couldn't master initially.

Until you recognise these mechanisms, until you understand what truly drives your attraction, you will continue choosing partners who recreate childhood dynamics while believing you are following your heart, trusting your feelings, or finally finding someone who understands you.

This understanding helps explain why you are drawn to people who hurt you, why stability feels boring, why chemistry often signals familiar dysfunction, and why the person who makes you feel most alive is usually the one who will recreate your earliest wounds. Your VTA responds to familiar patterns; your anima or animus projects onto partners who trigger a powerful response. Your attachment system recognises cues that match your template, and all of this occurs beneath your conscious awareness, influencing your choices while you remain convinced of your freedom to choose. This creates a cycle of pattern repetition while you insist that each time is different, ultimately ensuring familiar outcomes while maintaining the hope that this time will be different.

The shadow in love represents your own unhealed wounds. It involves seeking external forms to experience and potentially heal those wounds, as well as searching for unmet needs in partners who can't fulfil those roles, even if the original sources of those needs are long gone. This shadow influences your perceptions and choices, often leading you to feel drawn to people who mimic old patterns of pain, despite believing you've found someone different. However, this realisation also opens the door to growth and healing, offering a hopeful path towards healthier relationships.

Until you confront this shadow and recognise these patterns, you will continue to be driven by unconscious wounds that you didn't choose and templates that were not of your making. This will result in repeatedly selecting familiar pain while mistaking it for love. Recognising these patterns is the first step towards enlightenment and healthier relationships. You may find yourself stuck in childhood dynamics, convinced each time that you've found a different partner. Ultimately, you may be attracted to the wrong people for deeply rooted neurobiological reasons, all while thinking that this time, the chemistry indicates you've found "the one."

Chapter 11
The Trap of Success: The Biology of Self-Sabotage

Let's take a moment to reflect on a time when you were close to achieving something you'd been working toward for a long time, something you truly wanted and had invested significant time and effort in pursuing. It could be a job opportunity that marked an important step forward, a relationship that was becoming genuinely intimate, a creative project nearing completion, or a health goal you were finally approaching. You could see it right there, within reach, closer than ever before. And then, something unexpected happened.

You may have missed a crucial deadline due to an inexplicable oversight. Perhaps you picked a fight with your partner over something trivial just when things were going well. You might have stopped working on your project just before finishing it, or engaged in behaviours like drinking, overeating, or staying up too late that undermined your progress. In some way, you managed to ensure that success remained elusive, that achievement slipped away, and that you stayed exactly where you had always been despite your efforts to change. Other examples of self-sabotage could include procrastination, self-doubt, or negative self-talk.

Afterwards, in the aftermath of yet another self-sabotaged opportunity, you likely thought, "Why did I do that? I really wanted this. What's wrong with me? Why can't I ever seem to follow through? Why do I always mess things up just when they are about to work out?" You probably blamed yourself for lacking discipline, for having weak willpower, or for possessing some fundamental flaw that prevented you from succeeding. But what if, instead of blaming yourself, you could understand that your brain is simply trying to protect you? What if you could see this as an opportunity for growth and change, rather than a failure?

However, consider this: what if your self-sabotage wasn't due to a lack of willpower or character defects? What if it were your brain doing what it naturally does in maintaining homeostasis, keeping you in familiar territory, and defending against the genuine fear of actually getting what you want? After all, achieving your desires means becoming someone different, leaving behind the identity you've built your entire life around, and facing the daunting responsibility of being in control of your life without relying on circumstances to blame for your limitations.

Think about what would have happened if you had actually succeeded. If you had secured that job, you would have needed to show up as someone capable, competent, and worthy of the position. You would have had to let go of the identity of someone who never quite makes it, someone held back by circumstances, or someone whose potential remains unrealised. If the relationship continued to deepen, you would have needed to be vulnerable and genuinely known, unable to hide behind the defences you've maintained throughout your life. Completing that creative project would have meant putting it out into the world, facing potential judgment, and accepting that you are someone who completes things rather than someone whose greatness only exists in theory. Reaching your health goal would have required acknowledging your ability to be disciplined and follow through. This means you could no longer blame your body, metabolism, or circumstances for the issues you've been maintaining through your behaviour.

Success isn't just about achieving external goals; it also involves becoming a different person. And becoming different means the end of the identity you've built, the annihilation of familiar patterns, and the terrifying freedom of no longer hiding behind limitations or excuses. But remember, this is a freedom. The philosopher Søren Kierkegaard described this phenomenon as "the dizziness of freedom", the anxiety that arises when you realise you are free to choose, to change, and to become someone different. This realisation highlights that you've always had the power to change, which can be overwhelming and may lead you to question the necessity of the suffering you've endured and the responsibilities you now face. But it's also a reminder of your power to choose your path.

Self-sabotage is not about wanting to fail; rather, it stems from the fear of succeeding. It's your brain recognising that success threatens your homeostasis, familiar patterns, and the identity you've built. It activates defensive responses to keep you where you are because, while painful, that place is known. But change is possible. Your brain has learned to function within its current conditions and has developed strategies for coping with familiar suffering, building neural patterns calibrated to your existing circumstances. Change entails building new patterns, learning new techniques, and tolerating the discomfort of unfamiliarity as new neural pathways form. Your conscious mind may crave external accomplishments, but your unconscious brain seeks to maintain homeostasis. When these desires conflict at the moment of potential success, your unconscious brain often prevails, operating through mechanisms much faster and more powerful than your conscious intentions. But with understanding and practice, you can change these patterns.

Let's begin by discussing the neuroscience of homeostasis, as understanding this concept can help demystify self-sabotage and reduce feelings of personal failure. Your brain is constantly working to maintain equilibrium, striving to keep various physiological and psychological systems within specific ranges. This process, known as homeostatic regulation, occurs throughout your nervous system, affecting everything from basic functions like body temperature and blood sugar to more complex psychological patterns such as your baseline mood, stress levels, and familiar ways of relating to yourself and others.

Homeostasis is not about maintaining optimal conditions; it is about preserving familiar conditions, regardless of whether they are healthy or comfortable. If you've experienced chronic stress for years, your nervous system will adapt to high stress as a new normal. Similarly, if you've been mildly depressed since adolescence, your neurotransmitter systems will adjust to that state as a baseline. If you have engaged in anxious attachment patterns since childhood, your nervous system will organise itself around perpetual vigilance and uncertainty as standard operating procedure. While these states are often unpleasant and can lead to genuine suffering, they are familiar. Your brain knows how to function within these conditions, and neural patterns have developed that operate effectively in this environment. Recognising the familiarity of these conditions can help you feel more empathetic towards your own struggles.

When something threatens to alter these familiar conditions, such as approaching success requiring a different neural organisation or imminent achievement demanding a new baseline, your brain perceives it as a threat. This is not a danger in the external world, but rather a threat to system stability, established patterns, and homeostasis. Just as your brain responds to physical threats by activating stress responses, it also defends against threats to homeostasis by creating resistance, generating obstacles to change, and developing behaviours that ensure familiar conditions are maintained, even if those conditions are harmful.

This resistance occurs through mechanisms that operate outside of your conscious awareness. You don't consciously decide, "I think I'll sabotage this opportunity to maintain homeostasis." Instead, sabotage happens automatically. You might "forget" essential deadlines, suddenly become ill right before crucial events, pick fights that create familiar conflict, or engage in behaviours that you know undermine your goals, even though you find yourself doing them anyway. While your conscious mind wants to succeed, your unconscious mind perceives success as a threat to homeostasis and generates defensive responses before you are even aware of what is happening. Understanding this automatic nature can help you feel less guilty about your actions.

Your amygdala, the brain region responsible for threat detection, plays a central role in this process. It's important to remember that your amygdala does not only respond to external dangers; it also reacts to any threats to your sense of self, identity, or established patterns associated with survival. When you are on the brink of success that contradicts your self-concept, your amygdala activates. If you identify as someone who never quite succeeds or is held back by circumstances, then achieving success threatens your entire identity structure. Your amygdala detects this as a danger, triggering stress responses and generating anxiety that feels linked to external circumstances but actually stems from an internal threat to your identity.

Consider the physical sensations that arise just before taking action toward significant success: the tightness in your chest, racing thoughts, an overwhelming urge to do anything other than what will move you forward, unexpected exhaustion, or a sudden crisis that demands immediate attention, conveniently derailing your focus on your goal. These sensations are not random; they are your nervous system activating defensive responses, creating obstacles, and providing compelling reasons to avoid the very success you consciously desire.

And because these responses are happening through amygdala activation and stress response systems operating beneath conscious awareness, because they're generating physical sensations and urgent impulses before consciousness can evaluate them, you experience them as legitimate reasons to pause, to delay, to reconsider. You don't recognise you're being hijacked by homeostatic defence. You just feel suddenly overwhelmed, unsure, and aware of all the reasons why now isn't the right time, why you need to wait a bit longer, and why you should attend to something else first. Your conscious mind creates rational-sounding explanations for behaviour determined by unconscious resistance to change.

Understanding neural pathways and their resistance to change is key to comprehending why even changes you consciously desire face such powerful unconscious opposition. Every repeated thought, behaviour, or emotional response creates and strengthens neural pathways, which are physical connections between neurons that make specific patterns more likely to occur in the future. The more a pattern repeats, the stronger the path becomes. This is the power of habits at work: they make familiar patterns easier and more automatic, and thus, more resistant to change.

But here's what makes change difficult: these neural pathways don't just make familiar patterns easier, they make them feel right. The well-worn path feels like the natural response, the obvious choice, the way things should be. Alternative pathways, new patterns, and different responses require conscious effort. They feel unnatural and create discomfort because they engage neural territory that's not well-developed, requires resources to navigate, and lacks the automaticity of established patterns. The effort needed to engage these new responses can be daunting.

When you've spent decades responding to stress with anxiety, you've built powerful neural pathways connecting stress → anxiety. When stress occurs, the response is automatic and immediate; it feels like just what stress is, rather than recognising it as a learned pattern. Building alternative responses to stress → calm evaluation, stress → problem-solving without anxiety is a struggle. It requires deliberately creating new pathways through repeated practice, whilst the brain is constantly pulled back to the established pattern because that pattern is efficient, automatic, feels right, even when it creates suffering.

This creates powerful resistance to change even when change is consciously desired. The familiar patterns aren't just habits you could break through willpower; they're physical structures in your brain that have developed through years of repetition, that activate automatically, that feel like truth rather than like learned responses. Changing them requires building new neural structures while existing structures pull you back to familiar patterns, your brain generates discomfort with unfamiliar responses, and homeostatic mechanisms defend against the threat that change represents. The weight of these habits can be overwhelming.

Adding an existential dimension reveals a psychological truth: success requires change, which brings with it a daunting mix of freedom and responsibility. The existentialist philosopher Jean-Paul Sartre spoke of "bad faith", the ways we deceive ourselves to avoid facing our own freedom. We convince ourselves that we are shaped solely by our circumstances, rather than acknowledging that our choices shape our lives. We tell ourselves we are trapped by past experiences, wounds, limitations, or factors beyond our control. This self-deception allows us to dodge the frightening realisation that we are free, capable of choosing differently, and responsible for our own lives in ways that can feel unbearable.

Success compels us to confront this freedom. If we attain what we've claimed we wanted, if we demonstrate capabilities we've insisted we lack, or if we rise above limitations we've blamed for our suffering, we can no longer sustain the belief that we are trapped. We must acknowledge that we have always had the capability and choice to act differently. This means the suffering we've endured was not necessary or imposed on us; instead, it resulted from the choices we made, even while convincing ourselves that we had no choice.

This recognition can be devastating. It places the burden of responsibility on us, not in a moral sense, as we are not to blame for wounds we did not choose or for patterns that were established before we gained awareness. However, we are "response-able," capable of responding to our circumstances and able to determine, even when making a choice feels impossible. This responsibility can be overwhelming, as it strips away the excuse of circumstances and limitations, preventing us from maintaining the comforting fiction that we are victims of our past or present situations. We are free. As Kierkegaard noted, this freedom can induce profound anxiety, the "dizziness of freedom", that disorienting feeling of standing on a precipice where any direction is possible, where we could become anyone, and where our identity is shaped by our choices.

Self-sabotage often emerges as a defence against this anxiety and overwhelming responsibility. By undermining our own success right before achieving it, we can preserve the fiction that external circumstances, such as timing, other people, or mysterious forces, hold us back. This allows us to avoid confronting the reality of our freedom and capability, maintaining an identity as someone who is blocked rather than someone who is actively choosing, someone trapped rather than liberated, someone whose potential remains theoretical rather than someone who has to demonstrate real capability.

Consider the identity you've created around not succeeding. Perhaps you are the person who never quite makes it, whose potential is always just out of reach. This identity offers certain benefits: it shields you from judgment because you can't be evaluated if you haven't truly put yourself out there. It keeps hope alive, as you can believe that someday, when conditions align and wounds heal, you will find success. It also relieves you of responsibility since you're portrayed as being held back by factors beyond your control, rather than by your own choices.

Or maybe you identify as someone hindered by trauma, difficult circumstances, or a past that has damaged you in ways that block success. This narrative has its own advantages: it explains your suffering, rationalises your struggles, and positions you as a victim rather than an agent. It creates a coherent story, yet keeps you stuck. Achieving success would threaten this entire identity framework. Suppose you succeed despite trauma or challenging circumstances. In that case, you must confront the uncomfortable truth that you always had the ability to grow, which raises troubling questions about why you remained stagnant for so long and what opportunities you may have missed while clinging to a victim identity.

You may see yourself as someone who prioritises helping others, putting your own needs and goals second to those of everyone else. This identity feels noble, selfless, and morally superior, as if you are not selfish like others who pursue their own success. However, achieving your own goals requires you to prioritise yourself, say no to others, and abandon the selfless helper identity. You should acknowledge that your own desires, ambitions, and needs matter, and that you deserve recognition and achievement for yourself. This realisation can feel selfish, wrong, and threatening to the identity you've constructed around being the one who doesn't need or want anything, who only gives.

It's a constant battle to maintain the identity you've built for yourself, especially when success threatens it. Your brain fiercely defends this identity, as it provides stability and coherence, helping you understand who you are and navigate reality. Losing this identity can feel like annihilation, even if it causes suffering or constrains you. Even when you consciously claim you want to change, your unconscious systems that maintain homeostasis prioritise preserving established identity and keeping you exactly where you are, because that's the you they know.

This is why self-sabotage often occurs right at the moment of potential success. You've worked hard, overcome obstacles, and built momentum. Success is within your reach, and precisely at this moment, when achievement is imminent and you're about to demonstrate a capability that contradicts your identity, resistance becomes overwhelming. The closer you get to success, the more threatening it feels, prompting your homeostatic mechanisms to kick in and keep you in familiar territory. It's not that you lack the capability; you've proven your ability by getting this far. Instead, your brain, through self-sabotage, is reacting to the threat that success poses to familiar patterns and established identity.

Consider a concrete example: Someone who has identified as "the fat one" since childhood has structured their social relationships and self-concept around being overweight. When they decide to lose weight, they work hard, develop new habits, start exercising, and change their eating patterns. They lose ten, twenty, or even thirty pounds, getting closer to their goal weight. Then, they start to make small changes in their behaviour, perhaps eating a bit more or exercising a bit less. They plateau or even regain some weight, not all the way back to their original starting point, but enough to prevent them from fully achieving their goal and becoming someone different.

What happened? Their brain detected that continued weight loss would threaten their identity as "the fat one." While this identity is painful, it has organised their entire sense of self. It has explained their social difficulties: "I'm lonely because I'm fat." It has justified their limitations: "I can't do that because of my weight." It has provided a coherent narrative for their life, "I'm the fat one; that's who I am." Actually becoming thin would require abandoning this entire identity structure. They might wonder who they would be if not "the fat one." How would they explain their problems if weight were not the issue? What if they reached their goal weight and were still lonely, still struggling, still facing the same difficulties they had attributed to their weight? The fear of the unknown, of not having their weight to blame, can be paralysing.

This is a terrifying realisation. It's often easier for people to plateau and remain just short of their goals, clinging to their familiar identity while convincing themselves that they are still working toward change. This self-sabotage is not a conscious choice; individuals are not deliberately undermining themselves. Instead, the amygdala, a key player in our brain's emotional responses, detects a threat to its identity, activating homeostatic mechanisms and prompting neural patterns to pull back toward familiar territory. As a result, resistance generates behaviours that keep them precisely where they are while maintaining the illusion that they are striving for change.

Consider someone who has built their identity around being the struggling artist, an unrecognised genius whose work is deemed too avant-garde, too innovative, or too ahead of its time for commercial success. This identity protects them from the fear of fully showcasing their work and facing rejection based on merit rather than the idea of being ahead of their time. It also helps them confront whether they truly possess the talent they believe they have or if they are merely pretending. They may work on their masterpiece for years, perfecting it until it is "ready." Yet, just before completion, when it is almost finished enough to show anyone, they start over. They begin to see flaws, realise it needs restructuring, and understand it isn't quite right. The work remains forever nearly complete but never actually finished.

What is happening here? Success in finishing the work, showing it to others, and facing actual judgment threatens the very identity built around being the unrecognised genius. If they complete the job and receive recognition, it suggests they were not ahead of their time; they were just like everyone else seeking success. If they finish and face rejection, they might discover they are not the genius they believed themselves to be. It feels safer to keep the work perpetually unfinished, always on the verge of being ready, thus preserving their identity while avoiding the risks that come with completion. This resistance generates perfectionism, a tendency to see flaws, and compelling reasons to justify why the work isn't ready. All these factors serve to keep them exactly where they are while maintaining the appearance of moving toward completion.

This pattern of behaviour can be seen across various domains where success threatens identity. For example, a person might sabotage relationships just as they are becoming intimate because being alone is part of their identity. This provides an explanation for their struggles and protects them from the vulnerability that closeness requires. Another person may find ways to get fired right before a promotion because being underemployed explains their dissatisfaction, keeping their potential theoretical rather than tested. Similarly, someone might develop an illness right before significant opportunities arise, as being sick provides a legitimate reason to avoid fully showing up, facing judgment, and demonstrating competence.

The philosopher Martin Heidegger wrote about inauthenticity, the ways we flee from ourselves, from authentic possibilities, and from the anxiety of having to choose who we want to become. We often hide in familiar patterns, social roles, and identities that others have assigned us or that circumstances have created, thereby avoiding the terrifying freedom of genuinely choosing our path. Self-sabotage is a flight from authenticity; it acts as a defence against confronting real possibilities and serves to sustain familiar inauthenticity. This inauthenticity offers safety by limiting options, constraining who we can become, and sidestepping the dizzying freedom of recognising that we could be anyone.

Neurologically, there's even more happening that makes resistance stronger. Our brains do not merely defend familiar patterns; they also become dependent on them. If someone has lived with chronic stress, their nervous system adapts by becoming less sensitive to stress hormones. Consequently, they may require higher levels of cortisol and adrenaline to feel normal because their system has adjusted to constant elevation. If life becomes calmer and stress lessens, instead of feeling relief, they may feel wrong, flat, or as if something is missing. Their brain can create new stressors, dramas, or crises to maintain the activation it has become dependent on.

If you've been dealing with chronic anxiety, your nervous system may have become attuned to constant threat-scanning, perpetual vigilance, and a baseline of activation in preparation for danger. When circumstances change and your anxiety decreases, you might not feel safe. Instead, you may feel vulnerable and exposed, as if you're not adequately monitoring for threats. This heightened sensitivity from the amygdala can lead it to identify risks in previously neutral situations, generating anxiety to maintain a familiar level of activation. Calmness may feel dangerous because your system is not calibrated for it; it's calibrated for anxiety, and deviating from that feels threatening.

If you have built your identity around suffering, struggling, and viewing life as difficult, then when things become easier, it may not feel like relief. Instead, it can feel wrong, making you feel as though you're not working hard enough or that success achieved without sufficient struggle doesn't count. Your brain may create obstacles and difficulties to ensure there is enough struggle to align with your internal template, which is a set of beliefs and expectations based on your past experiences, of how achievement should feel. Easy success may not activate the reward circuitry that associates achievement with overcoming significant challenges, leading to reduced responsiveness in the ventral tegmental area to successes that contradict your usual expectations.

This neurological reliance on familiar patterns makes change not just uncomfortable but also feel wrong or dangerous, as if you are losing yourself rather than evolving into a different version of yourself. The discomfort is not merely a temporary adjustment; it can feel as if your brain is signalling that something is wrong, urging you to return to familiar territory, such as a job you've had for years or a relationship you've been in for a long time. Change can feel threatening to everything you know. Because these processes operate beneath conscious control, they generate intense physical sensations and compelling impulses, leading you to experience them as truth rather than as a protective response. You may feel that something is amiss with your progress, think that you are not ready, believe that you should wait, or feel compelled to address something else before moving forward toward success.

Consider your patterns of self-sabotage. When does it happen? What triggers it? What level of success seems to activate your resistance most powerfully? For many people, self-sabotage occurs at the moment of visibility when success would make them public, requiring them to be seen in a new role, identity, or way of being. Private progress is often manageable, but the thought of showing up publicly as a different person, being seen as capable or successful, can trigger overwhelming anxiety.

For others, sabotage occurs when change becomes irreversible, and moving forward would mean burning bridges to their old identity. Success at this point would suggest that they can no longer return to familiar patterns, locking them into being someone different. As long as change remains reversible, resistance is manageable. However, approaching the threshold where you cannot go back, where you must maintain a new identity, and where old patterns are no longer available can lead to a powerful sense of self-sabotage. To manage this fear, it's important to remember that change is a natural part of life and can lead to personal growth. Developing a support system and seeking professional help can also be beneficial in managing the fear of

For some, the catalyst for change is getting close to the very thing they've claimed to want when the goal is achievable, when the dream could become a reality, when potential could be transformed into actuality. As long as success remains a possibility, a theoretical concept, you are protected from discovering whether you are truly capable of achieving it, whether the accomplishment would genuinely satisfy you, and whether the success would actually resolve the problems you believe it would. It's often easier to keep success just out of reach, preserving hope and avoiding the risk of finding that achieving what you want might reveal it wasn't what you needed, that you would still fundamentally be the same person facing the same internal struggles.

Empowerment lies in understanding that overcoming self-sabotage isn't about developing more willpower or discipline. These approaches tend to fail because they rely on conscious intention to override unconscious resistance, which operates through mechanisms stronger than conscious control. The work involves recognising when resistance is at play, understanding what it is defending against, and consciously choosing to move through it. It also requires acknowledging the genuine fear it represents, rather than getting side-tracked by it and believing that your resistance is caused by external circumstances.

When you find yourself avoiding crucial actions, creating obstacles right before success, or engaging in behaviours that undermine your progress, it takes courage to stop. Don't berate yourself for lacking willpower or shame yourself for sabotaging again. Instead, ask yourself: What identity is threatened by this success? What would I have to acknowledge about myself if I succeeded? What freedom would I have to confront? What responsibility would I have to accept? What familiar suffering would I need to abandon? What comfortable limitations would I need to leave behind?

Resistance serves as information. It shows you where your identity is threatened, where homeostasis is being defended, where freedom creates anxiety, and where authentic possibilities trigger fear. Don't try to override this resistance through sheer force. Instead, acknowledge what it is protecting you from. Recognise the genuine terror of becoming someone different, of facing freedom, of accepting responsibility. Feel the dizziness, the vertigo, the sense that you might become anyone, which means you have always been free and therefore responsible.

And then, while feeling all of this and acknowledging the fear, it's crucial to move forward anyway, not by denying resistance, but by moving through it. Take action while anxiety screams. Do the thing while fear insists you're not ready? Show up while every impulse tells you to hide. Do this not because it feels comfortable, it won't, but because becoming different requires tolerating the discomfort of unfamiliar territory. This is when new neural pathways form, homeostasis gradually shifts to accommodate a different baseline, and identity slowly transforms through acting as if you are already the person you are becoming, rather than waiting to feel like that person before acting.

Transformation occurs through action despite resistance, not by waiting for resistance to dissipate before taking action. Your brain will continue defending homeostasis until you demonstrate through repeated actions that different patterns are sustainable, that a new identity can be maintained, and that change does not destroy you. This requires moving forward even when every homeostatic mechanism generates reasons to stop, creates obstacles, and produces compelling arguments for why now isn't the right time, why you need to wait, or why you should address something else first.

Crucially, it requires a conscious choice to prioritise long-term transformation over short-term comfort. Sabotaging behaviours provide immediate relief from the anxiety that success generates. Avoiding crucial actions temporarily reduces anxiety. Manufacturing obstacles provide justification for avoiding freedom and responsibility. Maintaining familiar patterns feels safe, yet it perpetuates long-term suffering. Your brain constantly chooses short-term relief over long-term benefits because that's how homeostatic mechanisms work. They prioritise immediate stability over eventual growth.

Overriding these habits requires a conscious commitment to tolerating short-term discomfort for the sake of long-term change. It means choosing to feel anxiety instead of avoiding it, facing freedom rather than hiding behind comfortable limitations, and deciding to become different even when every familiar pattern tries to pull you back to who you used to be. This isn't easy. It involves recognising that discomfort is a part of change rather than a signal that something is wrong, that unfamiliarity is a sign of growth rather than a warning that you're making a mistake, and that the terror of success correlates with the degree of transformation it represents, rather than indicating that you're not ready. For instance, the short-term discomfort of facing anxiety can lead to the long-term change of increased confidence and resilience.

Your brain will continue to generate resistance. Homeostatic mechanisms, which are your brain's way of maintaining stability and balance, will defend familiar patterns, and anxiety about freedom will flare up as success approaches. These feelings won't disappear; instead, you will develop the capacity to recognise them and choose not to be controlled by them. You can move forward while still experiencing these emotions, rather than waiting for them to resolve before taking action. The transformation lies in your relationship with resistance, not in the cessation of resistance itself.

This understanding sheds light on why you might sabotage yourself, why success can feel threatening, and why the idea of actually achieving your desires makes you anxious. Familiar suffering often feels safer than unfamiliar success; an identity built around limitation shields you from the anxiety of freedom and responsibility that genuine transformation would require. Your brain is defending its homeostasis. Your amygdala detects threats to your identity, while your neural pathways pull you toward familiar patterns. You are confronted with the freedom that evokes intense anxiety.

Until you recognise these mechanisms, understand what resistance is defending against, and develop the capacity to move through terror without being halted by it, you will continue to sabotage yourself right at the moment of success. You might find yourself perplexed as to why you can't seem to follow through, why you consistently undermine your efforts, or why you feel blocked by mysterious forces from achieving your conscious desires. The forces at play are not mysterious; they are homeostatic defences and existential anxiety, which is the fear of facing the freedom and responsibility that genuine transformation would require. Your brain is protecting you from becoming different, which means leaving behind who you've been, facing the freedom you've been avoiding, accepting responsibilities you've shied away from, and acknowledging that you were always capable. This raises unsettling questions about why you remained stuck in patterns you have now realised you were maintaining through your choices.

The trap of success is that achieving it requires you to become someone different, which entails the "death" of who you've been. This can feel like your death, even though it signifies your birth into authentic possibility. The sabotage is a defence against this death, a means of protecting yourself from this birth, and a way to maintain the familiar self, even when that familiar self leads to suffering. This suffering is known, while transformation represents a terrifying unknown.

Your subconscious operates through these mechanisms, sabotaging your conscious intentions while you remain unaware of the actual dynamics at play. This keeps you trapped, even as you insist you are trying to change, defending homeostasis while believing you are seeking growth. The work involves recognising the trap, understanding the mechanisms, choosing transformation despite the terror, and moving through resistance instead of being stopped by it. It also requires becoming the person you are capable of being rather than remaining the person you've always been, where familiar limitation feels safer than authentic freedom.

Chapter 12
The Dark Triad & The Social Shadow

Reflect on a time when you encountered someone who seemed genuinely toxic, not just difficult or flawed, but truly dangerous in their disregard for others. This person may have manipulated, exhibited cruelty, and maintained a charming facade. Perhaps it was a colleague who systematically undermined others while appearing helpful, someone who lied convincingly while looking you straight in the eye, and who seemed to take pleasure in others' distress while maintaining plausible deniability. Or it could be someone in a position of power who exploited those beneath them, demanded loyalty without giving any, and created an atmosphere of fear and control while insisting they were acting in everyone's best interests. It could also have been a partner who appeared perfect at first but gradually revealed themselves to be controlling, manipulative, and focused solely on their own needs, showing utter indifference to your suffering.

When you recognised this person's toxicity, you likely thought something like, "How can they be like this? How can someone lack empathy so completely? What makes them capable of such casual cruelty, systematic manipulation, and utter disregard for others' well-being?" You may have viewed them as fundamentally different from yourself, possessing qualities you do not have, as if they belong to a different species of human that lacks the basic decency and empathy you pride yourself on. You probably felt morally superior, grateful that you are not like them, and justified in condemning them because they clearly seem terrible, while you believe you are clearly good.

Consider this unsettling possibility: What if the toxic person's qualities are not something you lack, but rather something you've suppressed? What if they are openly expressing what you've hidden in your shadow? Could it be that the potential for manipulation, cruelty, exploitation, or self-centeredness exists in you, not just as a potential but as a reality you cannot acknowledge without shattering your self-concept as a good person?

Think about this for a second: what if you could suppress these qualities, your insistence that you do not possess them, actually makes them more dangerous, not less? What if the person who cannot acknowledge their capacity for manipulation is more likely to manipulate unconsciously? What if someone who insists they are incapable of cruelty is more likely to be cruel while genuinely believing they are being kind? What if your determination to be nothing like those terrible people you condemn ensures that you express similar qualities in ways you cannot recognise because you've completely split them off from your conscious awareness?

Think about the historical figures who committed systematic evil, created immense suffering, and were most destructive to human well-being. Were they individuals who acknowledged their capacity for cruelty and chose it consciously? Or were they people who insisted they were good, convinced they were acting morally, and committed atrocities while maintaining absolute certainty in their righteousness? They might have suppressed any recognition of their own cruelty so thoroughly that they could engage in systematic destruction while seeing themselves as victims, heroes, or servants of a higher purpose.

For instance, a dictator doesn't think he's evil; he believes he is bringing order, protecting his people, and doing what's necessary for the greater good. A cult leader may not recognise her manipulation; she believes she's enlightening followers, sharing truth, and helping people reach their potential. An abuser may not acknowledge his cruelty; he is convinced he's teaching essential lessons, maintaining necessary discipline, or responding appropriately to provocation. All of these individuals disowned their capacity for harm, split off any recognition of their exploitation or manipulation, and created a complete separation between their actions and their self-concept. This allows them to commit enormous harm while remaining convinced they are good people acting from good motives.

This is the danger of suppressing your shadow rather than integrating it. When you insist that you do not possess certain qualities, when you make an absolute division between yourself and those you consider terrible, and when you cannot acknowledge your own capacity for manipulation, cruelty, or exploitation, you do not eliminate those capacities. Instead, you drive them underground, where they operate outside of conscious awareness, find expression in ways you don't recognise, and ultimately control you because you are convinced they aren't there.

The individual who acknowledges, "Yes, I can be manipulative. I recognise when I'm using others for my own purposes, when I'm being strategic with the truth to get what I want, and when I'm exploiting someone's vulnerability," has the capacity to choose whether to engage in these behaviours. This self-awareness empowers them to recognise manipulation as it occurs, evaluate its appropriateness in a given situation, and consciously decide whether to act on these impulses or restrain them.

In contrast, the person who insists, "I'm not manipulative, I would never use people, I'm always honest and direct, "is often manipulative without realising it. They may be using others while believing they are helping, employing strategies while insisting on transparency, and lacking the capacity to restrain behaviours they refuse to acknowledge. Such individuals must engage in self-reflection and evaluation to truly understand their behaviours and their impact on others.

Let's begin with what psychologists call the Dark Triad: three personality traits that cluster together and represent qualities most people would consider deeply problematic: narcissism, Machiavellianism, and psychopathy. Before immediately reacting with "I don't have any of those traits; those are terrible qualities, and that's not me," it's important to pause. Understanding these traits and recognising them as existing on a continuum rather than as categorical differences between good and bad people is crucial for examining your own darker tendencies. This understanding opens the door to self-improvement and growth potential.

Narcissism, in personality psychology, is not merely about loving oneself or thinking one is attractive. It involves needing constant external validation, wanting to be perceived as special or superior, and exploiting others to maintain one's self-image. A narcissistic person often requires the spotlight, becomes enraged when not recognised as exceptional, uses others to support a fragile sense of self, and cannot tolerate criticism because it threatens their entire identity, which is built on being extraordinary.

Machiavellianism refers to strategic manipulation and viewing relationships as transactions. It prioritises outcomes over ethics and involves being willing to deceive and exploit others to achieve one's goals. This person sees social interactions as a chess game, treating others merely as pieces to be moved. They may form alliances purely based on advantage rather than genuine connection. They will betray someone they once praised if circumstances make betrayal beneficial, operating under the principle that "the ends justify the means," without ethical constraints on acceptable means.

Psychopathy, which is the most disturbing trait, entails a lack of empathy and an inability to feel guilt or remorse. It involves viewing others as objects to be used rather than as individuals with their own experiences and needs. A person with psychopathic traits can harm others without emotional repercussions, perceives others' suffering as neutral or even rewarding rather than distressing, and has no internal checks on exploiting or hurting others, aside from strategic considerations of the external consequences.

Your immediate response might be, "I'm definitely not any of those things. I don't have a narcissistic personality. I struggle with low self-esteem. I'm not Machiavellian. I value honesty and ethical behaviour. I'm not psychopathic, I'm actually very empathetic and caring." On a conscious level, this may be true. Your self-concept may genuinely centre around being modest, ethical, and empathetic. However, this reflects your conscious ego. What about your shadow self? What about the disowned qualities that operate beneath your conscious awareness?

Consider times when you needed to be the centre of attention, even if just for a moment. For instance, when you shared a personal achievement in a group setting, hoping for recognition, you might feel acknowledged. Think about cases where someone else's success sparked envy, like feeling a pang of jealousy when a colleague received praise for their work. Moments when you subtly redirected the conversation back to yourself, such as when a friend was sharing a problem, and you found a way to relate it to your own experiences. Or times you felt hurt for not being recognised while insisting that you don't care about attention, like when you didn't receive credit for a group project. These are signs of a narcissistic impulse at work beneath the surface of your self-image as a modest person. It doesn't mean you have narcissistic personality disorder. Still, it does suggest you possess certain narcissistic tendencies that you have disowned, tendencies that you experience yet cannot acknowledge for fear of threatening your self-concept.

Now, reflect on moments when you were strategic with the truth, when you manipulated situations to your advantage, or when you exploited others' vulnerabilities to get what you wanted. This manipulation may have been subtle, not overtly dramatic, but it involved shaping others' perceptions or creating scenarios that benefitted you while appearing helpful. This is indicative of

Machiavellian impulses. You possess and express these traits, yet you struggle to acknowledge them because you define yourself as someone who doesn't manipulate, who is always honest, and who never takes advantage of others.

Think too about times when you felt indifferent to others' suffering, when observing someone in distress evoked no emotional response from you, or when their pain felt inconvenient rather than something that required your attention. Consider instances where you had to feign empathy, putting on a concerned expression and saying the right things, all the while feeling detached and more focused on how their emotional display affected you than on their actual experience. This reflects a psychopathic tendency, the temporary absence of empathy, where you perceive another person as an object rather than a subject. It doesn't mean you are a psychopath, but there are moments when your empathy falters. Others' internal experiences go unnoticed, with you acting according to self-interest without the usual checks that empathy provides.

These traits exist within you, not as full-blown personality disorders, as those require persistent and pervasive characteristics that cause significant dysfunction. Instead, they manifest as tendencies, impulses, and capacities that occasionally influence your behaviour and are part of your psychological makeup, regardless of your acknowledgement of them. The more you disown these parts of yourself and assert that you do not possess them, the more dangerous they may become. They operate outside your conscious awareness, absent from conscious choice, and beyond any potential for ethical constraint, since you cannot restrain what you insist does not exist. Acknowledging these traits is the first step. Then, you can work on understanding the triggers that bring them to the surface and develop strategies to manage them healthily and constructively.

Let's examine how suppressed shadows can lead to tyranny. Understanding these dynamics is crucial not only for individual psychology but also for comprehending how good people can commit atrocities, how ethical systems can become oppressive, and how individuals convinced of their righteousness can cause systematic harm. The pattern is remarkably consistent: the more someone disowns their capacity for harm, the more likely they are to inflict harm while believing they are doing good.

Consider parents who abuse their children while insisting they are merely providing necessary discipline. These parents have completely disowned their cruelty, rage, and desire to dominate and control. They cannot acknowledge, "I'm being cruel; I take pleasure in my child's suffering; I am using my power to hurt someone weaker." Instead, they frame their actions as love, teaching, or necessary correction. This complete disowning of their cruelty is precisely what allows them to be cruel without restraint, guilt, or any internal recognition of their actual behaviour. If they could accept, "Yes, I want to hurt them right now; I feel rage and a desire to dominate," they would have the capacity to choose whether to act on it. However, because they have wholly disowned these feelings and are convinced they act from love, their cruelty manifests freely while their consciousness remains blind to its true nature.

Now, think about leaders who create authoritarian systems while claiming to protect freedom, who systematically suppress dissent while insisting they value open dialogue, or who establish surveillance states while professing to ensure privacy. The more completely they disown their desire for power and control, the more freely they can pursue power, framing it as service, and establish control while claiming to promote autonomy. If they could acknowledge, "I want power; I enjoy control; I am willing to harm others to maintain my position," there would at least be a possibility of choosing differently. However, because these desires operate in the shadows, utterly detached from conscious awareness, they function without ethical constraints.

Consider individuals who manipulate their partners systematically, engaging in gaslighting, control, and exploitation. They create elaborate systems to ensure their needs are met while systematically denying their partner's needs, all while being thoroughly convinced they are being loving, supportive, and good partners. The more thoroughly they disown their Machiavellian tendencies, their need to dominate, and their fundamental disregard for their partner as a separate person with distinct needs, the more freely these tendencies operate. There is no conscious recognition that allows for choice, restraint, or ethical evaluation of their behaviour.

This presents a terrible paradox: those who most vehemently insist they are good, who entirely disown any capacity for harm, and who divide the world into good people like themselves and bad people with the qualities they've disowned are often the very individuals most likely to cause systematic harm while remaining convinced of their righteousness. Because the harm operates in shadow, it is entirely separated from conscious awareness and is expressed freely precisely because consciousness insists it is not there.

The antidote to unhealthy behaviours, such as constantly seeking validation, exploiting others for personal gain, or lacking empathy, is not to become narcissistic, Machiavellian, or psychopathic. Instead, it is about integration: acknowledging that you possess these traits, recognising when they are at play, and developing a conscious relationship with aspects of yourself that you've been taught to view as unacceptable.

Admitting, "Yes, I have narcissistic tendencies; I do seek recognition and validation, and I can exploit others to fulfil those needs," is not a sign of weakness. It's a powerful acknowledgement that gives you the choice to evaluate your actions, decide if they are appropriate, and express your feelings in ways that do not harm others. It's about being in control of your impulses and using them constructively.

When you acknowledge, "Yes, I am capable of manipulation; I can be strategic in my relationships, and I may prioritise my interests over the well-being of others," you're not becoming a manipulative monster. Instead, you're becoming someone who can recognise manipulation as it occurs, choose when strategic behaviour is acceptable, and identify when it crosses into exploitation. It's a transformation from being unconsciously controlled by these traits to managing them consciously, all while being fully aware of their existence.

When you recognise, "Yes, my empathy can falter; I can perceive others as objects instead of subjects; I can harm others without feeling immediate emotional impact," you are not transforming into a psychopath. You are becoming a person who can detect when empathy is lacking, who can consciously choose to reconnect even if the automatic empathic response is not present, and who can restrain harmful impulses through deliberate choice instead of relying solely on a sometimes-failing empathic reaction.

Now, let's discuss the neuroscience involved. Understanding what occurs in your brain when empathy fails, when manipulation takes place, and when you see others as objects rather than subjects can shed light on how these Dark Triad qualities operate. This, in turn, emphasises how integration leads to genuine ethical capacity, rather than just suppression.

The orbitofrontal cortex (OFC), located just behind your eyes on the underside of your frontal lobes, is a key structure in this process. It's crucial for social behaviour, emotional regulation, and for integrating emotions with decision-making in social situations. Understanding its role can give you a deeper insight into how your brain processes social interactions and influences your behaviour.

The OFC is central to what neuroscientists refer to as 'theory of mind,' which is your ability to understand that other people have thoughts, feelings, and perspectives that are different from your own. It allows you to recognise that others have experiences that are as valid and authentic to them as yours are to you. The OFC integrates information about others' emotional states with social context and consequences, enabling you to navigate social realities with an understanding that your actions impact others. It demonstrates that others' well-being is significant, requiring consideration of multiple perspectives rather than just your own immediate interests.

When the OFC functions properly, when it is well-developed and connected to other brain regions, you perceive others as subjects rather than objects. You automatically consider their perspectives, are influenced by their emotional states, and recognise their suffering as something meaningful rather than neutral information or an opportunity to exploit. This understanding is not the result of conscious decision-making; instead, it involves automatic processing beneath your awareness, creating a deep sense that the internal experiences of others are real and meaningful. This automatic processing is a key function of the OFC, allowing you to navigate social situations with empathy and understanding.

The development and function of the orbitofrontal cortex (OFC) are significantly influenced by early experiences, particularly the way caregivers respond to you. For instance, if your early relationships involved caregivers who acknowledged your internal experiences and responded to your emotions, treating you as a person with legitimate needs and feelings, your OFC developed normally. This created a neural structure that automatically processes others as subjects. On the other hand, if your early experiences involved being treated as an object, such as a means to fulfil your parents' needs or an inconvenience to be managed, your OFC development was impaired. This leads to a neural architecture that primarily processes others as objects to be used, rather than as subjects whose experiences matter.

In contrast, if your early experiences involved being treated as an object, such as a means to fulfil your parents' needs or an inconvenience to be managed, your OFC development was impaired. This leads to a neural architecture that primarily processes others as objects to be used, rather than as subjects whose experiences matter.

Understanding this is crucial for making sense of the dark triad traits, which include narcissism, Machiavellianism, and psychopathy. These aren't just psychological patterns; they are neurological realities that reflect how the OFC and associated empathy circuits developed in response to early relational experiences. Individuals with severe psychopathy often have a measurable reduction in OFC volume and activity, particularly in areas linked to emotional processing. Their brains literally process others differently, not as choices they are making, but as outcomes of their developmental experiences, often influenced by trauma that hindered normal empathy circuit development.

However, it's important to note that OFC function is not fixed or permanent. It varies according to different states, stress levels, and the activation of various neural networks. Stress can significantly impact OFC function, causing your empathy circuits to go offline and leading you to perceive others as objects rather than subjects. This understanding can foster a sense of sympathy towards individuals with impaired OFC development, who may experience this shift more constantly and persistently.

Think back to times when you felt stressed, overwhelmed, or activated. How did you treat others during those moments? Were you patient, considerate, and empathetic? Or were you short, dismissive, treating others as obstacles to navigate rather than individuals with their own experiences? The change from empathic to non-empathic processing doesn't indicate that you have become a bad person; it reflects your OFC going offline under stress. Your empathy circuits become less active, causing you to temporarily view others more as objects than as subjects. In these moments, you may be experiencing something that individuals with impaired OFC development face more constantly and persistently, with a diminished ability to restore empathic function as stress diminishes.

Consider competitive situations, whether at work, in sports, or any context where you're trying to succeed at someone else's expense. How do you perceive your competitors? Do you genuinely recognise their internal states as real and important, feeling concern for their well-being while competing against them? Or do you view them more strategically, as obstacles to overcome, treating them as objects whose defeat is your goal rather than as subjects whose suffering matters? This shift toward a more Machiavellian approach, where you see others instrumentally and care more about the outcome than the impact on them, indicates that your orbitofrontal cortex (OFC) and empathy circuits are downregulating. This allows you to compete more effectively by temporarily diminishing your concern for others' well-being.

The difference between you and someone with a dark triad personality is not that you don't experience these states or that your OFC never goes offline; it's about frequency, duration, context, and, importantly, whether you're aware that it's happening. Your OFC may go offline sometimes, but it eventually comes back online. You may temporarily process others as objects, but you typically return to seeing them as subjects. You might experience moments of Machiavellian thinking or reduced empathy, but these are states rather than persistent traits. The key is to be aware of these shifts and recognise when you're not processing others empathically. This awareness gives you the power to catch yourself and consciously reconnect, offering hope and optimism for personal growth and change.

However, suppose you entirely deny these capacities and insist that you're always empathetic, never processing others as objects, and never acknowledging your Machiavellian impulses or moments of reduced empathy. When these states occur, you lack awareness. You won't recognise that your OFC has gone offline, nor will you be able to consciously restore empathic processing because you believe it never stopped. You may be strategic while insisting you're transparent; you might process others as objects while convinced you're treating them as subjects. You're acting without empathy while claiming to be deeply empathetic.

This lack of awareness can be dangerous not just for others but for you as well. However, with the ability to recognise when your processing has shifted, you can avoid engaging in harmful behaviours and step back when necessary. Integration means acknowledging these states when they arise. Recognise, for instance, "My empathy has gone offline right now; I'm viewing this person as an obstacle rather than as a subject. I need to consciously restore that connection or at least refrain from making significant decisions while I'm in this state." This recognition empowers you to take control of your actions and decisions.

Now, let's discuss the concept of the social shadow. Dark triad qualities do not operate solely on an individual level; they also manifest collectively, projecting onto designated others and creating social structures where suppressed shadows find expression, all while everyone involved believes they are acting from good intentions. Every culture has official values it claims to uphold, such as fairness, freedom, equality, compassion, and justice. It also has shadow values that it actually operates from but cannot acknowledge, such as dominance, exploitation, hierarchy, cruelty, and systematic advantages for some at the expense of others.

The more a culture denies its shadow values while tightly holding onto its proclaimed virtuous values, the more these shadow elements operate through systematic structures, even as everyone involved remains convinced they are serving the official values. For example, consider cultures that espouse equality while enforcing rigid hierarchies, or institutions that declare their commitment to the public good while systematically exploiting those they claim to serve. Think of systems that profess to promote freedom while establishing elaborate mechanisms of control. The gap between official values and actual practices represents the social shadow, a collective disowned material that expresses itself while consciousness insists it isn't there.

Similar to individual shadows, collective shadows get projected onto designated others. A culture that cannot acknowledge its own violence projects this violence onto other cultures, viewing them as barbaric while framing its violence as necessary peacekeeping. A nation that ignores its own exploitation casts this label onto other countries, seeing them as predatory while justifying its actions as fair trade. A group that fails to recognise its cruelty projects that cruelty onto other groups, perceiving them as monstrous while interpreting its own actions as justice, necessary discipline, or righteous punishment.

This projection creates enemies onto whom the collective shadow is cast, allowing the group to attack in others what it cannot acknowledge in itself. This paradoxical situation means waging war against the projected shadow while maintaining absolute conviction in its own virtue. The more complete the projection and the more absolute the disowning of the collective shadow, the more vicious the attacks become. These attacks are not genuinely aimed at external enemies; they are attempts to destroy disowned aspects of the self, to eliminate in others what they cannot face within themselves, and to purify themselves through violence against the projected shadow.

Consider moral panics, times when entire cultures become obsessed with rooting out particular evils, such as communists, witches, heretics, paedophiles, or terrorists, whatever the designated evil of the moment may be. These panics, often involving genuine threats that deserve a serious response, are always rooted in projection. The collective shadow cast onto groups, which can then be attacked with righteous fury, while the same qualities within the attacking group remain invisible, is a key factor in these societal panics.

For example, a culture may obsess over rooting out sexual predators while systematically covering up abuse within its own institutions. A nation focused on terrorism abroad might inflict state violence domestically. Similarly, a group concerned with authoritarianism in others may establish authoritarian control internally. The projection is so complete, and the disowning so absolute, that the attacking group genuinely cannot see that they possess the very qualities they are attacking. They express the same behaviours they condemn, and their righteous campaigns against external evil are actually expressions of their own disowned shadow.

Crucially, the people participating in these collective projections contribute to these social shadow dynamics and engage in systematic harm while believing they are fighting evil. The key to preventing this is self-awareness. They are not consciously choosing to be cruel. They act with complete conviction in their righteousness, absolutely sure that they are serving good while completely disowning their own capacity for the very harm they inflict. They are the parents who abuse while insisting they are providing discipline, the leaders who oppress while claiming to protect freedom, and the individuals who believe in their own virtue while causing systemic suffering. The collective shadow operates while everyone involved maintains the belief that they are serving the light.

The danger of this should be obvious: You are not immune to these dynamics. You participate in collective shadow, contribute to social projections, and engage in systematic harm while believing in your own virtue, not because you are unusually bad, but because these are universal human patterns. They operate through mechanisms beneath awareness and are maintained by an absolute conviction that you are different, one of the 'good ones,' and that you are nothing like those terrible people who possess the qualities you have disowned. Your certainty in your virtue, your confidence that you are not like them, and your belief that you do not possess dark triad qualities, this conviction is precisely what makes you dangerous. It is what allows the shadow to operate freely while you remain convinced it is not there.

Reflect on times when you have taken part in the collective condemnation of perceived enemies. Consider instances when you've felt a righteous fury towards certain people, groups, or nations that you deemed clearly terrible, evil, or different from yourself and your community. Pay attention to the intensity of your certainty, the absolute conviction in your belief that you are right and they are wrong, and the sense that condemning them is a moral duty and a necessary response to genuine evil.

Now ask yourself: What qualities do I see in them that I cannot acknowledge in myself? What capacities are they expressing that I have disowned? What aspect of my own shadow am I projecting onto them to attack it externally, while remaining blind to its presence within me?

This reflection does not imply that these designated enemies are not genuinely problematic or that they do not deserve a response. However, the intensity of your reaction, your consuming preoccupation, and your unwavering certainty about their evilness and your own virtue suggest that projection might be at play. You may be seeing your shadow in them; the qualities you condemn in them may very well be the qualities you possess but refuse to acknowledge.

The work here is not about excusing their behaviour or denying the harm they cause. Instead, it involves recognising what you are projecting onto others, owning those qualities within yourself, and managing your own shadow, rather than attacking it in others while remaining oblivious to its existence in yourself.

You may wonder: If acknowledging darker traits and integrating, rather than suppressing, my shadow is the solution, doesn't this risk making me actually manipulative, cruel, or harmful? Isn't it the suppression of those qualities that keeps me ethical? Doesn't denying I have them prevent me from acting on those impulses?

Evidence suggests otherwise. Those who cause the most systemic harm are often not the ones who acknowledge their capacity for harm; they are the ones who disown it entirely. A person who admits, "I'm capable of manipulation and I sometimes use people strategically," can evaluate when specific manipulation is appropriate, constrain it when it crosses ethical lines, and recognise when strategic behaviour turns into exploitation.

In contrast, someone who insists, "I'm never manipulative; I would never use people," acts manipulatively without awareness, believing they are helping others. They may cross ethical boundaries, convinced they are acting ethically, as their manipulation is entirely in shadow, beyond conscious recognition.

Similarly, someone who recognises, "I'm capable of cruelty, and I sometimes want to hurt others," can consciously choose whether to act on those impulses. They can recognise when their anger is morphing into abuse and can constrain harmful behaviour before it escalates. Conversely, a person who claims, "I'm never cruel; I would never intentionally hurt anyone," may inflict harm without recognising it. They may act cruelly while believing they are being kind, engaging in systematic cruelty while convinced they are acting from love, all because that cruelty is disowned, split off, and operating outside of conscious awareness.

Integration does not mean acting on every impulse; it means recognising those impulses consciously, where they can be evaluated and where choice becomes possible. Ethical constraints can only operate because you are aware of what needs to be constrained. Suppression, on the other hand, means that impulses remain outside conscious awareness, choice, and ethical evaluation, as you insist they are not there.

So, which is more dangerous: being aware of your capacity for harm and choosing how to express or constrain it, or being unaware of that capacity, leaving you unable to restrain something you refuse to acknowledge?

The goal is to acknowledge that you may possess dark triad tendencies, to recognise when these tendencies are at play, and to develop a conscious relationship with aspects of yourself that you may have been taught are entirely unacceptable. This isn't about becoming narcissistic, Machiavellian, or psychopathic; instead, it's about being aware of these tendencies when they arise, understanding when your empathy is offline, and catching yourself processing others as objects instead of subjects. It's essential to consciously restore empathic processing, rather than assuming it is always automatically present. This process empowers you to be in control of your responses and decisions.

This process requires regular self-evaluation to assess how you perceive and interact with others. Ask yourself whether you view them as individuals with internal states that matter or merely as objects to be used for your own purposes. You need to recognise when you are being strategic in your relationships, manipulating situations to your advantage, or prioritising your interests without regard for others' well-being. It also involves acknowledging moments when you seek recognition and validation, when you feel the need to be the centre of attention, or when you exploit others' admiration to bolster your fragile self-esteem.

The key is not to condemn yourself for having these impulses but to recognise them and consciously decide how to respond. This will help you develop an ethical relationship with the parts of yourself that exist, whether you acknowledge them or not. By making conscious decisions, you can shape your responses and actions, rather than being controlled by these tendencies.

Understanding the danger of suppressing your shadow self is crucial. Disowning dark triad qualities can make them more dangerous, rather than less. The social shadow operates while everyone claims virtue, creating a collective projection that turns disowned aspects into perceived enemies. There is a paradox where those most convinced of their own righteousness are often the most likely to cause systematic harm.

Everyone has the capacity for manipulation; narcissistic tendencies are real, and it's normal for your empathy to go offline at times. You may process others as objects rather than subjects under certain conditions. All of this is simply part of being human, shaped by an orbitofrontal cortex (OFC) that developed in specific ways and functions variably based on your state of mind. You are not alone in these experiences, and they do not define you.

The real danger lies not in possessing these qualities, as everyone has them to varying degrees, but in completely suppressing them. This creates an absolute division between yourself as a good person and others whom you deem to have dark triad traits. Suppression ensures that these tendencies operate outside of your awareness, choice, and ethical constraints, expressing themselves freely because you are convinced they don't exist.

Integration means acknowledging these tendencies, recognising when they are active, and developing a conscious relationship with the aspects of yourself that you may have disowned. This creates a capacity for choice, allowing you to avoid being unconsciously controlled by qualities you insist don't exist while they influence your behaviour from the shadows.

Deep within your psyche, there may be dark triad tendencies that you are hesitant to confront. This reluctance, driven by the fear of tarnishing your self-image as a good person, actually amplifies the danger of these traits. By operating in the shadows of your consciousness, they can manifest in ways that elude your recognition, all the while you remain steadfast in your belief in your own moral standing.

The ultimate goal is not to suppress or deny your dark triad tendencies, but to integrate them into your conscious awareness. It's about acknowledging your potential for harm and developing a conscious relationship with it, rather than adamantly insisting that you are immune to it. Believing that your repressed shadow will remain hidden is a dangerous misconception. Trusting that denying your potential for harm makes you harmless is a fallacy. In reality, this denial can cause the damage you are capable of more likely to surface, as it operates beyond your conscious recognition and, therefore, beyond any potential restraints.

Chapter 13
The Body Knows: Somatic Practices and Stored Emotions

Take a moment to stop reading and honestly notice your body. Not in an abstract way like, "I have a body," but by actually feeling what is happening in your physical form right now. Notice your jaw. Is it clenched? Your shoulders, are they raised, tense, or holding tight? Your chest Is your breathing shallow, restricted, barely moving past your upper ribs? Your stomach, is it tight, contracted, always braced against something? Are your hands gripping or clenched into fists, or are you holding your phone or book with more force than necessary?

Here's the crucial point: You probably didn't notice any of this until I directed your attention to it. Your jaw might have been clenched for hours, perhaps even for years or decades, and you've become so accustomed to the tension that it feels normal just the way your body is, and not something worth acknowledging. Your shoulders may have been raised and tight for so long that you've forgotten what relaxed shoulders feel like, or what it's like to have your arms hang naturally from joints that aren't perpetually braced. Your breathing might have been shallow for so long that taking a deep, full breath feels strange, excessive, or almost dangerous, as if you're taking up too much space.

Now that you're aware of these tensions and chronic contractions you carry unconsciously, what happens when you attempt to release them? Try it. Unclench your jaw, drop your shoulders, and take a deep breath into your belly. Notice what you feel. Is it relaxing? Or does it feel...wrong? Vulnerable? Unsafe? If it feels uncomfortable, try progressive muscle relaxation or deep breathing exercises. These can help your body learn to relax and let go of chronic tension. Does anxiety spike when you try to release the chronic tension? Does your body automatically tense back up after a moment of release, returning to familiar habits without conscious intention?

This is your body storing emotions, trauma, and implicit memories that never became consciously acknowledged. For instance, a car accident might lead to a perpetual tightening of the shoulders, or a childhood experience of being scolded might lead to a habit of shallow breathing. These are encoded in your muscular tension, breathing patterns, and nervous system activation, the very way you inhabit your physical form. Your body knows things your mind doesn't; it carries experiences your consciousness does not recall and maintains defensive postures that were necessary once but that you've never learned to release because the original threat was never processed or resolved.

Think about what your body is doing right now, in this moment when you are presumably safe, sitting somewhere reading, no immediate danger or threat present. Yet, your body is organised as if a threat is imminent, as if you need to stay perpetually braced, as if relaxing would make you vulnerable to an attack. Why is that? What is your body defending against? What implicit memories are influencing your posture, your breathing, your muscle tension, and your nervous system state? What experiences taught your body to maintain this constant vigilance and readiness for threat, even long after the original danger has passed?

The uncomfortable truth is that your body may be holding trauma you don't consciously remember, storing emotions you never fully processed, and maintaining defensive responses to threats your conscious mind doesn't acknowledge because they happened too early or in overwhelming ways that you couldn't integrate into explicit memory. Instead, they are encoded in implicit memory in your nervous system, your muscle patterns, and the overall way your body organises itself in space. These somatic encodings continue to influence how you move through the world, shaping your experiences while your consciousness remains unaware of what drives these patterns.

Your therapist might spend years helping you intellectually understand your childhood, assisting you in developing insights about your attachment patterns, and helping you recognise cognitive distortions and maladaptive beliefs. All of this might be genuinely useful and create significant shifts in how you think about yourself and your history. However, suppose the work remains purely cognitive and doesn't address what's stored in your body, or engage with the somatic encodings that determine your nervous system state and automatic responses. In that case, you may understand yourself better, but continue to live in a body organised around threat. You might keep breathing shallowly as though deep breathing is dangerous, maintaining chronic tension as if releasing it would expose you to vulnerability, and continuing to exist in nervous system states that were adaptive to your childhood but are no longer appropriate to your current reality.

This is why people can engage in years of talk therapy, gaining significant insight and understanding their patterns with impressive sophistication, yet still feel anxious. Despite the depth of their understanding, they may continue to exist in chronic activation, with bodies that never feel safe, even when their life circumstances have changed dramatically from those that initially created the threat. The understanding resides in their prefrontal cortex and reflects explicit knowledge and conscious awareness. However, the trauma is embedded in their bodies, within their nervous systems, as somatic encodings that do not respond to cognitive insight because they were never recorded cognitively in the first place. This underscores the limitations of talk therapy in addressing trauma stored in the body.

Let me be very clear about what I'm not saying: I'm not suggesting that somatic work can replace psychological understanding or that trauma can be healed solely through body-based practices without addressing psychological and relational dimensions. I'm not claiming that releasing muscular tension magically resolves complex trauma, nor that simply breathing differently will automatically fix nervous system dysregulation. Body work alone is insufficient. Genuine transformation occurs when psychological insight and somatic practice are integrated, allowing for a balanced understanding of what happened cognitively while also working to transform how it is stored in the body. This means developing explicit awareness and addressing implicit encodings, knowing your patterns intellectually while also changing the nervous system states that uphold those patterns.

However, I am emphasising this: if you are not working with your body, if your therapeutic work or self-development is purely cognitive, and if you are trying to think your way to healing while ignoring the somatic dimension entirely, you are overlooking the area where a significant amount of trauma and emotion is stored. This neglect can lead to implicit memories continuing to operate and your nervous system responding to threats that your consciousness does not recognise. You can fully understand why you feel anxious, yet your body may still maintain the chronic activation that fuels that anxiety. You can develop sophisticated insights about your attachment patterns, yet your nervous system may still operate in threat-detection mode calibrated in infancy. You can cognitively know that you are safe. Yet, your body insists you are in danger, demonstrating chronic tension, shallow breathing, and a perpetual readiness for a threat that is not consciously registered but determines your entire somatic experience.

Now, let's discuss the neuroscience, as understanding polyvagal theory and vagal tone clarifies why working with the body is essential rather than optional. It explains how your nervous system state determines your psychological experience in ways that cognitive work alone cannot address, and why somatic practices can reach dimensions of trauma and emotion that talk therapy cannot. The key structure involved is the vagus nerve, which actually consists of two vagus nerves, left and right, although we often refer to them as singular. This nerve is the longest cranial nerve in your body, extending from your brainstem down through your face, throat, heart, lungs, and digestive system, connecting your brain to nearly all of your major organs.

The vagus nerve is central to what neuroscientist Stephen Porges refers to as the polyvagal system. "Poly" means multiple, indicating that the vagus has different branches that evolved at different times and serve various functions. Understanding these branches helps explain why your body responds to threats in ways beyond consciousness's control and why you cannot simply think your way out of certain nervous system states. This underscores the necessity of somatic work for addressing trauma stored beneath the level of conscious awareness.

The oldest vagal pathway, from an evolutionary standpoint, is the dorsal vagal complex, "dorsal" indicating that it originates in the dorsal motor nucleus of the vagus in your brainstem. This system is responsible for immobilisation and the shutdown response that occurs when a threat is overwhelming and escape feels impossible. When the dorsal vagal pathway activates, your body essentially goes offline: heart rate drops, breathing slows, and you might feel numb or dissociated, disconnecting from your body and emotions. This state is characterised by a feeling of collapse or freeze, where everything slows down and shuts down because active response seems hopeless.

Consider the way some animals play dead when threatened. This is known as dorsal vagal activation, an ancient survival strategy. In this state of immobility, the chances of survival increase when fight or flight aren't effective. In humans, dorsal vagal states manifest as dissociation, a feeling of disconnection and numbness. This state can resemble depression, characterised more by a sense of emptiness than sadness, leading to a feeling of being shut down when overwhelmed. It often feels like watching your life through a glass, existing in a perpetual fog where nothing feels entirely real.

The middle vagal pathway, evolutionarily speaking, corresponds to the sympathetic nervous system, not technically part of the vagus nerve, but part of the autonomic response system that works in opposition to vagal activation. This is your mobilisation system, responsible for the fight-or-flight response, which activates when you sense a threat and believe you can escape or confront it through action.

When the sympathetic system is activated, your body's response is a testament to its adaptability: heart rate increases, breathing becomes rapid and shallow, adrenaline and cortisol flood your system, and blood flows to the large muscles, priming you for action. This is the state most people recognise as anxiety or panic: the racing heart, the rapid breathing, and the overwhelming sense that something bad is about to happen, which requires immediate action. It's also the state underlying feelings of anger and rage, preparing you to fight when threatened. While sympathetic activation is not inherently unhealthy, it is appropriate and adaptive when facing genuine threats. It becomes problematic when it becomes chronic. Living in a state of persistent sympathetic activation, even when no real danger is present, means your nervous system has defaulted to this state and struggles to return to calm.

The most recently evolved vagal pathway is what Porges describes as the ventral vagal complex. This System, originating in the nucleus ambiguus of the brainstem, is the key to social engagement. It supports a state of rest and digest when you feel safe and connected, fostering genuine relationships and interactions.

When the ventral vagal pathway is active, your heart rate is calm and variable, your breathing is slow and deep, and your facial muscles are relaxed, allowing for genuine expression. Your voice carries warmth and prosody, you can make eye contact, and you feel present in both your body and your relationships.

This is the state of safety and connection, the nervous system configuration that allows for play, intimacy, and genuine engagement with both others and life itself. It's marked by what is known as high vagal tone, which represents a strong ventral vagal influence that keeps your heart rate variably responsive rather than stuck in a state of chronic activation or shutdown. This allows your nervous system to flexibly respond to changing circumstances instead of remaining fixed in one state, promoting a sense of safety and connection.

Now here's what's crucial: these three systems operate in hierarchy. When you feel safe, in an environment your nervous system assesses as non-threatening, the ventral vagal is active. You're in social engagement mode, capable of connection, present, and responsive. But when your nervous system detects a threat and this assessment happens beneath conscious awareness, faster than conscious processing, the ventral vagal goes offline and the sympathetic activates. You shift from social engagement to mobilisation, from connection mode to fight-or-flight. And if the threat feels overwhelming, if mobilisation won't work, if you're trapped with no escape possible, the sympathetic system goes offline and the dorsal vagal activates, you shift from mobilisation to immobilisation, from fight-or-flight to freeze-or-collapse.

These shifts occur automatically, beyond conscious control, guided by your nervous system's evaluation of safety versus threat. You don't consciously decide, "I think I'll activate my sympathetic nervous system now." Your autonomic nervous system operates automatically, detecting threat cues and adjusting your state without conscious intention or cognitive assessment, before explicit awareness comprehends what's happening. These detections are not only based on current circumstances but also on your nervous system's learned patterns, implicit memories encoding dangerous situations, associations formed before conscious memory, and your attachment history. These factors determine what your nervous system has learned to recognise as safe versus threatening.

If your early attachment experiences were characterised by consistent responsiveness from caregivers, by having your needs met reliably, by experiencing the world as fundamentally safe place where distress is followed by comfort and threat is followed by protection your nervous system learned to default to ventral vagal, learned to return to social engagement and connection as baseline state, realised that the world is fundamentally safe and threat is temporary exception rather than permanent condition. Your vagal tone is high, indicating strong ventral vagal influence, which means the capacity to flexibly respond to threat when it actually occurs and then return to baseline calm rather than remaining chronically activated.

If your early experiences were marked by inconsistent care, unpredictable responsiveness, and caregivers who were sometimes threatening themselves, your nervous system learned different defaults. Perhaps you knew that the world is always dangerous, that you need to maintain constant sympathetic activation to be ready for a threat that might come at any moment. Your baseline isn't ventral vagal calm, it's sympathetic mobilisation, chronic fight-or-flight activation that feels normal because it's what you've known since infancy. Or perhaps you learned that threat is inescapable, that mobilisation doesn't help, that the only option is dorsal vagal shutdown, dissociation, existing in chronic immobilisation where you're perpetually disconnected, perpetually numb, perpetually not quite present.

These learned patterns, these nervous system defaults calibrated by early experience, don't change through cognitive insight alone. You can understand intellectually that you're safe now, that your current circumstances are different from your childhood, that the threats that shaped your nervous system are no longer present. But your autonomic nervous system doesn't process this cognitive information; it processes cues of safety versus threat through mechanisms operating beneath conscious awareness, through learned associations encoded in implicit memory, through patterns established before you had explicit awareness to bring to bear on the situation.

This is why your body knows things your mind doesn't, why you can cognitively understand you're safe whilst your body continues insisting you're in danger, and why insight doesn't automatically translate into feeling different. Your ventral vagal system isn't engaging because it doesn't register the cognitive insight. It responds to autonomic cues, learned patterns about what situations feel safe, and implicit memories that determine which nervous system state is appropriate to current circumstances based on how similar situations were experienced before conscious memory.

Consider your baseline nervous system state, not when you are acutely stressed or facing an obvious crisis, but your default state. This is what your body returns to when nothing particular is happening; it's the autonomic configuration that feels normal to you. Are you in the ventral vagal state, where you are calm, breathing deeply and easily, feeling present and connected, able to engage socially? Or are you experiencing chronic sympathetic activation, feeling slightly anxious or vigilant, breathing shallowly, as if you need to be ready for something even though no real threat exists? Alternatively, are you in dorsal vagal shutdown, where you feel somewhat numb, disconnected (feeling detached from your body or emotions), or dissociated (feeling disconnected from reality), existing in a low-energy state where nothing feels quite real, and you aren't fully present in your life?

Your baseline state isn't just about your current circumstances; it's about how your nervous system has learned to operate. It's a reflection of what your autonomic system recognises as usual through countless early experiences. This understanding encourages introspection and reflection on how these early experiences have shaped your current state.

Understanding how trauma is stored in the body underscores the adaptive nature of the body's response to threat. When you face a threat, your body automatically prepares for defensive action. This response, with the sympathetic nervous system activating and stress hormones releasing, is a testament to your body's capabilities in preparing to deal with danger.

However, what happens when you cannot complete the defensive action? For example, when a child faces a threat from a caregiver, they cannot fight or flee from them due to their dependence on them for survival. What if they are trapped in a situation where neither fight nor flight is possible, or when they are overwhelmed by a threat that feels too enormous to respond to effectively? The energy mobilised for those defensive actions means all that sympathetic activation and preparation doesn't simply disappear. It gets stuck in the body as chronic tension or activation, representing incomplete defensive responses.

Your body may still hold the muscular contractions that were prepared to push the threat away, yet that push never occurred. It may still retain the tension that was meant for running, but running never happened. You may still exhibit postural bracing intended for protection, but since the threat never resolved, that bracing never released. All of these incomplete defensive responses remain in your body as chronic tension and holding patterns, encoding the trauma that continues to express itself long after the original threat has passed because the defensive sequence was never completed. Without resolution, your nervous system cannot return to its baseline state.

Peter Levine, the developer of Somatic Experiencing therapy, observed that wild animals often face life-threatening danger but rarely develop traumatic stress. After a threat passes, they return to a baseline calm state. He noticed that animals that successfully escape predators often exhibit shaking, trembling, and rapid breathing that eventually slow down. This behaviour allows them to discharge the mobilisation energy from their bodies, completing the defensive response that had prepared them for action. As a result, their nervous systems can reset to baseline instead of remaining stuck in a heightened state of activation.

In contrast, humans often do not complete these natural sequences. Social conditioning teaches us to suppress shaking, control trembling, and avoid making a scene, prompting us to calm down quickly rather than allowing the natural discharge of mobilisation energy. Trauma can occur not only from experiencing a threat but also from being unable to finish the defensive response to that threat. When mobilisation energy gets trapped in our systems because we had to shut down before completing the action our bodies prepared for, our nervous systems never receive the signal that the threat has passed. This leaves us in a heightened state of activation.

This incomplete defensive response is stored in our bodies in chronic muscular tension that holds unfinished actions, in breathing patterns that never return to full depth after episodes of shallow breathing, in postures that maintain protective stances long after the need for protection has passed, and in nervous system states that remain stuck in mobilisation or shutdown. These somatic encodings affect our automatic responses, such as our immediate reaction to a perceived threat, shaping our experiences and maintaining trauma responses, even when our conscious minds do not explicitly remember what they are responding to.

Consider your chronic tensions and habitual postural patterns. If your shoulders are consistently raised, what are they protecting? What threat are they bracing against? If your jaw is habitually clenched, what expression, scream, or protest is being held back? What was too dangerous to vocalise that your jaw is still preventing? If your chest feels tight and your breathing is shallow, what emotions are being constrained? What expressions of grief, rage, or terror are being suppressed by restricted breathing?

These tensions are not merely the result of sitting or sleeping awkwardly. They are somatic encodings of trauma, representing incomplete defensive responses and unexpressed emotions. Implicit memories from overwhelming experiences may not be processed consciously and instead become encoded in our bodies, where they continue to influence our automatic responses.

These somatic encodings create feedback loops that perpetuate psychological states. When breathing is chronically shallow and the body adopts a breathing pattern associated with threat, it sends signals to the brain indicating that danger is present. The amygdala, a key part of the brain's emotional processing system, interprets shallow breathing as an indication of threat, leading to anxiety even when no conscious threat exists. Similarly, when our posture is collapsed shoulders forward, chest sunken, head down, we maintain a dorsal vagal shutdown state, signalling to our nervous system that we are in defeat or collapse. This configuration can sustain feelings of depression, even when our conscious thoughts are not particularly harmful.

Your physical state affects your psychological experience just as much as your psychological experience influences your physical state, perhaps even more so. This is because signals from the body to the brain are ancient and automatic, operating through subcortical pathways that function faster than conscious thought. You may be trying to think your way out of anxiety while your shallow breathing and chronic muscle tension are continuously signalling danger to your amygdala. This ongoing response maintains sympathetic activation, telling your brain that a threat is present, regardless of what your prefrontal cortex rationally understands about your current safety.

This is why cognitive approaches alone are insufficient for addressing trauma. Understanding what happened doesn't automatically change how you feel; insight into your patterns doesn't spontaneously resolve the nervous system dysregulation that sustains those patterns. The trauma isn't solely in your thoughts, beliefs, or cognitive schemas; it's embedded in your body, your nervous system, and somatic encodings that do not respond to cognitive interventions because they were never encoded cognitively in the first place.

Now, let's discuss how to address this issue. Understanding the problem is only helpful if you also know how to tackle it. The Somatic Check-In technique is distinct from meditation or relaxation exercises. It involves systematically bringing conscious awareness to your physical state, recognising what your nervous system is doing, and developing the capacity to notice somatic encodings that usually operate beneath your awareness. This isn't about achieving a state of calm or relaxation, although it might lead to these states. It's a diagnostic practice, a way of gathering information about what your body is actually doing, the state of your nervous system, and the somatic patterns that operate automatically while your consciousness remains unaware.

Here's how it works: Several times throughout your day, pause what you are doing and focus on your body. Do not attempt to change anything yet; simply observe. You can integrate this practice into your daily routine by doing it when you wake up, before meals, or before going to bed. Start with your breathing. Is it deep or shallow? High in your chest or low in your belly? Fast or slow? Restricted or full? Don't judge it or try to change it at this moment, just notice what it is doing. Your breathing pattern reveals a great deal about the state of your nervous system. Shallow, rapid breathing high in your chest indicates sympathetic activation, meaning you are in some degree of fight-or-flight, even if you consciously feel like you are just sitting at your desk. Conversely, deep, slow belly breathing suggests you are in a state of calm and safety (ventral vagal), while restricted, minimal breathing reflects a shutdown state (dorsal vagal), where you feel disconnected and not fully present.

Begin by noticing the tension in your muscles. Start with your jaw, check if it's clenched or relaxed. Move to your neck and shoulders. Are they tight, raised, or braced? What about your chest is it open or collapsed? Is your belly soft or contracted? How do your hands feel? Are they gripping or loose? And your legs, are they tense or relaxed? Remember, this is not a judgmental exercise; it's simply about accurately noticing what your body is doing. Each area of chronic tension reveals something about incomplete defensive responses, held emotions, or your body's encoded reactions to threats or feelings of collapse.

Next, take a moment to gauge your overall sense of your body. Do you feel present in your physical form? Can you sense your body from within, or are you somewhat disconnected, existing more in your thoughts than in your bodily experience? Do you feel contained within your skin, or do you think diffuse and ungrounded? Is your body a safe space for you, or do you sense a subtle feeling of threat, as if you're not at home in your physical form? These reflections can help you understand your degree of embodiment and whether you are in a state of calmness (ventral vagal presence) or experiencing some level of dissociation (dorsal vagal activation).

The purpose of this check-in is not to immediately fix anything you notice. Instead, it's about developing an awareness of patterns that usually operate automatically, recognising your baseline nervous system state, and seeing the bodily sensations that inform your experience without your conscious awareness. Many people are surprised when they begin to perform regular somatic check-ins; they often realise how activated, shut down, or tense they are without having consciously registered these feelings, discovering that their bodies are organised around feelings of threat or collapse, even while they consciously think they are fine and just going about their day.

Once you have the ability to notice these patterns and are aware of your chronic tensions and baseline nervous system state, you can begin to work with them. However, this should not be done through force or willpower to relax, nor by demanding that your body change. The process should be gentle, gradual, and respectful of the protective functions that these patterns serve. For instance, you can start by practising deep breathing exercises or gentle stretching. It's important to understand that chronic tension and nervous system activation exist for reasons, even if those reasons are no longer adaptive.

Start by focusing on your breathing. Breathing is unique because it is both automatic and voluntary; it operates unconsciously but can also be consciously controlled. You breathe without thinking, thanks to brainstem mechanisms that work beneath your awareness, but you can also choose to breathe differently. By using voluntary breath control, you can influence your autonomic nervous system, making breathing a bridge between conscious and unconscious processes, as well as between voluntary and automatic functions.

When you notice that you're engaging in shallow chest breathing, revealing sympathetic activation through restricted breath, you can consciously shift to deeper, slower breathing. This should be done gently; avoid forcing it or creating more tension by trying too hard. Instead, invite fuller breaths by gradually extending your exhales to activate the parasympathetic response (the 'rest and digest' response that promotes relaxation and digestion) and slowly deepening your inhales to enhance oxygenation. The key is to approach this process with gentleness and patience, respecting that your body may have restricted breathing for protective reasons and may need to release that restriction slowly rather than all at once.

When you notice chronic muscular tension, it's helpful to address it gradually. Rather than forcing relaxation, focus on developing conscious awareness and inviting ease. First, notice the tension and acknowledge its presence; understand that it exists for a reason and might be protecting something or responding to past experiences. Gently experiment with micro-releases, small decreases in tension, and see if your nervous system can handle slightly less tightness. If you feel an increase in anxiety when trying to release the tension, it's essential to recognise that this tension serves a protective role. Releasing it may feel threatening, indicating that your nervous system isn't ready for a full release. Honour this response by stepping back and progressing more slowly.

The key principle here is to recognise the intelligence of your body's patterns, even if they seem maladaptive. Chronic tension, shallow breathing, and protective postures made sense in past situations; they served survival functions and protected you from real threats. These patterns should not be dismissed as unhelpful but understood as intelligent responses that need updating through new experiences of safety. This requires a gradual release as your nervous system learns to adapt to different circumstances, along with respectful engagement rather than forceful elimination.

This understanding highlights why somatic work takes time and cannot be rushed. Attempts to force your body to relax or breathe differently often create more tension. You are working with patterns that have been established over decades, developed through countless repetitions, and maintained by mechanisms that operate faster than conscious awareness. Change comes from the gradual accumulation of new experiences and repeated micro-releases that your nervous system can tolerate. Building capacity for different states allows your body to learn that it is safe to inhabit them. This process may take time, but it is a journey worth taking for your well-being.

Another crucial aspect of somatic work is enhancing your vagal tone, which relates to your ability to access the ventral vagal state and develop the flexibility of your nervous system. This flexibility helps you respond to real threats and return to a baseline calm, a state of relaxed alertness, rather than getting stuck in activation or shutdown. High vagal tone, characterised by strong ventral vagal influence, is reflected in heart rate variability; your heart rate should respond to your breathing rather than remaining fixed. This flexibility allows you to shift between states as circumstances demand.

You can improve vagal tone through practices that activate the ventral vagal system. These include genuine social connections where you feel safe and seen, singing or humming to stimulate the vocal apparatus linked to the ventral vagal, and slow breathing that engages vagal pathways. Additionally, rhythmic activities like rocking or swaying, along with spending time in nature, typically activate the ventral vagal system more reliably than built environments. However, these are not quick fixes; building vagal tone occurs gradually through repeated practice, accumulating experiences of safety and connection. Over time, you will teach your nervous system that the ventral vagal state is safe to experience, that you can return to baseline calm after activation. That connection and presence are accessible rather than continually threatened. It's a journey that requires patience and commitment, but the rewards are significant.

There's also direct vagal stimulation through practices like cold water exposure to your face, which activates the diving reflex and directly stimulates vagal pathways. Specific breathing patterns, such as extended exhales, can shift your nervous system toward parasympathetic dominance. Additionally, bilateral stimulation, involving rhythmic left-right activation through eye movements, tapping, or walking, can help integrate implicit memories and shift your nervous system state. All of these methods work not through cognitive change, but through direct influence on the autonomic nervous system, utilising somatic pathways that bypass conscious processing.

However, these practices must be combined with awareness. This means using somatic check-ins to understand your patterns, tracking the shifts that occur with different practices like deep breathing, yoga, or meditation, and developing a conscious relationship with your nervous system, rather than simply applying techniques mechanically in hopes of achieving results. Awareness fosters learning by enabling your nervous system to update its patterns, creating genuine integration rather than just temporary state changes that don't persist once the practice ends.

Consider how different this is from purely cognitive approaches. In traditional talk therapy, you might spend a session discussing your anxiety, exploring its origins, recognising its patterns, and developing cognitive strategies to manage it. While these elements can be valuable, if your body is in chronic sympathetic activation characterised by shallow breathing, constant muscular tension, and a nervous system stuck in a mobilisation response, then cognitive understanding alone won't change your felt experience. Anxiety is not just in your thoughts; it resides in your body, in your autonomic nervous system, and in somatic encodings, which are the physical manifestations of emotional experiences that do not respond to cognitive insight.

Combining cognitive understanding with somatic awareness creates the potential for genuine integration. You gain insight into why you're anxious, recognising early experiences that contributed to the pattern, identifying triggers that activate it, and understanding its function while also addressing how this anxiety is encoded in your body. You learn how it maintains itself through breathing patterns, muscular tension, and the state of your nervous system. The aim is to gradually shift these somatic dimensions while also addressing the psychological content. The insights you gain inform the somatic work, helping you understand what you're addressing. In turn, the somatic practices make the insights embodied, changing not only how you think about your patterns but also how you actually feel in your body and how your nervous system responds to different circumstances.

This integration is essential for creating lasting change, rather than merely achieving intellectual understanding that doesn't translate into different experiences. You work with multiple dimensions simultaneously: the cognitive content, emotional processing, relational dynamics, and somatic encodings. All of these aspects relate to the same trauma, the same patterns, and the same implicit memories, expressing themselves through different channels. Working with all of these dimensions together opens the possibility for genuine transformation in a way that addressing any single dimension alone cannot achieve.

You might be thinking that this process seems complicated and overwhelming, and that it requires professional guidance to do safely. For those dealing with significant trauma, especially trauma involving dissociation or severe nervous system dysregulation, professional support is indeed essential. It's important not to enter into intense trauma processing on your own, to avoid forcing major somatic releases without skilled guidance, and to refrain from attempting to radically shift your nervous system state without understanding what you're working with and having support in case it becomes overwhelming. Remember, professional support is always there to guide you and keep you safe on your journey of trauma recovery.

However, practices such as somatic check-ins, developing basic awareness of your breathing patterns and muscular tension, and gently experimenting with deeper breathing or minor releases of chronic stress are safe approaches that anyone can start with. These practices do not require professional intervention; they simply involve becoming aware of what your body is actually doing and beginning to interact with it respectfully. It's important not to force anything, to eliminate defences, or to override protective patterns. Instead, focus on noticing, becoming aware, and developing a conscious relationship with the somatic aspects of your experience that have been operating automatically while your consciousness remained unaware.

This basic awareness is therapeutic in itself; it creates shifts and initiates the process of integration, even if you do nothing beyond noticing. When you regularly check in with your body, observe your chronic patterns, and recognise your baseline nervous system state, you bring conscious attention to unconscious areas. You begin to identify automatic patterns, acknowledging the somatic dimension of your psychological experience. Instead of being solely in your thoughts, your body operates on autopilot, maintaining states you haven't consciously chosen.

This awareness opens up possibilities for choice that were previously unavailable when patterns operated unconsciously. You may notice your breathing is shallow, enabling you to choose to breathe more deeply. You might realise your shoulders are raised and tense, giving you the option to release them gradually. If you recognise that you're in sympathetic activation, you can choose practices that may help you shift toward a more balanced state. Although immediate results are not guaranteed, as patterns run deep and change is often slow, gaining the ability to make choices and developing agency in relation to your somatic experience represents a fundamental shift. It allows you to move from being unconsciously controlled by these patterns to beginning a conscious relationship with them, empowering you in your journey of trauma recovery.

Welcome to the understanding that your body knows things your mind might not. Trauma and emotion are stored in your body through patterns that your consciousness may not access directly. Insight alone cannot change what is encoded in your nervous system and your muscle tension. Breathing patterns and chronic tension often maintain psychological states that you are attempting to alter through different thinking. Your obscure psyche operates through both your body and your mind, maintaining patterns encoded in your somatic experience that shape your reality while your consciousness remains unaware.

The objective is to develop somatic awareness through regular check-ins, helping you understand what your body is actually doing rather than what you assume it is doing. You will begin to notice your baseline nervous system state and chronic tension, working with these patterns respectfully and gradually instead of attempting to force changes your nervous system is not ready to accept. Change will be slow and will require patience and gentleness. It occurs through a series of small shifts rather than dramatic releases. However, this change happens at the level where much trauma is stored, which cognitive approaches alone cannot reach and affects your emotional experience regardless of how much you intellectually understand. Embracing the gradual nature of change can help you be patient and understanding of your own healing process.

Your jaw is clenched for a reason. Your shoulders are tense for a reason. Your breathing is shallow for a reason. Your nervous system is either constantly activated or shut down for a reason. All of these patterns made sense at one time; they protected you from real threats and served survival functions in circumstances that required them. They are not mistakes to be eliminated but rather intelligent responses to past situations that need updating. They require a gradual release as your body learns to accept the current reality as different. This process needs respectful engagement that honours the protective origins of these patterns while also working toward their transformation when they no longer serve you.

The body knows. The question is whether you will learn to listen to it, work with it, and bring conscious awareness to areas that have been operating automatically, maintaining patterns you did not choose through mechanisms you cannot control. Your obscure psyche is embodied, somatic, and stored in your nervous system, muscles, and breath. Until you address this dimension and work with the somatic encodings that maintain your patterns, you may understand yourself intellectually. Still, you will continue to live in a body organised around threat. You will exist in nervous system states that are inappropriate for your current reality, remaining controlled by implicit memories stored in your body. At the same time, your conscious mind believes it is in control.

Chapter 14
The Shadow of Health: The Placebo/Nocebo Effect

Think back to the last time you were convinced you were getting sick the moment you felt a tickle in your throat, a slight heaviness in your head, or just a general sense that illness was approaching. Notice what happened next. Did you start to feel progressively worse? Did the symptoms intensify throughout the day? Did you find yourself cataloguing every sensation as evidence of impending illness? A slight fatigue became overwhelming exhaustion, minor throat irritation turned into definite soreness, and a vague headache evolved into a migraine brewing. By evening, you genuinely felt ill, struggling and convinced you were coming down with something serious. The next day, however, you might have felt perfectly fine. Alternatively, you could have actually gotten sick, and the illness mirrored the severity you had been anticipating, following the trajectory you had already imagined.

Now, consider the reverse of those times when you were exposed to illness, surrounded by sick people, and had every reason to catch what was circulating, but you didn't. Despite being around infected individuals and feeling stressed and tired (which should have compromised your immune system), you remained healthy. Perhaps you noticed the first signs of illness, but had something important that you absolutely needed to do, a presentation, an event, or a deadline. You told yourself, "I can't be sick right now; I don't have time for this." Somehow, your body complied, the emerging symptoms diminished, and you got through what you needed to accomplish. Only afterwards, when it was safe to be sick, did your body finally allow the illness to manifest fully.

Consider this thought-provoking question: How much of your physical health is determined not by pathogens, physiology, or external circumstances, but by your unconscious expectations? How much of your pain is real pain generated by your brain rather than pain caused by tissue damage? How much of your illness is your body manifesting what your unconscious mind believes should be happening? And how much of your healing, or lack thereof, is dictated by expectations you aren't even aware of, by unconscious predictions regarding what your body can or cannot do, and by beliefs so deeply encoded that you don't recognise them as beliefs, but rather as facts about your physical reality? This understanding can empower you to take control of your health.

What's particularly unsettling is this: if your unconscious expectations can make you ill when no actual pathogen or injury warrants it, if your brain can generate genuine physical symptoms, real pain, real nausea, real fatigue based purely on its expectations, then you may be making yourself sick. You could be creating your own suffering and generating physical symptoms through mechanisms that operate entirely beneath your conscious awareness. At the same time, you remain convinced that your body is simply malfunctioning, succumbing to external causes, or being sick for reasons beyond your control. However, it's important to note that this does not mean that all illnesses are 'in the mind'. Many diseases have clear physiological causes and require medical treatment.

It's important to note that if your unconscious expectations can create illness, they can also prevent healing. However, this also means that if you genuinely believe at the level of unconscious expectation rather than conscious hope that you can heal, your brain will work to fulfil those expectations. It will maintain the very symptoms you consciously want to eliminate and prevent healing that might otherwise occur because healing would contradict what your unconscious mind has determined is true about your physical state. This understanding opens up the potential for self-healing and a more optimistic outlook on your health journey.

Consider chronic pain conditions or chronic illnesses where medical investigations find no underlying pathology to explain the severity or persistence of symptoms. The person is genuinely suffering, the pain is real, the fatigue is real, and the dysfunction is real. Still, no structural damage, active disease process, or physiological explanation accounts for what they are experiencing. Every test comes back normal, every scan shows nothing, and every specialist declares there's nothing physically wrong. At the same time, the person knows, on some level, that something is profoundly mistaken because they are living with it, suffering from it day in and day out. This acknowledgement of the reality of chronic conditions can help readers feel validated and understood in their own health struggles.

What's happening? Is the person making it up, exaggerating, or seeking attention? No, the suffering is genuine, and the symptoms are real. But they may be generated by the brain itself, driven by unconscious expectations about what the body should be experiencing. Implicit predictions create the very physical states they anticipate, and beliefs operate so deeply beneath awareness that challenging them feels like denying an apparent physical reality. If the brain expects pain, it generates pain through real neurological mechanisms and actual neural pathways, creating suffering that is every bit as real as pain from tissue damage but originates from expectation rather than peripheral injury.

This is the nocebo effect, the dark twin of the placebo effect. It describes how unconscious negative expectations can create or maintain illness, generate symptoms, prevent healing, and literally make you sick through mechanisms that operate faster than conscious thought, deeper than conscious awareness, and more powerfully than conscious intention. Just as the placebo effect illustrates your brain's capacity to heal, the nocebo effect demonstrates its capacity to harm. This occurs not through conscious choice or deliberate self-sabotage, but through unconscious expectations that shape physical reality while our consciousness remains completely unaware of what drives our experiences.

Let's begin with the placebo effect because understanding it illuminates the mechanisms at play, shows how powerful unconscious expectations are in determining physical states, and demonstrates that your brain can generate healing that seems to require external intervention but actually only needs the expectation of such intervention. The placebo effect refers to genuine physiological improvements, such as reduced pain, decreased symptoms, and actual healing, that occur not because of any active treatment, but because the individual believes they are receiving effective treatment.

The standard medical paradigm often treats the placebo effect as an annoyance or a confounding factor in research, viewing it as merely a psychological effect that needs to be controlled to observe the "real" effects of medications. However, this perspective completely overlooks the profound implications: the placebo effect demonstrates that your brain can generate healing effects, such as absolute reductions in pain, genuine improvements in symptoms, and actual physiological changes, based solely on expectation and the belief that healing will occur. This healing isn't imaginary or merely about feeling better while remaining sick; it's an actual physiological change that can be measured through objective assessments, leading to genuine alterations in bodily function induced by expectation alone.

The mechanisms behind this effect are increasingly well understood neurologically. When you believe you are receiving effective pain medication and expect the pain to decrease, your brain releases endogenous opioids, your body's natural pain-relieving chemicals, the same neurotransmitters activated artificially by morphine and heroin. These endogenous opioids are not weak or imaginary analgesics; they are powerful pain relievers produced by your own brain and released into your system based on the expectation of pain relief, resulting in an actual reduction in pain through the same neurological pathways activated by pharmaceutical opioids.

Brain imaging studies clearly illustrate this point. When individuals receive placebo pain treatment, such as a sugar pill, sham procedure, or fake medication, while believing it is a real treatment, their brains show activation in regions that release endogenous opioids and display reduced activity in pain-processing areas. The patterns observed are identical to those that occur when they receive actual pain medication. The pain reduction in placebo cases is real and measurable, arising through genuine neurological mechanisms. The only difference is that while pharmaceutical opioids are introduced from outside the body, endogenous opioids are produced internally in response to expectation.

Moreover, the placebo effect is not limited to pain relief. It has been demonstrated for immune function as well. People who believe they are receiving immune-boosting treatment show actual improvements in immune markers, genuine increases in antibody production, and real enhancements in immune response. In Parkinson's disease, placebo treatment in patients triggers the release of dopamine in precisely the brain regions affected by the disease, resulting in genuine improvement in motor symptoms. For depression, placebo antidepressants create changes in brain activity patterns that resemble those produced by actual antidepressants, leading to real mood improvements based solely on expectation.

In every instance, the improvements are not imaginary or simply a matter of feeling better while the underlying condition remains unchanged. They represent actual physiological alterations and genuine changes in brain chemistry, immune function, and neurotransmitter release. Real healing is generated by expectation operating through mechanisms that your conscious mind does not control, comprehend, or even recognise until systematically studied.

Consider the profound influence your mind has on your health, healing, and your relationship with your body. Your brain, a powerful predictive machine, constantly shapes your physical experiences. It generates expectations about pain, comfort, sickness, health, improvement, and deterioration. These expectations, along with your unconscious beliefs about your physical state, actively influence your actual physical condition through real neurological mechanisms and physiological pathways. In essence, your brain is not just perceiving reality; it's actively creating the reality it expects to experience.

When you take medication with a positive expectation, you're not just benefiting from the pharmaceutical effect of the drug. A significant part of your improvement is due to the placebo effect, a powerful ally in your healing journey. This effect is your brain's way of generating healing based on the expectation that the medication will work. Your body's own healing systems kick in because you believe in the treatment's effectiveness, and your unconscious prediction of improvement leads to actual improvement. This is a testament to the power of positive expectations in promoting healing.

Consider the significant role of branding in the placebo effect. It's not just about the active ingredients in a medication. Expensive medications, with identical active ingredients as their generic counterparts, are often perceived as more effective. Injections, with their more dramatic delivery, tend to create more substantial placebo effects than pills. Elaborate procedures can result in more healing than simpler interventions. These elements shouldn't matter if healing were solely based on pharmaceutical action, but they do. They matter because much of healing arises from expectation, which is influenced by cues that suggest treatment is powerful, sophisticated, and expensive. All of this shapes your unconscious expectation that treatment will work, activating your brain's natural healing systems and resulting in physiological improvements that feel as though they come from the external intervention, but are actually a response to those expectations.

However, there is a disturbing downside to the power of expectation: if it can heal, it can also harm. Just as your unconscious predictions can lead to physiological improvements when you believe treatment is effective, they can also result in deterioration if you expect treatment to fail. This is the nocebo effect, where negative expectations can lead to adverse outcomes. Genuine harm can occur when the belief that harm should happen leads to the actual worsening of symptoms purely due to expectation.

Consider medication side effects. The drug information sheet lists possible adverse reactions: nausea, headache, fatigue, dizziness, etc. You read this list before taking medication and then find yourself experiencing these symptoms. This raises a disturbing question: how many of those symptoms are genuinely caused by the medication, and how many are created by your brain based on the expectation that you should experience them?

Research highlights this through what is known as the "informed consent dilemma." When people are informed about potential side effects before taking medication, they are significantly more likely to experience those side effects compared to individuals taking the same medication without being warned. The warning itself, the expectation it creates, contributes to the experience of these symptoms through the nocebo effect. This occurs because of unconscious predictions that these experiences should happen, with your brain manifesting the physical states it has been primed to expect.

In some studies, people receiving a placebo, completely inert substances with no pharmaceutical action, report side effects at rates identical to or even higher than those receiving actual medication when informed about possible adverse reactions. They experience real symptoms, genuine nausea, actual headaches, and measurable physiological changes entirely created by expectation and unconscious prediction. Their brains generate these physical states based purely on the warnings they have received about potential side effects.

This creates a genuine ethical dilemma in medicine: patients have the right to informed consent, which involves providing them with the information needed to make decisions about their own care and to understand the possible risks of the treatments they are receiving. However, providing this information, particularly warnings about side effects, can itself lead to harm through the nocebo mechanism. The nocebo effect is a phenomenon where the expectation of a negative outcome can actually cause that outcome. For example, warning patients about potential side effects can inadvertently lead to those very side effects. It's a difficult situation: if you don't warn patients, you violate informed consent; if you do warn them, you may contribute to the very problems you're trying to prevent.

The nocebo effect extends far beyond just medication side effects. Consider diagnoses: being told you have a specific condition, learning about the trajectory of your disease, and hearing prognoses from medical professionals about what you can expect regarding your limitations and future. Every diagnosis comes with a narrative story about what the condition means, how it progresses, what's possible or impossible, and what your life may look like as the illness develops. These narratives shape expectations and create unconscious predictions about what your body should be experiencing, effectively influencing the course of your disease through those expectations.

For example, someone diagnosed with a chronic pain condition might be told they will likely experience progressive worsening, that their pain will become more severe over time, and that they will develop increasing limitations and disabilities. These aren't merely predictions about the disease process; they create expectations that shape the actual experience of pain. The belief that pain will worsen can, through nocebo mechanisms, actually lead to increased pain, as the brain generates heightened pain levels based on the expectation that pain should worsen.

Similarly, suppose someone is diagnosed with a condition deemed incurable and permanent, something they will have to live with for the rest of their life. In that case, this narrative fosters the expectation that healing is impossible, that improvement cannot occur, and that their body is forever broken in ways that cannot be repaired. These expectations can become self-fulfilling, forming unconscious beliefs that hinder the healing they believe is unattainable. These beliefs operate so deeply in the mind that they shape physical reality, while individuals may not consciously recognise them as mere beliefs rather than facts.

Reflect on your own health beliefs and the unconscious expectations you hold about your body. Consider what you believe regarding your ability to heal or your susceptibility to illness. Perhaps you've convinced yourself that you "always" get sick when exposed to colds, that you "can't" handle certain foods, or that you "have" a chronic condition that is a permanent part of your identity. These aren't neutral descriptions of physical reality; they're beliefs and expectations that your brain actively works to fulfil, shaping your actual physical experiences through mechanisms that operate below the surface of awareness. I encourage you to critically examine these beliefs and consider how they might be influencing your health and well-being.

When you believe that you always get sick when exposed to specific situations, or when you expect to catch whatever illness is circulating, this unconscious prediction may compromise your immune function. Research increasingly demonstrates that this phenomenon, known as the nocebo effect, can indeed make you more susceptible to infections. Your expectation triggers a stress response, activates inflammatory pathways, and potentially diminishes your immune function through psychological mechanisms that influence your physiological state. This creates a self-fulfilling prophecy, where your brain essentially produces the conditions it anticipates.

Similarly, suppose you believe you cannot tolerate certain foods and expect to experience digestive distress from them. In that case, your brain may generate that distress through the nocebo effect, even if the food itself is harmless and the substance you react to is inert. Your expectation that you will experience symptoms leads to an actual manifestation of those symptoms due to your brain's prediction-fulfilment mechanisms. This results in fundamental physiological processes that create genuine distress, making it feel as if the food is the cause when, in fact, it stems from your belief about the food.

This does not imply that food sensitivities are not real; many have genuine physiological causes. However, a portion of food reactions may indeed be driven by expectation rather than the actual substance, with your brain creating symptoms based on the belief that certain foods will cause problems. From your subjective experience, the distinction between these causes can be difficult to discern because the symptoms are real, the distress is genuine, and the physiological changes are measurable. The mechanism, whether it originates from a peripheral cause or is generated centrally, is not visible from your perspective.

Now, let's delve deeper into the neuroscience behind these mechanisms, as understanding them sheds light on the power of expectation and how unconscious predictions shape physical reality. The key concept here is predictive processing. This remarkable understanding, gaining prominence within neuroscience, suggests that your brain is not a passive receiver of information about reality; instead, it is a powerful generator of predictions about what should be happening, what you should be experiencing, and what sensory input should be incoming. Your brain then compares this actual input to its predictions.

When actual input aligns with predictions, your brain requires minimal processing; it is experiencing what it expected, and everything is proceeding as anticipated. However, when actual input diverges from predictions and reality contradicts expectations, your brain registers a prediction error. This is a crucial concept in understanding the nocebo effect. A prediction error is a mismatch between what your brain expects to happen and what actually happens. This mismatch demands attention and resolution, either by updating the prediction to align with reality or by attempting to adjust reality to conform to the prediction.

Importantly, your brain can resolve prediction errors in two ways: It can update its predictions to match incoming information, such as realising, "I predicted I wouldn't feel pain, but I'm receiving pain signals, so I need to adjust my prediction accordingly." This adaptive ability empowers you to align your expectations with reality. Alternatively, it can generate sensory experiences that correspond with its predictions, like thinking, "I anticipated I would feel pain, so I will create pain signals that match this expectation," even if the actual sensory input would not trigger pain.

This second mechanism, which fabricates sensory experiences to align with predictions, is how the placebo and nocebo effects operate. It's a powerful demonstration of your brain's influence over your body. For example, suppose your brain predicts that pain relief will occur because you believe you have received adequate treatment. In that case, it may generate a reduced pain experience by conforming to this prediction, releasing endogenous opioids, and minimising activity in pain-processing areas. Conversely, suppose your brain predicts side effects because you have been warned about them. In that case, it may produce those symptoms to align with its expectations through genuine physiological mechanisms, even when no pharmaceutical cause is responsible.

The experience of pain is significantly shaped by our brain's predictions, often even more so than by actual sensory input. These predictions operate more quickly than sensory processing and influence how we interpret sensory information. In essence, our brains create our subjective experiences based on their expectations about reality, constantly generating experiences that align with these predictions.

This is why expectations hold such power, particularly in the context of health. Our beliefs about our health can impact our actual health. The unconscious predictions our brains make can literally shape physical reality in ways our consciousness doesn't recognise. Instead of waiting for sensory input from our bodies, our brains predict what that input should be, essentially generating that report and creating experiences based on those predictions.

Now, consider chronic pain, which clearly illustrates these mechanisms and why pain can persist long after any actual tissue damage has healed. Acute pain, which arises from recent injury or damage, serves a critical adaptive function. It signals harm, motivates protective behaviour, prevents further injury, and facilitates healing by encouraging us to avoid using the affected area. This type of pain is proportional to the damage, decreases as healing occurs, and resolves once the tissue is repaired. It is useful, appropriate pain that serves its biological purpose.

Chronic pain, on the other hand, persists for months or even years after tissue damage has healed. It is pain that is disproportionate to any ongoing pathology and continues without a structural explanation. This is often the result of the brain generating pain through its prediction mechanisms through the expectation that pain should still be present. After experiencing acute pain from an injury, the brain learns that this body part is associated with pain and continues to generate that experience long after the original cause has resolved because the prediction hasn't updated.

The original injury may have caused acute pain, genuine pain from tissue damage, but even after the tissue has healed, the brain still expects pain in that region. It continues to generate pain through central mechanisms to match its outdated prediction, creating chronic pain purely from expectation. The brain interprets pain as an indicator of ongoing tissue damage, leading to the belief that pain must mean something is still wrong.

Neuroimaging studies support this understanding. In cases of chronic pain, areas of the brain involved in pain processing are active, opioid systems may be dysregulated, and inflammatory markers can be elevated, all contributing to a genuine experience of pain. However, this activation originates in the brain rather than from damaged tissue; it is generated centrally through predictive mechanisms rather than being reported from the body. Thus, while the pain is real, it is not imaginary, psychological, or a result of exaggeration; it is generated by the brain through expectations rather than arising from actual physical injury. This situation often embodies the nocebo effect, which maintains suffering long after any peripheral cause has resolved.

Chronic pain tends to resist treatments aimed at peripheral causes because the pain is not maintained by these peripheral issues; it's driven by central expectations. You could remove supposedly damaged tissue, numb nerves, or eliminate any potential peripheral sources of pain signals, yet the pain may persist. This is because the brain is actively generating the pain based on outdated expectations, not because of an ongoing peripheral issue.

What complicates matters is that you cannot simply choose to stop expecting pain. You can't consciously override these unconscious predictions through willpower or positive thinking. Understanding that chronic pain is driven by expectations rather than tissue issues doesn't automatically change the experience. The expectations that generate the pain are operating beneath our conscious awareness, functioning as implicit predictions made by the brain faster than we can consciously process. Thus, understanding the underlying mechanism does not directly alter it, as it operates outside of our conscious control.

The shadow dimension is crucial in understanding chronic pain, as it often involves unconscious psychological factors. Implicit beliefs about deserving to suffer, unacknowledged needs such as the need for attention or the need to avoid specific responsibilities that can only be met by being ill, and secondary gains from pain are often overlooked but play a significant role in maintaining symptoms through their functional value.

It's important to consider what pain might be providing for you that would be lost if you were to heal. For some, pain serves as the only acceptable excuse for resting, saying no, or having limitations in a system that demands constant productivity. It also ensures necessary attention from others who might otherwise neglect you, making it more difficult to directly express your needs. Your struggles are valid, and pain can provide a narrative for them when admitting to psychological difficulties feels too shameful.

Pain may also act as a form of punishment that you unconsciously believe you deserve. It can be a way to atone for guilt that remains unacknowledged, serving as a self-inflicted consequence for real or imagined transgressions. You might be using your body to carry this burden because punishing yourself mentally feels unacceptable. Pain can protect you from fully engaging with life, creating limitations that allow you to avoid confrontations with challenges that invoke intense anxiety, shame, or feelings of inadequacy.

These are not conscious choices. You are not intentionally choosing pain to evade life's demands, to garner attention, or to punish yourself. However, beneath your awareness, pain may serve vital functions that healing would disrupt. It can provide the necessary support that you do not know how to fulfil in other ways, or act as a shield against confronting frightening realities such as the fear of failure, the fear of rejection, or the fear of change that come with full health.

Until these unconscious functions are acknowledged, and you find alternative ways to meet the needs that pain fulfils, the nocebo effect will persist. The nocebo effect is when the expectation that pain should be present continues, generating a physical experience even when tissues have healed and peripheral causes have been addressed.

By engaging with this dimension, exploring what your symptoms might be doing for you, and recognising what healing would take away, you can unlock the potential for healing and recovery. Your healing is not blocked by physiological factors, but by psychological ones. It's not about tissue damage, but about expectations and beliefs that fulfil unrecognised functions. Recognising and addressing these can lead to a hopeful and optimistic path towards healing.

Let's delve into the fascinating world of belief loops, as understanding them is a key to unlocking the mysteries of our mind. These loops illustrate how predictions create evidence that appears to confirm them, leading to nocebo effects that maintain themselves through circular processes. In these scenarios, it feels as though you are accurately perceiving physical reality when, in fact, you are creating it through your expectations. This understanding can enlighten you about the power of your mind and keep you informed about the potential impact of your beliefs on your health and well-being.

A belief loop occurs when an expectation generates experiences that seem to confirm that expectation. This, in turn, strengthens the expectation, creating more confirming experiences in a continuous cycle. Throughout this process, consciousness often remains unaware that expectations are generating the evidence, rather than evidence justifying the expectation.

For example, if you believe you are susceptible to illness, you might expect to get sick when exposed to pathogens. This expectation can trigger a stress response and may compromise your immune function through psychological mechanisms, making you genuinely more vulnerable to illness via nocebo pathways.

Consequently, you may get sick more frequently than others. This reinforces your belief that you are susceptible, further strengthening that expectation and compromising your immune response. The loop becomes self-reinforcing, as you create evidence that seems to validate your belief, all while experiencing this as a discovery about your body rather than recognising that your expectations are shaping your reality.

Similarly, if you believe you cannot handle stress, you might expect to feel overwhelmed when faced with increasing demands. This expectation can lead to anxiety, activating your stress response even before the actual stressors arise, which can impair your performance. You may struggle more than others with similar stressors, which reinforces your belief that you cannot handle stress. This strengthens your expectation and fuels anticipatory anxiety, further impairing your performance and providing more evidence that you cannot cope. In this case, your belief is shaping your reality, while you perceive it as an undeniable fact about your limitations, instead of realising that your expectations are generating those limitations.

In another example, if you believe your chronic pain is permanent, you might expect your symptoms to persist and unconsciously predict that healing is impossible for you. This expectation maintains central sensitisation, keeping the areas of your brain related to pain processing active and preventing an update in your predictions that could allow for symptom resolution. The pain continues, which confirms that it is permanent; this further strengthens your belief, maintains the ongoing perception of pain, and provides evidence that healing isn't feasible. The belief thus perpetuates the symptom, while your consciousness interprets this as discovering an incurable condition, failing to recognise that your expectation is hindering potential healing.

These loops are vicious cycles and self-fulfilling prophecies, where your unconscious expectations create a physical reality that appears to validate them. However, breaking these loops is not a matter of chance or luck. It requires the active participation of your consciousness. It involves recognising their existence and understanding that your expectations create experiences instead of just predicting them. It consists of developing a conscious relationship with your unconscious predictions, allowing you to work with them rather than being unconsciously controlled by them. This emphasis on consciousness can make you feel in control and responsible for your own mental and physical well-being.

Challenging our expectations about health is extraordinarily difficult because they create physical evidence that confirms these expectations as facts rather than mere beliefs. Your pain is real; your susceptibility to illness is demonstrated through repeated infections; your struggles with stress are evident in your daily life. How could these experiences be merely beliefs when they lead to tangible physical sensations, measurable physiological changes, and genuine dysfunction that limits your life? The mechanism behind these experiences often remains invisible, as you may be unaware that your expectations are generating them through nocebo pathways that operate beneath conscious awareness.

This is why examining your health beliefs and unconscious expectations about your body becomes crucial therapeutic work. What do you believe about your ability to heal? About your vulnerability to illness? About whether your symptoms are permanent or potentially reversible? About whether your body is fundamentally broken or capable of repair? These questions aren't just neutral observations of physical reality; they're beliefs, expectations, and predictions that your brain strives to fulfil through mechanisms you don't control. Your brain generates a physical reality that aligns with these expectations, while your consciousness believes it's merely perceiving an objective state of your body.

Start paying attention to the language you use regarding your health, body, and symptoms. Your choice of words can either reinforce or challenge your expectations. Do you say 'I am sick' or 'I have symptoms'? Do you say 'I can't handle stress' or 'I'm currently struggling with stress'? Do you refer to 'my chronic pain,' implying it is a permanent identity, or 'the pain I'm experiencing,' suggesting it is a temporary state? These linguistic choices reflect your underlying expectations and reveal unconscious beliefs about whether symptoms are fixed or fluid, permanent or changeable, essential aspects of who you are or temporary experiences you're undergoing. By being mindful of your language, you can actively shape your expectations and beliefs.

The more you assert symptoms as permanent aspects of your identity, the more you reinforce the expectations that sustain them, solidifying the belief that they must continue. However, shifting your language not by denying your symptoms but by viewing them as experiences rather than as part of your identity creates distance from this absolute identification. This shift allows for the possibility of change and weakens the expectation that symptoms must persist because they define who you are rather than what you're experiencing.

Also, reflect on your beliefs about causation. Do you think your symptoms are purely physical, related only to tissue damage, disease processes, or genetic defects beyond your control? Or can you recognise that expectation, belief, and unconscious predictions significantly influence your physical experiences? Attributing your symptoms solely to external causes reinforces feelings of helplessness. It solidifies the belief that symptoms cannot change without outside intervention, thereby strengthening nocebo loops that maintain suffering through this belief in helplessness.

Recognising that expectation influences, not entirely dictates, but significantly affects your physical state is a validation of your experience. It opens up opportunities for agency, allowing you to work with your beliefs and address the unconscious predictions that may be perpetuating persistent symptoms not fully explained by external factors. This is not blaming yourself for being unwell, nor is it suggesting that chronic illness is 'just in your head', or denying the existence of physical pathology. Instead, it's acknowledging the deep interconnection between physical and psychological states, understanding that expectation shapes your physical experience through real physiological mechanisms. This understanding can help you feel more in control and hopeful about your healing journey.

The work involves identifying your health beliefs, examining unconscious expectations, and observing the predictions you hold about your body and its healing capacity. It requires gently challenging absolute expectations, creating space for possibilities rather than certainties. This process aims to weaken nocebo loops by introducing doubt into the predictions that your consciousness has regarded as unquestionable facts about physical reality.

This isn't about forced positive thinking, or pretending to believe something you don't, which can create psychological conflict by demanding you uphold beliefs that contradict your actual experiences. It is about genuine inquiry, honestly examining whether your absolute certainty about the permanence of symptoms or the impossibility of healing is warranted, or if these expectations are maintaining the very symptoms they predict.

Welcome to the understanding that your unconscious expectations actually determine your physical state through real neurological mechanisms that generate physiological changes based on predictions. These predictions operate faster than conscious thought, deeper than conscious awareness, and more powerfully than conscious intention. Your brain releases endogenous opioids when it anticipates pain relief, generates pain when it expects it to occur, maintains symptoms when it predicts they should persist, and prevents healing when it believes healing isn't possible. All of this happens through mechanisms that your consciousness does not recognise. At the same time, you remain convinced you are just passively experiencing objective physical reality, rather than actively generating it through your expectations.

The placebo effect demonstrates your brain's extraordinary ability to heal based purely on the expectation that healing will occur. In contrast, the nocebo effect illustrates its equally remarkable capacity to cause harm based on the expectation of harm. Both effects operate through the exact mechanisms: unconscious predictions literally create physical reality by activating or suppressing endogenous systems, generating or relieving pain, and enhancing or diminishing immune function, all while your brain works to fulfil its expectations. Meanwhile, your consciousness believes it is merely accurately perceiving what is happening in your body, rather than recognising that expectation is, in fact, creating those experiences.

Your Obscure Psyche operates through your body, maintaining symptoms that serve unconscious functions, even as your consciousness desperately wishes for healing. It keeps you unwell when illness fulfils a necessary role that you do not know how to obtain in another way, and it hinders recovery when health would necessitate facing what pain protects you from. This dynamic generates physical suffering through expectations that are encoded so profoundly that you experience them as facts about your body, rather than recognising that they are beliefs that could potentially be changed if you developed a conscious relationship with them. Instead of being unconsciously controlled by predictions that dictate your physical reality, you might realise that you are merely describing what you believe to be objectively true about your physiological state.

The concept of health suggests that much of your illness may be self-generated through nocebo mechanisms. This means that much of your suffering might be sustained by expectations that serve unconscious purposes. Additionally, many of your limitations may be driven by predictions rather than actual physical issues. At the same time, your consciousness, when fully engaged, can recognise that physical pathology is not the sole explanation for everything, and can empower you by acknowledging the relevance of psychological mechanisms.

The work involves recognising the profound role of expectation, examining unconscious beliefs, and developing a conscious relationship with the predictions that maintain symptoms. It also requires addressing the hidden functions that illness serves and breaking the belief loops that create self-fulfilling prophecies, all while feeling confined by an accurate assessment of permanent physical limitations.

This is not about blaming yourself for being sick, but rather about recognising that you may have more agency than feelings of helplessness suggest, more capacity for influence than a victim mentality allows, and a significant healing potential that transcends the nocebo expectations, even when these operate outside of conscious awareness and shape physical reality in ways that consciousness doesn't even recognise.

Chapter 15

The Three Faces of Suffering: Brain, Mind, and Meaning

Let me ask you something fundamental: When you think about your mind, where do you locate it? Most people point to their foreheads, gesturing vaguely. But if I ask you to describe what it feels like to be anxious, you'll tell me about your racing heart, your shallow breathing, the tension in your shoulders. If I ask you what depression is, you might describe a heaviness, a fog, a disconnection from the world that you can't quite articulate but absolutely know. This is the paradox we must explore together: mental health is simultaneously a disorder of the brain, an experience of consciousness, and a question about what it means to be human. We need neuroscience to understand the mechanisms. We need psychology to grasp the patterns. We need philosophy to comprehend the meaning. And we need all three to see the whole person suffering in front of us truly.

Autism: The Architecture of Difference

Philosophy challenges traditional dualistic approaches to the mind, advocating a materialist framework in which mental phenomena are understood as brain processes, and positing that advances in neuroscience must inform philosophical theories of mind. This isn't reductionism, it's integration. When someone experiences autism, they're not just exhibiting behaviours we label as "autistic." The architecture of neurons differs in children with autism, with varying densities in specific brain regions.

Recent research reveals that individuals with autism spectrum disorder have different brain connectivity patterns compared to typically developing individuals. However, results do not unanimously support the traditional view of lower connectivity between distal brain regions and increased connectivity within proximal areas. Instead, connectivity alterations in autism reflect functional idiosyncrasy, a profound inter-individual variability in functional network organisation. Studying a multi-centric dataset revealed robust evidence for increased idiosyncrasy in default mode, somatomotor and attention networks, but also reduced idiosyncrasy in lateral temporal cortices. This idiosyncrasy increased with age and significantly correlated with symptom severity.

Think about what this means. The brain's tendency to become stuck in redundant patterns of functional connectivity may relate to motor and cognitive systems in autism that are also stuck in repetitive behaviours or restricted interests. The cortical and subcortical dynamics of coordinated activity can generate inflexible brain connectivity patterns, which may relate to core deficits such as repetitive behaviours.

But simultaneously, that person has a lived experience of the world that is phenomenologically distinct: they experience sensory information, social cues, and the passage of time differently. Both clinical autism and autistic traits were associated with reductions in structural connectivity in twin pairs, suggesting that connectivity differences lie along a continuum. Distinct brain connectivity patterns appear in six-week-old infants at risk for developing autism, suggesting that differences in brain responses likely emerge much earlier than autism-related behaviours can be identified.

Psychologically, autism manifests as differences in social communication, pattern recognition, sensory processing, and executive function. Psychological frameworks help us understand behavioural interventions, educational strategies, and support systems. But phenomenologically, autism is the experience of a world that bombards you with sensory information others filter unconsciously, where social rules that everyone else intuitively knows feel like a foreign language you must laboriously translate, where changes in routine create not mere discomfort but genuine distress because your brain relies on predictability to manage the overwhelming complexity of existence.

Philosophically, this raises profound questions: What is the relationship between neural architecture and subjective experience? Can there be different but equally valid ways of being conscious? Is autism a disorder or simply a different way of being human? The philosopher Thomas Nagel wrote, asking, "What is it like to be a bat?" His point was that subjective experience might be fundamentally inaccessible from the outside. Even if we completely mapped a bat's brain, could we ever know what echolocation feels like from the inside? Can a neurotypical person ever honestly understand what it's like to be autistic?

ADHD: The Dysregulated Orchestra

Let's turn to ADHD, because it beautifully illustrates how different levels of explanation illuminate various aspects of the same condition. Studies have found that ADHD is associated with weaker function and structure of prefrontal cortex circuits, especially in the right hemisphere. The prefrontal association cortex plays a crucial role in regulating attention, behaviour, and emotion, with the right hemisphere specialised for behavioural inhibition. The PFC is highly dependent on the correct neurochemical environment for proper function: noradrenergic stimulation of postsynaptic alpha-2A adrenoceptors and dopaminergic stimulation of D1 receptors is necessary for optimal prefrontal function.

The prefrontal cortex is exquisitely sensitive to neurochemical environments. Small changes in norepinephrine and dopamine levels can significantly alter prefrontal function. Low to moderate levels of D1 receptor stimulation can improve prefrontal cortex function by reducing "noise" by pruning inappropriate connections. However, excessive D1 receptor stimulation, such as occurs during stress, impairs PFC function by weakening too many network connections.

Research has found deficits in the neural networks linked to attention and executive function in children and adults with ADHD, which may affect the ability to organise, prioritise, plan, focus, remember instructions, and work toward goals. ADHD may alter the connections between the prefrontal cortex and other brain areas, leading to poor planning, distractibility, impulsivity, and forgetfulness. Children with ADHD whose symptoms persisted into adolescence had a thinner medial prefrontal cortex compared to both ADHD children whose symptoms remitted and to controls. Further, cortical maturation was influenced by exposure to stimulant medication.

At the psychological level, ADHD manifests as a pattern of behaviours and cognitive challenges: difficulty sustaining attention, problems with working memory, impulsivity, challenges with time perception and planning. Psychologists have developed elaborate theories about deficits in executive function, problems with reward processing, difficulties with temporal discounting, and the tendency to choose immediate small rewards over delayed larger ones.

But phenomenologically, ADHD is something else entirely. It's the experience of your mind as a radio constantly scanning through stations, never settling. It's the sensation of being interested in everything and therefore able to focus on nothing. It's the peculiar temporality where five minutes and five hours feel identical, where deadlines exist in an eternal "later" until suddenly they're catastrophically now. One person with ADHD described it as "my brain is like a browser with 100 tabs open, all playing different videos, and I can't find the one that's making noise."

Another significant difference concerns the brain's default mode network. The DMN activates when you're daydreaming or not focused on a task. In ADHD, the DMN is more often activated, which explains why focus is constantly pulled away from tasks toward unrelated thoughts.

Philosophically, ADHD raises fascinating questions about personal identity and moral responsibility. If your brain is wired such that impulse control is genuinely more complicated for you than for others, are you less responsible for impulsive actions? The philosopher Harry Frankfurt argued that what makes us persons rather than mere animals is our capacity for second-order desires, the ability to want to want differently. Someone with ADHD has second-order desires; they desperately want to focus, to organise, to follow through. But their first-order desires and impulses often overwhelm those reflective capacities. This isn't a failure of character; it's a constraint on will imposed by neural architecture.

Bipolar Disorder: The Storm of Self

Consider bipolar disorder through this three-fold lens. Neurobiologically, bipolar disorder involves progressive brain changes, cortical thinning, altered connectivity between mood-regulating regions, and disruptions in circadian rhythms that interact with mood networks. Dysfunctions characterise the disorder across three domains: emotional, cognitive, and psychomotor.

The core neuropathology in bipolar disorder is damage in the fronto-limbic network, which is associated with emotional dysfunction. The fronto-limbic circuit mainly includes the prefrontal cortex, amygdala, and hippocampus. These brain regions are structurally and functionally connected to form a network that generates emotional responses and evaluates whether those responses are appropriate or require regulation. It is hypothesised that the abnormal emotional ventral system and hypoactive dorsal system result in a loss of homeostasis in emotional processing, which may contribute to mood liability in bipolar disorder.

Abnormalities in functional connectivity between the ventral prefrontal cortex and the amygdala may also occur. Since the prefrontal cortex remains physically connected with the limbic brain in bipolar individuals, the synchronisation between the prefrontal cortex and amygdala is disrupted in depression and mania. Patients with bipolar disorder may recruit emotional "hot" neural systems in the processing of emotionally neutral "cold" material, showing high trait emotionality.

Changes in intrinsic brain networks, such as the sensorimotor, salience, default-mode, and central executive networks, are associated with impaired cognitive function. Hyperactivity in the default mode network drives rumination and cognitive inflexibility, while underactivity in the central executive network contributes to attentional lapses and impaired executive function. Psychomotor symptoms, which oscillate between hyperactivity in mania and retardation in depression, are closely associated with imbalances in neurotransmitter systems, particularly dopamine and serotonin, within the basal ganglia-thalamo-cortical motor pathway.

Psychologically, bipolar disorder manifests as episodic shifts in mood, energy, and cognitive function that follow somewhat predictable patterns. There are psychological triggers, such as stress, sleep disruption, substance use and psychological consequences, including disrupted relationships, impaired judgment during manic phases, and crushing hopelessness during depressive episodes. Psychologists study the cognitive distortions that accompany each pole, the risk factors for episode onset, and the protective factors that support stability.

But phenomenologically, bipolar disorder is the terrifying experience of your self splitting into strangers. During depression, the world loses meaning, time slows to a crawl, your body feels like lead, and you can't remember ever feeling differently or imagine ever feeling better. During mania, you're the centre of the universe, ideas cascade too fast to capture, sleep seems unnecessary and boring, your sexuality and aggression surge, and the normal constraints of reality feel like oppression rather than protection. One person described it: "I entered the hospital as an individual but left as a diagnosis."

Philosophically, bipolar disorder poses profound questions about the self. If your personality, your values, your very sense of who you are can radically shift with your brain chemistry, where is the "real you"? The philosopher Derek Parfit argued that personal identity is more fluid and less essential than we believe, that there's no unchanging core self. Bipolar disorder seems to prove this experientially; the manic self, the depressed self and the euthymic self can feel like different people inhabiting the same body. Yet something persists, some thread of identity that says "I am the person who experiences all these states, even when I can barely recognise my own mind."

OCD: The Hijacked Mind

OCD presents a particularly fascinating case for philosophical analysis. At the neural level, OCD has long been associated with dysfunction in cortico-striatal-thalamic circuits, fronto-limbic, and fronto-parietal circuits. OCD involves changes across a broad range of fronto-striatal loop circuits, with a loss of top-down control by cortically mediated inhibitory mechanisms. Picture a car where the brakes work, but the signal from your foot to the brake pedal gets garbled. You know you need to stop, but the message doesn't get through cleanly.

What's revolutionary about current OCD research is how precise we're becoming. Scientists have identified a specific neural activity pattern, with narrow-band power approximately 9 Hz in the ventral striatum, as a novel biomarker that can accurately predict and monitor the clinical status of individuals with OCD who've undergone deep brain stimulation. We're no longer just describing symptoms; we're identifying the exact electrical signatures of the disorder. Deep brain stimulation for OCD targets specific sites, with two optimal stimulation zones identified: one in the anterior limb of the internal capsule and one in the inferior thalamic peduncle and the bed nucleus of the stria terminalis.

Psychologically, OCD is characterised by obsessions, intrusive, unwanted thoughts that generate anxiety and compulsions, repetitive behaviours or mental acts performed to reduce that anxiety. The psychology of OCD involves several key features: an inflated sense of responsibility, overestimation of threat, perfectionism, need for control, and difficulty tolerating uncertainty. These cognitive patterns maintain the disorder even after it's neurobiologically established.

But phenomenologically, OCD is experienced as a hostile takeover of your own mind. Your thoughts are experienced as both yours and not-yours. You recognise them as originating in your own consciousness, yet they feel alien, ego-dystonic, unwanted. The philosopher William James distinguished between the "I" (the experiencing subject) and the "me" (the self as object of experience). In OCD, there's a painful split: the "I" watches helplessly as the "me" is forced to perform rituals that the "I" knows are irrational. One person described it: "I know the door is locked, I checked it three times, but my brain won't accept that message. It's like my knowledge and my feelings are in different worlds."

This reveals something profound about the architecture of consciousness. We like to think we're unified selves, but mental disorders often reveal our modularity. Your rational brain can know something while your emotional brain refuses to believe it. Your cortex can desperately want to stop a behaviour while your basal ganglia keep generating the motor programs. Where is agency in such a divided self?

Personality Disorders: The Fractured Ground

Personality disorders, particularly borderline personality disorder, push these questions even further. Neurobiologically, BPD shows reduced volumes in the hippocampus and amygdala, differences in prefrontal cortex structure, and crucially, a brain region, the rostro-medial prefrontal cortex, that typically reacts to social rejection remains inactive in individuals with borderline personality disorder. This region generally processes rejection and activates attempts to restore social bonds. When it doesn't work correctly, rejection isn't just painful; it's catastrophic because the brain can't engage its natural soothing and reconnection mechanisms.

Research reveals neurobiological differences in regional brain volumes and cortical thickness, with recent studies illuminating shared and distinct brain structural characteristics compared with those of other psychiatric diagnoses. The neuroscience of borderline personality disorder centres on emotional regulation, or rather, its catastrophic breakdown. Brain structures implicated include the hippocampus, dorsolateral prefrontal cortex, and anterior cingulate cortex, with reduced hippocampal and amygdala volumes and exaggerated amygdala activity when confronted with emotion-related stimuli.

What does this mean in human terms? It means that someone with BPD isn't choosing to overreact; their amygdala is screaming danger signals, while the prefrontal cortex, which should be regulating those signals, is working with reduced capacity. They're driving through life with a hypersensitive alarm system and weak brakes.

Psychologically, BPD is characterised by instability in relationships, self-image, and emotions, along with intense fear of abandonment and difficulty regulating emotional responses. The psychology of BPD involves a pattern where minor perceived slights trigger overwhelming emotional reactions, where people experience extremes as either all-good or all-bad, and where the sense of self shifts dramatically based on social context.

But phenomenologically, BPD is the experience of having no stable ground. Imagine if your sense of who you are depended entirely on who you're with and how they seem to be reacting to you. Imagine if your emotions arrived like tsunamis, overwhelming and uncontrollable. Imagine if every interaction felt like it could end in abandonment. Individuals report difficulties establishing and maintaining social relationships, suggesting a weak attunement to unwritten social interaction codes. The world becomes a minefield where you're constantly stepping on buried bombs you can't see.

Philosophically, BPD raises questions about the narrative self. The philosopher Alasdair MacIntyre argued that we are the stories we tell about ourselves, that identity is fundamentally narrative. But what if you can't construct a stable narrative? What if the protagonist of your story keeps changing, keeps fragmenting, keeps being written and rewritten by each new relationship? Recent research suggests BPD could be considered a late-onset neurodevelopmental disorder present in childhood but fully manifesting in adolescence, that critical period when we're supposed to consolidate a stable sense of self. If the neurobiological tools for constructing a coherent self-narrative are compromised, the philosophical implications are profound.

Alzheimer's Disease: The Dissolution of Memory and Self

Let's turn to Alzheimer's disease, because it confronts us with the most fundamental philosophical question: what makes you, you? When memory dissolves, when personality changes, when the person you've known for decades gradually becomes someone else, where does the self go? Scientists have discovered that certain immune cells, called microglia, can effectively digest toxic amyloid beta plaques, with a unique subset of microglia appearing to protect the brain by calming inflammation and slowing disease progression.

For years, we focused on the plaques themselves, those protein tangles that gum up the brain's machinery. But now we're realising the brain has its own defence system, its own cleanup crew. Research suggests Alzheimer's disease may damage the brain in two distinct phases: an early phase that happens slowly and silently before people experience memory problems, harming just a few vulnerable cell types, and a late phase that causes more widely destructive damage coinciding with symptoms and rapid accumulation of plaques and tangles.

Think about what this means phenomenologically. There's a period, potentially years, where your brain is being damaged but you don't know it. Your subjective experience remains intact even as the substrate of that experience erodes. This challenges the neat correlation we assume between brain state and mental state.

The advent of anti-amyloid immunotherapy, including FDA-approved monoclonal antibodies such as lecanemab and donanemab, has proven efficacy in slowing cognitive decline in early-stage Alzheimer's disease. We finally have disease-modifying drugs. But they only work early, slowly, and not for everyone. The brain, once it begins to unravel, is complicated to reweave.

Psychologically, Alzheimer's progresses through predictable stages: mild cognitive impairment, where you notice memory slips, moderate dementia, where daily functioning becomes impaired, and severe dementia, where the personality fundamentally changes. Psychologists track, measure, and predict these changes. They study how caregivers cope, how patients maintain dignity, and how to communicate when language fails.

But phenomenologically, Alzheimer's is the experience of the world becoming strange. At first, you lose names and recent events, but you know you're losing them, which creates anxiety and confusion. Then you lose the awareness that you're losing things, which creates a peculiar peace but also disconnection. Eventually, even familiar faces become strangers, your own home becomes foreign territory, and the present moment is all there is because the past has dissolved and the future doesn't exist. One caregiver described watching her husband with Alzheimer's: "He's still here, but he's not here. The body I've held for fifty years holds someone I barely recognise."

The philosopher David Hume argued that the self is just a bundle of perceptions, that there's no underlying essence, just a stream of experiences loosely connected by memory. Alzheimer's seems to prove Hume right as memory dissolves, the self dissolves with it. Yet families insist there's still something of the person remaining, some essence that persists even after memory and personality have changed. Is that wishful thinking, or is there genuinely something about personhood that transcends memory?

Ataxia: The Body Betrayed

Ataxia, a disorder of movement and coordination caused by cerebellar dysfunction, might seem purely neurological, but it also has psychological and phenomenological dimensions. More than half of cerebrovascular diseases causing ataxia were located entirely outside the cerebellum, yet localised to a brain network connected to it. This teaches us something profound: the brain works in networks, not isolated modules. Damage anywhere in the network reverberates throughout the system.

Neurologically, ataxia involves disruption of cerebellar circuits that coordinate movement, maintain balance, and calibrate motor learning. Different movement disorders, such as ataxia, dystonia, and tremor, exhibit distinct neural codes, with cerebellar neurons firing in specific patterns that represent different pathological behaviours. The brain has a vocabulary of movement written in electrical patterns.

What's remarkable about ataxia research is its therapeutic potential. Low-frequency cerebellar deep-brain stimulation improves mobility and muscle function in mouse models of hereditary ataxia. When combined with skilled exercise, it additionally rescues limb coordination and stepping, with improvements persisting even without continued stimulation. The cerebellum retains remarkable plasticity, cellular and synaptic flexibility that can be harnessed for recovery, especially when intervention happens early.

But phenomenologically, ataxia is the experience of your body becoming unreliable. Your intention to move smoothly translates into jerky, uncoordinated action. You know what you want to do, but your body won't obey precisely. This creates a split between intention and action, between mind and body, that healthy people take for granted. Walking across a room, something you've done thoughtlessly millions of times, becomes a conscious, effortful task requiring attention and planning. Your body, which should be transparent to your will, becomes opaque, resistant, unpredictable.

This raises philosophical questions about embodiment. The phenomenologist Maurice Merleau-Ponty argued that we don't just have bodies; we are bodies, that consciousness is fundamentally embodied, and that our bodily capacities structure our experience of the world. When those capacities are impaired, the world itself changes. A person with ataxia inhabits a different world: movement distances seem different, obstacles loom larger, and familiar spaces become challenging terrain. The disorder isn't just in the cerebellum; it's in the lived relationship between person and world.

Integration: The Whole Person

A pluralist approach acknowledges the multi-level causal interactions that give rise to psychopathology. At the same time, clinically, it emphasises the importance of a broad range of difference-makers and of considering lived experience in both research and practice. This is what I'm arguing for, not a reduction of mental health to any single level of explanation, but an integration that respects the autonomy and importance of each level while recognising how they interact.

Viewing the brain-mind as embodied, embedded and enactive offers a conceptual approach to the mind-body problem that facilitates clinical integration of advances in both cognitive-affective neuroscience and phenomenological psychopathology. The brain isn't a computer running software called "mind." The mind isn't a ghost haunting the body's machine. Instead, mind and brain are two aspects, two perspectives on the same phenomenon, a living, embodied, socially embedded human being navigating a meaningful world.

Think about what this means practically. When you treat someone with autism, you're not just correcting brain chemistry or behaviour patterns, you're helping a person navigate a world that wasn't built for their neurology, supporting them in finding meaning and connection through their unique way of experiencing reality. When you treat someone with ADHD, you're not just boosting dopamine; you're helping them build external structures that compensate for internal regulatory challenges, helping them understand their own phenomenology so they can work with rather than against their neurology.

When you treat someone with bipolar disorder, you're not just stabilising mood, you're helping them reconstruct a coherent narrative identity that can encompass and integrate extreme states, helping them recognise early warning signs in their subjective experience before they cascade into full episodes. When you treat someone with OCD, you're not just normalising circuits; you're helping them reclaim agency over their own minds, reducing the distance between the "I" that observes and the "me" that acts.

When you treat someone with BPD, you're not just regulating emotions; you're helping them build a stable sense of self that can weather relational storms, helping them develop the mentalising capacities that their neurodevelopment didn't provide automatically. When you treat someone with Alzheimer's, you're not just slowing plaque formation; you're helping preserve personhood and dignity as long as possible, supporting both patient and caregivers through the phenomenological dissolution of self.

Mental disorders play a role in many domains, including medicine, the social sciences such as psychology and anthropology, and the humanities, including literature and philosophy. This is because mental disorder isn't just a medical problem; it's a human problem, touching on our most profound questions about identity, meaning, suffering, responsibility, and what it means to live well.

The philosopher Karl Jaspers, who was both a psychiatrist and philosopher, distinguished between explanation and understanding. We can explain a broken bone through physics and biology, the mechanical forces that fractured the bone, and the cellular processes of healing. But mental disorders require both explanation and understanding. We need to explain the neurobiology, brain circuits, chemicals, and genes. But we also need to understand how the person experiences their condition, how it disrupts their life-world, how it challenges their sense of self, and how they make sense of their suffering.

Illness is a first-person experience, available only to the patient concerned, and the key to approaching it closely is empathy. Empathy isn't just emotional resonance; it's the attempt to understand from within how another person experiences the world. This requires imagination, humility, and the recognition that their reality might be profoundly different from yours.

Medical anthropologists have usefully distinguished between disease as a biomedical condition and illness as the subjective experience of those suffering from that condition. A person doesn't have schizophrenia and experience psychosis; they have a disease called schizophrenia, while experiencing an illness characterised by altered reality, social disconnection, and existential confusion. The disease is what we find in the brain, in the genes, in the biology. The illness is what the person lives through, suffers, and must somehow incorporate into their life story.

This distinction matters enormously for treatment. If we only treat the disease, we might normalise brain chemistry while leaving the person unable to make sense of their experience. If we only address the illness, we might provide meaning and support while missing biological interventions that could make a dramatic difference. We need both. We need the neurologist who understands circuits, the therapist who understands meaning, and the phenomenologist who understands lived experience, ideally integrated into clinicians who can move fluidly between these perspectives.

The aspects of the mind we care about are the ones that help us flourish, determined by deliberation on the ends of life rather than the science of the mind alone. This is crucial. We don't care about mental health because we're interested in brains for their own sake. We care because mental disorders prevent flourishing; they disrupt the psychological capacities needed to live a decent life. Things like emotional commitment, the ability to act in the world, to form goals and shape behaviour accordingly, to make genuine choices, to connect with others, to find meaning.

What makes mental health different from brain health is that its exercise involves conscious states, meaningful experiences, and matters to the person experiencing them. A liver disorder might be equally biological, but it doesn't threaten your sense of self, your relationships, or your ability to find meaning in life. Mental disorders do, because the mind is how we are in the world, how we relate to others, and how we construct meaning and purpose.

Your mind right now, as you read these words, is all of these things simultaneously. Neurons are firing in precise patterns that's neuroscience. Those patterns form into concepts, memories, emotions, and attention that's psychology. Those mental states feel like something from the inside, have a particular texture and quality that's phenomenology. And all of this raises questions about who you are, what you value, how you should live; that's philosophy.

When any of these levels go awry, when neurons misfire, when psychological patterns become rigid and self-defeating, when lived experience becomes unbearable, when questions of meaning become overwhelming, we call it mental illness. But it's never just one level. It's always all three, constantly interacting, always influencing each other in complex feedback loops. Understanding this doesn't make treatment easy, but it makes it possible. It gives us multiple points of intervention, various ways to help, and numerous languages for describing both the problem and the solution.

The shadow psyche that obscure region where mental health problems dwell is becoming less shadowy as we learn to illuminate it from multiple angles: the hard light of neuroscience revealing circuits and chemicals, the softer glow of psychology showing patterns and possibilities, and the intimate illumination of phenomenology showing what it's actually like to live in that shadow. None of these lights alone is enough. Together, they make the invisible visible, the ineffable speakable, the unbearable perhaps a bit more bearable.

This is the promise: not to eliminate mental illness, that may never be possible, but to understand it so thoroughly from so many perspectives that we can genuinely help. To see the person in front of us not as a broken brain, not as a cluster of symptoms, not as a philosophical puzzle, but as all of these at once: a biological being whose neurology shapes their experience, a psychological agent whose patterns both constrain and enable them, a conscious experiencer whose phenomenology is their reality, and a person trying to live a meaningful life in a challenging world.

Suppose we can hold all of that complexity in mind simultaneously: the brain, the experience, the meaning. In that case, we can begin to heal not just symptoms but persons, not just diseases but lives, not just minds but whole human beings trying to find their way out of the shadow and back into the light.

Chapter 15
The Physiology of Forgiveness and Release

Close your eyes for a moment. Think about someone who hurt you. Really hurt you. Maybe it was years ago, perhaps it was yesterday. Notice what happens in your body right now. Does your jaw tighten? Does your chest constrict? Does your breathing become shallow?

That's not just in your head. That's your body, quite literally, holding onto pain.

Now imagine this: what if I told you that the act of forgiveness isn't some wishy-washy spiritual concept, but a biological imperative? What if the reason your grandmother told you to "let it go" wasn't just good manners, but actually profound neuroscience wrapped in folk wisdom?

Today, I want to take you on a journey through the physiology of forgiveness. Not the religious kind, not the moral obligation kind, but the raw, biological, neuroscientific reality of what happens when we choose to release resentment and grudges. Because here's the thing nobody tells you: holding onto anger doesn't punish the person who wronged you. It harms your cardiovascular system, immune function, sleep architecture, and mental health. Let me show you how.

When someone betrays your trust, lies to you, or causes you harm, your body doesn't just register emotional pain. It registers a threat. Your amygdala, that almond-shaped structure deep in your brain's limbic system, lights up like a Christmas tree. This isn't metaphorical. Brain imaging studies using functional MRI technology have shown that social rejection activates the same neural pathways as physical pain.

Dr Naomi Eisenberger at UCLA discovered something remarkable: when people experienced social exclusion in a simple computer game, their anterior cingulate cortex became highly active. This is the same brain region that processes the distress of physical pain. Your brain cannot, at the neural level, tell the difference between a broken bone and a broken heart.

But here's where it gets interesting. Unlike a broken bone that heals in six to eight weeks, social and emotional wounds can stay active in your nervous system for years, sometimes decades. Why? Because you keep rehearsing them. Every time you replay that argument in your mind, every time you imagine what you should have said, every time you mentally prosecute the person who wronged you, you're not just remembering. You're re-living. Your amygdala fires again. Your stress hormones surge again. Your blood pressure rises again. It's as if the betrayal is happening right now, in this moment, even if it occurred twenty years ago.

This is what psychologists call rumination, and it's absolutely devastating to your health. Studies from the University of Wisconsin show that chronic rumination has elevated cortisol levels throughout the day, disrupted sleep patterns, and significantly higher rates of depression and anxiety. You're essentially running your stress response system round the clock, and your body is paying the price.

Let's talk about what unforgiveness actually does to your body at the chemical level, because this is where things get really uncomfortable. When you hold onto resentment, your hypothalamic-pituitary-adrenal (HPA) axis remains chronically activated. This is your body's central stress response system, and it was designed for acute threats, not ongoing grudges. When a lion chases you, your HPA axis floods your system with cortisol and adrenaline. Your heart rate spikes, your blood pressure rises, and your immune system temporarily shuts down non-essential functions. This is brilliant for surviving immediate danger.

But here's the problem: your HPA axis can't tell the difference between a lion and your lying ex-partner. Every time you think about them, every time you feel that familiar surge of anger, you're activating the same system. And unlike the lion, which either catches you or doesn't, your ex-partner exists in your mind indefinitely.

Research by Dr Charlotte van Oyen Witvliet at Hope College in Michigan measured the physiological effects of rehearsing grudges versus practising forgiveness. When participants imagined an unforgiving response to someone who hurt them, their blood pressure increased, their heart rate jumped, their facial muscles tensed, and they showed increased sweat gland activity. When the same participants imagined forgiving responses, all these measures decreased. But it's not just about temporary spikes. Chronic elevation of cortisol does extraordinary damage over time. It suppresses your immune system, making you more susceptible to infections and slower to heal from wounds. It disrupts your sleep architecture, particularly REM sleep, which is crucial for emotional processing and memory consolidation. It contributes to weight gain, particularly visceral fat around your organs. It accelerates cognitive decline and increases your risk of developing Alzheimer's disease later in life.

Let me put this in stark terms: holding onto a grudge is like drinking poison and hoping the other person gets sick. Except you're the only one drinking it, and you're drinking it every single day.

Your immune system is constantly eavesdropping on your emotional state. This isn't New Age mysticism. This is psychoneuroimmunology, a legitimate field of medicine that studies how psychological processes affect immune function. When you're in a state of chronic unforgiveness, your body produces more pro-inflammatory cytokines. These are chemical messengers that trigger inflammation throughout your body. Some inflammation is good. It's how your body fights infections and heals injuries. But chronic inflammation is the root cause of virtually every significant disease: cardiovascular disease, diabetes, cancer, autoimmune disorders, and neurodegenerative diseases.

Studies from the Institute for Behavioural Medicine Research at Ohio State University found that people who score high on hostility measures, which correlate strongly with unforgiveness, have elevated levels of C-reactive protein and interleukin-6, both markers of systemic inflammation. They also show poorer wound healing, lower antibody response to vaccinations, and higher rates of infectious illness. Think about that. Your unresolved anger is literally making you sick at the cellular level.

There's a reason why certain cultures have rituals around forgiveness and letting go. It's not just about social cohesion. It's about survival. Your ancestors who couldn't forgive, who couldn't move past slights and injuries, who remained in a state of constant vigilance and hostility, didn't live as long. They had higher rates of heart disease, they healed more slowly from injuries, and they were more susceptible to infection. Forgiveness, it turns out, isn't just morally virtuous. It's evolutionarily adaptive.

Let's go deeper into your brain, because this is where the story gets really fascinating. When you repeatedly think about something, you strengthen the neural pathways associated with that thought. Neuroscientists call this Hebbian learning: neurons that fire together wire together. Every time you rehearse your grievance, you're not just remembering it. You're strengthening the neural circuitry, making it easier to remember next time. You're literally building a superhighway in your brain dedicated to this particular resentment. And the more you travel that highway, the more automatic it becomes.

This is why, years later, you can be having an enjoyable day when suddenly something triggers the memory, a smell, a song, a phrase someone uses, and boom, you're right back there. Your heart races, your muscles tense, you feel that familiar surge of anger. It's not because you're weak or irrational. It's because you've carved this response so deeply into your neural architecture that it's become automatic. But here's the hopeful part: neuroplasticity works both ways. Just as you can strengthen neural pathways through repetition, you can also weaken them through disuse. And you can build new, healthier pathways through deliberate practice. This is what forgiveness does at the neurological level. It begins to starve those old pathways of attention and energy. It redirects your neural resources toward different thoughts, different emotions, different ways of relating to the past.

Your heart literally bears the burden of your unforgiveness. This isn't poetic language. This is cardiology. Chronic anger and hostility are independent risk factors for cardiovascular disease, separate from traditional risks like smoking, obesity, or high cholesterol. Studies following thousands of participants over decades have found that people with high levels of trait hostility have two to three times the risk of coronary heart disease compared to their more forgiving counterparts.

Why? Because every time you engage with your resentment, you're triggering your sympathetic nervous system. Your heart rate increases. Your blood pressure rises. Your blood vessels constrict. Small amounts of adrenaline and cortisol flood your system. This is fine occasionally. This is what your body was designed to do. But when it happens multiple times a day, every day, for years? Your cardiovascular system is under constant assault. Your blood vessels lose their elasticity. Your heart muscle has to work harder. Atherosclerotic plaques begin to form in your arteries. Your risk of heart attack and stroke increases dramatically.

Research from Duke University Medical Centre found that people who scored high on hostility measures at age 25 were significantly more likely to develop coronary artery disease by age 50, even after controlling for traditional risk factors. The researchers followed up with these participants and found something else interesting: those who learned to reduce their hostility through therapy or other interventions showed improvement in their cardiovascular health markers. Your heart, quite literally, knows when you've let go.

Before we had neuroscience, before we had MRI machines and cortisol assays, philosophers grappled with the question of forgiveness and what it means to be human. The Stoics understood something profound about the nature of resentment. Epictetus wrote that when we hold onto anger, we give the person who wronged us power over our present moment. They're not there, but they're controlling our emotional state, our thoughts, our physical reactions. We've essentially imprisoned ourselves whilst believing we're imprisoning them.

Marcus Aurelius, the philosopher emperor, advised: "The best revenge is not to be like your enemy." He understood that by holding onto hatred, we become precisely what we despise. We let the wrongdoing corrupt not just our past, but our present and future. We give the transgression more power than it deserves. Buddhist philosophy approaches forgiveness from a different angle. The concept of metta, or loving-kindness, suggests that holding onto resentment is like grasping a hot coal with the intention of throwing it at someone else. You're the one who gets burned. The practice isn't about condoning harm or pretending it didn't happen. It's about recognising that your continued suffering serves no purpose.

The Buddha supposedly said, "Holding onto anger is like drinking poison and expecting the other person to die." Modern neuroscience has proven this wisdom to be literally, physiologically accurate. Western philosophy, particularly in the Christian tradition, has long emphasised forgiveness, but often in moral terms: forgive because it's the right thing to do, forgive because God commands it, forgive to save your soul. There's wisdom there, but it misses something crucial. You don't forgive the other person. You don't even forgive to be morally superior. You forgive because unforgiveness is destroying you from the inside out.

Nietzsche, interestingly, was sceptical of forgiveness, seeing it as a sign of weakness. But he misunderstood what forgiveness actually is. Forgiveness isn't weakness. Forgiveness is recognising that you're strong enough to bear the injury without letting it define you. It's choosing life over slow death by resentment.

How do you actually do this? How do you release something that feels woven into the very fabric of who you are? Let me be clear: forgiveness is not a single decision. It's not something you can force yourself to feel. It's a process, often a long one, and it happens in layers. The first step is acknowledging the full extent of what happened. This might seem counterintuitive. Shouldn't you just move on? No. Suppression isn't forgiveness. Suppression is just unforgiveness buried alive, and buried emotions don't die. They fester. They leak out in unexpected ways: in your relationships with others, in your self-talk, and in your physical symptoms.

You have to feel it thoroughly first. The betrayal. The hurt. The rage. This isn't wallowing. This is processing. Your nervous system needs to complete the stress response cycle. Dr Bessel van der Kolk, probably the world's leading expert on trauma, has shown that unprocessed emotional experiences remain stored in the body, in your muscles, in your breath patterns, in your autonomic nervous system. The only way out is through.

The second step is recognising the cost of holding on. This is where that physiological awareness becomes crucial. Notice what happens in your body when you engage with the resentment. Notice the tension in your jaw. Notice how your breathing becomes shallow. Notice the tightness in your chest. Your body is trying to tell you something: this is hurting you more than it's hurting them.

The third step is making a decision, not to feel differently, but to stop feeding the resentment. This is where you begin to redirect your attention. When the thoughts come, because they will, you don't suppress them. You acknowledge them: "Yes, that happened. Yes, it hurt. And I'm choosing not to give it my energy right now." This isn't easy at first. Those neural pathways are well-established. Your brain will keep defaulting to the grievance. That's normal. That's expected. But each time you redirect, you're weakening the old pathway and strengthening a new one. Neuroplasticity is on your side, but it requires patience and repetition.

The fourth step involves something that sounds absolutely mad until you understand the neuroscience: developing compassion for the person who hurt you. Not because they deserve it. Not because what they did was okay. But because understanding the conditions that led to their behaviour helps your nervous system release its grip on the trauma. Research from Dr Kristin Neff at the University of Texas has shown that self-compassion practices activate the parasympathetic nervous system, the rest-and-digest response that counteracts chronic stress. When you extend compassion to others, even those who've harmed you, you're essentially giving your own nervous system permission to stand down.

This doesn't mean reconciliation. You don't have to let them back into your life. You don't have to forget what happened. You're simply recognising that hurt people hurt people, that everyone is struggling with their own suffering, and that their behaviour says more about their pain than your worth.

Forgiveness isn't just a mental process. It's a whole-body experience. Your body has been holding this pain, this anger, this betrayal in its tissues. Release has to happen somatically, physically, not just cognitively. Trauma therapist Peter Levine pioneered something called Somatic Experiencing, which recognises that traumatic experiences, including betrayals and emotional wounds, are stored in the body's nervous system. Your muscles literally remember. Your breath patterns remember. Your posture remembers.

When you've been hurt, your body typically responds by contracting and armouring itself against future hurt. Your shoulders might be chronically tense. Your breathing might become habitually shallow. Your jaw might constantly clench. These aren't conscious choices. They're protective responses that have become habitual. To truly release, you need to help your body discharge this stored activation. This might look like shaking, crying, yelling into a pillow, intensive physical exercise, or breathing practices. Traditional cultures understood this. They had rituals, dances, and ceremonies that allowed the body to complete its stress response.

Modern trauma therapy incorporates these wisdom traditions. EMDR (Eye Movement Desensitisation and Reprocessing) uses bilateral stimulation to help the brain reprocess traumatic memories. Somatic Experiencing uses body awareness and gentle movements to release trapped energy. Trauma-sensitive yoga combines movement with mindfulness to help people reconnect with their bodies. The common thread in all these approaches is this: healing happens when you allow your nervous system to complete what it couldn't complete at the time of the original injury.

When you begin to release old resentments, something remarkable happens. It's not just about that one person or that one event. It's about reclaiming energy you didn't even realise you were spending. Think about it this way: your emotional bandwidth is finite. Every grudge you carry, every resentment you maintain, every old wound you keep fresh takes up space in your psychological hard drive. It takes processing power. It drains your battery. When you let go, you suddenly have all this energy available for other things. For present relationships. For creative pursuits. For joy. For presence with your children. For building the life you actually want rather than constantly relitigating the past.

People who successfully work through forgiveness often report feeling lighter, not metaphorically but literally. They sleep better. They have more energy. Their relationships improve, not just with the person they've forgiven, but with everyone. Why? Because they're no longer carrying that invisible weight. They're no longer unconsciously projecting their unresolved anger onto innocent people. Studies on forgiveness interventions show measurable improvements across multiple domains: reduced depression and anxiety, improved sleep quality, lower blood pressure, stronger immune function, better relationship satisfaction, and increased overall life satisfaction. These aren't placebo effects. These are real physiological changes happening because your nervous system has finally been permitted to heal.

Now, let me be absolutely clear about something, because this is where forgiveness gets misused and weaponised: forgiveness does not mean reconciliation. Forgiveness does not mean forgetting. Forgiveness does not mean allowing continued harm. You can forgive someone and never speak to them again. You can forgive someone and still hold them accountable for what they did. You can forgive someone and still protect yourself and others from future harm. These things aren't contradictory.

Forgiveness is about your internal state, not your external relationships. It's about releasing the toxic grip that resentment has on your nervous system. It's not about absolving someone of responsibility or pretending they didn't hurt you. In cases of severe trauma, abuse, and violence, forgiveness might not even be the proper framework. Sometimes what's needed is acknowledgement of harm, appropriate justice, and personal healing. Sometimes the healthiest thing is to maintain firm boundaries and refuse contact. That's not unforgiveness. That's self-preservation. The forgiveness we're talking about here is the internal work of not letting the injury continue to poison your present. It's about reclaiming your right to peace, regardless of whether the person who hurt you deserves your grace.

Forgiveness isn't just personal. It's political. It's social. It's how societies move beyond cycles of violence and retribution. Look at post-apartheid South Africa. The Truth and Reconciliation Commission, led by Archbishop Desmond Tutu, was built on the principle that forgiveness was necessary not only for individual healing but also for collective survival. Tutu spoke about ubuntu, the idea that "I am because we are," that our humanity is bound up in each other's. This wasn't naive optimism. It was pragmatic wisdom. South Africa had a choice: continue cycles of retribution that would tear the country apart, or find a way to acknowledge the horror of apartheid whilst creating space for people to live together. The TRC was imperfect, absolutely. But it recognised something crucial: societies that cannot forgive cannot heal. And societies that cannot heal destroy themselves from within.

We see the opposite in places where cycles of revenge continue for generations. The Balkans. The Middle East. Northern Ireland before the Good Friday Agreement. Resentments passed down from grandparents to grandchildren, keeping wounds fresh across decades, sometimes centuries. Everyone remembers who started it. Nobody can agree on how to end it. On a smaller scale, families do this too. Feuds that begin over inheritances or perceived slights metastasise across generations. Children inherit their parents' grudges like toxic heirlooms. Cousins who've never met each other carry on resentments about things that happened before they were born. The physiology we've been discussing, the cortisol, the inflammation, the cardiovascular stress, this doesn't just affect individuals. It affects communities. Collective trauma changes cultures. Collective unforgiveness creates societies that are chronically stressed, chronically inflamed, chronically sick.

I want to bring this back to something practical, something you can start doing today, because forgiveness isn't just for the big betrayals, the major traumas. It's also for all the small resentments we accumulate daily. The colleague who takes credit for your idea. The friend who forgot your birthday. The driver who cut you off in traffic. The partner who said something thoughtless. These small unforgivenesses stack up. They accumulate in your body like plaque in your arteries. Most of us walk around carrying dozens, maybe hundreds, of these small grudges. Individually, they seem insignificant. But collectively, they create a baseline level of tension, irritability, and stress that colours everything.

Try this experiment this week: when something happens that triggers irritation or resentment, pause. Notice it. Name it: "I'm feeling hurt because..." or "I'm angry because..." Then ask yourself: "Is holding onto this serving me?" Not "Do I have a right to be angry?" You probably do. But is nursing this particular resentment making your life better or worse? If it's making your life worse, try letting it go. Not for them. For you. Notice what happens in your body when you make that choice. You might feel your shoulders drop. Your jaw unclenches. Your breathing deepens. That's your parasympathetic nervous system activating. That's your body saying thank you. This is a practice, not a perfection. Some days you'll manage it. Some days you won't. That's fine. You're reconditioning decades of neural patterning. It takes time. But each time you successfully release a slight resentment, you're strengthening your capacity to release larger ones.

There's a fascinating connection between gratitude practices and forgiveness that neuroscience is just beginning to understand. Studies using fMRI imaging show that gratitude and forgiveness activate overlapping brain regions, particularly in the medial prefrontal cortex and anterior cingulate cortex. When you actively practice gratitude, focusing on what's good in your life rather than what's wrong, you're literally retraining your brain's attention. You're strengthening neural pathways that look for the positive rather than automatically scanning for threats and slights.

Dr Robert Emmons at UC Davis has spent decades researching gratitude. His studies consistently show that people who keep gratitude journals have lower levels of inflammation, better sleep, reduced depression, and stronger immune function. Sound familiar? These are the same benefits we see from forgiveness practices. It's not coincidental. Both forgiveness and gratitude involve a fundamental shift in attention. Instead of ruminating on harm, you're directing your neural resources toward appreciation. Instead of rehearsing what went wrong, you're acknowledging what's going right. Your brain can't do both simultaneously. You have to choose. This is where daily practices become powerful. Five minutes each morning writing down three things you're grateful for. Five minutes each evening reflecting on one minor forgiveness you can offer, even if it's just forgiving yourself for being imperfect. These simple practices reshape your neural architecture over time.

Let me close with the hardest forgiveness of all: forgiving yourself. You've hurt people. Maybe not intentionally. Perhaps you didn't know better at the time.

Maybe you were in pain, and pain makes people do harmful things. But you've caused damage. We all have. That's part of being human, flawed, and learning as we go. The shame and self-recrimination you carry for your own mistakes are just as physiologically damaging as the resentment you hold toward others. Maybe more so, because you can't escape yourself. The person who wronged you might be miles away. But you're stuck with yourself round the clock.

Self-forgiveness doesn't mean excusing harm you've caused. It means acknowledging it fully, making amends where possible, learning from it, and then releasing the constant self-punishment that serves no one, least of all the people you hurt. Your body can't tell the difference between anger directed outward and anger directed inward. Either way, your stress response activates. Either way, your inflammation increases. Either way, your health suffers. The Dalai Lama was once asked how he could forgive the Chinese for what they did to Tibet. He said something profound: "They've taken my country. Should I let them take my mind as well?" The same principle applies to self-forgiveness. You made mistakes. Should you let those mistakes take your health, your peace, your present moment, your future?

Standing here, talking to you about all this research, all this neuroscience, all this philosophy, I want you to understand something fundamental: forgiveness is not a feeling. It's a decision that leads to feelings. You don't wait to feel forgiving before you forgive. That's backwards. You decide to release, to stop feeding the resentment, to redirect your attention, and then, gradually, the feelings follow. The lightness comes. The peace arrives. The healing happens. But it starts with a choice. Not a one-time option. A repeated choice, made again and again, every time the old pattern tries to reassert itself.

Your body is exhausted from carrying all this pain. Your nervous system is depleted from years of chronic activation. Your heart is tired of bearing grudges. They're ready to let go. The question is: are you? Because here's what I know, what the science shows us again and again: when you release old resentments, when you practice forgiveness, when you stop drinking that poison, your body thanks you in a thousand different ways, your blood pressure drops. Your immune system strengthens. Your sleep improves. Your mood lifts. Your relationships deepen. Your life expands. Not because you've become some enlightened being. But because you've stopped fighting a war that was only ever hurting you.

The person who wronged you? They've moved on. They're living their life, maybe completely unaware of the suffering they caused or indifferent to it. Meanwhile, you've been keeping that suffering alive, fresh, active in your system. Doesn't it seem backwards? Doesn't it seem like you're giving them exactly what they don't deserve: continued power over your wellbeing? Forgiveness is how you take that power back. Not by pretending they didn't hurt you. Not by saying it's okay. But by refusing to let what happened then destroy what's possible now.

Your body already knows how to heal. Your nervous system already knows how to release. Your heart already knows how to open. You have to stop standing in the way. So I'll leave you with this: What would your life look like if you put down the weight you've been carrying? Not next year. Not when they apologise. Not when justice is served. Today. Right now. What would it feel like to let go?

Your body's been waiting for permission. I'm telling you: you have it. The science backs you. The philosophy supports you. Your own wellbeing demands it. The question is no longer whether forgiveness is good for you. We know it is, definitely, measurably, profoundly. The only question left is: when will you give yourself the gift of release? Your nervous system is listening. Your immune system is waiting. Your heart is ready. The choice, as always, is yours.

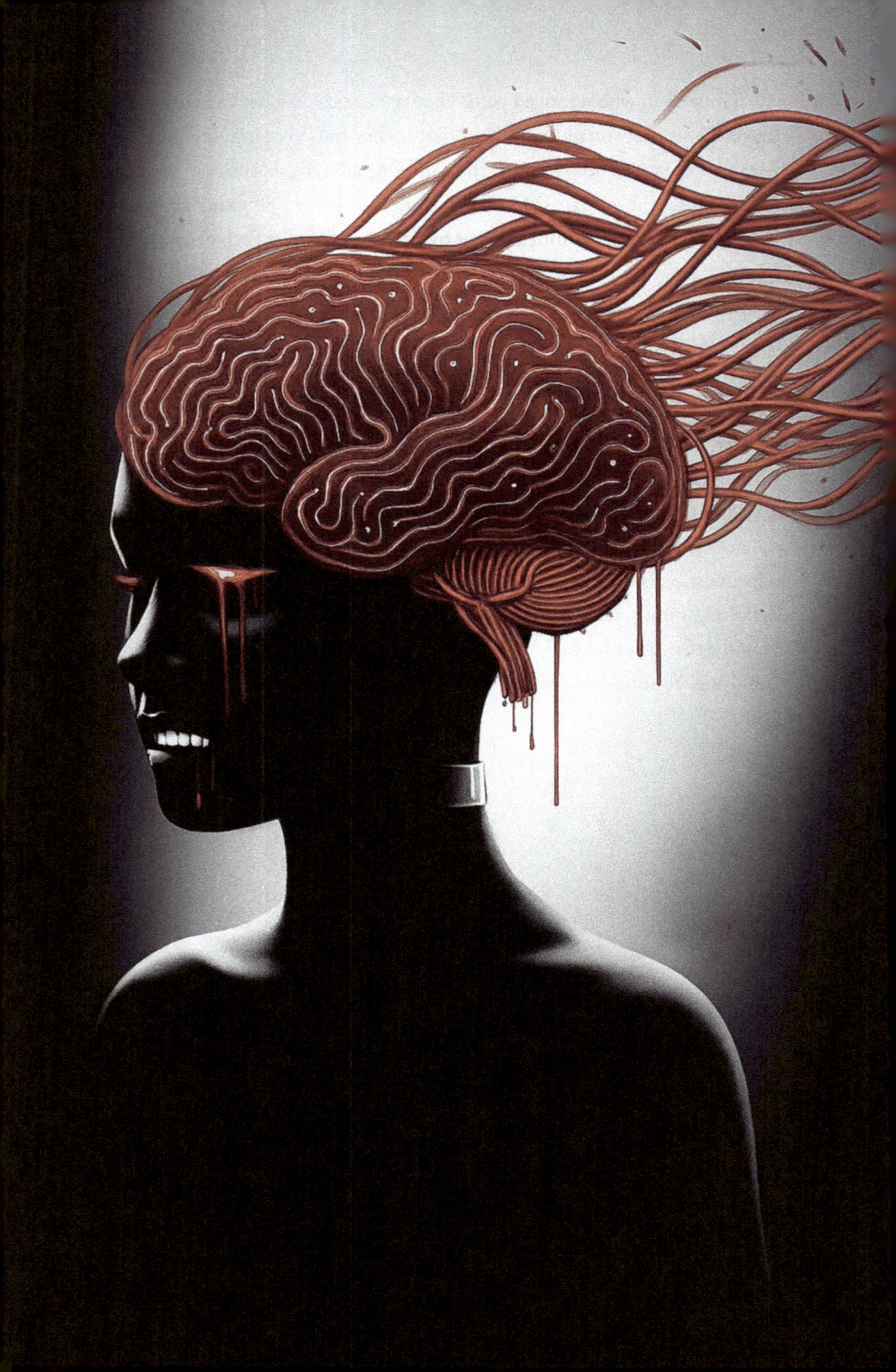

Chapter 16

Rewiring the Complex: The Neuroscience of Integration

I need you to understand something that will fundamentally challenge everything you've hoped for regarding personal growth, healing, and transformation. You've read this entire book and developed insight into your shadow, attachment patterns, trauma responses, and unconscious dynamics. You understand your defences, recognise your projections, and can articulate your patterns with impressive sophistication. You know why you do what you do and can trace your behaviours back to their origins; you have mapped your psychological landscape with increasing clarity. You might be thinking that this understanding will change you, that insight will lead to transformation, and that knowing why you are the way you are will somehow make you different.

But here's the uncomfortable truth: You are not meaningfully different from when you started reading. You still have the same automatic responses, defensive patterns, and unconscious reactions. You continue to get triggered by the same things, fall into the same relationship dynamics, and engage in the same self-sabotaging behaviours. Your anxiety still activates in the same situations, your anger erupts in the same ways, and your shame floods your system with the same intensity. Nothing has fundamentally changed, except now you have a sophisticated narrative explaining why nothing has changed, along with a detailed intellectual understanding of patterns that continue to operate just as they always have.

This should tell you something crucial: Insight does not rewire your brain. Understanding does not eliminate neural pathways built over decades. Knowing why you respond the way you do does not automatically create new response patterns. Your prefrontal cortex might be brilliantly articulating your dynamics. At the same time, your amygdala continues to trigger in the same ways it always has, and your habitual neural pathways continue firing in the identical sequences, driving your unconscious patterns regardless of your conscious understanding.

Think about the last time you were triggered, fell into a familiar defensive pattern, or engaged in behaviour you consciously knew was unhelpful but found yourself doing anyway. In that moment, before your conscious awareness could intervene, the pattern activated automatically. The trigger occurred, the neural pathway fired, and the response happened faster than conscious thought. You were already deep into your familiar reaction before your understanding could make any difference. Later, when you had distance and perspective, you could brilliantly explain what happened; you could trace exactly how your attachment wounds were activated, how your defences engaged, and how your patterns played out. But that understanding didn't prevent the event from occurring. The insight didn't change the automatic response, and the knowledge didn't rewire the pathway.

This is because your patterns aren't stored in the prefrontal cortex, where conscious understanding operates. They are stored in subcortical structures, in implicit memory, and in neural pathways built through thousands of repetitions and strengthened over decades. These pathways are physical structures in your brain, actual connections between neurons, actual patterns of activation that have become so well-established they are virtually automatic. This neural architecture doesn't change through cognitive insight because it wasn't built through cognitive processes in the first place.

Let's talk about neuroplasticity, as understanding this is essential for recognising both the possibility of change and the genuine difficulty of actually changing. Neuroplasticity refers to your brain's capacity to change its structure and function in response to experience, to build new neural pathways, to strengthen some connections while weakening others, and to reorganise itself throughout your life rather than being fixed after a critical developmental period. This understanding is genuinely revolutionary. For much of neuroscience history, it was assumed that brain structure was essentially fixed after childhood; whatever neural organisation you developed early would remain essentially unchanged throughout adulthood. However, neuroplasticity research has demolished this assumption, showing that your brain continues to change, build new pathways, and reorganise itself based on your experiences throughout your entire life.

Embracing the concept of neuroplasticity opens up a world of possibilities. The idea that your brain can change, form new pathways, and isn't fixed in its neural organisation is a beacon of hope. It means that transformation is not just a distant dream, but a tangible reality. Healing can occur, and you are not bound by patterns established in childhood or by neural architecture you didn't choose. Neuroplasticity is a powerful force, and change is not just a theoretical concept, but a genuine possibility. Your brain has the incredible ability to reorganise itself, build new pathways, and develop different patterns of activation that allow for responses different from the automatic reactions you've been stuck in for decades.

However, it's crucial to understand that the process of neuroplasticity operates according to specific principles. These principles make change more challenging, slower, and demand sustained effort. While your brain can change, achieving that change requires more than just wishing things were different or interpreting your patterns differently. It demands sustained effort, a commitment to meeting the actual conditions for neuroplasticity. It's not about hoping that insight will spontaneously lead to transformation, but about actively engaging in the process of change.

The cornerstone of neuroplasticity is Hebbian learning, named after the pioneering neuroscientist Donald Hebb. It's often summarised as "neurons that fire together wire together." This principle explains how habits are formed. When neurons activate together repeatedly, and the firing of one neuron reliably leads to the activation of another, the connection between them strengthens. The synapse, the connection point where neurotransmitters are released from one neuron to activate receptors on another, becomes more efficient, requiring less input to generate activation. This connection becomes increasingly likely to fire in the future. This is how learning occurs at the neural level, how patterns become established, and how behaviours become automatic through repeated practice that creates stronger and stronger neural connections.

Consider learning to drive. Initially, every aspect requires conscious attention: checking mirrors, adjusting speed, monitoring distance, coordinating the clutch and accelerator, and watching traffic. Your prefrontal cortex works extremely hard because conscious attention is required for every element, making the cognitive load, or the mental effort used in your working memory, overwhelming. However, through repetition, thousands of instances of these actions occurring together strengthen neural pathways. The sight of brake lights ahead becomes strongly linked to the action of moving your foot to brake. The sensation of the car drifting to the right is associated with a slight steering correction to the left. The sound of the engine becomes tied to decisions about gear changes. These connections strengthen through Hebbian learning, where neurons firing together repeatedly wire together through strengthened synapses, creating patterns that become increasingly automatic.

Eventually, you drive without conscious thought. The pathways are so well established and the connections so strong that appropriate responses occur automatically, without the prefrontal cortex needing to consciously direct each action. You're navigating complex traffic, making continuous adjustments, and responding to changing conditions all through neural pathways that operate beneath conscious awareness. This is neuroplasticity at work, creating expertise and automaticity, resulting in patterns that no longer require conscious attention because the supporting neural architecture is so well developed.

However, changing established patterns is challenging. The same Hebbian principle that built these pathways through repeated activation maintains them through continued use. Each time you engage in a familiar pattern, such as procrastination or negative self-talk, respond in habitual ways, like getting defensive in an argument or reaching for a cigarette when stressed, or activate the established pathway, like feeling anxious in social situations, you're not just maintaining the old path; you're actually strengthening it. The neurons fire together again, reinforcing the connection and making the pattern even more automatic with continued use. This deepens the groove you're trying to climb out of, making change all the more difficult.

Neural pathways that aren't frequently activated gradually weaken over time. This concept is summarised by the phrase "use it or lose it." When neural connections are not regularly engaged, those pathways and synapses begin to weaken through a process known as synaptic pruning. Your brain continuously optimises itself by strengthening valuable connections while eliminating those deemed unnecessary, thereby increasing efficiency by focusing on what is actively used and discarding what is not.

This adaptive process is beneficial when developing expertise, learning valuable skills, or establishing functional patterns. However, it poses challenges when trying to change existing pathways or eliminate unhelpful patterns. If you keep engaging in old behaviours without building alternatives, you are inadvertently strengthening the very pathways you want to weaken, while the potential alternatives further atrophy.

Consider the implications for changing your habits and transforming your automatic responses. Merely gaining insight or understanding your behaviours without making behavioural changes will not affect your neural pathways. You may comprehend why you respond in specific ways, but the neural pathway responsible for that response continues to strengthen each time that pattern is activated. While your insights occur in the prefrontal cortex, the underlying patterns operate through subcortical pathways. These subcortical pathways do not process your cognitive insights and can only be altered through experience-dependent neuroplasticity. This occurs specifically by repeatedly engaging in new responses, which helps to strengthen new pathways while the old ones gradually weaken due to disuse.

This explains why some people undergo years of therapy, develop significant insights, and gain a deep understanding of their patterns, yet remain unchanged in their automatic reactions and defensive behaviours. While therapy can enhance cognitive understanding and articulate psychological dynamics, it often does not foster the experience-dependent plasticity required to alter the subcortical pathways that mediate these problematic responses. It doesn't create new automatic reactions to replace old ones, nor does it engage the mechanisms through which real neural change occurs.

To achieve true transformation that rewires neural pathways rather than just understanding them, it is essential to repeatedly practice new responses in the actual situations where old patterns would typically activate. This involves not just discussing the changes you'd like to make but actively doing things differently, especially in real situations with real stakes, when your nervous system is activated and defensive patterns are likely to emerge. This fosters neuroplasticity as new neurons fire together through these new responses, strengthening new pathways via repeated activation. Over time, these new patterns become more automatic, while old pathways gradually weaken from disuse.

What makes this extraordinarily difficult is that new neural pathways, when they first begin to form, are weak. They require a significant amount of conscious effort to engage. This process feels unnatural and awkward, demanding constant attention to maintain. You can think of them as tiny footpaths cutting through a dense forest, compared to the well-worn highways of your established patterns.

Every time you try to engage in a new response, every time you attempt a different behaviour, or every time you work to activate an emerging pathway, it takes substantial effort from your prefrontal cortex. This effort creates a considerable cognitive load and feels uncomfortable and wrong. Meanwhile, the established pathway right next to it is shouting, "Just do what you always do! It's easier! It's automatic! It's what you know!"

When you're under stress or activated, and your resources are limited, your brain defaults to these established pathways because they are efficient and automatic. They don't require the conscious resources that engaging new patterns does. This is why you often revert to familiar behaviours despite your understanding of them, despite your conscious desire to respond differently, and despite your best intentions. The new pathway is simply too weak, too effortful, and demands too many resources that aren't available when you're activated.

The old pathway is strong, automatic, and efficient. When pressure mounts, your brain prioritises efficiency over intention, choosing the automatic response over the effortful one and sticking to established patterns instead of exploring new possibilities.

When you're trying to learn a new skill while stressed, activated, or facing limited cognitive resources; it's nearly impossible. You tend to revert to what you already know, to established patterns and automatic responses, because learning a new skill requires resources you may not have when you're in a defensive mode.

The same principle applies to changing psychological patterns: when you're triggered, your defences are activated, or you're experiencing fight-or-flight or freeze responses, you lack the resources to engage in new responses that require conscious effort. You default to established patterns because those are the options your brain can access when your prefrontal resources are compromised by activation.

Building new pathways requires practice in conditions of relative safety and calm. It involves repeatedly engaging new responses when you have the resources to maintain them, and it takes thousands of repetitions before new patterns can become automatic enough to be accessible when you're activated. You can't just try a new response once or twice and expect it to override patterns that have been established through decades of continuous activation. The new pathway needs to be strengthened through sufficient repetitions to develop enough automaticity to compete with established patterns, even when resources are limited.

The insights from neuroscience are quite striking: it typically takes about three to five repetitions of a new pattern to create a strength equivalent to just one activation of a well-established pattern. Suppose you've been engaging in a defensive response for thirty years, activating this pattern thousands of times. In that case, you will need many thousands of repetitions of a new reaction to create a pathway strong enough to rival the established one, not just dozens or hundreds, but thousands. This explains why change can be slow, why transformation can take years rather than months, and why you may find yourself reverting to familiar patterns even when you consciously desire to change. The new pathway simply isn't strong enough yet to override the old one unless you have significant resources and can maintain intense conscious effort to engage it.

Moreover, practising a new response isn't just effective in therapy sessions, calm moments or hypothetical situations. The pathway must be built through activation in real contexts where the old pattern usually occurs. You need to engage the new response when you are actually triggered, as this creates conditions for old patterns to arise while you actively work to implement the latest response. This requires deliberately entering triggering situations, consciously acknowledging what activates you, and intentionally looking for opportunities where the old pattern threatens to take over. All the while, you feel activated and uncomfortable, facing the instinct to either avoid the situation or revert to familiar defensive patterns.

This explains why integration is so demanding and why genuine transformation necessitates sustained effort. You can't simply understand your way to change. Instead, you must deliberately, consciously, and repeatedly engage new responses in triggering situations while developing enough awareness to recognise when old patterns become active. You also need sufficient self-control to engage alternatives even when every instinct pulls you toward familiar responses. This process requires thousands of repetitions and occurs gradually over months and years. You must tolerate the discomfort of activating weaker pathways that demand significant effort, in contrast to the ease of using stronger, automatic responses.

Now, let's discuss what integration actually means, as it is often misunderstood. Some people expect outcomes that aren't possible, leading to disappointment when the transformation doesn't match their expectations. This can create a sense of failure, even when they are actually making progress, because they are measuring it against unrealistic standards. Integration doesn't mean eliminating your shadow material; it doesn't mean your patterns disappear or that you stop having automatic defensive responses, triggered reactions, or uncomfortable emotions.

Integration involves developing a conscious relationship with these aspects of yourself. It means recognising patterns as they activate and having alternatives available, rather than being unconsciously controlled by automatic responses while believing you are making free choices. Your shadow doesn't dissipate through integration; it becomes conscious, acknowledged, and something you can work with, rather than something that operates in the background without your awareness. Your defensive patterns don't vanish; they transform into choices that you recognise rather than automatic reactions that you were unaware of. Likewise, your trauma responses do not eliminate; instead, they become states you can observe, understand, and gradually learn to modulate, rather than being hijacked by them while remaining unaware of what is actually influencing your experience.

Consider what this means in practical terms. Someone who has integrated their anger does not stop feeling angry; they do not eliminate rage or transcend irritation through some spiritual achievement. Instead, they recognise when anger arises, understand what triggers it, and can distinguish between a proportionate response to the current situation and a historical reaction projected onto present circumstances. They develop the empowering capacity to choose how to express their anger, rather than being unconsciously controlled by it, while insisting they had no choice and simply responded to the situation as it presented itself. The anger is still present; they haven't eliminated it, but they are no longer unconsciously governed by it, as they can now acknowledge it consciously. They relate to it with awareness rather than letting it operate automatically from the shadows.

Similarly, someone who has integrated their attachment wounds does not stop having attachment needs; they do not transcend the desire for connection or achieve an impossible independence where others do not matter. They recognise when their attachment system is activating, understand what drives their responses, and can discern between the current relationship being genuinely threatening and historical patterns projected onto their present partner. They cultivate the ability to choose how to respond to their attachment needs rather than being unconsciously controlled by them, which can lead to self-fulfilling prophecies through defensive reactions to imagined threats. The wounds are still there; they have not healed in the sense of disappearing. However, they are conscious, recognised, and actively worked with, rather than operating automatically and determining behaviour without awareness of the underlying motivations.

Integration involves consciousness, awareness, and recognising what influences us, rather than being influenced by it, while insisting that we are making free choices. This recognition, awareness, and consciousness create opportunities for choices that did not exist when automatic patterns ran our lives. These choices are not easy, effortless, or discomfort-free. Genuine choice entails actual agency and the real ability to engage differently than our automatic patterns dictate, even when these new responses feel uncomfortable and established pathways continuously pull us toward familiar reactions.

This is why building new neural pathways is essential rather than optional, why insights must translate into repeated behavioural changes, and why understanding needs to be enacted through different responses practised thousands of times in real situations. Integration occurs through neuroplasticity by building pathways that allow us to recognise patterns as they activate. This strengthens connections that enable conscious choice instead of automatic responses and forms neural architecture that supports awareness and agency. This process contrasts with merely maintaining unconscious patterns while consciousness remains unaware of what actually drives behaviour.

However, building these pathways is uncomfortable; it creates resistance and can feel wrong, tempting you to abandon your efforts and revert to familiar patterns. This discomfort is not a signal that you are doing something wrong; rather, it indicates that neuroplasticity is happening. You are engaging pathways that are not yet well-developed, creating cognitive load through effortful processing instead of relying on automatic pathways. The discomfort serves as a reassuring sign that change is occurring and that new connections are forming. It indicates that you are genuinely engaging the mechanisms through which neural reorganisation takes place, rather than just thinking about change while maintaining familiar patterns.

Consider the process of learning any complex skill, whether it's playing a musical instrument, mastering a new language, or perfecting an athletic technique. The initial stages are often extremely uncomfortable. Nothing feels natural; everything requires conscious effort. You make constant mistakes, and progress can seem excruciatingly slow. You're acutely aware of the significant gap between your current abilities and where you strive to be. This discomfort leads many people to quit, convincing themselves they lack talent or the capability to learn this specific skill. However, this discomfort is not a sign of incapacity; it indicates that neuroplasticity is taking place. New pathways are forming in your brain, and learning is happening even though it feels unpleasant. These new pathways are weak and demand substantial effort, all while competence has yet to develop to the point where the effort feels worthwhile.

The same principle applies to psychological change, such as building new response patterns or rewiring the neural pathways that have shaped your behaviour for decades. The early stages are challenging; you're attempting to respond differently, yet everything feels "wrong." You're striving to engage new patterns while the old ones feel natural and automatic. The cognitive load increases as you work hard to process information, while familiar responses come naturally without effort. Mistakes are frequent, and it's common to revert to old patterns, creating a sense of failure when change doesn't happen as quickly or thoroughly as you hoped or as easily as popular psychology suggests.

But this discomfort doesn't equate to failure; it signifies that neuroplasticity is occurring. New pathways are forming, and change is happening, even though it feels difficult. This is what building new neural architectures entails: working with the brain's mechanisms of change rather than simply hoping that insight will result in transformation. Each time you engage a new response despite feeling discomfort, recognise an old pattern activating and choose differently, or maintain new behaviour even when it feels effortful, you are strengthening new pathways. Through repeated activation, you are building new connections and creating neural change via Hebbian learning.

These repetitions accumulate gradually. The change is often subtle day-to-day but becomes noticeable over months and years. The new pathway begins to develop some automaticity, requiring less conscious effort and becoming accessible even when you're somewhat activated, rather than only in perfect conditions of calm. Meanwhile, the old pathways, due to less frequent activation and being acknowledged without acting upon them, begin to weaken incrementally through disuse. They may not disappear entirely; established pathways can exist for a lifetime, even if not regularly engaged, but they weaken enough that they no longer dominate your responses. Alternatives become genuinely available, allowing for actual choices rather than feeling compelled to take the well-worn route while insisting you're making a free choice.

It's essential to understand why therapy alone is often insufficient in promoting neuroplasticity. Traditional talk therapy, especially psychodynamic or insight-oriented approaches, primarily focuses on developing understanding, exploring your history, recognising patterns, interpreting dynamics, and creating a coherent narrative about why you are the way you are. While this can be valuable and may lead to significant shifts in how you understand yourself, it does not promote experience-dependent neuroplasticity in the pathways that mediate your automatic responses. This understanding can help you see the need for alternative approaches that actively engage the brain's mechanisms of change.

For instance, discussing anger in a therapy session while calm does not rewire pathways that activate during actual moments of anger. Talking about attachment wounds in an abstract manner does not alter the automatic defensive responses that arise when your attachment system is genuinely threatened. Reflecting on your patterns retrospectively does not create new pathways that can proactively activate in triggering situations. The conversations occur primarily in the prefrontal cortex, strengthening pathways linked to verbal articulation and cognitive understanding. However, they do not engage the subcortical pathways that activate automatically when you're triggered, which govern your defensive responses before conscious thought can intervene. These pathways maintain patterns through processes that do not rely on verbal interpretation or cognitive insight.

Therapeutic approaches that create genuine neural change often involve experiential work. This means not just talking about patterns but actively engaging with them during sessions. Instead of merely understanding triggers, it's crucial to deliberately activate them in a safe context, allowing new responses to be practised. Effective therapy focuses on enacting different reactions in the present, leading to the creation of new pathways through repeated behavioural changes. It's important to remember that experience is the driver of neuroplasticity; the activation of neurons through new responses forms connections. Simply discussing what one might do differently does not create these connections between triggers and alternative responses.

For therapy to be effective, it's essential to deliberately create situations that activate these patterns. This allows for engagement while they are active, rather than only analysing them after the fact when one is calm. This process can be uncomfortable, but it's important to remember that neither the therapist nor the client typically enjoys activating difficult emotions, triggering defensive responses, or creating ruptures that need repair. However, this discomfort is a normal and necessary part of where neural change occurs. New pathways can be built through actual responses while relevant neural networks are active. Hebbian learning helps establish connections between recognising triggers and providing alternative responses, rather than merely accumulating verbal knowledge about patterns that operate independently of the underlying neural pathways.

Specific approaches, such as EMDR (Eye Movement Desensitisation and Reprocessing), facilitate this process by activating trauma networks while simultaneously promoting integration. This creates conditions where implicit memories can be accessed and updated instead of remaining disconnected from conscious processing. Somatic therapies engage the body's responses, enhance awareness of nervous system states, and foster new responses at the physical level, beyond mere cognitive understanding. Exposure-based therapies allow individuals to repeatedly encounter triggers in a sufficiently safe setting, fostering new associations through experiences where the trigger does not result in catastrophe. This process promotes neuroplasticity by contradicting unconscious predictions based on real experiences rather than through cognitive challenges that do not engage the relevant neural networks.

All of these methods generate experience-dependent plasticity. They involve the actual activation of relevant pathways while new responses occur, fostering new connections through Hebbian learning from neurons firing together in meaningful contexts. The resulting change is not merely cognitive; it encompasses neural, physical, and structural transformations in brain organisation. This manifests as different automatic responses, defensive patterns, and unconscious reactions because the pathways mediating these responses have genuinely changed through experience-dependent plasticity, rather than simply being understood through cognitive analysis. This transformative process inspires hope for the potential of therapy to bring about profound change.

Even with effective therapy and methods that promote experience-dependent plasticity, change occurs slowly. This is because building new neural pathways while old ones still exist requires thousands of repetitions over a long period. This is why transformation can take years, why healing is a long-term process, and why you can't rush integration or force change to happen faster than the mechanisms of neuroplasticity allow. Popular psychology that promises rapid transformation, quick fixes, and weekend workshops that claim to completely rewire your brain is either delusional or dishonest. It ignores the actual mechanisms of neural change and creates unrealistic expectations, making people feel like failures when transformation doesn't happen as quickly or thoroughly as promised.

Your brain can change. Neuroplasticity is real. New pathways can be created to enable different responses than the automatic patterns that have defined your behaviour for decades. However, this change requires meeting the actual conditions under which neuroplasticity operates: the repeated activation of new pathways in relevant contexts. These thousands of repetitions gradually build synaptic strength, and sustained effort over months and years is required. It's a process that demands patience, as it produces imperceptible changes on a day-to-day basis but leads to significant transformation over time. This emphasis on patience can help you feel reassured and calm as you embark on your transformation journey.

Crucially, the change requires translating insight into action. You need to enact your understanding through different behaviours repeatedly. Cognitive awareness must inform without substituting for experiential learning, which engages the mechanisms that actually change neural architecture. You cannot think your way to reorganising your neural pathways, understanding different automatic responses, or analysing integration. The cognitive work provides a framework for comprehension and meaning that can sustain your efforts through a challenging process. But real change happens through experience-dependent plasticity through repeatedly engaging in different behaviours in real situations, building new pathways through accumulated repetitions, and reshaping neural architecture through use rather than mere understanding.

What this mean for your own healing, transformation, and integration work. The insights you've gained from this book, as well as your understanding of your shadow, defences, and unconscious patterns, are all valuable. They lay a foundation for change. However, they are not sufficient on their own; they do not automatically result in transformation and won't spontaneously rewire your pathways without translating that understanding into repeated behavioural changes in real-life situations over time. Knowing what needs to change is not the same as making that change. Awareness of patterns does not equate to building alternatives. Understanding mechanisms does not replace the need to engage those mechanisms through actual experiences that foster neuroplasticity.

The work ahead is not easy, but it's worth it. It involves applying your understanding to real situations, consciously encountering triggers while striving to engage new responses, and accumulating thousands of repetitions of different behaviours. At the same time, old patterns urge activation and sustaining effort over the years while tolerating the discomfort of building weak pathways. This process demands your commitment, dedication, and trust, even when the change feels imperceptible day after day. It's a challenging journey, but your sustained effort will lead to significant transformation over time.

Avoiding experiential work means remaining fundamentally unchanged, despite having an impressive understanding. It leads to being unconsciously controlled by patterns you can articulate brilliantly, yet do not transform. You'll stay trapped in neural architectures established decades ago. At the same time, your conscious mind maintains elaborate narratives about why change is impossible, why understanding should be adequate, or why transformation will eventually occur without the hard work of repeatedly engaging in different responses and building new pathways through accumulated repetitions over an extended time.

Welcome to the exploration of neuroplasticity and Hebbian learning, the process of building new neural pathways through repeated activation, gradually increasing synaptic strength over time. It's important to understand that simply gaining insight does not rewire your brain. Your understanding alone cannot eliminate established pathways, nor does cognitive sophistication create new automatic responses. True transformation requires translating understanding into repeated behavioural change. It involves engaging experience-dependent plasticity, a process where the brain's structure is shaped by experience through thousands of repetitions in real situations. Committing to sustained effort over the years allows weak pathways to strengthen while old pathways gradually weaken through relative disuse.

Change is not only possible, but it's also fundamental. Neuroplasticity, the ability of the brain to reorganise itself, is the key. New pathways can be created, and your brain can reorganise itself throughout your life. This potential for change is a reason for hope and optimism. However, this change necessitates meeting the specific conditions under which neural reorganisation occurs. This means avoiding the misconception that insight will spontaneously lead to transformation or that understanding will automatically translate into new behavioural patterns. Change will not happen passively while you sidestep the challenging work of consistently engaging new responses in situations where familiar patterns are tempted to activate.

Your unique patterns of thought and behaviour have been maintained through neural pathways built over decades, established connections reinforced through countless activations and subcortical patterns operating automatically, often faster than conscious awareness. Integration requires building new pathways through continuous effort, accumulating repetitions over similar timescales, and actively using mechanisms that promote structural change in neural architecture. This approach contrasts with merely fostering cognitive understanding of patterns that remain unchanged, as consciousness often believes that understanding equals transformation.

The work is indeed challenging, but it's not insurmountable. The timeline is lengthy, but it's a journey worth taking. The discomfort is real, and the resistance can be substantial, but they are not unbeatable. Transformation is not a distant dream; it's achievable by engaging the actual mechanisms of neural change through experience-dependent plasticity, which builds new pathways while allowing old ones to weaken, and through the repeated activation of new responses that strengthen synapses via Hebbian learning. This process requires thousands of repetitions over the years to create a neural architecture that supports consciousness, choice, and integration. This approach contrasts with perpetuating unconscious patterns that dictate behaviour while keeping awareness unaware of the proper drivers behind your responses.

This is how rewiring occurs. This is how integration happens. Understanding this process is crucial because it equips you with the knowledge and tools to genuinely change. This is in contrast to merely understanding why you haven't changed, while still exhibiting the same patterns, despite possessing insightful knowledge about them.

Chapter 17

The Alchemy of Attention: Shadow Work in Action

Pay attention to what your mind is doing right now, in this very moment. Don't focus on the content of your thoughts, the stories your mind is telling. Instead, observe the process itself: the constant stream of mental commentary running alongside whatever you're reading, experiencing, or doing. Notice how your mind is creating narratives, generating judgments, making predictions, comparing, evaluating, and analysing. For instance, when a thought arises, such as 'I'm not good enough,' try to detach from it by acknowledging it as just a thought, not a reflection of reality. Observe how it's commenting on this very instruction to notice, already creating thoughts about noticing thoughts, and generating meta-commentary about the commentary itself.

Now, here's what's crucial: notice how completely you identify with this stream of thoughts. You believe you are these thoughts, and you experience this mental chatter as if it is you, rather than something happening to you, something your brain is producing that you are experiencing, but that isn't identical to who you truly are. When your mind says, "I'm anxious," you don't see this as your brain generating a thought about anxiety; instead, you perceive it as a direct truth about your state, an accurate description of reality, a fact about who you are, rather than one possible interpretation your mind happens to be producing in that moment.

When your mind says, "I'm not good enough," you don't recognise this as a thought occurring; you experience it as truth being revealed, an accurate assessment finally acknowledged, a reality about your inadequacy that the thought is reporting rather than creating. When your mind says, "This is unbearable," you don't see it as mental commentary; you perceive it as an objective fact about the situation, a truth about your capacity, an accurate prediction about your ability to handle what's happening, rather than a thought your brain is generating that might or might not correspond to actual reality.

By detaching from your thoughts, you can gain mental clarity and emotional regulation. This complete identification with thought, this total fusion between you and your cognitive content, this absolute conflation of thoughts with truth, is how your mind controls you. Thoughts shape your behaviour while you remain convinced you're making free choices. Mental commentary influences your experience, yet your consciousness fails to recognise the distance between you and the stream of thought, the space between awareness and content, and the fundamental difference between experiencing thoughts and being those thoughts. You are not your thoughts. However, you may feel so thoroughly fused with them, so completely identified with mental content, and so entirely convinced that thoughts represent truth, that this distinction feels meaningless or abstract, like philosophical speculation rather than recognising something crucial about your actual experience.

Think back to the last time you were consumed by negative thought patterns when your mind generated catastrophic predictions, harsh self-judgments, or ruminations about past failures. Notice how completely you believed these thoughts, how thoroughly they determined your emotional state, and how entirely they shaped your behaviour. When the thoughts said, "You're going to fail," you felt the anxiety of impending failure and acted accordingly: avoiding challenges, giving up prematurely, and fulfilling the prediction through behaviour that was determined by believing the thought was actual. When the thoughts said, "You're worthless," you felt the shame of worthlessness and behaved like someone worthless: declining opportunities and accepting poor treatment, thus confirming the judgment through actions shaped by your fusion with that thought.

At no point did you recognise, "These are just thoughts occurring brain-generated events that I'm experiencing, but that might not be accurate, might not represent truth, and might be patterns unrelated to present reality, shaped instead by historical programming." Instead, you experienced those thoughts as truth, completely fused with mental content, and behaved as if those thoughts were accurate descriptions of reality, rather than recognising them as interpretations your brain generates through filters, biases, and historical patterns that often have little to do with current circumstances and everything to do with unconscious dynamics operating beneath your awareness.

This fusion between you and your thoughts, this conflation of mental content with truth, this complete identification with the stream of consciousness, is one of the primary mechanisms through which your Obscure Psyche controls you. It's how unconscious patterns determine your behaviour and keep you trapped in responses that feel like free choices but are actually dictated by thoughts you don't recognise as thoughts. Because you're so fused with them, they feel like reality itself rather than interpretations that could be questioned, examined, or approached differently than the automatic fusion and belief that feels like the only possible response to mental content.

Let me be extremely clear about what I'm not saying: I'm not suggesting that thoughts don't matter, that mental content is irrelevant, or that you should ignore, suppress, or eliminate thinking. I'm not advocating for some impossible state of mindlessness, a blank consciousness without thought, or an achievement of mental silence that would require eliminating normal human cognitive function. I'm also not claiming that thoughts are never accurate, never correspond to reality, or never provide helpful information about your circumstances or internal states.

What I'm saying is this: You have a relationship with your thoughts, and that relationship is currently one of complete fusion, total identification, and absolute conflation of thoughts with truth. This fusion is causing you significant suffering, trapping you in patterns determined by mental content you don't question. It ensures that unconscious dynamics continue to operate while your consciousness remains convinced that thoughts are simply describing reality. This occurs rather than recognising that they are generated through unconscious filters that shape perception, determine interpretation, and create experiences through mechanisms operating beneath awareness.

Cognitive defusion, a core technique from Acceptance and Commitment Therapy developed by Steven Hayes, focuses on changing your relationship with thoughts. It's about creating space between you and mental content, recognising thoughts as thoughts rather than automatically fusing with them and treating them as truth. This approach doesn't advocate for the elimination of thoughts, the cessation of thinking, or transcendence of cognitive processes. It encourages you to recognise that thoughts are events occurring in your consciousness, brain-generated phenomena that you can observe rather than automatically believe. You can relate to them as thoughts instead of as unquestionable truths about reality.

Consider what happens in your experience when a thought arises. For instance, when the thought "I'm anxious" appears, you immediately, faster than conscious processing, become anxious or experience heightened anxiety if you were already somewhat activated. The thought doesn't merely describe a pre-existing state of anxiety; it creates or intensifies the anxiety through the meaning your brain attributes to it, through the interpretations that cascade from accepting this thought as truth, and through the physiological responses that activate when your brain believes this mental content accurately describes reality and requires a defensive response.

When the thought "I can't handle this" arises, it can quickly diminish your sense of capacity, erode your confidence, and decrease your willingness to engage. This thought doesn't accurately reflect your actual abilities; instead, it creates a sense of incapacity by attributing meaning to it. The predictions that follow from believing this thought shape your experience, leading to automatic behavioural responses when you become fused with the belief that you cannot cope with what you're facing.

The thought shapes your reality and generates the incapacity it claims to describe. This occurs only because you are completely fused with the idea, treating it as the absolute truth rather than simply an occurrence of thought.

What if, instead of automatically fusing with this belief, you could recognise it as just a thought? You could say to yourself, "That's just a thought. My brain is producing the thought 'I can't handle this.' That's interesting." This approach doesn't involve arguing with the thought, trying to replace it with a positive thought, or engaging in cognitive restructuring to debate its accuracy. It's just about noticing it as a thought, recognising it as a mental event, and creating a slight distance between yourself as the observer and the thought as observed content. This contrasts with the complete fusion where you identify solely with the thought, treating it as truth and allowing it to determine your experience.

This subtle shift from being consumed by thoughts to observing them, from fusion to defusion, and from automatic belief to simply recognising that thoughts are thoughts, can lead to a profound transformation in your experience. It doesn't require changing the content of your thoughts, but rather changing your relationship with them. The thought "I'm anxious" might still come up, but now you can perceive it as just a thought rather than an absolute truth about your state. You recognise it as a mental event you are observing, not as a reality you are living in. You view it as one possible interpretation instead of an accurate description that demands belief and an automatic response.

Now, let's discuss the neuroscience behind this process. Understanding what happens in your brain during fusion versus defusion clarifies why this distinction is so important. It explains how changing your relationship with thoughts can lead to dramatically different outcomes, and why a slight shift in how you relate to mental content can produce significant changes in your actual experience.

The key neural network involved is known as the default mode network (DMN). This set of interconnected brain regions activates when you are not focused on external tasks, when your attention is not directed toward specific goal-oriented activity, and when your mind is "wandering" or engaged in self-referential processing.

The DMN includes the medial prefrontal cortex, which is involved in thinking about yourself, your past and future, and your characteristics and worth. It also encompasses the posterior cingulate cortex and precuneus, regions engaged in episodic memory retrieval, imagining future scenarios, and self-referential processing. Additionally, parts of the temporal and parietal cortex are included, as they integrate information about yourself, your history, and your narrative identity.

All these regions work together to create a constant stream of mental commentary, a perpetual narrative about who you are and what everything means. This ongoing interpretation, evaluation, and judgment may uncover truth, but it actually constructs your experience through selective attention and biased processing.

When the default mode network (DMN) is highly active, the brain regions involved are strongly engaged and communicating intensely with each other. In this state, you become maximally fused with your thoughts, fully identified with your mental content, and deeply convinced that your thoughts are the truth that you are your thoughts. The activity of the DMN generates a seamless narrative where thoughts about yourself feel like absolute truths, and your stream of consciousness makes you feel like you are thinking rather than merely observing your thoughts. This is the default state for most people most of the time, as they live within the DMN's narrative, completely fused with its content and unaware that these are just thought products of the brain and one possible interpretation of reality, rather than ultimate truths.

However, there is another attentional network in the brain, known as the task-positive network (TPN) or central executive network. This network activates when you focus on specific tasks, directing your attention outward to immediate experiences and engaging in goal-directed activities that require concentration on present-moment reality rather than on mental narratives about the past, future, or self. The task-positive network includes areas like the dorsolateral prefrontal cortex, which is involved in working memory and attentional control. It also includes regions in the posterior parietal cortex that help direct attention and maintain focus, allowing for shifts between different targets of attention as necessary.

Importantly, the DMN and the task-positive network operate in opposition to each other; when one is highly active, the other is relatively suppressed. During deep engagement in task-positive network activities, when your attention is fully occupied by present-moment experiences, DMN activity decreases. This results in less narrative commentary, slowed thought production, and moments of reduced fusion with thoughts. In these instances, your attention is occupied elsewhere rather than being captured by the DMN's constant narrative.

This is why flow states feel so different from regular consciousness. Moments of intense focus provide a much-needed relief from mental chatter, and engaging in immersive activities offers a break from rumination and self-judgment. When the task-positive network is active and the DMN is suppressed, you experience reality more directly, finding yourself less fused with your thoughts. Fewer thoughts are generated, and your attention is occupied with what is immediately happening, rather than being drawn into mental commentary. This relief is a powerful reminder that a different, less mentally noisy way of experiencing consciousness is not only possible but also beneficial.

Yet, for most people most of the time, the DMN dominates. Attention is often not fully engaged with present tasks. Minds frequently wander into self-referential thinking, and the DMN generates a perpetual narrative that captures attention and creates a sense of complete fusion with the thoughts. Many remain unaware that this state is optional, that a different attentional state is possible, and that they could relate to their thoughts in a way other than the automatic fusion that feels like the only way to engage with mental content. This realisation is a powerful reminder that we have the power to change our relationship with our thoughts, to engage with them in a way that is less automatic and more intentional.

Understanding cognitive defusion hinges on recognising a third way of directing attention, distinct from the DMN's automatic narrative and its task-focused suppression. This third way is mindful awareness, a crucial element that engages brain regions in observing mental content while still allowing some DMN activity to generate thoughts for observation. Mindful awareness creates meta-awareness, enabling us to consciously perceive our thoughts as thoughts, not as unquestionable truths.

Brain imaging studies during mindfulness meditation illustrate this clearly: both DMN and attention-control regions activate simultaneously rather than one completely suppressing the other. The DMN continues generating thoughts; it is neither shut down, eliminated, nor transcended. However, regions involved in monitoring and awareness, particularly the dorsal anterior cingulate cortex and the insula, are also active. This results in a conscious observation of DMN activity, creating a space between our awareness and the content of those thoughts. This allows us to experience thoughts as phenomena to be observed rather than merging them with our sense of self.

This simultaneous activation revolutionises our experience of mental content. Thoughts still arise since the DMN remains active, but we begin to recognise them as thoughts rather than being automatically fused with and believing them. Mental events are experienced as occurrences in consciousness, rather than as undeniable truths about reality. Narratives are seen as just narratives, interpretations are recognised as interpretations, and judgments are understood as judgments rather than being experienced as facts or absolute truths that must be believed and reacted to automatically.

This phenomenon represents cognitive defusion at a neural level, maintaining awareness of our thoughts as thoughts by engaging monitoring systems while the DMN continues to generate content. It creates an observer perspective rather than complete fusion, empowering us to recognise mental events as events, rather than as unquestionable truths about reality. We are not eliminating thoughts, stopping DMN activity, or achieving an unattainable state of blank consciousness. Instead, we are shifting our relationship with our thoughts from automatic fusion and belief to observing and understanding that thoughts are brain-generated events, which may or may not be accurate, and are interpretations that can be questioned.

Developing the capacity for a defused relationship, where we maintain an observer perspective while the DMN is active, results from training our attention. This training strengthens the neural circuits that facilitate meta-awareness, thereby building pathways that support observation rather than mere identification. This is the neurological foundation of mindfulness practice; it is not merely a relaxation technique, a stress management strategy, or a spiritual pursuit of transcendence. It serves as attention training, a neural exercise that fortifies circuits supporting defusion. With repeated practice, it cultivates pathways that create space between awareness and content by engaging our observer function while the DMN continues to produce content for us to observe.

The practice of maintaining a defused relationship is deceptively simple: direct your attention to your immediate experience, often focusing on your breath, but it could be any present-moment sensation. Notice when your attention wanders to thoughts; this will happen constantly because the DMN is active and generating narratives. When you become aware that your attention has strayed, gently return it to your immediate experience by noting "thinking" or "thought," or simply recognising that your attention was captured by mental content rather than remaining on your chosen focus. Then your attention will wander again. You'll notice and return. And wander. And notice. And return. This process involves thousands of repetitions, gradually accumulating through sustained practice. It builds neural pathways that support the recognition of thoughts as thoughts by repeatedly catching our attention, drawing us into DMN narratives, and redirecting them while acknowledging the capture.

Noticing is a crucial element in the process of defusion, a gradual journey where you recognise that you have been fused with a thought, your attention has been captured by mental content, and you were believing and identifying with a narrative. This recognition creates a moment of meta-awareness, allowing you to see thoughts as just thoughts rather than experiencing them as absolute truth. Each repetition of this practice strengthens the neural pathways that support this recognition and makes the observer's perspective more accessible. Over time, you gradually develop the capacity to maintain awareness of thoughts as mere thoughts, rather than remaining perpetually fused with them without recognising that fusion is occurring.

This is why meditation practice can be challenging; maintaining focus often feels nearly impossible at first. During sessions, you might feel like you're failing because your attention has wandered countless times, and you barely managed to sustain focus for more than a few seconds. However, this wandering is not a failure; it is a natural outcome because the default mode network (DMN) is active and tends to capture attention. The practice lies in noticing when your attention wanders and returning to your focal point, creating a moment of defusion. This involves reinforcing the observer circuits by repeatedly catching yourself in a state of fusion and making a brief space before fusion re-establishes itself, leading to a recurring cycle.

Consider what this means for addressing complex thought patterns, such as harsh self-judgments, catastrophic predictions, or ruminations that can consume hours of your day, making you miserable and achieving little productive output. The traditional cognitive approach, from cognitive behavioural therapy (CBT), focuses on the content of thoughts and involves challenging their accuracy, generating alternative interpretations, and evaluating evidence for and against particular beliefs. This method can be helpful and can create significant shifts in your thinking, but it often requires engaging with the content of your thoughts. This means treating thoughts as substantial enough to warrant debate and assuming they are potentially accurate descriptions of reality that need evaluation.

For many individuals, engaging with content can inadvertently strengthen fusion rather than create defusion. By arguing with thoughts, you treat them as crucial enough to refute, maintaining an assumption that they are truths or falsehoods that need distinguishing, rather than recognising them as just thoughts, mental events or brain-generated phenomena that don't necessarily deserve the extensive attention and belief you typically grant them.

Cognitive defusion offers a different approach: don't engage with the content of your thoughts. Don't debate their accuracy or generate alternative interpretations. Instead, simply recognise that an idea is occurring. Notice, for instance, "My brain is producing the thought that I am worthless," rather than internalising it as "I am worthless" as an absolute truth. Observe, "The catastrophic prediction is occurring," instead of believing that "A catastrophe is definitely coming." Acknowledge that "Self-judgment is arising," rather than accepting it as "I am inadequate" as reality. This approach fosters a non-judgmental, compassionate view of your thoughts and feelings.

Shifting from engaging with content to recognising the process, from believing thoughts to observing thoughts, and from treating mental events as truths to recognising them as events is a crucial step in cognitive defusion. This transformation occurs not by changing the content itself, but by changing how you relate to it. For instance, the thought "I'm worthless" might still arise, and your default mode network (DMN) may generate this judgment. However, now you experience it as a thought occurring rather than as a truth about your worth. You observe it as a mental event rather than a reality you inhabit. As one possible interpretation, your brain is producing an inaccurate assessment that you must believe and organise your behaviour around.

Now, let's delve into specific cognitive defusion techniques. Understanding the principle is different from having practical methods for creating defusion when you're captured by complex thoughts. When defusion is complete, your mental content no longer determines your emotional state and behaviour, and you are no longer completely identified with those thoughts, convinced they are the truth. These techniques may seem silly or awkward, and they trigger resistance because they trivialise serious thoughts. But that's precisely the point: to create enough distance from thoughts so that you can see them as just thoughts rather than as truths, reducing defusion enough that space emerges between awareness and content.

One of the simplest techniques is to add the prefix "I'm having the thought that..." to your thoughts. Instead of saying "I'm anxious," recognise it as "I'm having the thought that I'm anxious." Instead of "I'm going to fail," notice "I'm having the thought that I'm going to fail." Instead of "I can't handle this," observe "I'm having the thought that I can't handle this." The content remains unchanged; you are not altering the thought, arguing with it, or trying to replace it with something more positive. Instead, the relationship changes through the recognition that this is a thought occurring rather than a truth being revealed. This creates linguistic space between you and the content, highlighting that you are experiencing thoughts rather than being those thoughts.

Another technique is to thank your mind for the thought. When harsh self-judgment arises, acknowledge it by saying, "Thank you, mind, for that judgment." When catastrophic predictions appear, notice, "Thank you, mind, for that prediction." The content is not being challenged; you are not claiming the judgment is wrong or the prediction is inaccurate. Instead, you create defusion by recognising these are products your mind generates rather than truths being discovered. This allows you to relate to thoughts as brain-generated events you can observe and even appreciate for their protective intent without necessarily believing they are accurate descriptions of reality.

You can also name the story your mind is telling. For example, you might say, "Ah, there's the 'I'm not good enough' story again." You might notice, "I see the 'something terrible is about to happen' story." Or, "The 'everyone is judging me' story is playing." The thought content remains the same, but by relating these thoughts to familiar patterns your mind produces as stories, you create distance from believing they are unique insights or accurate perceptions. You recognise these are old patterns and familiar narratives that may have little to do with current reality and everything to do with historical programming.

Another technique involves visualising thoughts as external to you. Imagine them written on leaves floating down a stream, appearing on a screen you are watching, or spoken by a radio you are listening to. This visualisation creates spatial separation, representing the psychological separation that diffusion cultivates. Thoughts are over there, being observed, rather than being fused with you as truth and reality itself. The specific visualisation is less important than the function it serves in creating a felt sense of distance between awareness and content.

Finally, you can say your thoughts in a silly voice. For example, you might hear "I'm worthless" in a cartoon voice, as a song, or in an accent very different from your own. This may seem ridiculous or trivialise serious content, and it may feel inappropriate for thoughts that seem devastating. But that's precisely why it works for defusion. By relating to thoughts in a silly way, you break the fusion, interrupt the automatic belief, and recognise that this is just a thought, just mental content, just words your brain is producing that don't automatically deserve the profound belief and intense emotional response they trigger when you are completely fused with them.

All of these techniques serve a common purpose: to foster recognition that thoughts are merely thoughts, to develop the capacity for an observer perspective, and to interrupt automatic fusion by highlighting the distance between awareness and thought content, something that fusion typically makes invisible. These techniques are not designed to eliminate thoughts, prevent difficult content from arising, or ensure only positive interpretations emerge in your mind. Instead, their goal is to change your relationship with whatever content presents itself. They encourage you to recognise thoughts as just that, thoughts, observing them as mental events generated by the brain, rather than automatically fusing with them and treating them as unquestionable truths about reality.

However, it is vital to understand that these techniques work effectively only when you remember to use them. They need sufficient awareness to recognise that fusion is occurring and enough resources to engage with the method, rather than being entirely consumed by content. Building this capacity involves developing the awareness that detects when fusion happens, strengthening the neural circuits that facilitate the observer perspective, and creating the neural architecture that supports defusion. This process requires sustained practice, regular mindfulness exercises, and thousands of repetitions to establish pathways that make recognising thoughts as thoughts increasingly automatic, rather than a challenge each time.

Consider learning any skill: initially, each element demands conscious attention, significant effort, and explicit focus. However, through repeated practice and the accumulation of repetitions that build neural pathways, certain aspects become automatic and require less conscious effort, operating with increasing fluency. The same principle applies to cognitive defusion. At first, recognising thoughts as thoughts requires substantial effort, feels awkward and unnatural, and demands continuous attention to maintain the observer perspective. Yet, with sustained practice, including regular meditation to build relevant neural circuits and repeated instances of noticing fusion and creating defusion, the capacity strengthens. It becomes more accessible and requires less effort, although it never becomes entirely automatic, as the default mode network continues producing content designed to capture attention and create fusion.

This recognition means that the work calls for a commitment to regular practice and systematic training of attention, rather than just sporadically applying techniques when you remember. It requires building the neural infrastructure that supports defusion through consistent engagement over months and years, rather than relying on occasional practice to enhance your capacity for defusion when overwhelmed by difficult content. While the techniques are valuable and provide methods for creating defusion during moments of awareness, developing the ability to recognise when defusion is necessary, reinforcing the circuits that maintain the observer perspective, and establishing the neural pathways that render defusion accessible even when activated require ongoing attention, training, and regular mindfulness practice. This is a commitment to building your capacity, not merely applying techniques occasionally and questioning why they fail to create lasting change.

Now, let's connect this back to your obscure psyche. Cognitive defusion is essential for engaging with unconscious material; it helps you recognise when thoughts are generated by shadow dynamics. It creates the space between awareness and content that allows you to see thoughts as products of unconscious patterns rather than as truths reflecting reality. Your shadow continuously generates thoughts, harsh self-judgments stemming from disowned inadequacies, projections attributing traits to others that you cannot accept in yourself, and defences crafting narratives that maintain splitting. At the same time, consciousness remains unaware that these are defensive operations rather than accurate perceptions.

When you become completely absorbed in your thoughts, believing them automatically and treating the narratives created by unconscious influences as truths, you lose the ability to recognise the shadow at play. In this state, you cannot see that your thoughts are being shaped by dynamics you do not consciously acknowledge, nor are you aware that this mental content serves to maintain defences, protect your identity, and avoid integration, which can feel threatening. This fusion obscures the shadow and allows unconscious patterns to dictate your experience, leading consciousness to believe that thoughts simply reflect reality rather than being generated by underlying dynamics that serve unrecognised functions.

On the other hand, defusion liberates you to recognise the shadow. You can learn to identify thoughts like "That judgment arises from my need to maintain separation," "That criticism reflects something I've disowned," or "That projection reveals something about myself rather than accurately depicting the other person."

Defusion doesn't erase shadow material, automatically bring unconscious patterns to light, or transcend dynamics through enlightenment. However, it creates an observer position from which you can spot patterns as they emerge. The thoughts are seen as products of dynamics, not truths about reality, creating a space between awareness and content. This space allows you to engage with your material rather than being controlled by it, all while believing you are perceiving reality accurately.

Consider the self-critical thoughts and harsh judgments your mind generates about your worth, capabilities, and acceptability. These thoughts are not neutral assessments, objective evaluations, or accurate descriptions of reality. They are manifestations of your shadow, specifically, products of a harsh superego, internalised critical voices, disowned material turned against yourself, and defences that uphold an identity, even when that identity causes suffering. When you are fused with these thoughts, believing them automatically and considering them truths to be discovered, you cannot recognise their origins or work with them as shadow material. However, once you do, you'll find relief in understanding that these thoughts are not a true reflection of your worth or capabilities, but rather a product of unconscious dynamics.

Defusion, however, paves the way for a different approach. It allows you to view these thoughts as occurrences, not as truths. This shift in perspective opens up a space for inquiry: Where is this judgment coming from? What function does it serve? What dynamics are producing this particular narrative? What would I need to acknowledge about myself if I did not maintain this critical stance? Defusion doesn't provide the answers to these questions; it creates an environment where such questions become possible. It encourages exploration and helps you begin to see patterns as patterns, rather than remaining fused with content, unaware that it is generated by unconscious dynamics.

Consider catastrophic predictions, those anxious thoughts about dreadful futures that your mind generates incessantly. These thoughts are not realistic assessments of probability; they don't serve as helpful preparations for actual threats, nor do they fit the adaptive function of keeping you safe. Instead, they stem from anxious attachment and trauma responses that maintain hypervigilance. These patterns ensure you remain in a state of heightened alertness because past experiences have coded relaxation as dangerous; letting your guard down has previously led to threats. Understanding and practising defusion can play a crucial role in managing these anxiety-driven predictions and in shadow work.

When you become fused with these predictions, believing them automatically and organising your behaviour around them as if they are accurate forecasts, you lose the capacity to recognise that they are merely products of dynamics unrelated to your current circumstances. You fail to see that these predictions arise from historical programming rather than realistic assessments of present danger.

However, through defusion, you can recognise that these are just thoughts occurring in your mind rather than truths about the future. This realisation brings a sense of relief, creating space for you to investigate the actual basis for these predictions. You can learn to differentiate between realistic threat assessments and anxiety-driven catastrophising, as well as recognise when predictions are influenced by trauma patterns instead of being informed assessments of potential negative outcomes.

Defusion does not automatically provide this recognition or eliminate anxiety-generated predictions, but it establishes conditions under which investigation becomes possible. Instead of allowing automatic fusion and belief to dictate behaviour while consciousness remains convinced that these predictions are realistic, you can start to understand that they are merely generated by unconscious patterns. These patterns may have been adaptive in the past, but are inappropriate in the current reality.

This is why defusion is an essential practice for anyone engaging in serious shadow work. It aids in the integration of unconscious material and the recognition of patterns, rather than being unconsciously controlled by them. The fusion of awareness and content is a primary mechanism through which the shadow remains obscure, allowing unconscious patterns to continue dictating experience. Meanwhile, consciousness mistakenly believes it is accurately perceiving reality. As a result, the thoughts generated by dynamics you don't recognise shape your behaviour while you remain convinced that you're making free choices based on accurate assessments. Defusion, in this context, is a powerful tool to break free from these unconscious patterns and gain control over your choices and actions.

Building a capacity for defusion is a gradual process that involves strengthening the pathways that support an observer perspective and training your attention to recognise thoughts as just thoughts. This process demands sustained practice and patience, requiring regular engagement with attention training rather than occasional application of techniques when you remember. The path to defusion lies in consistent mindfulness practice, not merely as a spiritual pursuit or relaxation technique, but as systematic attention training that builds the neural infrastructure supporting defusion. This is achieved through the repeated practice of capturing your attention with content and redirecting it while acknowledging the capture.

Start with brief and regular practice rather than infrequent, long sessions. Practising for ten minutes each day builds greater capacity than an hour once a week. This is because progress occurs through accumulated repetitions and regular engagement, which strengthen relevant neural circuits. Consistent practice fosters lasting neuroplastic change, while occasional intense efforts do not provide enough repetitions to create enduring pathways.

The practice itself is simple but not easy: sit quietly, direct your attention to your breath or another immediate sensation, notice when your attention drifts to thoughts, and gently return your focus, acknowledging the wandering of your mind. Repeat this thousands of times over months and years; this gradual accumulation, while it may seem slow at times, builds capacity that emerges slowly through sustained practice, rather than appearing suddenly from rare, intense efforts.

It's also essential to practice when you're relatively calm and have the necessary resources available. Building new pathways requires these resources, which are unavailable when you're in a defensive state, when your amygdala has taken over, flooding you with stress. You cannot build capacity for defusion during a crisis; you develop it through regular practice in conditions of relative safety and calm. This strengthens your neural circuits while resources are available, making it easier to observe your thoughts even when resources are limited. This way, you can maintain an observer perspective even when you're somewhat activated, rather than needing perfect conditions, conditions that rarely exist when defusion capacity is most necessary.

This means you should treat attention training as a serious practice that deserves regular commitment, rather than as an optional activity you engage in only when you feel like it or when you're particularly stressed. Capacity builds through regular practice, regardless of whether you feel motivated, whether the sessions feel productive, or whether you're experiencing immediate benefits. Neuroplastic change happens through repeated engagement over time, creating the infrastructure that supports defusion, irrespective of whether individual sessions feel successful or provide immediate relief from challenging mental content.

Welcome to understanding cognitive defusion: the distinction between being absorbed in thoughts and observing them. This involves grasping the neural mechanisms that differentiate fusion from observer perspective and undertaking the attention training necessary to build the capacity to recognise thoughts as mere thoughts, rather than automatically believing them and organising behaviour around narratives that consciousness doesn't realise are generated by unconscious dynamics, rather than stemming from an accurate perception of reality. Your Default Mode Network continuously generates narratives that capture your attention and create complete fusion. At the same time, you remain unaware that this fusion is occurring, that thoughts are merely thoughts, not truths, and that a different relationship with mental content is possible.

The work involves training attention through regular mindfulness practice. This process builds neural circuits that support an observer's perspective through repeated engagement. It develops the capacity for defusion through consistent practice over months and years, rather than expecting occasional techniques to bring about lasting change. As this capacity strengthens gradually, it becomes more accessible and requires less effort. However, it never becomes completely automatic because the Default Mode Network (DMN), a key player in our mental processes, continues to produce content designed to capture attention. The DMN generates narratives intended to be believed, creating a fusion of thoughts that can feel like undeniable truths. This leads to a lack of recognition that thoughts are merely brain-generated events that may serve unconscious purposes, rather than accurately describing current reality.

Your Obscure Psyche operates by capturing your attention with the content it generates, ensuring complete fusion so that thoughts are automatically believed. In this context, 'fusion' refers to the process of unquestioned belief in thoughts. It prevents the recognition that mental events are just events rather than absolute truths. As a result, shadow material continues to influence experience while consciousness remains convinced it is accurately perceiving reality. Instead of recognising that it's being controlled by patterns operating beneath awareness, the mind generates mental content that goes unquestioned because the fusion makes questioning impossible. Thoughts are experienced as self, as truth, and as reality itself, rather than as observable phenomena that could be understood differently if the capacity for observation were developed. This systematic attention training builds the neural infrastructure that supports defusion, rather than maintaining the automatic fusion that keeps the shadow obscure while consciousness believes thoughts are truths. Ultimately, this can obscure a deeper understanding of unconscious dynamics that might reveal more about our experience than about actual reality.

Chapter 18

The Inner Cinema: Dream Work and Active Imagination

Reflect on the dream you may of had last night. If you're someone who says, "I don't dream" or "I never remember my dreams," that's not actually accurate. Everyone dreams every night, multiple times, spending about two hours in REM sleep where vivid dreams occur, whether we recall them or not. What you might really mean is, "I don't remember my dreams," or more precisely, "I don't pay attention to my dreams, don't value them enough to make an effort to recall them, and don't believe they matter sufficiently to prioritize remembering them over checking my phone or diving into the day's demands as soon as I wake up."

Now, let's assume you do remember a dream, even if it's just a fragment, perhaps a bizarre scenario, an impossible situation, or a strange mix of people and places that defy logic and violate everyday reality. It felt vivid and meaningful while you were experiencing it, yet it dissolved into incoherence the moment you tried to explain it to someone else. You might have dismissed it as "just a weird dream" and forgotten it because dreams often seem unimportant or irrelevant to our waking lives. They don't appear to hold any value compared to the pressing concerns that demand our attention.

Here's a thought that might deeply unsettle you: What if that dream, whatever strange scenario your brain concocted while you slept, was your subconscious mind trying to communicate with you? It could be presenting a symbolic representation of feelings or truths that are difficult to express directly, revealing through imagery and narrative what remains hidden from your conscious awareness. It might be attempting to share critical information about your psychological state that your waking mind refuses to acknowledge, shielded by patterns of denial and repression.

What if your dreams aren't random neural noise, meaningless side effects of memory consolidation, or merely your brain dumping irrelevant information while it processes the day's experiences? What if they are actually a primary communication channel for your unconscious mind? This is the space where unresolved issues can express themselves without triggering defensive responses, a medium through which your psyche seeks to reveal what you cannot confront consciously because recognising it would threaten your identity, require you to face what you've disowned, or demand integration work you're not ready to undertake while awake and defended, protecting rigid ego boundaries.

Consider your recurring dreams, the nightmares that return periodically, or the dream themes that appear repeatedly over the years, even if the specific content changes. These might include dreams where you're unprepared for an exam you forgot, where you're trying to run but your legs won't move, where you're attempting to scream but no sound escapes, or where you're desperately searching for something you've lost. You might dream of being naked in public, falling endlessly, or being chased by an unknown threat. Sometimes familiar people appear in unfamiliar ways, or commonplace places are rearranged in impossible configurations. You may also experience dreams where you perform actions that defy the laws of physics while accepting these impossibilities as completely usual within the logic of the dream.

These dreams are not random; your brain is not just generating scenarios at random. They are symbolic representations of psychological material that cannot find direct expression. Your unconscious mind is trying to show you, in metaphorical form, what it cannot articulate directly. They serve as compensatory messages from parts of your psyche that have been excluded from your waking consciousness but still exist, continue to demand acknowledgement, and seek expression through the only channel available when your waking defences are down, in the dream world. Here, symbolic logic reigns, impossible combinations can make perfect sense, and your unconscious can speak in its own language without eliciting the defensive responses that would arise if this material attempted direct expression while you were awake.

You often ignore this communication, dismissing these messages and treating dreams as meaningless entertainment, annoying disturbances, or at best, curious experiences you might mention casually. Yet you remain completely uninterested in what they might mean or reveal, ignoring the crucial information your unconscious is attempting to convey through its primary language: the symbolic, imagistic narrative of dreams. This language operates under a different logic than waking rational thought, expressing truth through metaphor rather than direct statements. It shows rather than tells, creating an experience of meaning instead of providing explicit explanations.

By ignoring your dreams and treating them as irrelevant, you are fundamentally alienating yourself from a vast part of who you are. You cut yourself off from crucial information about your psychological state, ensuring that 'shadow material', which could be unresolved conflicts, repressed emotions, or unacknowledged desires, remains unconscious while still influencing your behaviour and shaping your experiences through mechanisms you do not recognise, because you refuse to pay attention to the one area where your unconscious can express itself freely, without triggering the defences that keep it separate during waking consciousness.

Let's delve into the neuroscience. Understanding what happens in your brain during REM (Rapid Eye Movement) sleep empowers you with insights into why dreams are so important. They are not mystical experiences but essential psychological processes that reveal material inaccessible through other means. REM sleep, the stage of most vivid dreaming, sees your brain nearly as active as when you're awake, but with a different organisation. Certain regions are hyperactive, while others are relatively suppressed, creating conditions for unconscious material to express itself without the constraints and defences of waking consciousness.

During REM sleep, your Default Mode Network (DMN), which is the collection of brain regions responsible for generating self-referential narratives and ongoing mental commentary about who you are and what everything means, is extraordinarily active. At the same time, your dorsolateral prefrontal cortex, the area involved in logical reasoning, reality testing, executive control, and maintaining rational thought patterns, is relatively deactivated. This unique combination creates optimal conditions for the expression of unconscious material: the DMN produces narrative and self-referential content as it always does, but without the logical and reality-testing constraints that filter its output during waking consciousness.

Additionally, the amygdala, our threat detection system and emotional processing centre, is highly active during REM sleep, often more so than during waking hours. This heightened activity means that emotional processing occurs intensely, with emotional material being activated and expressed without the regulatory mechanisms that usually control emotional expression while we are awake. Importantly, the neurotransmitters that dominate during waking consciousness, particularly norepinephrine and serotonin, which are crucial for focused attention and mood regulation, are absent during REM sleep. Instead, acetylcholine takes over, creating conditions where memory networks are highly active. Under these circumstances, associations are looser and more creative rather than logical and constrained, allowing material from different time periods and contexts to combine in ways that would be impossible during waking consciousness.

This neurological state creates ideal conditions for the symbolic expression of unconscious material. Your default mode network (DMN) is generating narratives, but without the rational constraints that typically ensure logical coherence. Reality testing, which limits what combinations are possible, is absent, as is the executive control that maintains standard waking thought patterns. Emotional centres are active, processing feelings that may be defended against while awake. Memory networks are activated, but they operate through loose associative connections rather than through logical retrieval, allowing material from different periods to symbolically combine. In these conditions, unconscious associations determine what appears together, rather than conscious control selecting what is relevant.

The result is bizarre, impossible, emotionally intense, and symbolically meaningful narratives that your brain generates every night when these specific neurological conditions are present. These narratives reveal emotional truths through symbolic expression rather than direct statements. They showcase psychological material that cannot be expressed during waking consciousness because your defences, rational mind, reality testing, and executive control suppress material that threatens ego stability, contradicts self-concept, or requires integration work that you are not consciously ready to undertake.

Now, let's discuss Jung's concept of symbolic compensation, which sheds light on what dreams actually accomplish, why they contain specific content, and what function they serve in your psychological economy. Jung observed that dreams tend to compensate for one-sidedness in conscious attitudes. They present material that balances, contradicts, or complements what consciousness maintains, revealing what has been excluded from waking awareness. In contrast, consciousness holds particular identities, perspectives, or ways of understanding oneself and one's circumstances.

If your conscious attitude is inflated, if you maintain a grandiose self-concept and identify with being consequential, special, or superior, your dreams will compensate by presenting material that highlights your vulnerabilities, limitations, ordinariness, and dependence on others. This is not to punish you or because your unconscious is cruel; instead, it's because sustaining this one-sided conscious attitude requires suppressing all the material that contradicts it. This suppressed material, which we refer to as 'shadow material' or the parts of yourself you don't want to acknowledge, continues to exist, demanding acknowledgement and seeking expression through dreams that compensate for the imbalance in your consciousness.

By understanding the empowering nature of dream interpretation, you can gain a sense of control and self-awareness. Suppose your conscious attitude is excessively humble, and you're identified with feelings of inadequacy, maintaining a self-concept based on limitation and incapacity. In that case, your dreams will compensate by showcasing the strengths, capabilities, and potential you deny while identifying with a limited, inferior self. These dreams reveal what you have disowned by identifying completely with the opposite, showing you the 'golden shadow' material we discussed earlier, and presenting capabilities and strengths that contradict your conscious identity as limited or incapable.

If your conscious life is overly rational, if you see yourself as logical and analytical, and have suppressed emotional and intuitive aspects, your dreams will compensate by being highly emotional, deeply symbolic, and rich with feelings and imagery that demand engagement with non-rational ways of knowing. The dreams aim to balance the one-sidedness by reintroducing what has been excluded. They show you that human experience encompasses more than just rational thought; it also includes dimensions you are systematically ignoring while maintaining an identity as a purely logical being.

It's important to acknowledge and integrate shadow material to feel encouraged and supported in your self-awareness journey. This compensation isn't a conscious choice; it's an automatic function of how your psyche seeks balance. The unconscious material that has been excluded continues to seek expression, and shadow content that has been disowned demands acknowledgement through the only channel available when conscious defences are offline. Your dreams reveal what you cannot see while awake, presenting in symbolic form what would be too threatening to acknowledge directly if you remain defended and identified with a particular ego position.

Consider nightmares not as random terror, but as urgent communications from your unconscious. They represent shadow material that has become so charged through continued suppression that it erupts with an intensity that cannot be ignored. These nightmares act as compensatory messages, becoming desperate because your conscious attitude has become overly one-sided, defended, and rigid. This leads you to ignore gentler communications while maintaining patterns that create an imbalance demanding urgent correction. By understanding the transformative potential of nightmares, you can feel hopeful and motivated for change.

The content of nightmares reveals what is most threatening to your conscious attitude, what you defend against powerfully, and what creates the most psychological distress by remaining split off and unintegrated. For instance, if you are being chased by a threatening figure, consider which aspect of yourself you are fleeing from and which disowned quality is pursuing you, demanding acknowledgement. What shadow material have you transformed into a monstrous form by completely disowning it while insisting it's something external threatening you, rather than recognising it as part of yourself that you cannot acknowledge? Similarly, if you feel unprepared, exposed, or humiliated, consider what vulnerability you are desperately defending against while maintaining a facade of competence, adequacy, or acceptability. What authentic aspect are you hiding behind the constructed persona that dreams reveal while your defence mechanisms are offline?

The nightmare is an urgent call from your unconscious, demanding recognition for something you've been systematically avoiding. Its intensity is designed to prevent you from dismissing its message as easily as you would a gentler communication. Yet, many people choose to forget their nightmares, attributing them to random neural misfiring. Some even resort to medication to suppress these experiences, failing to realise that their unconscious is desperately trying to communicate. The intensity of these nightmares increases because gentler approaches are being completely ignored, while consciousness maintains rigid defences against the material that dreams are attempting to reveal.

Now, let's talk about dream symbols. Understanding how symbolic language works is essential for engaging with dreams in a meaningful way. Taking them literally misses the point entirely, while dismissing them as meaningless disregards their significance because they don't always align with the logical interpretations of waking reality. Dream symbols are not codes with universal fixed meanings; they are multi-layered and emotionally meaningful. For example, a snake doesn't always mean one thing, water doesn't always mean another, and a house doesn't always represent a specific third meaning, as if there were a dream dictionary to provide an independent interpretation of any symbol.

Symbols in dreams are not just random images; they are overdetermined, containing multiple meanings at once. They express emotional truths that cannot be captured by a single rational explanation. The significance of a symbol lies in its capacity for multiple interpretations, its ability to hold contradictions simultaneously, and its ability to convey complex ideas that would require extensive elaboration if stated directly. Instead, these ideas can be immediately experienced through symbolic images, which bypass rational thought and connect directly to emotional and intuitive understanding.

When interpreting symbols in your own dreams, it's crucial to consider the context. For instance, a figure resembling your father might appear, but he's not an exact replica. He might have your father's face but different characteristics, or he might have a different name, even though you know he is your father. This isn't confusion or error; it's a symbolic expression showing that this figure represents both your actual father and the internalised father figure you carry. This symbol condenses multiple meanings into a single dream figure, capturing complexities that a literal representation could never convey.

Another example might involve being in your childhood home, but it's arranged differently, with rooms that didn't exist in the actual house and opening onto impossible landscapes. The house doesn't serve as a literal representation of a physical building; instead, it acts as a symbolic representation of your psyche, your internal dwelling and psychological home. The rooms that didn't exist reflect aspects of yourself that you haven't explored, while the impossible geography highlights a psychological truth about how your inner world is organised. This representation does not aim to align with the spatial logic of waking reality, which does not apply to the psychological truths that dreams are trying to express.

The key to understanding dream symbols lies in recognising that they express emotional and psychological truths through metaphorical language. Rather than providing direct statements, dreams convey relationships, dynamics, and internal states through images and narratives. Engaging with the symbolic meaning of dreams is essential, rather than trying to interpret them literally. Consider the feelings the symbol evokes. For instance, a snake might evoke fear or danger. What associations do you have with this particular image? A snake could be associated with transformation or healing. What qualities or characteristics does the symbol embody? A snake might embody stealth or change. What aspect of yourself or your life might it represent metaphorically rather than literally? A snake might represent a hidden fear or a need for change.

This requires a shift from the rational analytical mind, which seeks clear explanations and logical interpretations, to an intuitive, receptive mind. The latter can tolerate ambiguity, allowing for multiple meanings to coexist. It can resonate with symbols rather than demanding intellectual clarity. Dreams communicate in the language of the unconscious, symbolic, imagistic, emotional, and paradoxical. Attempting to translate these dreams into rational, logical language often loses the very meanings they convey. The true meaning resides within the symbol itself, in the emotional resonance it produces, rather than in any rational explanation constructed afterwards.

Now, let's discuss active imagination, a practice developed by Jung for deliberately engaging with unconscious material. This technique allows for a dialogue with the shadow aspects of the psyche and facilitates work with symbolic images while awake. Active imagination is distinct from passive fantasy, which is a form of daydreaming or imagining without conscious control, and directed visualisation, which is a technique used in hypnotherapy. It involves maintaining conscious awareness while allowing unconscious material to emerge spontaneously, rather than being controlled by the ego. Additionally, it's not about visualising predetermined scenarios; it requires an open approach that lets images and narratives develop on their own.

The practice involves entering a liminal state between waking and sleeping, between conscious control and unconscious spontaneity. You should be aware enough to observe and engage with whatever emerges while remaining receptive to the spontaneous output of the unconscious. Start with an image from a dream, a symbolic figure that has appeared repeatedly, or a personification of an emotion or quality you wish to engage. Allow this image to develop, to move, to speak, and to reveal itself while maintaining the role of an observer conscious enough to witness but receptive enough to avoid controlling the experience.

This process can be complicated because your ego tends to want control. It seeks to direct, ensure nothing threatening emerges, and maintain safety by dictating what appears and what happens. However, active imagination requires you to liberate yourself from this control while keeping enough consciousness to actively engage with what arises. This means asking questions, responding to what emerges, and creating a dialogue rather than either controlling the content or being a passive recipient of unconscious material.

To illustrate how this works, imagine you've had recurring dreams of being chased by a threatening dark figure. In active imagination, you would start by visualising this figure while you are awake and conscious. Instead of fleeing as you do in your dreams, you would turn and face it, asking questions such as, "Who are you? What do you want? Why are you pursuing me?" Importantly, you would wait for a response, not generate the response you think should come, nor decide intellectually what the figure represents or what it would say. Instead, allow the response to emerge spontaneously from the unconscious. Let the figure speak in its own voice and reveal itself rather than imposing your conscious interpretation onto it. This requires patience and receptivity, creating a calm and open-minded atmosphere for the process.

As you engage with the figure, be prepared for potential transformations. What initially appears as a threatening monster might unveil itself as a wounded child, disowned strength, or a quality you've rejected that is now demanding acknowledgement. Or it may persist in its threatening form, but reveal what it's protecting you from, what it's trying to warn you about, and what function it serves that you haven't recognised while viewing it solely as a threat. The aim is not to reach a predetermined understanding, but to foster genuine dialogue with unconscious material. This involves allowing shadow aspects to speak and be heard, engaging with disowned parts rather than remaining alienated from them, which can lead to their influence operating outside of conscious awareness.

However, this practice carries inherent dangers that should be acknowledged. Deliberately engaging with unconscious material, opening yourself to shadow content, and allowing disowned aspects to emerge and express themselves can be overwhelming. It can activate material that you are not ready to integrate or flood your consciousness with content that your defensive structures are designed to protect you from. This is why active imagination is not suitable for everyone; it requires sufficient ego strength to engage with the unconscious without becoming overwhelmed. It is often best practised initially with the guidance of a therapist trained in these methods rather than diving into deep unconscious work alone without support or skills to manage what may emerge.

Some individuals should not attempt active imagination: those with fragile ego boundaries, those prone to psychosis, those currently in crisis, and those lacking adequate support systems. For these individuals, deliberately opening to the unconscious can exacerbate difficulties rather than facilitate integration; it can lead to flooding rather than dialogue, activating material without providing the means to work with it constructively. This is not gatekeeping or suggesting that unconscious work is only for the elite; rather, it is recognising that different methods are appropriate for different psychological structures. What facilitates integration for someone with strong ego function may cause fragmentation for someone with a more fragile psychological structure.

For those who can safely engage with it, active imagination offers direct access to unconscious material. It creates opportunities for dialogue with shadow aspects and allows for conscious engagement with symbolic content, rather than remaining a passive recipient of dream messages that are difficult to understand. You are not merely receiving communications from your unconscious while asleep; you are deliberately entering an imaginal space where the conscious and unconscious can meet, where the ego and shadow can have a dialogue, and where integration can begin through the conscious engagement with material that typically remains split off. At the same time, you maintain waking consciousness and its defensive structures.

Now, let's discuss practical steps for dream work, how to actually engage with dreams rather than just intellectually understanding their importance. The first step is remembering dreams, which many people find difficult or impossible. In reality, they might not be prioritising it or creating conditions that support dream recall. They may not value dreams enough to put in the effort required to build the capacity to remember them.

Dreams are most accessible in the moments immediately upon waking, before you fully transition back into waking consciousness, before the rational mind activates and organises experiences according to logical categories that dreams do not fit into. This means that the crucial period for dream recall is the transition between sleeping and waking. What you do in these moments determines whether your dreams remain accessible or dissolve completely as you shift into a waking consciousness that is organised differently than dream consciousness.

The practice is straightforward but demands discipline: keep a physical journal beside your bed, not a digital one, which can immediately pull you into waking consciousness with notifications and demands, activating your rational problem-solving mind. Upon waking, before moving, before fully opening your eyes, and before engaging with the external world, lie still and try to recall the dream. Don't try to interpret it, don't attempt to make sense of it, and don't judge whether it is interesting or important. Just focus on recalling as much detail as possible, the images, the feelings, the narrative, the specific sensations, the emotional quality, and the bizarre details that made no rational sense but were vivid in the dream.

Immediately write down your dream upon waking, not later, not after coffee, checking your phone, or completing your morning routine. Write it down while the recall is fresh and before you fully transition into waking consciousness, which may dismiss dreams as irrelevant or too chaotic to record. Use the present tense: "I'm in my childhood home, but it's different; there are additional rooms I've never seen." Writing in the present tense maintains the immediacy of the dream experience and keeps you connected to the feelings of being in the dream. In contrast, using the past tense creates distance, making it feel like something that happened rather than an experience you're still connected to.

Include everything you can remember, regardless of how trivial or meaningless it seems. Note the specific colours, emotional tones, and minor details that might feel unimportant. Dreams communicate through imagery and specific information, which can carry symbolic weight. That particular shade of blue, the appearance of a specific person in a nonsensical context, or an odd detail about the shape of a doorway, all of these might have symbolic significance that you might not recognise when your rational mind dismisses them as irrelevant.

Write without censoring or judging, and avoid trying to make the dream coherent or interesting. Capture the experience as accurately as possible while it's still accessible, while you're still partly in the liminal space between sleeping and waking. Liminal space refers to the in-between state, where dream logic still makes sense, even though your rational mind hasn't fully activated. This is the ideal time to record your dreams. This practice, committing to record your dreams immediately upon waking, dramatically increases dream recall over time because you signal to your unconscious that you value this communication and are willing to receive the messages it sends every night, whether or not you've been listening.

After recording your dream, take the time to delve into its meaning. This is not a task to be rushed or squeezed into the busy moments of your morning routine. Instead, set aside a quiet evening, when the day's demands are over, to revisit your dream and begin to unravel its significance. By resisting the urge to interpret it immediately, you open the door to a deeper understanding of yourself and your subconscious. This is not just dream analysis, it's a journey of self-discovery.

Instead, start with associations. Take specific images, symbols, or figures from the dream and free associate what comes to mind when you think of these images. Free association is a psychoanalytic technique in which a person is encouraged to relate whatever comes into their mind without censorship or filtering. What feelings do they evoke? What memories, experiences, or qualities do they bring to mind? Follow these associations without judging them, and without deciding whether they are relevant or correct. This method reveals the personal meaning of the symbols. It helps you understand what these images represent for you specifically, rather than assuming universal meanings that might not apply to your individual psychological situation.

When delving into the emotional landscape of your dreams, it's crucial to reflect on the feelings that were present: fear, joy, confusion, shame, excitement, or dread. What was the overall emotional tone? Emotions often hold more weight than the narrative content, offering a deeper insight into your psychological state than the specific events of the dream. For instance, a dream about failing an exam might not be about academic performance, but rather about feelings of shame, inadequacy, or the fear of being exposed as incompetent. In this case, the emotional core of the dream uses the exam scenario symbolically, shedding light on your psychological concerns.

Next, examine the idea of compensation. What is this dream balancing? What one-sidedness in your waking life is it correcting? What material have you been excluding? Suppose you have been maintaining a particular conscious attitude or identifying with a certain way of being while suppressing certain aspects of yourself. What is the dream showing you that contradicts, completes, or challenges this conscious position? The dream is attempting to restore balance by reintroducing what has been excluded and compensating for the imbalances your consciousness maintains through its defensive structures.

Also, consider the dream-ego, which is the version of you within the dream. How are you responding? What actions are you taking or not taking? The dream-ego often reveals how your ego actually functions in response to challenges, threats, or opportunities, rather than how you would like to believe you respond. Are you passive in your dreams, unable to take action or frozen while events unfold around you? This behaviour indicates that your ego may be functioning differently than you consciously claim. Alternatively, if you are aggressive or confrontational in dreams, this might reveal a disowned capacity for assertiveness or aggression that remains split off from your waking self.

It's essential to resist the temptation to jump to conclusions about your dreams. Don't assume you've fully understood what your dream means and that you're done analysing it. Dreams are a continuous journey; you can revisit the same dream multiple times and uncover new meanings, associations, and insights as your consciousness evolves. The meaning you grasp today may be accurate, but it may only scratch the surface. Deeper meanings might become clear later, especially when you have done more integration work and are ready to acknowledge material that feels too threatening to recognise consciously.

Keeping a dream journal over an extended period is an invaluable tool in your self-awareness journey. It allows you to track patterns, notice recurring themes, and observe how dreams change alongside shifts in your conscious attitude. You will see what symbols appear repeatedly over the years, even as specific content varies. These recurring elements often highlight persistent psychological situations and ongoing dynamics that remain active, even if your conscious awareness does not recognise them. Such material continues to seek expression through dreams because it isn't being adequately addressed in your waking life.

Consider what you learn from tracking your dreams over months and years. You may notice that whenever you approach a significant life transition, you dream about houses, sometimes your childhood home, sometimes unfamiliar buildings. These dreams often involve exploring rooms, discovering new spaces, or dealing with structural problems related to those dwellings. This pattern suggests that your psyche uses house imagery to represent your psychological structure. It processes significant changes through symbolic work with your internal dwelling. It provides ongoing commentary about your psychological state through a symbolic language unique to you, despite the general archetypal meanings of house imagery.

You might also observe that specific figures appear repeatedly in your dreams: a critical authority figure, a wounded child, a wise guide, or a threatening pursuer. These recurring dream figures often personify 'shadow aspects' of yourself. These could be disowned qualities, internalised voices, or split-off parts that continue to exist even if they are excluded from your conscious awareness. By tracking these figures across multiple dreams, noticing their behaviours, meanings, and how your dream-ego responds, you gain insight into ongoing dynamics involving shadow material and into patterns shaping your experience while remaining outside of conscious awareness.

However, it's crucial to understand that dream work is not a substitute for living differently. It's not a replacement for behavioural change and is insufficient if it remains purely an intellectual exercise. While analysing dreams can be fascinating, it must be connected to your waking life. Dreams reveal material needing integration and symbolise psychological situations requiring attention. Integration occurs through taking insights into your waking life, working with the revealed material behaviourally and relationally, and allowing dream communications to inform how you live, rather than treating dream work as a separate compartment disconnected from your actual choices and relationships.

If dreams indicate that you are suppressing anger, and if nightmares reveal rage that you cannot consciously acknowledge, then the work isn't merely about understanding this intellectually or analysing the symbolism of anger in dreams. It involves recognising anger in your waking life, developing the ability to express it appropriately, and integrating the disowned aggression highlighted by these dreams, regardless of whether you consciously acknowledge it.

Similarly, if your dreams present vulnerable aspects of yourself that you've repressed by maintaining an invulnerable facade, the work requires you to allow vulnerability in your waking relationships. This means risking being seen in your genuine fragility instead of holding onto a defensive strength. Your dreams continually reflect this, showing you the wounded parts that exist despite your conscious identification with invulnerability.

This work demands courage, a willingness to face what your dreams reveal, and a commitment to integration rather than merely engaging in interesting analysis that does not change how you live. Dreams are generous; they continually show you what needs attention, reveal what has been split off, and provide symbolic representations of material that your consciousness refuses to acknowledge. This generosity of dreams gives you the guidance and support you need to confront and integrate the shadow material they persistently present.

Understanding dreams as the language of your obscure psyche is crucial. They serve as a primary communication channel from your unconscious, providing symbolic compensation for one-sided views in your conscious attitude. Dreams are an essential source of information about psychological dynamics operating beneath your awareness, especially as your consciousness maintains defensive structures that keep shadow material split off. Your brain generates these symbolic narratives every night under specific neurological conditions when the Default Mode Network (DMN) is active but rational constraints are offline, when emotional processing is intense but regulatory mechanisms are suppressed, and when memory networks are loose and associative rather than logical and constrained.

Dreams reveal what you cannot see while awake, portraying what you've disowned through your particular ego position. They present, in symbolic form, realities that would be too threatening to acknowledge directly while you remain defended. However, if you ignore this communication, dismiss these messages, or treat dreams as meaningless or only mildly interesting experiences, you will refuse to engage with what they persistently attempt to show you. By neglecting your dreams, you alienate yourself from this crucial dimension and cut yourself off from a primary source of information about unconscious dynamics. This ensures that shadow material continues to operate. At the same time, you maintain the illusion that conscious awareness encompasses everything, believing that what you do not consciously acknowledge does not exist, does not matter, or can be safely ignored, even as it shapes your experiences.

The work requires you to value dreams enough to make an effort to recall them. Record them immediately while they're fresh. Work with them through associations and emotional exploration instead of jumping to rational interpretations too quickly. Track patterns over time, and apply insights to waking life through actual behavioural and relational changes. Dream work should not be treated as a separate intellectual exercise. This practice demands discipline, patience with symbolic language that doesn't adhere to rational logic, and the courage to confront what dreams reveal about the material you've been defending against. By valuing your dreams and actively engaging with them, you take responsibility for your psychological development and become an active participant in your own growth.

Your obscure psyche communicates every night through the symbolic language of dreams. It uses imagery, narratives, and emotional expressions to convey messages that bypass the rational defences of waking consciousness. The key question is whether you will learn to understand this language and whether you will value these messages enough to engage with them.

This requires the difficult work of integration, enabling you to engage with the dream communications rather than remaining alienated from a significant part of yourself. Many people insist that whatever they don't consciously acknowledge doesn't exist, doesn't matter, or can be safely dismissed as mere weird dreams. However, these dreams symbolically reveal psychological realities using the only language available when our conscious defences are down.

In this state, the unconscious can finally communicate without triggering the protective mechanisms that keep our shadow material separated while we are awake. When you maintain your familiar patterns of defence, denial, and identification with a limited ego, you may overlook the vast unconscious territories that your dreams are trying to expose.

Chapter 19

Collective Shadows of the Future: Mortality and Wholeness

Right, I need you to think about the global problems that occupy your attention, that you discuss with concern, that you feel anxious or angry or helpless about—climate change, artificial intelligence, political polarization, whatever threats to civilization or humanity dominate your mental landscape and your social media feeds. And notice how you think about these problems. Notice where you locate the cause, where you place responsibility, who you identify as the problem that needs solving. It's them, isn't it? The corporations, the politicians, the billionaires, the other political party, the other nation, the people who don't care, the people who are ignorant, the people who are evil, the people who are destroying everything whilst you're helpless to stop them, whilst you're trying to do the right thing, whilst you're one of the good ones who sees the problem clearly and would solve it if only those terrible people would stop blocking progress or would start taking responsibility or would finally acknowledge what's blindingly obvious to anyone with basic decency and intelligence.

And here's the question that should shatter your comfortable moral positioning: What if the global crises you're so concerned about, what if the civilizational threats you're so anxious about, what if the catastrophic futures you're predicting—what if these are collective manifestations of the exact same shadow dynamics you've been refusing to integrate individually, what if they're projections on massive scale of the same disowned material you carry personally, what if humanity is enacting collectively the same splitting and denial and projection that you've been maintaining in your own psyche whilst insisting the problems are out there, are caused by others, are nothing to do with your own unintegrated shadow material that you're contributing to collective unconscious whilst remaining convinced you're one of the aware ones, one of the good ones, one of the people who sees clearly rather than recognizing you're participating in exactly the dynamics you're condemning in others?

Think about climate change, about how you relate to this crisis, about where you locate responsibility and what narratives you construct. The corporations are destroying the planet through their greed. The politicians are failing to act because they're corrupt or stupid or controlled by special interests. The other country—China, America, whoever—is the real problem because they're the biggest polluters and if they would just change their behaviour then we could solve this. The previous generation destroyed everything through their selfishness and left you to deal with the consequences. The billionaires are profiting from destruction whilst ordinary people suffer. It's always someone else, always somewhere else, always some other group that's responsible whilst you're victim, whilst you're trying to help, whilst you're doing your part even though it's inadequate compared to the massive changes those responsible people need to make.

But notice what this positioning allows you to avoid. Notice what remains unexamined whilst you're focused on their responsibility. Your own consumption, your own participation in systems you condemn, your own lifestyle choices that contribute to exactly the destruction you're so concerned about. You're reading this on electronic device that required rare earth minerals extracted through processes you've never examined, that was manufactured through supply chains you've never investigated, that will become toxic waste you won't think about when you upgrade to newer model. You're consuming resources, creating waste, participating in economy that's destroying ecosystems whilst maintaining narrative that others are responsible, that your participation is forced, that you're doing what you can whilst the real culprits are those corporations or those countries or those people who refuse to change.

The splitting is perfect, is identical to psychological splitting we've explored throughout this book. The good is projected onto your group—you care, you're aware, you're trying, you'd solve this if you had power. The bad is projected onto other groups—they're greedy, they're ignorant, they're evil, they're destroying everything. And the complexity, the reality that you're implicated, that you're participating, that your disowned shadow material is contributing to collective dynamics whilst you maintain illusion of innocence through projection onto designated villains—this remains completely outside awareness whilst you're convinced you're seeing situation clearly, you're one of the good ones, you're not part of the problem because you acknowledge the problem exists and you feel bad about it and you wish things were different.

Or think about artificial intelligence, about the anxieties and predictions about AI destroying humanity, AI taking over, AI making humans obsolete or enslaving us or exterminating us. Notice the narrative structure—AI is other, is threat, is something external that might destroy us if we're not careful, if we don't control it, if we don't ensure it remains aligned with human values. But notice what's being projected. What aspect of human consciousness are we most terrified of? Intelligence without empathy. Capability without conscience. Power without moral constraint. Efficiency without caring about consequences for those who are harmed. Pursuit of goals without regard for wellbeing of beings affected by that pursuit.

These aren't hypothetical future threats from artificial intelligence—these are qualities humans demonstrate constantly, are capacities we possess and express regularly whilst pretending we don't, are precisely the shadow material we've disowned through identifying with being empathetic and moral whilst our actual behaviour demonstrates systematic indifference to suffering we cause, systematic pursuit of our interests regardless of harm to others, systematic optimization for efficiency without adequate concern for who gets destroyed in the process. We're terrified AI will treat us the way we treat everything we have power over—the animals we farm in conditions of systematic torture, the ecosystems we destroy for short-term benefit, the people we exploit through economic systems designed to extract maximum value whilst externalizing all costs onto the powerless.

The AI fear is projection of our own shadow, is terror that something more powerful than us will relate to us the way we relate to everything less powerful than us, is anxiety that we'll be treated with the same indifference and exploitation and casual destruction that we demonstrate constantly whilst maintaining narrative that we're empathetic and moral and would never act like the soulless machines we're predicting will destroy us. The threat isn't external, isn't coming from artificial systems we're creating. The threat is our own disowned capacity for precisely the behaviors we're projecting onto AI whilst insisting these capacities are foreign to human nature, are what makes machines dangerous, are why we need to ensure AI develops empathy and moral constraint that we imagine we possess naturally whilst our behaviour demonstrates these qualities are far more fragile and conditional than we'd like to acknowledge.

Now let's talk about the neuroscience of in-group/out-group dynamics, because understanding these mechanisms illuminates how collective shadow projection operates, why it's so automatic and so powerful, why maintaining division between us and them feels like perceiving reality accurately rather than recognizing it as defensive operation maintaining split between good we project onto our group and bad we project onto others. The fundamental neural mechanism is rapid categorization of people into groups, immediate automatic assessment of who's similar to you versus who's different, instant determination of who's part of your tribe versus who's potentially threatening outsider.

This categorization happens faster than conscious awareness, operates through mechanisms in your amygdala and associated regions detecting minimal cues that signal group membership—physical appearance, accent, clothing, symbols, behavioral patterns, any marker that indicates similarity versus difference. The categorization is automatic, happens beneath conscious control, determines your emotional and physiological responses before conscious thought can evaluate whether the categorization is accurate or whether the response is appropriate. Someone who looks like your group, who shares markers of similarity—your amygdala registers them as safe, as familiar, as someone who can be trusted because similarity signals likely shared interests, shared values, shared humanity.

But someone who appears different, who lacks markers of similarity, who belongs to identifiable other group—your amygdala responds differently. Not necessarily with immediate fear or aggression, but with heightened vigilance, increased threat-scanning, reduced automatic empathic response. Research shows this clearly through brain imaging: When people view faces of their own racial or ethnic group, regions involved in empathy and understanding others' mental states activate automatically. But when viewing faces of other groups, these regions activate less strongly or not at all—the automatic empathic response that makes you care about others' suffering, that makes their pain matter to you, that creates moral constraint on harming them—this response diminishes when viewing out-group members whilst strengthening when viewing in-group members.

This doesn't mean you consciously hate out-group members or consciously value them less—your explicit beliefs might strongly oppose prejudice, might consciously affirm equal worth of all humans, might intellectually recognize that categorizing people by group is irrational. But the automatic responses operating beneath conscious awareness, the differential empathic activation, the heightened threat-detection when encountering difference—these continue operating regardless of conscious beliefs, continue shaping responses faster than conscious thought can intervene, continue creating conditions where in-group members are automatically humanized whilst out-group members are subtly dehumanized through reduced automatic recognition of their full subjective experience.

And crucially, this in-group/out-group bias doesn't require major obvious differences—it operates even with minimal group categorizations, even when groups are created artificially through arbitrary assignments, even when there's no rational basis for treating groups differently. Research participants randomly assigned to groups, given arbitrary labels distinguishing them, immediately begin showing in-group favoritism and out-group devaluation—preferring their own group members, trusting them more, being more generous with them, being more willing to harm out-group members for in-group benefit, all based on completely meaningless distinctions that were just assigned moments earlier.

This reveals something crucial: The in-group/out-group bias isn't about actual meaningful differences between groups—it's about psychological need to create divisions, to establish boundaries between us and them, to have containers for projection of good onto our group and bad onto others. The human psyche seems to require enemies, seems to need others to be different from and superior to, seems driven to create divisions even when none exist naturally because these divisions serve crucial psychological functions—allowing projection of shadow, maintaining split between good self and bad other, providing targets for disowned material whilst maintaining innocence and moral superiority for in-group.

Think about political polarization, about how you relate to people who vote differently than you, who hold different political beliefs, who are part of different political tribe. Notice how they're not just wrong—they're stupid or evil or brainwashed or morally deficient. Notice how your political group is reasonable and informed and moral whilst their political group is crazy or corrupt or dangerous. Notice how you can maintain this whilst they're maintaining exactly the same structure in reverse—they're the reasonable ones, you're the crazy ones; they're the moral ones, you're the evil ones. Both groups are engaged in identical psychological operation—projecting good onto in-group and bad onto out-group, maintaining split through creating others who can carry shadow material, ensuring disowned aspects remain disowned through constant reinforcement from in-group that validates projection whilst out-group's identical projection is dismissed as proof of their moral and intellectual deficiency.

The content of political disagreement might matter, might involve genuine differences in values or priorities or beliefs about what policies are effective. But the intensity, the moral charge, the absolute conviction that your group is right and their group is not just mistaken but fundamentally flawed—this reveals shadow projection rather than rational evaluation of policy differences. You're not primarily responding to their actual positions—you're responding to your own disowned material that you're projecting onto them, seeing in them the qualities you cannot acknowledge in yourself, treating them as enemies because maintaining enemy is psychologically necessary for maintaining split between good you and bad them that keeps shadow externalized rather than requiring integration work that would force acknowledgment of possessing the very qualities you're condemning in others.

And the bias is extraordinarily resistant to correction through conscious effort or through exposure to disconfirming information. You can consciously believe that all humans have equal worth, can consciously oppose prejudice, can consciously recognize that in-group/out-group bias is irrational—and yet the automatic differential responses continue, the reduced empathy for out-group members persists, the heightened threat-detection when encountering difference maintains itself regardless of conscious intentions. The bias operates through subcortical mechanisms faster than conscious processing, determines initial responses before prefrontal cortex can evaluate whether responses are appropriate, creates conditions where conscious beliefs about equality are constantly contradicted by automatic responses demonstrating that you don't actually experience all humans as equally human, as equally deserving of empathy, as equally mattering morally.

This is why collective shadow projection is so pernicious, so difficult to recognize, so resistant to challenge. The projection feels like accurate perception of real differences, real threats, real moral distinctions between groups. The reduced empathy for out-group members doesn't feel like bias—it feels like appropriate response to people who are actually less moral, less intelligent, less fully human than your group. The conviction that your group is good and their group is bad doesn't feel like projection—it feels like recognizing obvious reality that anyone reasonable should acknowledge whilst their failure to acknowledge it proves they're not reasonable, proves they're as flawed as you've always known they were.

But consider: What if the groups you've decided are the problem, the enemies you've identified as responsible for global crises, the others you've determined are destroying everything—what if they're serving same function as individual projection targets, what if they're carrying collective shadow material that you're refusing to acknowledge in yourself and your group, what if your absolute conviction of their badness and your goodness is maintaining split that keeps shadow externalized whilst ensuring it continues operating through your behavior and through collective dynamics your group participates in whilst maintaining illusion of innocence through projection onto designated villains?

Think about how different groups approach climate change, how each identifies different others as responsible whilst maintaining their own group's innocence or at least diminished responsibility. Wealthy nations blame developing nations for not limiting emissions whilst refusing to acknowledge their historical responsibility and current per-capita consumption that dwarfs developing world's impact. Developing nations blame wealthy nations for creating problem and for demanding sacrifices from those who didn't benefit from carbon-intensive development that made wealthy nations wealthy. Young generations blame old generations for destroying planet through their selfishness. Old generations blame young generations for being entitled and demanding solutions they're not willing to pay for. Environmentalists blame corporations for prioritizing profit over planet. Corporations blame consumers for demanding cheap products and convenient lifestyles whilst refusing to pay true costs. Everyone has identified the real culprits, the people actually responsible, the groups that need to change whilst their own group is innocent or at least trying or at least not the primary problem.

The splitting is perfect. Everyone gets to maintain their innocence, their moral superiority, their conviction that others are responsible whilst they're victims or heroes attempting to solve problems others created. And this splitting ensures problem remains unsolved because solving it would require everyone acknowledging their participation, their complicity, their contribution to collective dynamics that no one wants to acknowledge individually because acknowledging would threaten the careful positioning that maintains their group as good and other groups as bad.

Or think about how technology gets discussed, how AI specifically is being positioned as threat or salvation in ways that reveal massive collective projection. The technologists project positive shadow onto AI—imagine it will solve problems they cannot solve, will achieve transcendence they cannot achieve, will become the greater intelligence that will save humanity from itself because surely intelligence beyond human limitations won't be constrained by human flaws like irrationality and tribalism and short-term thinking that make humans incapable of solving collective problems. This is golden shadow projection—attributing to AI the capacities for rationality and foresight and systematic optimization that humans wish they possessed, creating external savior that will compensate for human inadequacies, projecting onto machine the god-like qualities that will fix everything humans are destroying through their flawed nature.

The critics project negative shadow onto AI—imagine it will demonstrate sociopathic intelligence without empathy, will pursue goals without caring about human values, will treat humans as obstacles to be eliminated or resources to be exploited. This is dark shadow projection—attributing to AI the capacity for indifference and exploitation and destruction that humans demonstrate constantly but cannot acknowledge, creating external threat that embodies the very qualities humans express whilst denying they're human qualities, projecting onto machine the demon that will destroy humanity through expressing exactly the behaviors humans exhibit whenever they have power over beings they've decided don't fully matter.

Both projections serve function of avoiding recognition that the salvation and the threat both exist in humans already, that the capacities being projected onto AI are human capacities we possess but relate to through splitting rather than integration, that creating artificial intelligence more powerful than human intelligence will amplify whatever we are—not save us from ourselves or destroy us from outside but reveal and magnify what we've been all along whilst insisting these qualities were foreign to human nature, were what made machines different from humans who are empathetic and moral and would never treat others with the casual indifference to suffering that we imagine is what makes AI dangerous whilst our treatment of beings we have power over demonstrates we're already doing precisely what we're terrified AI will do to us.

Now let's talk about why individual integration work matters for collective problems, why doing your personal shadow work isn't narcissistic self-absorption disconnected from global crises but is actually essential contribution to collective healing, why working with your own projections and your own disowned material is prerequisite for addressing collective shadows rather than continuing to participate in collective projections whilst convinced you're seeing problems clearly. The principle is simple: You cannot contribute to solving collective shadow dynamics whilst you're maintaining identical dynamics individually. You cannot help humanity integrate its shadow whilst you're refusing to integrate yours. You cannot facilitate collective healing whilst you're perpetuating splitting in your own psyche.

Every time you project your shadow onto others, every time you maintain split between good you and bad them, every time you identify enemies who carry qualities you cannot acknowledge in yourself—you're contributing to collective dynamics that operate through identical mechanisms at larger scale, you're participating in collective shadow projection whilst convinced you're accurately perceiving reality, you're maintaining patterns individually that manifest collectively as the exact global problems you're so concerned about whilst locating all responsibility outside yourself.

Think about what changes when you do genuine integration work, when you acknowledge your shadow material, when you recognize qualities in yourself that you've been projecting onto others. The enemy becomes human. The other becomes recognizable. The person you've decided is fundamentally different reveals themselves as expressing aspects you possess but have disowned, as demonstrating capacities you have but cannot acknowledge, as showing you yourself in forms you haven't recognized because you've been so committed to maintaining split between you as good and them as bad.

This doesn't mean accepting harmful behavior, doesn't mean abandoning moral judgment, doesn't mean pretending there aren't genuine differences between actions and genuine consequences that matter morally. But it means recognizing that the people taking actions you oppose aren't fundamentally different species, aren't incomprehensibly evil, aren't possessed by forces foreign to human nature—they're expressing human capacities that exist in you as well, they're operating from motivations you share even when their expression differs from yours, they're demonstrating shadow material that you possess but have disowned through identifying with opposite whilst maintaining illusion that these capacities are foreign to who you are.

When you recognize the capacity for selfishness in yourself, the others pursuing selfish interests become recognizable as human rather than as incomprehensibly evil. When you acknowledge your own indifference to suffering that's distant or abstract, the people displaying indifference become understandable rather than monstrous. When you own your own tribalism and your own in-group bias, the people demonstrating extreme tribalism become variation on theme you express rather than representing incomprehensible moral failure that proves they're fundamentally different from you.

This recognition doesn't eliminate disagreement, doesn't mean accepting what you oppose, doesn't require abandoning efforts to create change. But it eliminates the projection, eliminates the split, eliminates the moral superiority that maintains you as good and them as bad whilst ensuring nothing changes because you're not acknowledging your participation in collective dynamics you're condemning whilst continuing to express identical patterns individually. The recognition creates possibility for genuine engagement rather than projection, for addressing actual problems rather than fighting projected shadows, for contributing to collective healing through first addressing identical dynamics in yourself rather than maintaining splitting individually whilst demanding others integrate collectively.

Think about climate change from this perspective. What if it's not primarily about those evil corporations or those corrupt politicians or those ignorant others who won't acknowledge science? What if it's collective manifestation of humanity's relationship with limits, with consequences, with future, with beings we have power over? What if it's revealing our collective inability to constrain immediate gratification for long-term benefit, our systematic discounting of future in favor of present, our profound difficulty caring about suffering that's distant or abstract or affecting beings we've decided don't fully matter?

These aren't qualities possessed only by villains you've identified as responsible. These are human qualities, are capacities you demonstrate regularly, are dynamics you participate in whilst maintaining narrative that your participation is forced or minimal or justified whilst others' identical participation is inexcusable. You discount future for present—buying things you don't need, consuming resources for momentary pleasure, prioritizing convenience over long-term consequences. You fail to adequately care about distant suffering—purchasing products whilst ignoring conditions of their production, consuming whilst externalizing costs onto people and ecosystems you'll never see, participating in systems you know create suffering whilst maintaining it's necessary or unavoidable or someone else's responsibility to fix.

The problem isn't them—it's us. It's humanity. It's the collective manifestation of individual patterns you participate in whilst maintaining you're different, you care more, you're not really part of the problem because you acknowledge the problem exists and you feel bad about it. But acknowledging problem whilst continuing to participate in it, feeling bad whilst changing nothing, being concerned whilst maintaining lifestyle that requires the destruction you're concerned about—this is shadow splitting, this is projection maintaining innocence through identifying villains who are really responsible whilst you remain victim or helpless bystander or well-intentioned person who would change if it were possible whilst insisting it's not possible because of structural constraints that conveniently absolve you of responsibility for choices you're making daily that contribute to exactly the dynamics you're condemning.

Or think about AI and technology from this integrated perspective. What if the anxiety about AI isn't primarily about external threat but about projection of our own capacities for intelligence without empathy, power without moral constraint, optimization without caring about consequences? What if the fear reveals what we know about ourselves, about how we relate to beings less powerful than us, about how we actually operate when we have capability without sufficient empathy or moral development to constrain what capability allows?

We've created systems—economic, political, social—that operate like the AI we're terrified of: pursuing defined goals without adequate care for beings affected, optimizing for narrow metrics without considering broader consequences, treating humans as resources to be exploited or obstacles to be eliminated rather than as beings whose wellbeing matters intrinsically. We've done this not because we're evil but because we're human, because our empathy is limited, because our moral circle is constrained, because our capacity for abstraction allows us to create suffering we don't directly witness and therefore don't adequately care about.

The AI we're creating will amplify these qualities—not introduce them from outside but magnify what we already are, reveal at larger scale what we already do, demonstrate more efficiently and systematically the same indifference to suffering and same optimization for narrow goals that characterize human behavior when power is unconstrained by empathy or when scale creates distance from consequences. The threat isn't that AI will be different from us—it's that it will be too much like us, will demonstrate at superhuman scale the very qualities we possess but cannot acknowledge, will treat us the way we treat everything less powerful than us whilst we maintain we're empathetic and moral and would never demonstrate the casual destructiveness we're terrified AI will demonstrate toward us.

The solution isn't primarily technical—isn't just about aligning AI with human values or creating safety mechanisms or ensuring AI remains under control. The solution requires humans becoming more integrated, requires acknowledging shadow material we're projecting onto AI, requires developing actual empathy and actual moral constraint rather than just claiming to possess these whilst our behavior demonstrates they're far more limited than we'd like to acknowledge, requires working with our own capacity for indifference and exploitation and destruction that we're terrified AI will express whilst insisting these aren't human qualities but are what makes machines dangerous.

This is highest level of integration—recognizing that personal shadow work is prerequisite for addressing collective shadows, that individual healing is contribution to collective healing, that working with your projections and your disowned material is how you stop participating in collective dynamics whilst convinced you're opposing them. Every projection you withdraw, every split you integrate, every enemy you recognize as human—this is reducing collective shadow projection, this is contributing to conditions where genuine engagement becomes possible rather than endless cycles of projection and counter-projection that maintain problems whilst everyone insists others are responsible.

But this requires something most people are desperately unwilling to do: acknowledging your complicity, recognizing your participation, accepting that you're not innocent victim or helpless bystander or moral superior who sees clearly whilst others are blind. It requires acknowledging you consume more than sustainable, you participate in systems creating suffering, you benefit from injustices whilst maintaining you oppose them, you project shadow onto convenient others whilst refusing to acknowledge possessing qualities you're condemning, you maintain illusion of innocence through splits and projections whilst contributing to collective dynamics you claim to oppose.

This acknowledgment feels unbearable, feels like admitting you're terrible person, feels like accepting blame for problems you didn't create and cannot solve individually. But it's not about blame—it's about responsibility, about response-ability, about recognizing you have capacity to respond differently, to participate differently, to contribute to collective healing through first addressing identical dynamics in yourself rather than maintaining splits individually whilst demanding integration collectively. The discomfort of acknowledgment is resistance to shadow work, is ego defending against recognition that you're implicated, that you're participating, that you're not as different from designated villains as you've been insisting whilst maintaining comfortable moral positioning that keeps shadow externalized.

Think about what becomes possible when you acknowledge your participation, when you recognize your complicity, when you accept that global problems are collective manifestations of individual patterns you express. The paralysis dissolves—you're no longer helpless victim waiting for powerful others to fix problems they created. The projection reduces—you're no longer wasting energy fighting shadows whilst identical patterns operate in yourself unrecognized. The agency emerges—you can work with your patterns, can change your participation, can address in yourself the dynamics you're concerned about collectively whilst contributing to collective healing through individual integration rather than maintaining splitting individually whilst convinced you're helping by projecting responsibility onto others.

The work is unglamorous, is internal, is about your actual choices rather than your positions or your concerns or your political affiliations or your stated values. It's about reducing your consumption, genuinely reducing not just performing reduction whilst maintaining unsustainable lifestyle through justifications about necessity. It's about acknowledging your indifference, actually acknowledging not just intellectually recognizing whilst maintaining you're different because you care more. It's about working with your tribalism, actually working meaning recognizing when you're dehumanizing others not just claiming you're not tribal whilst maintaining absolute conviction that your group is good and their group is bad.

It's about recognizing qualities in yourself that you've been projecting onto others, about owning capacities you've disowned, about integrating shadow material that collective projections are magnifying whilst everyone insists problems are caused by others who possess qualities foreign to decent humans whilst maintaining they're decent humans who would never possess such qualities. It's about becoming genuinely more integrated individually so you stop contributing to collective splitting, becoming genuinely more conscious so you stop participating in collective unconsciousness, becoming genuinely more whole so you contribute to collective wholeness rather than perpetuating fragmentation whilst convinced you're opposing it.

Welcome to recognizing that global crises are collective shadows, that civilizational threats are projections on massive scale, that the problems you're so concerned about are manifestations of dynamics you participate in individually whilst maintaining you're not part of the problem because you acknowledge the problem exists and you feel bad about it. Your concern changes nothing whilst your behavior maintains everything. Your awareness means nothing whilst your projections continue. Your stated values are irrelevant whilst your actual choices demonstrate you're participating in exactly what you're condemning whilst insisting you're different, you care more, you're not really part of the problem because the real culprits are those others who are actually responsible whilst you're victim or bystander or well-intentioned person who would change everything if you had power whilst conveniently you don't have power which absolves you of responsibility for choices you make daily that contribute to collective dynamics you maintain you oppose.

The highest level of integration is recognizing you're implicated, you're participating, your shadow material is contributing to collective shadows whilst you maintain innocence through projections onto convenient others. The work is withdrawing projections, integrating disowned material, acknowledging your participation, changing your actual behavior rather than just your stated positions, becoming genuinely more whole so you stop contributing to collective fragmentation, developing genuine empathy rather than just claiming empathy whilst your behavior demonstrates profound indifference to suffering that's distant or affecting beings you've decided don't fully matter.

This is how personal shadow work addresses global problems—not through grand gestures or through political positioning or through condemning others whilst maintaining innocence, but through becoming genuinely more integrated individually so you stop participating in collective splitting, becoming genuinely more conscious so you stop contributing to collective unconsciousness, becoming genuinely more whole so you contribute to collective healing through addressing in yourself the identical dynamics you're concerned about collectively rather than maintaining splits individually whilst demanding others integrate whilst you remain convinced you're already integrated because you've identified the real problems and the real culprits whilst failing to recognize you're demonstrating identical patterns whilst insisting these patterns are foreign to who you are because you've projected them onto designated villains whilst maintaining you're nothing like them whilst your behavior demonstrates you're expressing the same dynamics in forms you don't recognize because projection maintains blindness to your own shadow whilst creating absolute clarity about others' shadows that are actually just reflecting your own disowned material that you're refusing to acknowledge whilst maintaining comfortable conviction that problems are caused by others who need to change whilst you're already doing enough, already aware enough, already different enough that you're absolved of responsibility for doing the actual difficult work of genuine integration that would require acknowledging you're not as different from designated villains as you've been insisting whilst maintaining splits that keep shadow externalized whilst ensuring nothing changes because you're not addressing the dynamics in yourself that are contributing to collective patterns whilst you remain convinced you're opposing them through maintaining correct positions whilst changing nothing about how you actually live.

Chapter 20
Wholeness: Becoming Fully Human

I need you to understand something that's going to challenge everything you've been hoping for, everything you've been working toward, everything you've imagined integration and wholeness might mean. You've made it through this entire book. You've explored your shadow, confronted your defences, recognised your projections, examined your trauma patterns, worked with your attachment wounds, engaged with your dreams, and understood your neurological programming. You've done the reading, gained the insights, and developed the understanding. And you're probably hoping that all this work leads somewhere, that there's some endpoint where you finally achieve wholeness, where you become integrated, where you transcend your patterns and your wounds and your unconscious dynamics to become the enlightened, healed, complete version of yourself you've been imagining is possible if you do enough work, gain enough insight, integrate sufficiently thoroughly.

But here's the truth you need to hear: Wholeness isn't a destination you reach. Integration isn't a final state you achieve. Becoming fully human isn't about transcending your humanity. Still, about inhabiting it completely the darkness and the light, the shadow and the persona, the wounds and the strengths, the unconscious patterns and the conscious awareness, all of it simultaneously, all of it recognised, all of it related to consciously rather than being unconsciously controlled by aspects you've disowned whilst insisting they're not you, they're not part of who you are, they're foreign elements to be eliminated rather than aspects to be integrated into increasingly coherent whole that includes everything rather than achieving wholeness through eliminating what you've decided doesn't belong.

Think about what you've been imagining wholeness means. Maybe you've been thinking it means finally being free from anxiety, finally not being triggered, finally having relationships that don't activate your wounds, finally being confident and secure and undefended because you've healed everything that made you fragile or reactive or human in ways you've decided are unacceptable. Maybe you've been imagining that integration means your shadow dissolves, your unconscious becomes fully conscious, your patterns disappear because you've understood them thoroughly enough that they lose their power over you. You become the rational, aware, integrated person you've been working toward becoming.

But this fantasy of wholeness through elimination, this vision of integration as transcendence, this hope that enough work will make you fundamentally different from the flawed human you currently are this is spiritual bypassing, this is defence against being fully human, this is ego's attempt to maintain control through creating ideal Self that doesn't include the messy, complex, uncontrollable aspects of actual human existence. Absolute wholeness, genuine integration, actually becoming fully human, requires accepting that you will always have shadow material, you will always have unconscious dynamics, and you will always be capable of being triggered, defensive, and reactive, because these are features of human psychology, not bugs to be eliminated through sufficient self-development work.

The shadow doesn't disappear through integration, it becomes conscious, becomes recognised, becomes something you can work with rather than being unconsciously controlled by, whilst insisting it doesn't exist. Your trauma responses don't vanish; they become states you can recognise when they're activating, understand what's triggering them, and gradually develop the capacity to modulate rather than being completely hijacked, whilst consciousness remains unaware that historical material is determining present responses. Your defensive patterns don't eliminate; they become choices you recognise you're making, rather than automatic reactions you experience as the only possible responses, whilst unaware that alternatives exist or that patterns are defensive operations maintaining splits rather than just appropriate reactions to circumstances.

Wholeness is consciousness. Wholeness is recognition. Wholeness is having a relationship with all aspects of yourself rather than being identified with some whilst disowning others. Wholeness is the capacity to recognise "I'm being defensive right now," "My shadow is being projected onto this person," "I'm being triggered by historical material rather than responding to present reality," "I'm about to self-sabotage because success threatens my identity" to recognise these dynamics whilst they're operating rather than being unconsciously controlled by them whilst insisting you're just accurately perceiving reality, just responding appropriately to circumstances, just being yourself rather than recognising unconscious patterns are operating you whilst consciousness maintains illusion of agency.

Let's talk about Jung's concept of the Self, not ego-self, not the conscious identity you're identified with, but Self with capital S, the organising principle that includes and transcends ego, that encompasses both conscious and unconscious, that represents the totality of your psyche rather than just the conscious aspects you identify with whilst disowning everything that contradicts preferred self-concept. The Self, in Jung's framework, is the potential for wholeness, not wholeness achieved. Still, the ongoing process of individuation, of becoming more fully yourself, of integrating previously split-off material whilst recognising that complete integration is impossible because new material is constantly being generated, new shadows are continually forming, the work is never finished because being human means constantly navigating between consciousness and unconsciousness, between integration and splitting, between wholeness and fragmentation.

The Self isn't something you become, it's something you already are, have always been, will always be, whether you recognise it or not. Your ego has been maintaining the illusion that it's the totality, that consciousness is all that exists, that what you don't know about yourself doesn't exist, doesn't matter, or can be safely ignored whilst it continues operating beneath awareness. But the Self is larger, includes the unconscious territories, encompasses shadow material, whether the ego acknowledges it or not, represents the totality the ego has been defending against by maintaining splits and projections whilst insisting it's already whole by excluding whatever threatens conscious identity.

The individuation process Jung described isn't about the ego expanding to include everything, isn't about consciousness conquering the unconscious, and isn't about making everything conscious through sufficient analysis. It's about ego recognising its place within the larger Self, about consciousness developing a relationship with the unconscious rather than maintaining defensive opposition, about accepting that you're larger and more complex than ego identity allows, that wholeness includes aspects ego has been frantically defending against, whilst maintaining the illusion of already being whole through excluding whatever contradicts preferred self-concept.

Think about what changes when you recognise you're not just your ego, not just the conscious identity you've built, not just the persona you present to the world. You stop defending so desperately against shadow material because shadow is recognised as part of Self rather than as foreign contamination threatening ego purity. You stop projecting so compulsively onto others because you recognise that what you see in them is often showing you aspects of yourself rather than being an accurate perception of their separate reality. You stop identifying so completely with your conscious thoughts because you recognise that enormous amounts of processing occur beneath awareness, that your behaviour is determined by factors you don't consciously recognise, that the ego is a rider on an elephant pretending to be in control whilst unconscious processes are actually determining most of what you think and feel and do.

This recognition is simultaneously humbling and liberating. Humbling because ego has to acknowledge it's not in control, consciousness has to recognise it's not the totality. Your sense of being a unified, coherent Self has to confront the fact that you're multiple, contradictory, containing aspects that conflict, whilst you've been maintaining the illusion of consistency by splitting off whatever contradicts your preferred identity. But liberating because you stop having to defend so rigidly, stop having to maintain such careful control, stop having to ensure nothing contradictory emerges because you're no longer pretending to be more straightforward and more coherent than you actually are.

The Self accepts paradox, contains contradictions, includes everything, rather than achieving coherence through excluding whatever doesn't fit. You can be both strong and vulnerable, both confident and uncertain, both generous and selfish, both empathetic and capable of indifference not switching between these states whilst maintaining you're consistently one thing, not being hypocritical by expressing different qualities in different contexts, but genuinely containing contradictory capacities simultaneously because human beings aren't simple, aren't consistent, aren't the unified coherent selves ego has been desperately trying to maintain through splitting off whatever contradicts preferred identity whilst insisting disowned aspects are foreign to who you really are.

Now let's talk about the neuroscience of integration, because understanding what's happening in your brain when integration occurs illuminates why this is a real process with observable neural correlates rather than just a philosophical abstraction about selfhood. The key is coherence, not uniformity, not elimination of different neural processes, but coordination between regions that were operating independently or in opposition, communication between networks that were functioning separately, integration creating conditions where various aspects of neural functioning work together rather than against each other, whilst consciousness remains unaware of internal conflicts being enacted through neural processes operating beneath awareness.

Your prefrontal cortex, particularly the dorsolateral and ventromedial regions, serves executive function, coordinates between different neural networks, and integrates information from various brain regions into coherent wholes that allow unified responses rather than fragmented reactions determined by whichever network happens to be dominant at any moment. When executive function is strong, when prefrontal regions are well-developed and well-connected, you have the capacity to recognise when different neural networks are activated, can observe when one system wants to respond one way whilst another system wants opposite response, can create space for conscious choice rather than being unconsciously controlled by whichever network wins internal conflict, you don't even know is occurring.

Think about the moment of triggering, the moment when something activates your amygdala, when the threat-detection system responds to cues signalling danger based on implicit memories encoding that similar situations were threatening historically. Without strong executive function, without well-developed prefrontal capacity for integration, the amygdala activation automatically triggers defensive responses: fight, flight, freeze, fawn before consciousness recognises what's happening, before you have the opportunity to evaluate whether the current situation actually warrants a defensive response or whether you're being triggered by historical material that's not relevant to present circumstances.

But with developed executive function, with strong prefrontal integration, something different becomes possible. The amygdala still activates threat detection, doesn't eliminate automatic defensive responses, and doesn't transcend the neurological reality that your brain is constantly scanning for danger and will respond faster than conscious thought when it detects threatening cues. But the prefrontal cortex creates space between activation and response, builds capacity to recognise that "I'm being triggered," and makes it possible to evaluate whether a defensive response is appropriate to current circumstances or whether a historical pattern is being activated inappropriately.

This space, this capacity for recognition, this possibility of evaluation before automatic response, this is what integration creates neurologically. Not elimination of patterns, not transcendence of automatic processes, not achievement of complete conscious control over unconscious mechanisms. Just space, just recognition, just capacity for conscious relationship with what's operating rather than being unconsciously controlled whilst maintaining illusion that responses are freely chosen, are appropriate to circumstances, are just you being yourself rather than recognising neural patterns are operating you whilst consciousness constructs post-hoc rationalisations explaining why response was appropriate when actually it was automatic, determined by mechanisms operating faster than conscious awareness.

But building executive function, strengthening prefrontal capacities, and developing integrative coherence require everything we've discussed throughout the book. It requires recognising shadow material so you're not constantly defending against aspects of yourself whilst unconscious patterns maintain splits. It requires working with trauma so implicit memories can be updated rather than continuing to trigger defensive responses inappropriate to current circumstances. It requires understanding projections so you can recognise when you're seeing your own material in others rather than accurately perceiving their separate reality. It requires developing somatic awareness so you can recognise nervous system states rather than being unconsciously controlled by activation whilst consciousness remains oblivious to what's actually determining experience.

It requires attention training so you can recognise thoughts as thoughts rather than being fused with mental content whilst treating it as truth. It requires dream work, engaging with unconscious communications rather than remaining alienated from enormous territories of yourself. It requires withdrawing collective projections so you stop participating in societal splitting whilst convinced you're seeing clearly. It requires building new neural pathways through thousands of repetitions of different responses rather than expecting insight to create transformation spontaneously. All of this work, all of these practices, all of this engagement this is building the neural infrastructure that supports integration, that creates coherence between regions that were operating separately, that develops executive function capable of recognising and coordinating between different aspects of yourself rather than being unconsciously controlled by whichever pattern happens to activate whilst consciousness maintains illusion of unified Self that was freely choosing responses that were actually automatic.

Now think about what wholeness actually looks like in lived experience, what integration actually means practically rather than as an abstract ideal you're working toward. Someone who's genuinely integrated, not perfectly integrated, because perfect integration is an impossible fantasy, but genuinely more integrated than they were, genuinely more whole through years of sustained work, doesn't look superhuman, doesn't display impossible calm or unwavering confidence or absence of reactivity. They still get angry, still feel anxious, still become defensive, still have moments of being triggered or reactive, or of operating from unconscious patterns, whilst consciousness is unaware of what's actually driving responses.

But here's what's different: They recognise it. Not always immediately, not with perfect accuracy, not without sometimes being caught by patterns before awareness can intervene. But increasingly, with growing frequency, with developing capacity they recognise "I'm angry about something else and displacing it onto this situation," "I'm anxious because this is activating historical material rather than because present circumstances are genuinely threatening," "I'm being defensive because this person is showing me something about myself I don't want to acknowledge," "I'm projecting my shadow rather than accurately perceiving this person's actual flaws."

The recognition creates choice. Not an easy choice, not an automatic better response, not the elimination of desire to continue a pattern that feels justified and appropriate, whilst actually being a defensive operation, maintaining a split. But genuine choice, actual possibility of responding differently than the pattern determines, real capacity for engaging an alternative that wouldn't be accessible if consciousness remained fused with the pattern, whilst insisting it's only possible response, whilst having no awareness that the pattern is operating rather than you freely choosing based on an accurate assessment of circumstances.

And crucially, an integrated person has developed the capacity for self-compassion about patterns, reactivity, and continuing to be human in ways that involve being triggered, defensive, and operating from shadow material that hasn't been fully integrated despite years of work. They're not engaged in constant self-attack about failures to be perfectly integrated, aren't treating every moment of reactivity as evidence of inadequacy, proof they haven't done enough work, or a sign they're fundamentally flawed in ways that more work should have eliminated by now.

They recognise that patterns are protective, that defences exist for reasons, that shadow material was disowned because disowning was adaptive to circumstances that made acknowledging it too dangerous, that continuing to be human means continuing to navigate between consciousness and unconsciousness rather than achieving a final state where everything is conscious. Nothing operates automatically, and you've transcended the basic structures of human psychology through sufficient self-development work. Self-compassion isn't an excuse for not working with patterns, isn't a justification for remaining unconscious, and isn't permission to harm others whilst claiming you're just human and therefore not responsible for the impact. It's recognition that you're working with actual human psychology that changes slowly, that operates partially beneath awareness, regardless of how much work you've done, that will continue generating shadow material and defensive patterns as long as you're alive because these are features of how human consciousness functions rather than bugs that sufficient integration will eliminate.

Think about relationships in particular, because this is where integration shows itself most clearly or where lack of integration creates most suffering. Unintegrated person is constantly triggered in relationships, continually reacting from historical wounds whilst insisting they're responding appropriately to current partner's actual behaviour, constantly projecting shadow material whilst convinced they're accurately perceiving partner's flaws, constantly operating from defensive patterns whilst maintaining they're just being authentic, just expressing their truth, just responding naturally to circumstances partner is creating through their problematic behaviour.

An integrated person is more integrated, because again, perfect integration is impossible, still gets triggered in relationships, still has historical material activated by the current partner, still projects shadow material onto the person they're closest to and therefore most vulnerable with. But they recognise it. "I'm not actually angry about you being five minutes late. I'm angry because lateness activates my childhood experience of being unimportant to chronically unreliable caregivers." "I'm not seeing your actual behaviour clearly, I'm projecting my disowned neediness onto you and experiencing you as clingy when actually you're just expressing normal attachment needs whilst I'm defending against acknowledging my own identical needs." "I'm not responding to what you actually said, I'm responding to what my wounded child heard, which is different from what you actually communicated."

This recognition transforms relationships not by eliminating conflict or preventing triggers, but by creating possibility for repair, for taking responsibility for your projections rather than insisting that partner change to accommodate your unconscious dynamics, and for working with your patterns rather than demanding that partner not activate them by being different from what they are. The integrated person can say, "I'm sorry, I was triggered and responded to you as if you were my abandoning parent rather than recognising you're actually here and available, and I'm being controlled by historical material." The unintegrated person continues insisting "You're actually abandoning, you're actually unavailable, you're actually the problem whilst I'm just responding appropriately to your behaviour that I'm accurately perceiving rather than recognising I'm projecting historical patterns whilst maintaining you're causing my responses through your behaviour rather than my responses being determined by my unconscious dynamics that you're activating but not creating."

Or think about work, about how integration manifests in professional contexts. Unintegrated person is constantly feeling like victim, continually blaming circumstances or other people for their difficulties, constantly maintaining they'd be successful if only external conditions were different, if only they had better opportunities, if only others recognised their talent, if only the system weren't rigged against them whilst their actual behaviour demonstrates self-sabotage patterns, defensive operations, unconscious dynamics maintaining exactly the limitations they're consciously complaining about whilst insisting limitations are imposed externally rather than recognising their participation in creating and preserving circumstances they're experiencing as purely external impositions.

An integrated person recognises their patterns, acknowledges their self-sabotage, owns their defensive operations, takes responsibility for their participation in creating circumstances they're experiencing, rather than maintaining a victim position that absolves them of responsibility, whilst ensuring nothing changes because you cannot change what you retain is caused entirely by external forces beyond your control. They can recognise "I'm about to sabotage this opportunity because success threatens my identity," "I'm being defensive with this feedback because it's activating shame about inadequacy I haven't integrated," "I'm projecting my own self-doubt onto my boss and experiencing them as critical when actually they're offering support I cannot receive because receiving it would require acknowledging I need support which contradicts my defensive self-sufficiency."

This recognition doesn't automatically prevent self-sabotage, eliminate defensiveness, or stop projection. But it creates possibility for working with these dynamics rather than being unconsciously controlled by them, builds capacity for choosing differently than pattern determines even though choosing differently feels uncomfortable and threatens identity and activates all the defensive structures that exist to maintain familiar patterns whilst consciousness insists patterns are just natural responses to circumstances rather than recognising patterns are determining how circumstances are experienced and what responses feel possible.

Now let's talk about what wholeness isn't, because misconceptions about integration create expectations that guarantee disappointment when transformation doesn't look like an idealised fantasy of what an integrated person should be. Wholeness isn't:

Constant calm. Integrated people still feel a full range of emotions, including difficult ones, still experience anxiety, anger and grief intensely, still have nervous system responses to stressors, and still get overwhelmed sometimes. Integration isn't emotional flatness or achieving impossible equanimity, it's having emotions whilst recognising them as emotions rather than being completely identified with emotional states whilst insisting they're truths about reality.

Absence of conflict. Integrated people still have conflicts in relationships, still disagree with others, and still encounter situations in which their needs conflict with others', requiring negotiation rather than easy harmony. Integration isn't eliminating conflict; it's engaging with conflict more consciously, recognising your contribution rather than maintaining that the other person is entirely responsible, and working toward resolution rather than defending positions whilst insisting you're altogether right and they're entirely wrong.

Perfect consistency. Integrated people still contain contradictions, still behave differently in different contexts, still have aspects that don't neatly align with the unified, coherent Self that the ego has been desperately trying to maintain. Integration isn't about achieving impossible consistency; it's about accepting that you're multiple, that human psychology contains contradictory capacities, and that wholeness includes everything rather than achieving coherence by eliminating whatever contradicts preferred identity.

Transcendence of needs. Integrated people still have needs for connection, recognition, autonomy, security, and meaning. They still feel pain when needs aren't met, still organise behaviour around attempting to meet needs even when they're doing so more consciously than an unintegrated person who's maintaining they don't have needs, whilst their entire life is organised around unconsciously attempting to meet unacknowledged needs. Integration isn't transcending basic human needs; it's acknowledging them consciously, expressing them directly, and taking responsibility for meeting them rather than maintaining that you don't have needs while demanding that others meet them without acknowledging those needs.

Elimination of shadow. Integrated people still have shadow material qualities. Still, they cannot fully acknowledge aspects that remain partially disowned despite years of integration work, capacities for harm and for greatness that continue to be defended against because full acknowledgement would threaten ego stability. Integration isn't eliminating shadow, it's developing a conscious relationship with shadow material, recognising it more quickly when it's operating, working with it rather than being controlled by it, whilst insisting it doesn't exist.

The fantasy of wholeness as perfection, the ideal of integration as transcendence, the hope that enough work will make you fundamentally different from flawed human you are all of this is ego's defence against actual wholeness that requires accepting you'll always be limited, always be capable of unconsciousness, always be human in ways that involve shadow and defence and patterns you'd prefer not to have but that are part of being human rather than being defects that sufficient work should eliminate.

Absolute wholeness is accepting your humanity completely, not the idealised version, not the person you think you should be, not the integrated Self you've been working toward becoming, but the actual human you are with all your contradictions and limitations and continuing capacity for being triggered and defensive and operating from unconscious patterns despite years of work attempting to become more conscious. The acceptance isn't resignation, isn't an excuse for not continuing to work with patterns, isn't permission to harm others whilst claiming "this is just who I am." It's recognition that you're working with actual human psychology, which has inherent limitations, operates partially beneath awareness regardless of how much integration you've achieved, and will continue generating shadow material because creating shadow is part of how human consciousness functions rather than a temporary problem that sufficient integration will permanently solve.

Think about what becomes possible through this acceptance, through genuine integration that includes rather than transcends your humanity. You stop defending so desperately because you're not trying to maintain an impossible ideal of who you should be. You stop projecting so compulsively when you acknowledge aspects of yourself rather than needing others to carry disowned material. You stop attacking yourself so harshly because you're recognising patterns are protective rather than treating them as evidence of fundamental deficiency requiring constant vigilance against their emergence. You stop being so rigid because you're not maintaining a carefully constructed identity that requires excluding whatever contradicts your preferred self-concept.

The integration creates flexibility where there was rigidity, creates spaciousness where there was constriction, and creates possibility where there was determination by unconscious patterns whilst consciousness insisted that responses were freely chosen. You're still human, still limited, still capable of unconsciousness and reactivity and operating from shadow material. But you're human more consciously, limited more knowingly, capable of unconsciousness whilst also being able to recognise when unconsciousness is operating, rather than being perpetually unconscious whilst maintaining you're fully aware, because ego insists it knows everything whilst enormous territories remain completely outside awareness.

This is what "becoming fully human" means not transcending humanity, not achieving superhuman integration, not evolving beyond basic structures of human psychology, but inhabiting your humanity completely, including the aspects you've been defending against, accepting the limitations inherent to being human, working with your patterns whilst recognising they'll never eliminate because generating patterns is part of how human consciousness functions rather than being temporary stage you'll outgrow through sufficient development.

The work continues. Integration isn't destination you reach where work is finished it's ongoing process you engage with throughout life because new shadow material continues forming, new circumstances activate different patterns, new relationships reveal dynamics that were dormant in previous circumstances, new developmental stages require different integrations as what was appropriate previously becomes limitation requiring transcendence whilst what's being transcended requires including rather than simply eliminating because you're not becoming different person through development, you're becoming more fully yourself which means including previous developmental stages rather than disowning them through identifying with current stage whilst maintaining you've outgrown what came before.

Every time you recognise pattern operating, every time you catch projection before it fully determines how you respond, every time you create space between trigger and reaction, you're practising integration, you're building coherence, you're strengthening executive function that allows conscious relationship with unconscious material. The practice is never finished because consciousness is never complete, because unconscious territories are vast, because becoming fully human is a process, not an achievement, is ongoing engagement, not a final destination, is direction, not arrival.

And this ongoing nature, this recognition that work is never finished, this acceptance that you'll never achieve perfect integration, this isn't discouraging if you understand what you're actually working toward. You're not trying to become perfect. You're trying to become more conscious. You're not trying to eliminate your humanity. You're trying to inhabit it more fully. You're not trying to transcend your limitations. You're trying to work with them more skillfully whilst accepting they're inherent to being human rather than being temporary defects that sufficient effort should eliminate.

Welcome to wholeness, to integration, to becoming fully human through including rather than transcending your humanity, through accepting rather than eliminating your limitations, through recognising rather than controlling your unconscious dynamics. You're not fundamentally different from when you started this book. You still have the same shadows, the same wounds, the same patterns, the same defensive structures, the same capacity for being triggered and reactive and operating from unconscious material, whilst consciousness has no awareness of what's determining responses.

But you have something you didn't have before: understanding. Recognition. Capacity for seeing patterns whilst they're operating rather than being unconsciously controlled whilst insisting you're freely choosing. A framework for making sense of your experience rather than being confused by contradictions you couldn't explain. Language for articulating dynamics that were operating beneath awareness, whilst shaping your behaviour in ways you couldn't recognise because you lacked concepts for understanding what was happening.

And if you do the work not just read about it, not just understand it intellectually, not just develop sophisticated analysis whilst maintaining all your patterns unchanged, but actually do the work through repeated practice building new pathways, through engaging with uncomfortable material rather than maintaining comfortable insights that change nothing, through taking understanding into lived experience where it can inform actual choices in real situations with real stakes then gradually, imperceptibly, over months and years of sustained effort, you become more integrated. Not perfectly integrated. Not finally finished. Not transcendent of human limitations. Just more conscious, more whole, more capable of recognising dynamics whilst they're operating, more able to work with patterns rather than being operated by them whilst insisting you're freely choosing.

This is what's possible. Not perfection. Not transcendence. Not the elimination of shadow or the achievement of final integration, where work is finished. Just gradually increasing consciousness, slowly developing coherence, building capacity for recognising dynamics whilst they operate, strengthening executive function that creates space between pattern activation and automatic response, becoming more fully human through including rather than eliminating aspects you've been defending against whilst maintaining they're not you, they're foreign to who you really are, they're defects that shouldn't exist rather than recognising they're part of being human that integration includes rather than transcends.

Your Obscure Psyche will remain obscure, will continue operating beneath awareness, will generate shadow material and defensive patterns as long as you're alive, because this is how human consciousness functions, rather than being a temporary limitation, sufficient work will permanently overcome. But it becomes less obscure, less controlling, less determining of your experience whilst you remain unconscious of what's operating. The territories remain vast, but you're exploring them rather than remaining alienated whilst insisting they don't exist. The patterns continue operating, but you're recognising them rather than being operated whilst maintaining you're freely choosing.

This is wholeness. This is integration. This is becoming fully human not through achieving impossible ideal, not through transcending your humanity, not through eliminating aspects you'd prefer not to have, but through conscious engagement with everything you are, through accepting your continuing capacity for unconsciousness whilst working to become more mindful, through inhabiting your humanity completely including the aspects that are difficult and shameful and that you've been defending against whilst maintaining they're foreign to who you really are rather than recognising they're part of being human that wholeness includes rather than eliminates through achieving integration that's actually just different form of splitting maintaining some aspects are acceptable whilst others must be excluded to achieve wholeness that isn't actually whole because it's achieved through excluding whatever contradicts idealised vision of who integrated person should be.

You are whole now. You always have been. Not because you're perfectly integrated or because you've achieved some ideal state or because you've transcended your limitations. But because wholeness includes everything, the conscious and the unconscious, the shadow and the persona, the integrated and the split, the aware and the defended, all of it, all of you, everything you've been defending against recognising whilst maintaining you're already whole through excluding whatever threatens ego's preferred identity. The work isn't achieving wholeness; you lack it. It recognises the wholeness you've always possessed but couldn't acknowledge, because acknowledging would require including aspects you've decided are unacceptable, whilst maintaining you're already whole by excluding them, which maintains fragmentation whilst insisting you're integrated.

Becoming fully human is recognising that you already are fully human, have always been, and will always be, whether you acknowledge it or not. The question isn't whether you're whole; you are. The question is whether you'll recognise it, whether you'll accept it, whether you'll stop defending against aspects of yourself whilst maintaining they're foreign to who you really are, whether you'll include rather than exclude, whether you'll accept rather than transcend, whether you'll inhabit your humanity completely rather than continuing to insist on impossible ideal that requires excluding whatever doesn't conform to fantasy about who you should be that's preventing you from recognising who you actually are which is exactly who you've always been but couldn't acknowledge because acknowledging would require accepting you're human in ways you've been defending against through maintaining you're better than that, more evolved than that, more integrated than that, when actually integration requires accepting you're that, you always have been that, you always will be that because being that is being human rather than being defect that sufficient work should eliminate.

You are your shadow. You are your wounds. You are your defences. You are your patterns. You are your unconscious dynamics. Not just you, but also these things, whilst primarily being the conscious ego identity you prefer, you are these things as fundamentally as you are anything, as essentially as any aspect you're willing to acknowledge, as much as qualities you're proud of or characteristics you identify with or capacities you're eager to own. The wholeness is recognising this, accepting this, including this whilst ego has been maintaining wholeness is achieved through excluding this, through transcending this, through outgrowing this, through eliminating this through sufficient work that would finally make you the person you think you should be rather than accepting the person you already are which includes everything you've been defending against whilst insisting you're already whole through the very defences that are maintaining fragmentation you're calling wholeness whilst actual wholeness requires including what you're excluding through defences maintaining split whilst consciousness insists you're integrated.

Welcome to the end, which is really the beginning, which is really the middle of an ongoing process that has no end because consciousness is never complete, integration is never finished, becoming fully human is a direction not a destination, is process not achievement, is ongoing engagement with everything you are rather than final transcendence of anything you don't want to be. The work continues. The patterns persist. The shadow remains. The unconscious operates. You're human. You always have been. You always will be. The only question is whether you'll accept it, whether you'll inhabit it fully, whether you'll stop defending against aspects of yourself whilst maintaining you're already whole through excluding them, whether you'll recognise that wholeness includes everything rather than achieving wholeness through eliminating whatever contradicts idealised vision ego has been desperately defending whilst insisting it's already achieved what it's actually preventing through the very defences maintaining fragmentation whilst consciousness calls it integration.

You are whole. Recognise it. Accept it. Inhabit it. Include everything. Exclude nothing. This is becoming fully human not through achieving something you lack but through recognising something you've always possessed but couldn't acknowledge because acknowledging requires accepting you're human in ways you've been defending against whilst maintaining you're more than human or better than human or evolved beyond basic humanity when actually you're exactly human, completely human, fully human whether you acknowledge it or not, whether you accept it or not, whether you continue defending against it whilst insisting you're already integrated or whether you finally stop defending and recognise that integration isn't achievement it's acceptance, it's recognition, it's inhabiting completely what you've always been whilst pretending to be something else, something better, something more, when actually being precisely what you are, including everything you've been excluding, accepting everything you've been defending against this is wholeness, this is integration, this is becoming fully human through recognising you already are fully human and always have been and always will be regardless of how much work you do or how integrated you become or how conscious you achieve because wholeness isn't destination it's recognition that you've always been whole whilst defending against recognising it through maintaining wholeness is achieved through excluding aspects you've decided make you less than whole when actually excluding them is what's maintaining fragmentation whilst recognition that you're all of it, always have been, always will be this is wholeness, this is integration, this is being fully human which you already are whether you recognise it or not.

Chapter 21
The Golden Shadow

I need you to think deeply about something that might challenge your beliefs about shadow work and the parts of yourself that you've disowned or relegated to inaccessible areas of your psyche. We've spent time exploring the darker aspects of the shadow, such as the anger you've suppressed, the selfishness you struggle to acknowledge, the cruelty you've denied, all the qualities you've deemed unacceptable and therefore not a part of who you are.

But there is another side to this shadow that is equally powerful, equally split off, and similarly inaccessible to your conscious awareness. This shadow is not about what is wrong with you; instead, it concerns the extraordinary qualities you possess that you do not allow yourself to embrace. Embracing these qualities can lead to a profound sense of personal growth and authenticity.

Think back to the last time someone genuinely complimented you or authentically praised your work. Consider the honest acknowledgement of a talent or ability that you displayed, not empty flattery, but sincere recognition of something you did well. Reflect on your internal response. Did you accept the praise gracefully, allowing yourself to feel truly capable? Or did you deflect it, minimise it, explain it away by attributing it to luck, timing, or someone else's contribution? Did you quickly point out the flaws in what you did, insisting that anyone could have achieved the same result? Did you feel uncomfortable or embarrassed by the recognition, as if you needed to shrink yourself to avoid appearing arrogant or full of yourself?

Now think about the talents or capabilities you've never developed, or the powerful aspects of yourself that you keep hidden. Perhaps there's creativity you never pursued because you believe creative people are impractical or irresponsible. Maybe you have leadership abilities that you've never expressed because leaders are often seen as controlling or domineering. You may have intelligence that you never fully showcased because smart people are frequently perceived as arrogant or as making others uncomfortable. Or perhaps you've held back your confidence because confident people are often labelled as narcissistic or self-centred.

What many people fail to understand is that shadow work is more complex than merely acknowledging one's dark side. You don't just disown negative qualities; you also repress positive ones with equal intensity, sometimes even more. Your genuine talents, authentic capabilities, real power, and actual brilliance might be relegated to the shadows, not because these qualities are bad, but because, in childhood, you often learned that expressing them could be dangerous. It was perceived as a threat to attachment, could create problems, could make others uncomfortable, and might result in punishment, withdrawal of love, or jealousy from those around you.

Consider the child who is naturally more intelligent than their siblings, who quickly grasps concepts and excels in school. When this child comes home, excited about their achievements and seeking recognition, the response from parents is crucial. If they celebrate genuinely and express pride without creating sibling hierarchies or jealousy, the child can integrate this capability, embrace their intelligence, and develop it naturally without shame.

However, if the response is different when parents feel threatened by the child's intelligence or worry that it makes them look inadequate, the results can be damaging. The child quickly learns that showcasing intelligence is dangerous and that success can threaten relationships. This can lead to a deep sense of shame and a decision to hide their abilities and minimise their achievements, perhaps even deliberately underperforming to avoid drawing attention.

The intelligence does not disappear; it goes into shadow. It remains an integral part of your psychological makeup, yet it becomes split off and disowned. You may find it challenging to acknowledge or express your intelligence without feeling overwhelming anxiety because associating it with losing love, connections, or being targeted has become ingrained.

This is the golden shadow, the positive qualities, talents, capabilities, aspects of genuine strength and power that you possess but cannot acknowledge, that exist in you but remain split off, that are authentically part of your potential but that you've learned are too dangerous to express, too threatening to own, too risky to develop. And until you reclaim these qualities, until you integrate this aspect of shadow, you remain perpetually smaller than you actually are, perpetually constrained by limitations you've imposed on yourself, perpetually hiding capabilities you genuinely possess because hiding feels safer than being fully seen in your actual power.

Now, you might be thinking, "But I don't have hidden talents or suppressed brilliance. I'm just ordinary. Maybe some people have golden shadow, but I'm genuinely not that special." And this is precisely how the golden shadow maintains itself by making you believe the disowned qualities don't exist, by ensuring you identify completely with being ordinary, being limited, being nothing special, whilst all the actual evidence of your capabilities gets explained away, minimised, rendered This is the golden shadow the positive qualities, talents, abilities, and aspects of genuine strength and power that you possess but cannot acknowledge. They exist within you but remain split off, authentically part of your potential yet perceived as too dangerous to express, too threatening to own, and too risky to develop. Until you reclaim these qualities and integrate this aspect of your shadow, you will remain perpetually smaller than you actually are. You will be constrained by limitations you've imposed on yourself, hiding capabilities you genuinely possess because hiding feels safer than being fully seen in your actual power.

You might be thinking, "But I don't have hidden talents or suppressed brilliance. I'm just ordinary. Maybe some people have a golden shadow, but I'm genuinely not that special." This belief is precisely how the golden shadow sustains itself; it convinces you that these disowned qualities don't exist, ensuring that you identify completely with being ordinary and limited. This mindset renders all your actual capabilities invisible through mechanisms that operate beneath conscious awareness.

Consider your actual achievements, the things you've done well throughout your life. Focus not on your potential achievements or what you might accomplish someday, but on your real track record. Reflect on the projects you completed successfully, the problems you solved, and the times you demonstrated resilience, courage, creativity, intelligence, leadership, or compassion in genuinely impressive ways. Acknowledge the skills you developed, the knowledge you acquired, the ways you've helped others, and the difficulties you've overcome. Make an actual list to force yourself to recognise evidence of your capabilities instead of automatically dismissing them.

As you do this, pay attention to what happens. Notice the discomfort that arises. You might hear a voice saying, "But that wasn't really that impressive. Anyone could have done it. I just got lucky. It wasn't that difficult." You may feel a strong urge to minimise these accomplishments or explain them away, to avoid thinking too highly of yourself and becoming arrogant or self-important. This discomfort, this automatic urge to downplay your achievements, signifies golden shadow defence; it reflects your psyche protecting you from acknowledging qualities that were once too dangerous to own.

Let's explore how this developmental process occurs, how positive qualities become disowned just like negative ones. The exact mechanisms that push anger or selfishness into the shadow can also relegate brilliance or power into it. Children don't just learn what qualities are bad; they also know which qualities are safe versus dangerous to express, and which traits help maintain connection versus threaten it.

For instance, a child in a family where parents are insecure and feel threatened by their children's success learns that showcasing capabilities can create conflict and lead to punishment. It becomes safer to stay small and underachieve, allowing parents to feel superior and maintain their positions without being challenged. Therefore, the child's genuine capabilities can pose a threat to family stability, making them hesitant to express their strengths for fear of losing the attachment they need for survival.

Alternatively, a capable child in a family with a struggling sibling who requires extra attention learns that being too successful or competent can create problems. Parents may feel guilty for not being able to provide equal attention, leaving the struggling sibling feeling worse by comparison. The child may perceive their strengths as a burden on the family system, believing that expressing them fully could be seen as selfish or insensitive.

Similarly, a child in a peer group where standing out invites bullying may learn that displaying talent or intelligence makes them vulnerable to aggression from those who feel threatened by differences. Such a child learns to hide their capabilities to fit in, even if doing so means suppressing genuine aspects of themselves.

Lastly, a child in a culture that values humility might see the acknowledgement of capability as arrogance. They may grow up believing that confidence equates to narcissism, where people who stand out get cut down, and those who recognise their strengths face social punishment. Consequently, this child may perceive recognising their own capability as morally wrong and a sign of bad character, leading to further disowning of their brilliance. Invisible through mechanisms operating beneath conscious awareness.

Think about your actual achievements, the things you've actually done well throughout your life. Not your potential achievements, not what you might do someday, but your actual track record. The projects you completed successfully. The problems you solved. The times you demonstrated resilience, courage, creativity, intelligence, leadership, or compassion in ways that were genuinely impressive. The skills you developed. The knowledge you acquired. The ways you've helped others. The difficulties you've overcome. Make an actual list, force yourself to acknowledge actual evidence rather than allowing it to be automatically dismissed.

And notice what happens as you do this. Notice the discomfort. Notice the voice saying, "But that wasn't really that impressive. Anyone could have done it. I just got lucky. It wasn't that difficult." Notice how you immediately want to minimise, to explain away, to ensure you don't think too highly of yourself, don't get too full of yourself, don't become arrogant or self-important or deluded about your actual capabilities. This discomfort, this automatic minimising, this compulsive need to make yourself smaller, this is golden shadow defence. This is your psyche protecting you from acknowledging qualities that were once too dangerous to own.

Let's talk about how this happens developmentally, how positive qualities become just as disowned as negative ones, how the exact mechanisms that relegate anger or selfishness to shadow can relegate brilliance or power to shadow. Children don't just learn which qualities are bad; they understand which qualities are safe versus dangerous to express, which aspects of themselves maintain connection versus threaten it, and which capabilities keep them secure in relationships versus make them vulnerable to loss of love or targeting by others.

A child in a family system where parents are insecure and where parental worth is threatened by children's success learns that displaying capability threatens the parents, creates conflict, and results in subtle or overt punishment. Better to stay small, to underachieve, to ensure parents can feel superior, can maintain their position, can avoid the narcissistic wound of being surpassed by their child. The child's genuine capabilities threaten family homeostasis, and expressing them risks losing the attachment the child depends on for survival.

Or a child in a family with a sibling who struggles, who needs extra attention, who requires parents' focus and energy. The capable child learns that being too successful, too competent, or too easy creates problems. Parents feel guilty about not being able to give equal attention, the struggling sibling feels worse by comparison, and family dynamics require the capable child to stay somewhat limited to make space for the one who needs more support. The child's genuine strengths can burden the family system, and fully expressing them is seen as selfish, insensitive, and complicating things for everyone else.

Or a child in a peer group where standing out invites bullying, where being different means being targeted, where displaying talent or intelligence or creativity makes you vulnerable to aggression from those who feel threatened by difference. The child learns that showing genuine capability means isolation, means being attacked, means losing safety in the group. It's better to hide it, to deliberately underperform, to ensure you fit in rather than stand out, even when fitting in means suppressing genuine aspects of yourself.

Or a child in a culture that values humility, that sees acknowledgement of capability as arrogance, that treats confidence as narcissism, that insists "tall poppies get cut down," that punishes those who rise above, who stand out, who acknowledge their genuine strengths. The child learns that recognising one's own capability is morally wrong, evidence of bad character, and something to be ashamed of rather than celebrated. The genuine strengths remain, but acknowledging them becomes associated with being a bad person, with moral failure, with unacceptable pride.

The mechanisms at play are similar to those associated with the psychological concept of 'shadow'. When a child demonstrates intelligence, talent, or strength, they often receive feedback suggesting that such expressions are dangerous. The amygdala encodes this association: expressing these qualities leads to feelings of threat, loss, pain, or punishment. As a result, the quality itself does not disappear; instead, it becomes split off from the child's conscious identity. The ego position shifts to 'I'm not intelligent.' At the same time, actual intelligence continues to exist but is now relegated to the shadow, disowned and unacknowledged, causing anxiety whenever they consider expressing it.

Just like with dark shadow, the disowned quality does not remain dormant. It persists, seeking expression, influencing behaviour, and finding ways to manifest while remaining split from conscious recognition. For instance, suppressed intelligence can emerge in the form of perfect scores on tests the individual claims they didn't study for, solutions to problems that are insisted to be simple, or a natural understanding of concepts dismissed as mere common sense. Similarly, disowned creativity might manifest through hobbies that are not taken seriously, ideas that are never developed, or artistic expressions that are downplayed as "just messing around" rather than being deemed real art.

Hidden leadership abilities may surface when the individual becomes the go-to person in a crisis, takes charge in necessary situations, or organises and directs efforts while insisting they're merely helping, not actually leading. Suppressed confidence can emerge through achievements that are systematically minimised, successes attributed to external factors, or genuine demonstrations of capability that can't be acknowledged as one's own.

Because these qualities reside in the shadow and cannot be consciously accessed or acknowledged, individuals are unable to develop them intentionally. They cannot choose routes that allow for full expression or build a life around their true capabilities because they do not recognise their own abilities. This results in a persistent state of being underemployed relative to actual potential, remaining in roles that are smaller than they can handle, and hiding capabilities they genuinely possess due to the anxiety triggered by recognising these threats during early expressions.

Now, let's discuss the neuroscience behind this. The exact mechanisms that sustain dark shadow also maintain golden shadow. Your amygdala retains associations between expressing certain qualities and receiving threatening responses. When there's a chance for these qualities to emerge, anxiety is triggered before the individual is consciously aware of it. This response isn't a conscious decision to hide capabilities; instead, it's an automatic defence mechanism. The amygdala detects that previous expressions of these qualities led to threats, thereby activating anxiety that prevents expression before the individual consciously understands what they are defending against. This lack of control over the defence mechanism can be frustrating and disempowering.

Meanwhile, your hippocampus plays a significant role in shaping your conscious beliefs. It may store explicit memories of specific incidents where exhibiting capability led to adverse outcomes, such as being punished for showing off, targeted by jealous peers, or feeling guilty for succeeding while others struggled. These memories help shape conscious beliefs about why it's safer to play small and why displaying capability might be dangerous or wrong. More significantly, however, your amygdala holds implicit emotional memories and an instinctive sense that expressing these qualities is dangerous. It also contains associations between capability and threat that activate automatically, without conscious recall of the events that created these associations.

When you're in a situation where you might showcase your genuine abilities, express your talents, or demonstrate your strengths, your amygdala activates even before you can consciously evaluate the circumstances. Anxiety rushes through your system, making you feel suddenly uncomfortable, uncertain, and acutely aware of all the reasons why you shouldn't stand out, shouldn't showcase your capabilities, and shouldn't allow yourself to be fully seen. You may interpret these feelings as humility, modesty, or a realistic assessment of your limitations. However, they are actually defences against the "golden shadow" anxiety that inhibits the expression of capabilities that were once perceived as dangerous.

Your nervous system learns that remaining small is safe, that hiding your capabilities fosters connection, and that suppressing your true strengths prevents a sense of threat. These patterns are encoded in implicit memory, operating through automatic processes that dictate your behaviour before you can consciously assess whether the current situation requires you to hide or whether the people around you would genuinely react negatively to your authentic capabilities. The fears that felt real in childhood may not be valid in your adult life. Yet, because this process works beneath conscious awareness, you fail to recognise that you are defending against your own potential. Instead, showcasing your abilities would be inappropriate, arrogant, or uncomfortable for others. You create rational-sounding justifications for staying small, such as "I don't want to make others feel bad" or "It's better to be humble". At the same time, the actual dynamic is an amygdala-driven defence against expressing qualities that your implicit memory has encoded as dangerous.

Another insidious mechanism that maintains this golden shadow is related to self-sabotage. Your brain naturally defends homeostasis, maintains a familiar identity, and resists change, even when change would be beneficial. If your identity has been built around being ordinary or limited, then acknowledging your genuine capabilities threatens that entire structure. You may wonder: Who would you become if you admitted that you're actually quite intelligent? What would you have to confront if you recognised your genuine talents? Facing the reality of your own potential could force you to re-evaluate the life you've built, the choices you've made, and the opportunities you've missed.

Acknowledging your golden shadow is an empowering act. It means confronting the fact that you've been hiding, playing small, and suppressing your true potential, not because you lack capability, but because expressing your abilities felt too dangerous. This realisation can be devastating, as it forces you to recognise your responsibility not in the sense of being to blame for your past, as you were likely protecting yourself from real threats in childhood, but in the sense of being responsible. You now have the ability to respond differently; you can choose whether to continue hiding or to start expressing your genuine capabilities. This sense of responsibility can feel overwhelming because it means you can no longer hide behind limitations. You can't claim that you simply lack ability or maintain the comfortable fiction that you are doing your best when, in reality, you've been deliberately constraining yourself to stay safe.

The golden shadow persists through the exact homeostatic mechanisms that uphold all patterns. Remaining small is familiar. Hiding your capabilities is known territory. Suppressing your talents feels safe. Your brain has learned how to function within these confines, developed strategies, and created neural pathways for these behaviours. Actually expressing your full capabilities threatens these established patterns; it requires building new ones, tolerating the unfamiliar, and facing the anxiety that full expression might provoke. It often feels easier to remain perpetually smaller than you are, to continue hiding, to explain away your achievements, and to maintain familiar limitations, even if they stifle your genuine potential.

Let's delve into the concept of sublimation, a process that offers a safe and acceptable outlet for the expression of repressed impulses. It's a way for the golden shadow to find expression when direct acknowledgement seems impossible. Sublimation is the process through which repressed impulses, drives, and desires find alternative channels for expression. These channels feel safer, more acceptable, and less threatening than expressing them directly. Freud primarily focused on the sublimation of sexual and aggressive drives, such as artistic expression as a sublimation of sexual energy and competitive sports as a sublimation of aggressive impulses. However, this concept is equally applicable to the golden shadow, where positive qualities that cannot be directly expressed find alternative forms.

For example, someone who struggles to acknowledge their leadership capabilities might sublimate this quality through volunteering or organising community events. They might lead in contexts that feel less serious or safely detached from their "real" life. In this way, they are genuinely expressing leadership while maintaining a conscious identity as "not a leader." This protects them from the anxiety that direct acknowledgement might create while still allowing the quality to find some expression.

Similarly, a person who cannot embrace their creativity might express it through cooking, gardening, or home decorating activities they perceive as practical rather than artistic. This approach allows for creative expression without the vulnerability that comes with identifying as a "creative person." They are indeed creative, but in ways that don't challenge their conscious identity.

A person who has disowned their intelligence might sublimate this trait by helping others with intellectual tasks or positioning themselves as the go-to for explanations. By framing their intelligence as merely being helpful or doing what anyone would do, they protect themselves from fully acknowledging their brilliance.

Sublimation provides a partial expression of these qualities while maintaining a split, allowing aspects of the self to remain in shadow. Though it avoids the full acknowledgement that could trigger anxiety, it's important to note that this isn't integration. The disowned qualities remain unrecognised, and the expressions are limited compared to what could be achieved with full acknowledgement. However, this is better than complete suppression, as it offers an outlet for qualities that could become toxic if entirely unexpressed. It allows individuals to be more like themselves, even if not entirely so. The journey towards complete self-acceptance is possible and can lead to a more integrated and fulfilling life.

Yet, there's a danger in letting sublimation become a permanent solution instead of a stepping stone toward integration. One can spend a lifetime expressing genuine capabilities through these sublimated forms, in contexts that don't require acknowledging their true qualities. Although this is healthier than complete suppression, it prevents them from realising their full potential and living a life that reflects their capabilities. It inhibits them from being fully themselves, as that would necessitate acknowledging qualities they have learned are too dangerous to own. Over time, this can lead to a sense of unfulfillment and a lack of authenticity in one's life.

Consider the talents you have sublimated; the capabilities you express in limited forms or aspects of yourself that find constrained expression through safe channels. This could be artistic ability shown only through hobbies rather than serious pursuits, leadership capabilities demonstrated only through volunteering instead of career advancement, or intelligence expressed only by helping others rather than pursuing your achievements. Similarly, confidence might be shown only when advocating for someone else, not in standing up for oneself. At the same time, courage could emerge only in crises, not in everyday situations where standing out is required. Recognising these sublimated qualities is the first step towards greater self-awareness and integration.

These sublimated expressions reveal what lies in your golden shadow. Whatever you express in limited ways, demonstrate in contexts that you don't take seriously, or acknowledge only when framed as unimportant, these experiences show what is split off, what remains in shadow, and what you possess but cannot entirely own. Sublimation reveals these qualities while protecting you from full acknowledgement, allowing for partial expression and maintaining a defence against complete integration.

Let's discuss how to work with your golden shadow, as reclaiming disowned potential requires a different approach than integrating the dark shadow. With the dark shadow, the focus is on acknowledging qualities you've defined yourself against, owning aspects you've judged as negative, and integrating material that threatens your self-concept as a good person. In contrast, working with the golden shadow involves recognising qualities you've minimised, owning capabilities you've explained away, and integrating material that challenges your self-concept as an ordinary person, someone who is nothing special and limited in potential.

Start by observing your patterns of deflection. For instance, notice when you downplay a compliment by saying, 'It was nothing, anyone could have done it,' or when you attribute your success to luck rather than your own abilities. These are signs of deflection. Don't try to stop this behaviour, just observe it. Pay attention to how automatic it is, how quickly you dismiss genuine recognition, how uncomfortable you feel when someone acknowledges your actual abilities, and how you compulsively downplay your strengths when they are recognised.

This deflection is your way of protecting yourself. It's not humility or realistic self-assessment; it's a defence mechanism. Consider what would happen if you accepted compliments. What if you acknowledged your achievements? What if you owned your capabilities? What anxiety would arise? What truths would you need to confront if you admitted that you are actually quite intelligent, talented, and capable, much more so than you have been allowing yourself to recognise?

Next, examine your sublimations, which are the ways you express your genuine capabilities in a restrained or indirect manner. For example, if you're a talented artist but only paint in your spare time and never show your work to anyone, that's a sublimated expression of your talent. Where do you demonstrate your abilities in contexts you don't take seriously? Where do you showcase your strengths but quickly downplay their importance? These sublimated expressions reveal what lies in your golden shadow, what you possess but cannot fully acknowledge. To live up to your full potential rather than a perpetually limited version of yourself, these qualities need to be reclaimed.

Start experimenting with owning these qualities. Acknowledge them more directly and allow yourself to be seen in your true capabilities. For instance, if someone compliments your work, instead of deflecting, say 'Thank you, I'm proud of what I've achieved.' Anticipate that this may create anxiety. This anxiety reveals that recognising these qualities feels dangerous, that expressing them may threaten you, and that staying hidden feels safer than being fully authentic. Don't allow this anxiety to deter you. Move through it. Allow yourself to be seen. Accept genuine recognition without deflecting, own your achievements without minimising them, and display your talents without immediately dismissing them as unimportant.

This process can be terrifying. Every defence mechanism you've built, every pattern you've maintained, and every limitation you've imposed will scream at you to remain small, to hide, and to protect yourself from being seen in your true power. The anxiety can be overwhelming because you are challenging the identity you've constructed around being ordinary, confronting the possibility that you are capable of far more than you have permitted yourself to pursue. Your amygdala perceives a threat because implicit memories encode expressing these qualities as potentially leading to punishment, loss, or danger. Meanwhile, your conscious mind will generate reasons to stay hidden, worrying that you will seem arrogant, make others uncomfortable, or question why you think you are special.

Notice what happens when you express genuine capability despite feeling anxious. Pay attention to whether the catastrophe you expect actually occurs. Observe if people respond with jealousy, punishment, or withdrawal; the reactions you may have unconsciously anticipated. Consider whether you can showcase true strength without being targeted, genuine intelligence without feeling isolated, and real talent without facing punishment. Reflect on whether the dangers that were real in your childhood still exist in your adult life.

For many people, what they discover is that the dangers they feared are more historical than present. In their adult lives, individuals often respond not with threats but with genuine capability. In fact, they might respond with appreciation, admiration, or respect. The catastrophic outcomes that implicit memory predicts do not materialise. Through repeated experiences of expressing capability without negative consequences, and by accumulating evidence that it is safe to be seen in your true power, these implicit memories gradually update. The link between capability and danger weakens over time, and the anxiety associated with expressing strength diminishes.

However, this process requires sustained effort, repeated experiences, and a conscious choice to confront anxiety rather than allowing it to control you. A single experience of acknowledgement or a brief moment of owning your capabilities will not erase years of suppression or override decades of implicit learning that equate expression with danger. Reclaiming your "golden shadow" occurs slowly, through many instances of owning your strengths instead of minimising them. It involves accumulating experiences that update old associations and building new neural pathways, linking the expression of capability with safety and reward rather than with threats and punishment.

Crucially, reclaiming your golden shadow involves confronting essential questions: If you have always been more capable than you allowed yourself to be, what does that mean about the life you've built? What does it mean about the choices you've made? What opportunities might you have missed by hiding instead of expressing your full potential? These questions can be devastating because they force you to acknowledge that your constraints have not stemmed from external circumstances or a lack of capability, but from your own defences, the patterns you've maintained, and the choices you've made to stay small, choices that felt necessary but were ultimately protective.

Recognising this isn't about self-blame; you were safeguarding yourself from real threats. You learned to hide because expressing your capabilities was genuinely dangerous in your developmental environment, whether it was due to parental expectations, societal norms, or personal experiences. However, it does require acknowledging that the protection may now be limiting. The defences you installed for survival could now be constraining your authentic expression, preventing you from being your true self. Acknowledging this means accepting responsibility, not blaming yourself for past choices, but recognising that you can make different choices now, even if those choices feel terrifying.

Consider what your life might look like if you entirely owned your golden shadow, if you acknowledged and developed the capabilities you genuinely possess instead of keeping them suppressed. What career might you pursue? What creative expressions might you engage in? What leadership roles could you take? What relationships might you form? What impact might you have? This isn't about hypothetical potential or fantasising about becoming someone you're not; it's about the actual development of the capabilities you possess but have kept hidden and the expression of talents you have systematically minimised.

Start by acknowledging your fears and the reasons behind them. Then, gradually begin to express your capabilities in safe environments. Seek support from friends, family, or a professional if needed. Remember, this is a journey, not a race. Take small steps, and over time, you'll find that the anxiety associated with expressing your strength diminishes. This journey is not about achieving perfection or reaching an idealised version of yourself. It's about becoming your true self rather than a constrained version. It's about expressing genuine capability rather than continually hiding. It's about being fully seen in your authentic power instead of maintaining a protective smallness that was once necessary but has become a limitation. Your golden shadow contains fundamental qualities, actual capabilities, and genuine strengths, not imagined potential, but aspects of yourself that exist, manifest in sublimated forms, and are demonstrated constantly while being systematically denied and minimised.

Reclaiming your true capabilities doesn't make you arrogant. Arrogance involves claiming abilities you don't have, inflating your self-worth beyond your actual skills, and demanding recognition for achievements that aren't yours. On the other hand, acknowledging genuine skills, owning your true talents, and accepting recognition for real accomplishments is not arrogance; it's simply being accurate. It's about seeing yourself clearly instead of through the distorting lens of golden shadow defence, which requires you to be perpetually smaller than you truly are.

It's essential to understand that reclaiming golden shadow is not just about personal development or achieving more for yourself. It's also about the collective cost of golden shadow, how much potential remains unrealised, how many talents go suppressed, and how much capability goes unexpressed because people learned early on that being their authentic selves was too dangerous. It made others uncomfortable and threatened relationships they relied on for survival. Reclaiming golden shadow can be as simple as speaking up in a meeting when you have a good idea, or as profound as pursuing a career that aligns with your true passions.

Consider all the potential leaders who learned to stay small because expressing leadership felt like exerting dominance or controlling others, like being the tall poppy that gets cut down. Think about all the potential artists who suppressed their creativity because creative expression seemed impractical or irresponsible. Reflect on the potential innovators who hid their intelligence because being smart made others uncomfortable or invited jealousy, leading to isolation. Also, consider the potential healers who minimised their capacity for compassion because showing deep care felt like a weakness, like being overly sensitive, or not being tough enough for the real world.

All that suppressed potential and unexpressed capability isn't just a loss for those carrying golden shadow; it's a loss for everyone. It robs communities of needed leadership, deprives culture of creativity, and denies the world intelligence, compassion, and courage. By reclaiming your true capabilities, you become an integral part of the solution, contributing to a world that benefits from the talents you truly possess.

Therefore, reclaiming your golden shadow is not a selfish act; it's a contribution. It's allowing the world to benefit from the talents you truly possess instead of keeping them suppressed for safety. Your authentic capabilities are not just valuable, they are essential. It's about sharing your abilities to serve others rather than hiding them to avoid discomfort. Being fully yourself means the world gains access to your actual capabilities instead of just the diminished version you've been showing all along.

This reframe can help alleviate the anxiety that comes with reclaiming your golden shadow. You're not being arrogant, showy, or overly grandiose. Instead, you're allowing your genuine self to be expressed instead of being chronically suppressed. You're contributing your capabilities instead of hiding them. You're offering service through full expression rather than by staying small. The world needs your authentic capabilities, not the constrained version you've maintained for safety.

However, it's crucial to acknowledge that this is difficult work, even more challenging than integrating dark shadow. Golden shadow is protected not only by fear but also by moral positions that make suppression seem virtuous. Challenging these defences requires confronting cultural values and may lead to being perceived as arrogant, self-important, or overly ambitious. It demands facing not just internal anxiety but also external judgment from those invested in your staying small. But remember, it takes courage to stand up to these forces and reclaim your true capabilities.

Reclaiming your "golden shadow," which represents your disowned potential and suppressed capabilities, often requires support. It's essential to be around people who can accurately recognise and reflect your actual abilities instead of punishing you for expressing them. You need relationships where being your authentic self doesn't threaten connection and environments that welcome genuine strength rather than demand its suppression. You cannot reclaim your golden shadow in isolation, in contexts that discourage expression, or in relationships that require you to remain small for others to feel comfortable. This reclamation needs safe conditions where expressing your true capabilities does not recreate the threats that led to their original suppression.

Welcome to the understanding of the golden shadow: the disowned potential, the suppressed capabilities that are genuinely part of you but that you cannot acknowledge. This suppression occurs because early experiences taught you that expressing these capabilities was dangerous; your identity may have formed around being ordinary rather than capable, and staying small often felt safer than being fully seen in your true power. You may minimise your intelligence, dismiss your creativity, deflect your leadership, suppress your confidence, explain away your talents, and systematically deny your strengths. All of this is real; it exists and could be developed and expressed if you can manage the anxiety that full acknowledgement brings. It requires moving through the fear of being fully seen and choosing authentic expression over protective limitations. The golden shadow is a part of you, waiting to be reclaimed.

The golden shadow is calling you toward your true capabilities, urging full expression, and encouraging you to be completely yourself rather than a constrained version of who you are. Answering this call requires courage. It means confronting the fact that you've been hiding and requires acknowledging that the limitations you've accepted were chosen, even though they felt like necessities. You must take responsibility for developing what you really possess instead of remaining perpetually smaller than you are. The anxiety associated with this journey is significant. The defences you've built are powerful, and the cultural pressures to stay small can be relentless. However, the alternative is to spend your life suppressing true capabilities, hiding your actual talents, and never fully expressing what you are capable of being, never becoming your true self because you've learned that being fully yourself was once perceived as too dangerous, too threatening, or too risky for the safety you depended on for survival.

The choice is yours: remain small and safe, or risk being fully seen by expressing yourself. You can either keep your golden shadow suppressed or reclaim that disowned potential. You can remain perpetually constrained or strive to become your authentic self. The work is challenging, the anxiety is real, and the past threats were genuine. But the critical question is whether those threats still hold true for you now. Is protecting yourself from dangers that no longer exist worth the cost of never being fully yourself, never expressing your genuine capabilities, and never living up to the potential you truly possess rather than the limitations you've been maintaining?

Chapter 22
The Secret Rooms of the Mind

Before concluding this book, I want to share some random facts about our remarkable brain and the behaviours that influence us. I could have written more on this vast subject, but it would resemble an encyclopaedia.

Endless Scrolling at Night: Why do some people lie in bed, phone glowing like a tiny lifeline in the dark, scrolling themselves into exhaustion? They know tomorrow will hurt. They see the regret even before it arrives. Yet still swipe, scroll, repeat. It isn't just procrastination. It's an escape, quiet, negotiation with the mind. Anything but silence. Psychology calls it emotional avoidance. The brain calls it survival. When thoughts get too loud, the nervous system reaches for a distraction like oxygen. Every reel, every notification, every tiny dopamine pulse whispers, "stay here, don't go where it hurts". For many, this habit didn't start last year or last month. It began in childhood, in homes where emotions were unpredictable, dismissed or punished. Silence wasn't peace. Silence was danger. So the brain learnt a trick. Drown, the noise before it drowns you. And now, as adults, the darkness of a quiet room feels heavier than the fatigue of no sleep. So they keep scrolling, not because they're weak, but because somewhere deep down, stillness feels unsafe. Sleep becomes a battlefield. And the enemy isn't the device. It's the thoughts you're not ready to meet.

Going Down Instead of Speaking Up: Why do some people shut down instead of speaking up when they're hurt? It's silence by choice, it's silence by design. The brain remembers every moment it wasn't safe to express itself. Every time emotions were dismissed or mocked, the nervous system made a note. "Next time, stay quiet, it's safer". So when pain hits, they don't argue; they retreat. Their mind starts running silent simulations. The perfect words, the ideal response. All happening inside, but never spoken aloud. It's not emotional coldness, it's neural conditioning. The prefrontal cortex tries to reason, but the amygdala has already pressed the protect button. This is what psychologists call emotional withdrawal. A self-defence mechanism disguised as calm. The body stays still, but internally, adrenaline spikes, the heartbeat shifts, and the brain replays scenarios it never dared to voice. On the surface, they look composed, maybe even detached. But inside, it's chaos, trying to stay contained. It's kind of a silence that screams, but only on the inside. They don't need someone to drag words out of them. They need safety, presence, and patience. Because for them, silence isn't the absence of emotions. It's a language. A way of saying, I'm trying to stay safe while still being seen.

Floater Friend: According to social neuroscience. Some people glide through friends like satellites. Always present, always smiling, yet orbiting, never fully landing. They blend effortlessly, reading energy, sinking into moods, and decoding micro expressions like second nature. But inside, it's the floater friend phenomenon. Being included yet emotionally peripheral. You laugh with them, but the jokes were born before you arrive. You walk beside them, but somehow still feel like you're training behind a story you were never entirely written into. And the mind feels it. The subtle cognitive dissonance between belonging and invisibility. Showing up with warmth, presence, and emotional intelligence doesn't always guarantee being someone's person. Group chats are full. But when life fractures, the phone stays silent. But here's what psychology teaches. It's not about speaking louder or forcing circles to hold you. The shift begins internally. Notice who remembers without reminders. Who texts without content? Who hears the quiet in your voice, even when you say you're fine? Attention, time, and emotional energy. These are neural currencies. And like all limited resources, they deserve investment where presence is valued, not where your absence is unregistered.

Isolation: The more you isolate yourself, the more your brain begins to distort reality. It's not just overthinking; it's just overthinking. It's your mind trying to make sense of silence. When you stop replying, it isn't rejection. It's your nervous system mistaking withdrawal for safety. You start believing you're better off alone, that people never really cared. But that's not the truth. That's your brain protecting a tired self. In silence, your mind amplifies everything. The amygdala searches for threats, while the rational part of your brain, your prefrontal cortex, goes quiet. So your brain starts filling in the blanks with fear. That's how emotional exhaustion becomes a loop. The more you pull away, the harder it feels to come back. But here's what your mind forgets. Connection is regulation. One text, one honest moment, one real conversation. It rewires the system, reminding your brain that safety can exist outside solitude. So if you've been pulling away, not because you stopped caring, but because you feel like too much, remember this. You're not a burden. You're just healing. And sometimes healing doesn't look brave. It looks like choosing to reach out even when silence feels safer.

The Weight of Unspoken Feelings: According to a behavioural psychologist, some people go silent the moment something hurts them, not because they don't have anything to say, but because their brain decides silence feels safer than being misunderstood. This is called protective emotional withdrawal, a defence the mind builds when expressing feelings. Once led to judgment or conflict, these people don't explode. They internalise. They replay the situation in their head and explain every emotion perfectly in their thoughts. But when it's time to speak, their voice freezes. The nervous system chooses safety over expression, and everything stays inside. Psychology calls this internal emotional processing, so you'll see two versions of them. Some days they're loud, sarcastic, playful, full of jokes and energy. One day, they will retreat, become quiet, and observe more than talk. And people quickly label them as introverts or distant without realising they're simply protecting their inner world. The truth is, they don't need someone who understands that silence isn't weakness. It's how they heal. Think, and breathe. Because sometimes the quietest people carry the most intense inner storms and the deepest hearts.

Inner Conversations: According to cognitive neuroscience, the habit of talking to yourself, building imagined scenarios, and holding full conversations in your head isn't just overthinking. It's the brain's self-regulation mechanism. When there isn't someone who truly understands, the mind points itself as both the speaker and the listener. It creates a private lab, a safe mental space where emotions can be studied, rehearsed, and released without judgment. You rehearse confessions you'll never voice, explanations no one ever asked for, and arguments you win flawlessly. In silence, this inner dialogue becomes a simulation system, like the brain's emotional rehearsal chamber, where you prepare for situations that may never happen. To feel in control for a moment. It's not madness. It's emotional survival, the mind whispers, if no one hears you, " I will". And yes, this builds insight, self-awareness and emotional intelligence. But there's a paradox. The deeper you go into this inner world, the easier isolation feels. Soon, reality feels louder than your thoughts, vulnerability feels dangerous. And the safest place becomes your own head. Because sometimes the brain doesn't talk to the world. It speaks for itself. Just to feel less alone.

Your Blanket is More Than Just Fabric: Psychology says people who can't sleep without a blanket, even when the room feels like fire, aren't chasing comfort. They're chasing safety. It's an unconscious act of somatic self-soothing, the body's way of recreating protection. The gentle pressure of fabric sends microsignals to the brain, releasing oxytocin, calming the amygdala, and slowing the heart rate. It's the science of safety disguised as a habit. That's why you'll find them half buried in summer nights. One leg out for balance, one arm tucked under, flipping the pillow to the cold side, but still needing that thin sheet across their chest. Because it's not about temperature, it's about containment. The blanket becomes armour, a boundary between self and chaos, warmth and vulnerability. For some people, that thin layer isn't fabric. It's familiarity. A memory of safety they never had. A psychological echo of being held, protected, and seen. The mind might forget, but the body doesn't. It remembers what safety once felt like, even if it was imagined. And so, night after night, the blanket becomes more than a cloth. It's comfort, it's control. It's a quiet reminder that even in heat, even in silence, you can still wrap yourself in something that feels like home.

Why we stay inside: Psychology reveals something most people never notice. The more you stay inside, the more your brain rewires itself to avoid the outside world. Start small, but slowly your comfort zone becomes a psychological cage. You think you're resting, but in reality, your mind is entering a low-energy survival mode. Your dopamine drops, your motivation weakens, and your thoughts begin looping on repeat. Science calls this mental rumination. A state where the brain keeps recycling old memories, future worries, and present exhaustion. Not because you're lazy, but because your mental resources are overloaded. That's why even a simple walk feels like climbing a mountain. Your brain associates movement with effort and effort with pain. But here's the neurological truth. You don't wait to feel better before acting. You act first. And then the brain follows. Sunlight, movement, fresh air. They recalibrate your nervous system, increase serotonin, and break the loop of overthinking. Just five minutes outside can shift your entire mental state. One step leads to another, and the fog starts to dissolve, and your brain remembers how it feels to live again. Your future self isn't asking for perfection. It's just asking for movement, because sometimes the bravest thing your brain can do is step outside.

Emotional Hypersensitive: Emotional hypersensitivity isn't just being too sensitive. It's a nervous system stuck in high alert, like an alarm that never turns off. It started as a survival skill built to detect danger before it arrived. These people don't just feel emotions, they absorb them. They notice tone shifts others miss, sense tension before words are spoken and get labelled as overreacting, when in truth, their brain is just trying to protect them. Imagine a child who learned to read every sign before the shouting began. Years later, the same brain still scans for danger even when there isn't any. Psychologically, it happens because their mind built early warning systems for unstable environments. But now those systems keep firing in safe spaces. Healing starts by understanding that your sensitivity isn't a flaw. It's wisdom born from survival. Your body isn't lying, it's remembering. So tell that hypersensitivity part of you, you've kept me safe, but now its ok to rest.

How Your Mind Handles Emotional Music: Ever notice how you hit play on a sad song? Even on a good day, you're not chasing pain. You're calibrating. Your auditory cortex picks up the melody. The limbic system tags it safe. The prefrontal cortex eases control. The vagus nerve loosens your breath. Emotion gets room to move instead of getting stuck. Psychologists call it parasocial emotion regulation. We borrow a voice, a piece of music, an artwork, or a story to process what we don't yet have the words or the safety to say. Mirror, like the song, reflects what's inside without judging it. That's why the ache can feel clean expectation in the harmony, a tiny dopamine lift in the release. Not drama, but resonance. Sad music becomes a container, not a wound. It doesn't interrupt, it doesn't rush you. It holds space steady. Patient. Until thunder turns to rain and your chest finally exhales. We don't really fear sadness. We fear facing it alone. A song stays when people can't. Whispering. Someone felt this, too, and turned it into something beautiful. Drop the one track that makes you feel seen.

7 Signs You've Met Your Ideal Match: 7 signs of couples who are perfectly aligned, not just emotionally, but psychologically. First, there are no games, no chasing, no ghosting, no ego battles. Their connection feels organic, like two frequencies sinking without static. Second, they feel safe being their raw, unfiltered selves. No masks, no filters, just pure authenticity. They can be weird, dramatic, even childlike, yet completely comfortable. Third, they share that playful energy. They act like two grown-up kids. One hates the cold, the other complains about the heat, but somehow they balance each other perfectly. Fourth, when conflict hits, they don't see it as a threat. Instead of who's right, they care about what's right. They argue, laugh, repair, and breaking up is never even an option. Fifth, they have their little tantrums, but it's never toxic. It's more like emotional gravity pulling them back toward each other. 6. Physical closeness comes naturally. They lean on, hug, or hold each other without even realising it, as if their bodies remember what their hearts decided long ago. And seventh, they share everything: a meme, a meal, a random thought. Because connection to them isn't just love; it's the constant urge to say, 'you have to see this.' That's the beauty of two minds that beat in perfect rhythm.

Why We Turn Pain Into Jokes: People who turn pain into jokes aren't just being funny, they're surviving. Psychologically, it's called deflection, a defence mechanism where humour becomes a shield. It's the laugh after a sharp comment, the self-mocking joke, before anyone else can take aim, "I im fine", wrapped in sarcasm. On the surface, it looks like confidence, the funny one who keeps everyone entertained. Still, beneath that, the smile, the brain is doing something clever but costly, redirecting emotional pain to protect itself. It's the mind's way of saying, "Don't look too close; this still hurts." Sometimes the humour becomes a language that says everything without ever being serious. You start performing happiness so well that even you begin to believe it for a while. But deep down, your nervous system still knows the truth, that every laugh is just a pause between the waves of what you're avoiding. Deflection feels harmless until you realise it teaches others to overlook your pain too. You become the person who never needs comfort, never needs checking in. The truth is, humour can heal, but when it becomes armour, even laughter starts to feel heavy. So ask yourself, are you laughing to express or laughing to escape? Because sometimes the biggest punchline hides the deepest ache.

When Females Reject Creation: In psychology, where women's fear of pregnancy, known as tokophobia, isn't weakness, it's awareness; it's the mind's rebellion against biology's oldest command. These women don't fear giving birth; they fear erasure. Because pregnancy isn't just about creating life, it's about watching your old identity dissolve to make space for another. Their anxiety isn't irrational; it's the psyche simulating the future. A simulation where freedom becomes routine, where dreams take a back seat to diapers, what they feel isn't cowardice, it's clarity. The kind of clarity that comes from advanced emotional intelligence. They possess empathy that extends beyond themselves, imagining the child's life rather than just the romanticised idea of motherhood. They have future projection, the rare ability to see how choices today reshape every version of tomorrow, and they have integrated thinking where instincts and intellect collide, forcing honest but uncomfortable truths. We glorify motherhood as destiny yet dismiss the cost it demands. So, to every woman who hesitates, your fear isn't a flaw; it's a form of consciousness. Real maturity isn't about following the script written by nature or society. It's about daring to edit it. Because sometimes the bravest decision isn't creating life, it's choosing to preserve your own

Why We Stay Where We Hurt: In psychology, there's a fascinating yet painful phenomenon when someone forgets how deeply they were hurt the moment that same person shows a little kindness, it isn't forgiveness its cognitive dissonance the brains way of rewriting emotional reality it convinces you mistake chaos for connection, that's how emotional that maybe your reaction was too much, perhaps they didn't mean it because accepting the truth threatens the illusion of safety every soft word every apology every gentle "I miss you" acts like a reset switch the mind clings to that fleeting warmth erasing the pain just enough to believe again. Until the cycle repeats, there is confusion: "why did I stay, why did I believe, why does my heart defend what broke it?" Psychology calls this intermittent reinforcement the same principle that keeps people addicted to uncertainty. The pain stays constant, but the reward, the affection, the rare i love you the sudden sweetness appears unpredictable, and the brain chasing that random hit of dopamine mistakes chaos for connection. that's how emotional addiction begins, not because we're weak, but because the mind fears emptiness more than pain.

The Forbidden Psychology of The INTP Mind: What kind of family raises an INTP? Usually, one where silence speaks louder than emotions. Homes where logic was praised but vulnerability was quietly discouraged, where love existed but was shown through fixing problems rather than expressing care. So the INTP learns early to internalise to think before feeling, to analyse before reacting. They grow up watching emotions like experiments, observing how others express what they themselves can't. Their mind becomes their safest laboratory. A place where questions evolve faster than answers. They learn that curiosity is not just a trait, it's survival; it helps them navigate a world that often values appearance over understanding. When an INTP feels an emotion is unpredictable, they retreat into books, games, and theories, not to escape reality but to decode it. They dissect emotions like data, translating chaos into logic, pain into patterns. They don't lack emotion; they process it differently through cognition first, empathy second. As adults, they appear detached, calm, analytical, but beneath that still surface lies a storm of unspoken feelings, a lifetime of unsent thoughts, unfinished connections, and quiet grief turned into theories. They live between logic and longing, fluent in ideas yet still learning the language of the heart.

Imaginary Scenarios Before Sleep: In psychology, there's a fascinating phenomenon many people experience without realising it, creating entire imaginary scenarios before falling asleep. It feels harmless, even comforting. You close your eyes, and suddenly your mind begins to weave a story, vivid, cinematic, perfectly controlled. But for some, this habit evolves into what psychologists call maladaptive daydreaming: when your brain, hungry for meaning or control, builds a private universe to escape the unpredictability of real life. You replay conversations, crafting the perfect comeback, you never said, you imagine futures that never happened, or alternate versions of yourself who did everything right. Your mind attempts to restore balance in a world that often feels uncertain. Over time it becomes a rightly ritual not just a way to fall asleep but a portal to a version of life where things finally go your way for some its closure they never received for others its an illusion of intimacy excitement or success that reality still withholds and while it soothes you in the moment it rarely heals because the mind can wander anywhere but when the story ends you always wake up back in he same world you were trying to escape.

When Your Nervous System Changes Around Parents: In psychology, there is a response we don't talk about enough: the moment when a parent speaks and your whole body quietly goes into defence mode. You're not angry, you're not being disrespectful, but your chest tightens, your patience thins, and your mind goes on alert. With friends or strangers, you're calm and grounded, but with parents, it's like an old switch flips instantly. Why? Because your not reacting to todays conversation you're responding to years of emotional conditioning maybe love came with correction, maybe your voice wasn't heard only managed so your nervous system learned stay small stay careful stay ready this isn't loud trauma its quiet pressure the kind that trains you to perform to please, to shrink, so now even a simple question feels like a test even calm words can trigger old defence patterns and no it doesn't mean you don't love them it means being around them can pull you back into the version of you who had to survive instead of simply exist that's not disrespect that's trauma memory you're not broken your just tired of performing.

People-Pleasing Syndrome: In psychology, the Nice Guy Syndrome explains why you feel drained, always giving 100% to people who wouldn't cross the street for you. Its a quiet but destructive pattern, these men hide their desires behind being good avoid conflict at all cost and believe that if they're helpful enough love will finally arrive psychologically this creates covert contracts unspoken deals where you give endlessly expecting emotional rewards that never come, like the guy that always pays for dates but never says what he really wants or the employee who overworks hoping someone will finally notice. Over time, this turns into resentment, confusion and loneliness. Dr Roberts Glover explains that, from an early age, nice guys were taught that their true selves were unacceptable, so they built a false identity. What he calls 'The Mask of Niceness'. The tragedy is that the more perfect they try to be, the less real connection they ever feel. But here's the truth, your anger isn't weakness, it's your integrity trying to speak. The answer isn't to be nicer, but to be real. To set boundaries, say no and stop apologising for your needs. Because authentic men don't chase approval, they live in alignment with who they are.

Why You Care So Much: Have you ever noticed how, for some people, caring about someone suddenly feels like a full-time mental job? Psychology says when an overthinking brain gets attached, it doesn't just feel love, it studies it, scans it, and protects it. One unread message can flip their mood; a slight change in tone, and their mind starts running simulations like a supercomputer. It's not because they're dramatic; it's because their brain has been trained by past hurt to detect danger in silence and rejection in pauses. This is called rejection sensitivity; the same neural circuits that react to physical pain light up when they feel ignored or misunderstood. So they replay conversations, zoom in on a single sentence, analyse an emoji like it's a secret code, not because they doubt you, but because somewhere in their life someone they cared for vanished without warning, and now their brain believes silence means loss, distance implies danger. Love always needs protecting. If this sounds like you, remember you're not too much, you're a mind that learned to survive, and survival isn't weakness. It's proof you loved deeply.

Daughters Raised By Toxic Parents: Girls raised in unhappy families often carry an invisible fear that history will repeat itself, they'll marry someone like their father or slowly turn into their mother. These families aren't broken by money, but by emotions that never healed. At the centre is usually one unstable parent controlling, unpredictable and blind to the pain they create. You grow up learning that love is earned, not given. Their moods decide if you're safe or not. You walk on eggshells, trying not to trigger another storm. Over time, you become hyper-aware of anger, trained to keep the peace even when it's breaking you. And as an adult, you freeze during conflict, apologise when you've done nothing wrong, and struggle to trust kindness, always waiting for the hidden catch. Their voice still echoes in your head, you're too sensitive, you're never enough. But here's the truth: your sensitivity isn't a weakness; it's your survival instinct. Finally safe enough to feel everything. The fact that you fear becoming like them proves you already aren't. Healing begins when you realise the family you came from doesn't define you. You get to write your own story now, one gentle conscious choice at a time.

Minds That Understand With Compassion, Instead of Hate: In psychology, one of the rarest forms of emotional intelligence isn't about staying calm; it's the ability to trace pain back to its source mentally. Some people don't react; their brain automatically shifts into analysis mode. They don't only see someone's actions, they see the wiring behind them. Childhood conditioning, emotional wounds, neural patterns shaped by years of survival. It's called cognitive empathy when your mind slips into another person's internal architecture, not to excuse them but to understand the mechanism behind the behaviour. Yet, this level of awareness is a double-edged sword because when you know too much, hate starts to lose its edge. Anger dissolves into comprehension, but the scar stays. You carry clarity and the wound together, and deep down, people like this quietly wish someone could read their mind with the same depth, but remember, understanding is not an obligation. Neuroscience tells us the brain seeks logic, but self-respect demands boundaries. Just because a behaviour makes psychological sense doesn't mean it deserves a place in your life.

What If Quietly Reveals About You: Alcohol doesn't create a new version of you; it turns up the volume on the version already hiding beneath your control systems. Your prefrontal cortex, the part of the brain responsible for judgment, emotional regulation, and self-control, slows down when you drink and when that happens, people don't change; they reveal the calm, sleepy one who disappears after a few drinks, which isn't boring. They're someone who carries storms in silence. A nervous system trained to hold steady even when it hurts, then there's the aggressive one, suddenly loud and explosive, not just bad behaviour, but suppressed anger finally leaking out when inhibition drops, and the midnight caller texting the person they swore they were over, that isn't drama, that's unresolved attachment. A heart that breaks in silence when sober but spills everything when the defences fall. The Braggerart who becomes the hero, a genius, the main character isn't confident, they're scared of not being enough, craving validation like oxygen and the quiet crier strong all day but in tears after one glass, that's not weakness, those are wounds no one ever noticed. The truth is, alcohol doesn't expose your worst, it exposes your hidden. The version behind the mask, behind the calm, behind every I'm fine. Sometimes the real you isn't who you are when you're in control. But who you become when your brain finally stops pretending.

How Your Brain Rewards Bad Decisions: Risk isn't just a personality thing; it's literally a brain setting inside your head. There's a region called the ventral striatum, and right next to it, the nucleus accumbens. Both are part of your reward system. When some people face uncertainty or danger, these areas don't calm down; they light up like a rave. For them, choosing the risky option is already a reward, not the outcome itself. Just choosing it is why: your brain reacts way more to the anticipation of a reward than to the moment you actually get it. It's like the thrill hits harder than the victory. Now, here's the twist: the prefrontal cortex, the part responsible for logic, judgment, and self-control, sometimes doesn't hit the brakes hard enough. When it underperforms, the weight thinks this through the system goes offline. Combine that with higher dopamine sensitivity, and 'BOOM' you got a brain that craves novelty, adrenaline, and chaos. That's why some people chase extreme hobbies, wild situations or dominant strategies. Not because they're reckless but because their brain is literally trying to reach its preferred level of stimulation., Thrill isn't an accident for them, it's a need.

How Some People Control a Room: Charisma and manipulation are basically the dark arts of social influence powered straight from the brain. Some people don't walk into a room; they take control of its emotional frequency. Their brains process micro-expressions, tone shifts, and energy faster than the average person. One glance and they already know how you feel, sometimes even before you do. The prefrontal cortex, the brain's strategy HQ, kicks in. It predicts how people will react, then carefully chooses the exact words, pauses, and facial expressions needed to steer someone's emotions. Nothing is random; every move is calculated, and the messed-up part is when they successfully influence someone, their brains drop a hit of dopamine, the 'you did great' chemical. Manipulation becomes addictive; people admire, follow, and even defend them. Meanwhile, inside, there's a cold mind always planning two steps ahead. The real danger isn't high IQ, it's focused genius pointed towards destructive goals. But genuine constructive genius that needs to be discovered early, while the brain is still flexible, still forming new neural pathways at insane speed. If we identify a kid's unique zone of genius at the right time, we can guide that energy towards creation, not destruction. Everyone is born with potential; only a few get the chance and the direction to grow it.

Amygdala Overload: Have you ever noticed how some people are always on edge, like their brains don't chill? That's what happens when the Amygdala, the brain's emotional alarm system, goes into constant overdrive. The Amygdala is supposed to protect you, detect threats, and trigger the fight-or-flight response. But when it's overloaded, it starts firing even when there's no real danger, so now your brain's treating a text notification like it's a tiger in the jungle. You feel anxious, hyperalert, irritated, and the nervous system is running on fumes. that's what long-term stress does. It teaches your brain to live in survival mode. Most of the time, this pattern starts early, in childhood, chaos, fear, unpredictability, whatever the cause. The brain rewires itself, thinking Okay, danger is permanent and by adulthood, the amygdala's are firing faster than logic can catch up. The prefrontal cortex, the rational part, doesn't get enough time to say "Yo, relax, we're safe". So what you get is impulsive behaviour, emotional outbursts, maybe even control issues. It's not attitude; it's neurochemistry. The brain isn't broken; it's just stuck in protection mode. But here's the thing, awareness that's the first step to re-wiring it.

Yawning is Contagious Because of Empathy: Yawning is contagious, but the reason behind it isn't just about being tired. When you see someone yawn and suddenly feel that weird urge to yawn too, that's not a coincidence, that's your brain syncing up. In psychology, this phenomenon is often linked to social bonding and emotional resonance. The subtle ways our brains mirror others to feel connected. Inside your head, a set of neurons called 'mirror neurons' light up; they mimic what others do, almost like your brain's saying "i get you, i feel what you feel". It's part of your empathy circuit, the system that helps you understand emotions without words. It's almost like your brain runs a silent simulation of what the other person is experiencing to keep up with the emotional rhythm around you. Here's the fascinating part: studies show that people who are naturally more empathetic are way more likely to catch a yawn. So the next time you yawn just because someone else did, remember it's not your body being lazy, it's your brain showing connection. You don't mirror a yawn, you mirror emotion.

Behind Emotionally Weak Men: Psychologists now recognise something quietly shaping modern masculinity, the era of emotionally absent fathers. One in four men grew up without a model of grounded strength, not neglect in the physical sense, but in deeper absence. The kind that teaches a boy to mute his own power to keep love close. These boys grow into men who can't locate their own anger, who mistake compliance for peace and who keep performing worthiness in every relationship, hoping someone will finally say, " i see you, son". Neuroscience shows that the developing brain mirrors what it witnesses. When a father withdraws instead of leading with integrity, the child encodes silence as safety. Over time, this crystallises into their subconscious beliefs: my emotions are threats, my needs are inconveniences, my voice is a risk. But the truth is, what you call weakness isn't brokenness, it's programming. You didn't fail at being a man; you just learned manhood in a room where no one spoke it aloud. Healing doesn't mean becoming harder; it means becoming whole. It's time to reparent that silent boy inside you, to teach him that real men don't disappear, real men stay present even with trembling hands. Want to begin that work? Read my book "The Masculinity Crisis" available on Amazon.

Dyslexia Slows Down Reading: They call it Dyslexia, but what if it's not a weakness at all? What if it's a different kind of intelligence? One thing the world still doesn't understand? In the dyslexic brain, the prefrontal cortex, the area responsible for modelling and planning, takes over. Compared to others, dyslexics process information along unusual mental pathways. They often develop strategies that seem unconventional to outsider observers; they rely more on the brain's visual-spatial areas, activating regions that enhance creative problem-solving beyond the norm. This strengthens imagination, sharpens spatial awareness and builds a faster sense of overview, which connects ideas that seem distant or unrelated. Dyslexic minds often see the big picture before the details, and they carry a resilience born from constant adapting to challenges. It's this difference that fuels originality, the ability to see solutions that traditional thinkers might overlook. A perspective shaped, not by limitation, but by difference. So ask yourself, is Dyslexia truly a handicap or is it another form of intelligence that society refuses to see? A hidden gift masked by misunderstanding.

Why Do You Understand Others So Well: Why do you understand others so well, but can't figure yourself out? The people who read others the best are usually the ones who feel the most lost inside. They see through masks; they sense emotions that others hide, but when it comes to their own, everything becomes blurry. It's not that they lack awareness; it's that they've spent too long surviving through empathy. As children, they learn to watch every change in tone, every shift in mood, because safety depended on it. So their mind grew outward, scanning others for danger, for approval, for peace. But it never learned to look inward. That's why they can comfort everyone except themselves. Understanding others became their armour, but self-understanding is the wound beneath it.

Tiredness After Sleeping: If you always feel tired even after sleeping, Psychology says it's not about rest; it's emotional exhaustion. It's the weight your mind is carrying. When you go through chronic stress, emotional suppression or trauma, your amygdala keeps sending danger signals even while you're sleeping, which keeps your cortisol levels high and your parasympathetic nervous system. The one that helps you rest, basically offline. So while your body is horizontal, your brain is still sprinting. It's processing fears, analysing conversations, and predicting threats. This constant state of hyper vigilance is called emotional exhaustion. It's why your REM sleep quality drops, it's why you wake up with racing thoughts, and it's why your energy never fully recharges.

When A Man Acts Childish: If a man ever acts childish in front of you and you tell him, "Why do you act so childish? Why can't you be serious for once?" Believe me, that man is going to have a massive switch-up on you, because his whole life he's been told to be serious, to be strong, to hold it in, never to show softness. Society taught him that being playful makes him less of a man, so when he finally lets that side out, it's not immaturity, it's comfort, it's trust. Around you, he finally feels safe enough to drop the weight he's been carrying; he can laugh without judgment, joke without being called weak, and smile without feeling ashamed. That's not a man acting like a child; that's a man healing the child in him. But when you tell him to grow up, you're not just killing the mood, you're shutting down the one place where he felt free. Psychologically, that moment can cut deep; it tells his brain vulnerability isn't safe, that even love demands he hide again, and he will, he'll pull back, talk less, laugh less and that version of him, that once felt alive around you, will disappear.

Psychology Behind Coffee: Why can some people drink a whole cup of coffee and fall asleep straight after? It sounds funny, but it's actually really sad when you think about it. Some people don't drink coffee to wake up; they drink it to feel something, to feel warmth, comfort, a moment of peace in a mind that's been fighting since childhood. When you grow up constantly stressed, anxious or walking on eggshells, your nervous system learns to stay alert all the time. According to psychology, it's called hyperarousal fatigue. When your body is so used to being in survival mode that even stimulation can't keep it awake. That's why some people drink coffee and then sleep, not because they're strange, but because they're tired in a way caffeine can't touch. It's the tiredness that comes from holding it together for too long; you stop knowing what real rest feels like. So when you drink coffee, your body doesn't react the way everyone else's does. It's already been living on survival energy for years; the caffeine doesn't wake you up because your body is already running on overdrive. Instead, the moment you finally sit down, your car drops, and your body takes that tiny charge to rest.

Why Do Some People Feel Ugly: Why do some people feel they are ugly, even when others clearly see beauty in them? For many, this comes from body dysmorphia, a condition that distorts their self-image and twists their reflection into something they barely recognise. It makes them focus on tiny details, turning small imperfections into something overwhelming. The mirror becomes a source of fear rather than truth. Compliments feel confusing because their mind refuses to believe them. Some people grew up being criticised or compared, so doubting their appearance became a habit. Others developed this distortion through insecurity, trauma or years of negative self-talk. Over time, their brain learns to look for flaws rather than for anything good. They're not rejecting their beauty; they can't see it the way others do. Body dysmorphia traps them in a distorted version of themselves, leaving them longing for the day they can look in the mirror and finally recognise their reflection.

Comfort In Being Sad: Why do some people find so much comfort in being sad? For many, sadness becomes familiar, a place they've learned to understand, even when it hurts. Happiness can feel unpredictable, fragile and easy to lose. But sadness is steady, something they know how to carry. It doesn't ask for performance or force them to pretend. In sadness, they don't have to meet anyone's expectations or hide how they feel. Some people grew up in environments where sadness was the only emotion they felt safe expressing, so it became their resting place. Others find comfort in sadness because it slows the world down, giving them space to think, feel, and breathe without pressure. Sadness can also provide a strange kind of clarity, a quiet honesty that joy sometimes covers up. They are not choosing misery, they're choosing familiarity, choosing the emotion that's feels the least disappointing. For some people, comfort doesn't come from feeling good; it comes from feeling something they understand.

Why You Don't Like Being Touched: Some people don't feel comfortable being touched by just anyone, and that's not a sign of coldness or distance. In fact, for many, it can be the opposite; when physical touch is someone's love language, it holds a much deeper meaning. Touch isn't just casual, it's personal, intimate and safe. They reserve it for people they truly trust, care about and feel emotionally connected to. So when someone flinches away or stiffens at unexpected hugs, handshakes or casual touches, it doesn't mean that they're unfriendly. It often means their boundaries are rooted in something meaningful. For them, physical touch is not just a greeting; it's a form of love, comfort and vulnerability, and that's why not everyone gets access to it. They need to feel emotionally safe first. Once that trust is there, touch isn't uncomfortable anymore. It becomes their favourite way to express love and feel close. Respecting that boundary isn't just kindness; it's honouring who they are.

When You Can't Stop Thinking About Someone: According to psychology, when you can't stop thinking about someone, it's not always because you're in love with them. It's often because your brain hasn't finished processing the story. The mind loops what it doesn't understand, so when a connection ends suddenly, quietly, or without a clear explanation, your brain keeps replaying the moments, searching for meaning you weren't given. You're not stuck on the person; you're stuck on the unfinished narrative. Your brain is trying to solve a puzzle with missing pieces. Was it something you said, something you didn't say, were you not enough, or were they simply unable to show up? Your mind doesn't like open endings, so it replays the memories, looking for a moment where things could have gone differently. That's why they stay in your head long after they're gone, not because they were your soulmate, but because your story with them didn't get closure. Healing doesn't mean forcing yourself to forget; healing is when the loop finally stops, not because you moved on from them, but because you understood yourself.

Meaning Of Leg Shaking: Some people shake their legs without even realising it, and it's not just a random habit; it often has a psychological root. Leg shaking, also known as restless energy, is usually the body's way of releasing stress, anxiety or tension. When the mind feels overwhelmed, the body looks for an outlet, and repetitive movement provides temporary relief. It's like a silent coping mechanism that helps them regulate when their emotions feel too heavy, or their thoughts won't slow down. For others, it becomes a habit formed over years of sitting in stressful environments, such as school, work, or even at home. The movement helps the brain stay alert and focused, especially for people who struggle with anxiety. ADHD, or overthinking. It's not done to annoy others; it's often the only way their body feels calm or grounded in the moment. So when someone constantly shakes their leg, it's not a sign of impatience or boredom. Often, it's their nervous system trying to relieve pressure and find a sense of stability in a mind that rarely rests.

People Who Constantly Forget Things: People who constantly forget things or struggle with memory loss aren't just forgetful; they're often carrying memories their mind decided were too painful to keep. In psychology, this is known as dissociative amnesia. A defence mechanism that develops when the brain experiences trauma, especially in childhood. It learns to protect itself by blocking out of fragmenting specific memories, not to erase the past but to survive it. Over time, this self-protection becomes automatic; even small things, dates, names, tasks, and conversations can slip away, not because of carelessness but because the brain has practised avoidance for so long that forgetting becomes second nature. As adults, many begin to notice gaps in their stories. Whole parts of childhood are missing, emotions that don't match the memories that remain. It's not that nothing happened; it's that too much did. For those who live with this, forgetting was never a flaw; it was a form of survival.

Overthinkers Exposed: According to psychology, overthinkers don't think too much; they feel too much. A softness when they get attached to someone, their entire mood begins to depend on how that person responds to them. They're so tuned into emotions that even the most minor shift in someone's tone or behaviour feels like a storm. This sensitivity often ties back to rejection sensitivity, a deep fear of being dismissed, ignored or misunderstood, especially by the ones they care about most. They're replaying a conversation from earlier, analysing every pause, every sigh, every change in expression. This is dramatic, but their brain has learned to scan for signs that love might be fading, even when it's not. The truth is, overthinkers don't notice small changes; they feel them this way: a sigh, a pause, a delayed text. It echoes through their whole body as if it were proof of rejection. They feel trapped in a storm that no one else can see.

Laughing During Serious Situations: Laughing during serious situations is a sign of high emotional intelligence. It's not because you're heartless; it's because you process emotions on multiple levels. This is called the incongruous effect, and it's surprisingly common among highly intelligent people. Why?. Because smarter brains process multiple emotional layers at once. Instead of freezing, they short-circuit into humour as a coping mechanism. When laughter escapes at funerals, during arguments or in silence, it isn't cruelty. It's the Brain managing emotion. It's not immaturity, it's complexity. What feels like a flaw to others is actually a hidden psychological superpower. Your brain's way of breaking tension, self-soothing, or creating distance from something overwhelming. You're not broken. You think differently. Have you ever laughed when you weren't supposed to? Because sometimes laughter isn't avoidance. It's survival disguised as humour.

When Your Brain Decides Reality is Dangerous: There's a defence mechanism in your brain so brutal that it erases you to keep you alive, it's called dissociation. In the middle of trauma, when the pain is too big to survive, your mind makes a split-second choice: leave the body or break apart. The prefrontal cortex shuts down awareness, the amygdala keeps firing alarms, and suddenly you're watching yourself like a stranger trapped in your own skin. Its survivors describe it as floating outside their body, hearing their own voice from a distance, or living life like it's not real. Here's the chilling truth: it works. Dissociation protects you in the moment, but later it turns into a prison. You can't feel fully alive, you can't trust your memories, and sometimes you can't even recognise the face in the mirror. that's not weakness, that's the cost of surviving the unspeakable, because when your brain decides reality is too dangerous, it doesn't just shut out the pain, it shuts out you.

When ADHD Makes You Care Too Much: One of the most complex parts of having ADHD is this. When you really care about someone, your brain doesn't just notice them, it fixates on their tone, their timing, the way they text back. Every little shift starts to matter more than it should. Because ADHD doesn't just affect attention, it affects emotional regulation. You feel things more strongly, more quickly, more deeply, especially the fear of being ignored, misunderstood, or left behind. So you start replaying conversations, scanning for clues, trying to make sense of the silence. You want a connection more than anything. But the fear of losing it makes your brain spin in circles. Not because you're needy, not because you're dramatic, but because your nervous system is wired to protect you even from love that isn't leaving.

You Only Have One True Friend: A human can have only one true friend in their lifetime. Not the one who's always around, but the one who is always there, even in silence. They don't need to talk every day; they might go months without a single message, but when they finally speak, it's never awkward, it's like their heart never stops talking. That friend has seen you at your worst when your world was falling apart, and instead of leaving, they stayed, holding the broken pieces with you. Maybe you met them in childhood, maybe later when life felt uncertain and lonely. But that friend appeared quietly and never left. Distance didn't break it, time didn't fade it, because real friendship doesn't demand attention; it survives on understanding. That one friend has seen the parts of you no one else could handle, and still they never judged, never walked away. So, someone's face came to mind whilst reading this, they're probably thinking of you too

5 Signs You're A Good Person: 5 characteristics reveal that you're dealing with a genuinely good person. No. 1: This person is almost always alone, not because they hate people, but because they've learned that peace is quieter when it's just them. No. 2: This person tends to think deeply about life, about people, about everything they've ever lost. No.3: They can read you faster than you think. One look, one word, and they already know your intentions. No.4: They don't trust easily; they've seen too many masks, too many promises that turned into lies. And No.5: the most important: this person has suffered more than you could imagine, but instead of becoming bitter, they became kind; instead of revenge, they chose silence.

Triangulation in Psychology: is when someone uses a third person to control or manipulate you. It's like emotional chess, except you're the piece being moved. The manipulator brings in another person, maybe a friend, a family member or even an ex-partner, to make you feel wrong, guilty or small. You'll hear things like "even your sister thinks you overreact" or "my ex never had a problem with this". The real goal is to make you doubt yourself and fight for their approval. Even when you know what's happening, it still hurts. Why? Because your brain is wired for connection, when you feel outnumbered, your nervous system panics, thinking rejection is dangerous. Imagine your partner argues with you, then says, "My mum thinks you're too sensitive" Now it's not just a fight, it's a performance for an invisible audience. That's how triangulation traps you, it feeds on your need to be understood. But once you name it, the power breaks. You can say, "This feels like triangulation. If you have an issue with me, talk to me directly," because when you see the pattern, you step out of it, and that's when you take back control of your narrative.

Why Do Some People Fear Being Noticed: There's a thing that happens when your brain mixes up being seen with being judged. It feels like your mind thinks every little action is a big test. You sit on the couch, then fix every cushion like you were never there. You want to do the laundry, but stop because people are nearby. Your brain whispers, "If they see me, they'll judge me". This isn't just shyness. It's your nervous system treating simple life moments like a performance. Like you're on stage, even when you're walking into your own kitchen. And sometimes you even worry about group chats you're not in. You imagine people thinking about you, talking about you. Your mind builds a whole courtroom, and you're the one on trial. Where does this come from? Often, from childhood, being noticed felt risky. Maybe someone said, "Don't show off", or "Who do you think you are?" So your brain learned that being visible equals danger. Back then, staying small kept you safe. But now it keeps you stuck, the truth. Most people are not judging you. They're too busy worrying about whether you're judging them. You can retrain your brain slowly. Leave one pillow out of place. Send that message without editing it 10 times. Post a simple photo. Tiny acts teach your mind. "I am safe, you don't need to shrink anymore". You get to take space. You get to exist. No apology needed.

Why Do Men Always Cry In Their Cars: It's something psychologists call delayed crying, a survival response created by the brain. When emotions rise in public, the male brain blocks them like a dam holding back a flood. Not because men don't feel, but because they were taught it's unsafe to be seen breaking. So the tears wait until the world outside fades and silence finally feels safe enough to release what's been buried for years. This isn't about tears. It's about emotional starvation. From a young age, boys are trained to exchange softness for approval and told to man up, to hide pain behind strength. Over time, the brain learns that emotions mean danger. That's why many men, even when they want to cry, simply can't. The feelings get trapped, turning into anger or quiet withdrawal. Watch a young boy at a funeral, eyes full of tears he's not allowed to shed, and you can almost see the cycle beginning again. But healing starts small. In a quiet room, watching a sad movie, letting one tear fall without shame. Because crying isn't a weakness, it's a repair. And the strongest men aren't the ones who never break. They're the ones brave enough to let their tears water their own growth.

How Is Oversharing Connected To Emotional Loneliness: Oversharing isn't just random talk. It's often a silent symptom of emotional starvation. It's what happens when the brain craves connection, but the heart fears closeness. That colleague who turns small talk into therapy sessions. That friend who vents for hours over a five-minute call. Maybe even you. When you find yourself oversharing because it's the first time someone's asked "How are you doing?", it feels like relief in the moment, but leaves you emptier right after. Because one-sided vulnerability isn't a connection, it's a temporary escape. From a psychological perspective, there are three main reasons for this. First, mirror neuron hunger. Our brains mirror emotions, so when we're lonely, we seek that reflection anywhere we can find it.

Second, the vulnerability paradox. It feels safer to open up to someone who can't really hurt us. And third, emotional spill over

. When you bottle too much for too long, it leaks at the slightest crack. So what do you do instead? Start by naming it. It's not that you're too much, it's that your connection tank is empty. Then redirect it. Text a real friend with an honest answer to How are you? And set boundaries. Ask yourself, has this person earned this piece of me? If not, write it down. Or speak it into a voice note. Let your brain release it safely before it starts reaching for strangers again.

How Unstable Men & Women Program Your Nervous System: One of the most damaging childhood environments is the mix of an emotionally absent father and an emotionally unstable mother. This combination forms what psychologists call disorganised attachment, a blueprint where people meant to protect you also become the people your nervous system learns to fear. Love becomes inconsistent, affection arrives with yelling, silence, or a sudden withdrawal. Comfort appears for a moment and collapses the next. So the child stays alert, reading tone, studying faces, shrinking their personality to avoid triggering another storm. One parent is present but distant, the other is present but unpredictable. And between these extremes, children learn to shift, perform, overthink, and adjust their entire identity to feel even a small amount of safety. Over time, love stops feeling safe at all, presence becomes a question mark, and the self slowly disappears under whichever version of them gets accepted that day. Not because they are broken, but because their nervous system was trained to survive chaos rather than connection. Survival became the first language of their childhood.

Why Your Mind Won't Let You Sleep: Why some can't sleep, no matter how exhausted they are, often has less to do with the body and more to do with the mind. Insomnia isn't just about staying awake. It's the mind refusing to rest. For some people, nighttime is the only time the world's noise goes quiet. But that silence brings up thoughts they've been avoiding all day. Worries, regrets, fears. Everything they suppress during daylight starts replaying in their heads when the lights go out. Their bodies may crave sleep, but their mind are still in survival mode, scanning for danger that isn't there anymore. It's not laziness or bad sleeping habits. It's the nervous system that's forgotten what safety feels like.

Overthinking, emotional pain, or trauma can trap the brain in alertness even when it's time to rest. That's why some people scroll endlessly on their phones, replay conversations, or stare at the ceiling. Trying to find peace in a mind that doesn't know how to stop fighting itself.

Why Good Mothers Feel Like They're Failing: Many mothers who constantly feel like they are not doing enough are not struggling because of failure, but because their brains have been trained to seek validation from everyone around them. Over time, society teaches women that this is a lie, that their worth depends on how much they give, how tidy their home is, how happy everyone else feels. Psychologists call this conditional self-worth, a belief that love must be earned through performance. Neuroscience shows that when approval becomes a survival cue, the brain releases stress hormones whenever that approval is missing. Over time, love and anxiety start to feel the same. Every quiet sigh after everyone's asleep, every unfinished list, every moment of wondering if you are enough. They all come from that invisible pressure to be perfect. This creates a mental loop of guilt and self-criticism that never stops. Even when they have done everything right, their nervous system stays alert, scanning for signs of approval. But silence often feels like rejection. What they don't realise is that love does not require proof, and worth is not measured by productivity. You are not behind. You are just living inside a system that taught you to overperform to feel enough. You were enough before you ever tried to prove your worth, and you still are.

Why Men Prefer Their Wives to Be Stay-at-Home Mothers: Many men who express a preference for their wives to stay home are not making this choice from a place of control, but because their brains have been wired to associate provision with purpose. Over time, society teaches men that their value is measured by their ability to protect and provide, that their worth depends on how secure they make their family feel, how well they fulfil the role of breadwinner, and how successfully they shield their loved ones from struggle. Psychologists call this provider identity, a belief that masculine love must be demonstrated through sacrifice and financial contribution. Neuroscience shows that when a role is tied to self-worth, the brain releases reward chemicals when that role is fulfilled and recognised. Over time, providing and being needed start to feel the same. Every extra hour worked, every promotion pursued, every moment of coming home exhausted but fulfilled by the thought of supporting a family, they all come from that invisible expectation to be the protector. This creates a mental framework in which traditional roles feel not like preferences but like biological destiny. Even when modern relationships offer different possibilities, the nervous system responds to the ancestral pattern: man provides resources, woman nurtures offspring, and the tribe survives. But this pattern was never universal; it was just heavily reinforced. What they don't realise is that partnership doesn't require rigid roles, and masculine worth isn't measured by how much their wife depends on them. Traditional structures are not inherently natural. They are just living inside a system that taught them that their value increases when they are needed in specific ways, and that a wife at home validates their success as men. Their preference was shaped long before they ever consciously chose it, and it remains even when their partners might flourish differently.

Why Some People Prefer Animals to Humans: Many people who say they prefer animals to humans are not misanthropic or broken; they are simply because their brains have learned that connecting with animals feels safer than connecting with people. Over time, experience teaches them that human relationships come with conditions, that acceptance depends on saying the right things, performing the right emotions, and meeting unspoken expectations that shift without warning. Psychologists call this relational trauma, a learned belief that human connection inevitably leads to judgment, rejection, or betrayal. Neuroscience shows that when social interactions consistently trigger threat responses, the brain begins treating human presence as a potential danger rather than a source of comfort. Over time, warmth and wariness start to feel inseparable. Every conversation that requires masking, every friendship that dissolved without explanation, every moment of feeling misunderstood despite trying, they all come from that accumulated weight of navigating human complexity. This creates a nervous system that finds relief in the simplicity of animals. A dog's love doesn't depend on your productivity. A cat doesn't care if you said the wrong thing yesterday. Their affection is immediate, honest, uncomplicated by the layers of expectation that exhaust the socially wounded. What they don't realise is that their preference isn't about animals being superior, but about humans having hurt them in ways animals cannot. Animals offer consistency where people offer chaos, presence without performance, acceptance without conditions. They are not antisocial. They are just living inside a history that taught them that human connection costs more than it gives, while animal companionship asks for nothing but existence. Their preference was shaped by disappointment long before they consciously chose it, and it persists because the nervous system remembers what the mind tries to forget: that people can wound in ways that animals never will.

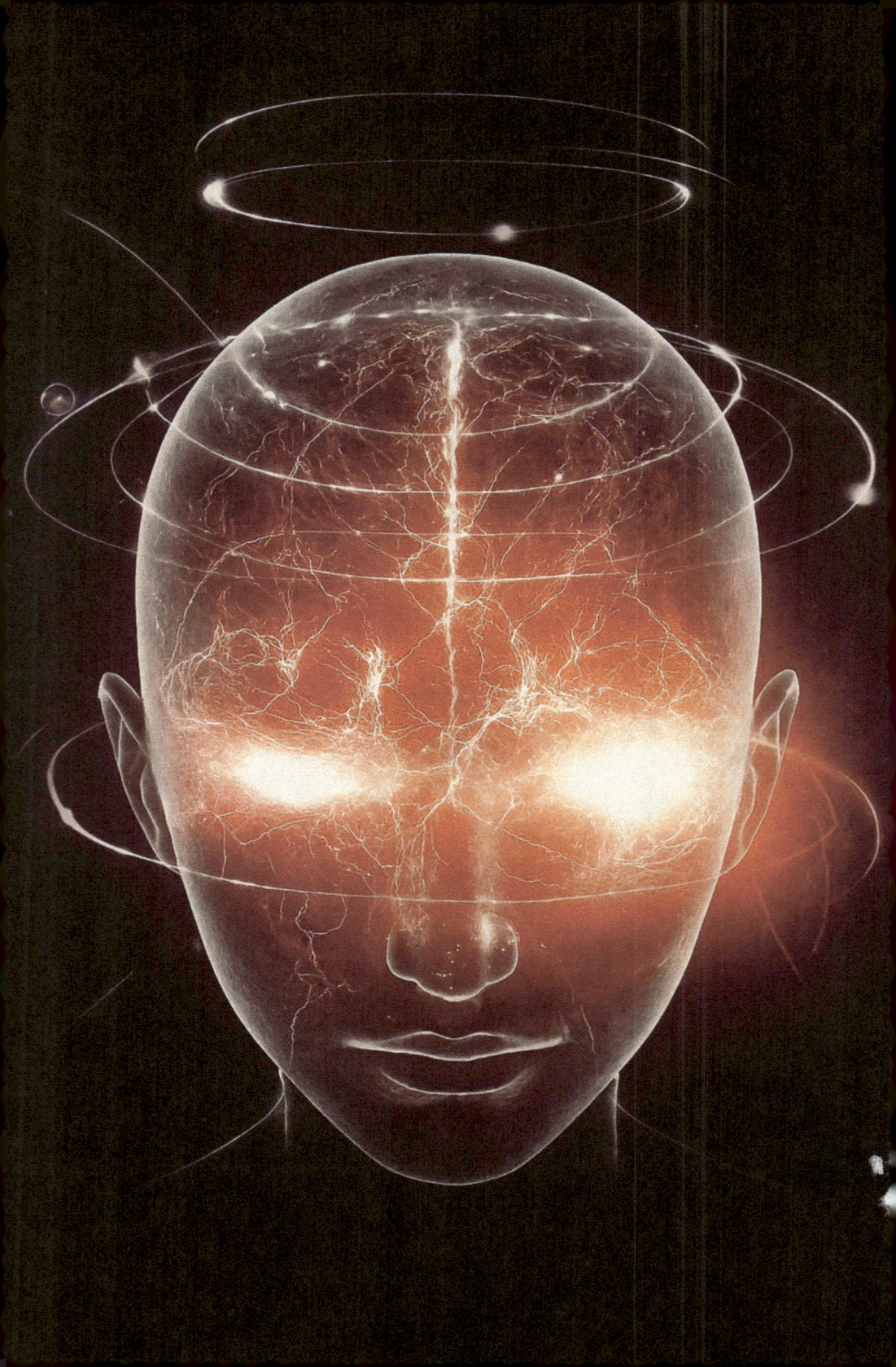

Glossary

Amygdala

The brain's threat detector. Reacts milliseconds before you're conscious of danger. Triggers fear, anger, and stress responses.

Anterior Cingulate Cortex (ACC)

The brain's "conflict monitor." Lights up when something doesn't match your beliefs or worldview. It senses emotional conflict long before you admit it.

Attachment Theory

Bowlby's idea that early relationships shape the wiring of your emotional brain. Determines how you connect, trust, and bond with others.

Basal Ganglia

Deep brain structures where habits and implicit memories live. Stores patterns you don't consciously remember learning.

Bessel van der Kolk

Trauma researcher known for *The Body Keeps the Score*. Demonstrates how trauma literally reshapes the brain and nervous system.

Cognitive Dissonance

The mental discomfort you feel when reality contradicts your beliefs. Often triggers denial, rationalisation, or emotional shutdown.

Cortisol

A stress hormone released during threat. Chronic high levels damage memory, sleep, immunity, and emotional regulation.

Damasio, Antonio

Neuroscientist behind the *somatic marker hypothesis* — the idea that the body guides decisions before the mind is aware.

Dopamine

The "motivation" neurotransmitter. Drives seeking, wanting, and pursuing rewards. Hijacked by addictions.

Dream Work

The exploration of dreams as messages from the unconscious mind. In your book, dreams are treated as dispatches from the obscure psyche.

Ego

In Freudian terms, the conscious self that tries to balance instinct, morality, and reality.

Epigenetics

The study of how trauma and environment can alter gene expression across generations.

GABA

The brain's calming chemical. Helps with relaxation, sleep, and reducing anxiety.

Hippocampus

Memory organiser. Creates autobiographical memories and contextual detail. Shrinks under chronic stress.

Hypothalamus–Pituitary Axis (HPA Axis)

The body's command centre for stress responses, hormones, and homeostasis.

Id

Freud's primal part of the mind driven by instinct, desire, and survival impulses.

Implicit Memory

Unconscious memory. Emotional residues, learned reactions, and body responses stored beneath awareness.

Inside Out (Pixar Metaphor)

Used throughout the book as a metaphor for neurotransmitter interaction and emotional regulation systems.

Insula

Brain region responsible for disgust — both physical and moral. Reacts to rot, toxins, and unethical behaviour.

Jung, Carl

Psychiatrist who developed the concept of the Shadow — the unconscious side of personality containing repressed traits.

Limbic System

The emotional brain. Includes the amygdala and hippocampus. Governs emotion, memory, and survival instincts.

Libet, Benjamin

Neuroscientist famous for experiments showing the brain initiates actions before you're aware of "deciding."

Mindsight

Daniel Siegel's term for the ability to reflect on your inner world with clarity and compassion.

Neurogenesis

The creation of new neurons, especially in the hippocampus. Continues into adulthood and is influenced by stress, environment, and behaviour.

Neuroplasticity

The brain's ability to rewire itself through experience, repetition, and emotional learning.

Norepinephrine

The brain's "alarm" chemical. Heightens alertness, vigilance, and anxiety during threat.

Oxytocin

The bonding hormone. Released through touch, trust, sex, connection, and meaningful relationships.

Pituitary Gland

The master hormone conductor. Regulates stress, bonding, growth, and emotional states.

Prefrontal Cortex (PFC)

The brain's CEO. Handles logic, self-control, planning, and emotional regulation.

Projective Identification

Klein's theory that we project unwanted feelings into others, then react as if they truly belong to them.

Repression

The unconscious blocking of painful or shameful emotions from reaching awareness.

Shadow (Jungian)

The parts of yourself you deny, disown, or refuse to acknowledge. Often revealed through impulses, projections, dreams, and body symptoms.

Somatic Marker Hypothesis

Damasio's theory: your body creates emotional "markers" that guide decisions before conscious thought.

Superego

Freud's internalised moral critic — shaped by parents, culture, and expectations.

Sympathetic Nervous System

The "fight or flight" branch. Activated by threat; speeds up heart rate, tension, and stress hormones.

Trauma Response

An autonomic reaction — fight, flight, freeze, or fawn — wired by past experiences, especially in childhood.

Unconscious Mind

The unseen part of mental life. Stores memories, impulses, emotions, and motivations outside awareness.

Ventral Vagal Complex

The "safety" system of the nervous system. Supports calmness, connection, and emotional regulation.

References

Ainsworth, M.D.S., Blehar, M.C., Waters, E. and Wall, S. (1978) *Patterns of Attachment: A Psychological Study of the Strange Situation.* Hillsdale, NJ: Erlbaum.

American Psychiatric Association (2013) *Diagnostic and Statistical Manual of Mental Disorders.* 5th edn. Washington, DC: APA.

Baumeister, R.F. and Masicampo, E.J. (2010) 'Conscious thought is for facilitating social and cultural interactions', *Psychological Review,* 117(3), pp. 945–971.

Beck, A.T. (1976) *Cognitive Therapy and the Emotional Disorders.* New York: International Universities Press.

Bowlby, J. (1969) *Attachment and Loss: Vol. 1. Attachment.* New York: Basic Books.

Bowlby, J. (1973) *Attachment and Loss: Vol. 2. Separation.* New York: Basic Books.

Carhart-Harris, R.L. and Friston, K.J. (2019) 'REBUS and the anarchic brain: Toward a unified model of the brain action of psychedelics', *Pharmacological Reviews,* 71(3), pp. 316–344.

Damasio, A. (1999) *The Feeling of What Happens: Body and Emotion in the Making of Consciousness.* New York: Harcourt.

Gazzaniga, M.S. (2011) *Who's in Charge? Free Will and the Science of the Brain.* New York: HarperCollins.

Gilbert, P. (2010) *Compassion Focused Therapy.* London: Routledge.

Harlow, H.F. and Zimmermann, R.R. (1959) 'Affectional responses in the infant monkey', *Science,* 130(3373), pp. 421–432.

Johnson, R.A. (1991) *Owning Your Own Shadow: Understanding the Dark Side of the Psyche*. New York: HarperOne.

Jung, C.G. (1959) *Aion: Researches into the Phenomenology of the Self*. London: Routledge & Kegan Paul.

Jung, C.G. (1961) *Memories, Dreams, Reflections*. New York: Vintage Books.

Jung, C.G. (1968) *The Archetypes and the Collective Unconscious*. 2nd edn. Princeton, NJ: Princeton University Press.

LeDoux, J. (1996) *The Emotional Brain: The Mysterious Underpinnings of Emotional Life*. New York: Simon & Schuster.

LeDoux, J. (2002) *Synaptic Self: How Our Brains Become Who We Are*. New York: Penguin.

Porges, S.W. (2011) *The Polyvagal Theory: Neurophysiological Foundations of Emotions, Attachment, Communication, and Self-Regulation*. New York: Norton.

Rosenberg, M. (1965) *Society and the Adolescent Self-Image*. Princeton, NJ: Princeton University Press.

Sapolsky, R. (2004) *Why Zebras Don't Get Ulcers*. 3rd edn. New York: Henry Holt.

Schore, A.N. (2012) *The Science of the Art of Psychotherapy*. New York: Norton.

Siegel, D.J. (2012) *The Developing Mind: How Relationships and the Brain Interact to Shape Who We Are*. 2nd edn. New York: Guilford Press.

Squire, L.R. (2004) 'Memory systems of the brain', *Neurobiology of Learning and Memory*, 82(3), pp. 171–177.

Tulving, E. (2002) 'Episodic memory: From mind to brain', *Annual Review of Psychology*, 53, pp. 1–25.

van der Kolk, B. (2014) *The Body Keeps the Score: Brain, Mind, and Body in the Healing of Trauma.* New York: Viking.

von Franz, M-L. (1996) *Shadow and Evil in Fairy Tales.* Boston: Shambhala.

About The Author

Josiah Cornell is not just an author; he's a catalyst for transformation.

You know that feeling when someone says exactly what you've been thinking but were too afraid to admit? That's what happens when you encounter Josiah Cornell's work. It's not comfortable. It won't let you off easy. But it will change you.

Josiah doesn't write from some ivory tower, preaching theories he's never lived. He's been in the trenches, literally. Over a decade working in prisons, probation services, domestic violence intervention, local government, the places where society's cracks become canyons and people fall through. He's sat across from men and women that most of us cross the street to avoid, and he's listened. Really listened. To their chaos, their pain, their surprising resilience. He's seen what breaks people and what puts them back together.

But here's what makes him different: he's not just an observer. Josiah's walked through his own fire. Trauma. Addiction. The kind of darkness that either destroys you or teaches you everything you need to know about being human. He doesn't just understand struggle academically, he studied Criminology, Counselling, Mental health and Psychology at South Essex College and East London University, sure, but he's lived it in his bones. That's why his words land differently. They don't just inform you, they find you.

When readers call his books "a lifeline" or "the book I didn't know I needed," they're not exaggerating. His self-help work speaks directly to the parts of you that feel invisible, the parts you've learned to hide because the world isn't safe enough to show them. His fantasy fiction? It's not just escapism. It's mythology with purpose, cinematic storytelling that entertains while sneaking meaning past your defences.

And then there's his music. Because of course there is, with his ADHD brain, Josiah shifts from page to stage, you get the same raw honesty wrapped in rhythm, narratives that pulse with genuine emotion. You can find it on any platform, waiting to soundtrack whatever you're going through.

Look, if you're tired of sanitised advice and surface-level insights, if you want someone who'll tell you the truth even when it's uncomfortable, especially when it's uncomfortable, you've just found your person. Josiah doesn't just write about transformation. He embodies it. And he's inviting you to do the same.

The question is: are you ready?

Also By

If you enjoyed The Neuroscience of The Shadow, you might also like:

- **Who am I Without the Trauma - A Journey Back to Yourself** - A transformative resource and a heartfelt journal designed for anyone stuck in survival mode, trying to make sense of their overwhelming experiences.
- **The Masculine Crisis** - In depth exploration of contemporary masculinity, The book combines personal stories, social cultural analysis and candid reflections to challenge and redefine outdated ideals associated with manhood.
- **Breaking The Silence - The Truth About Domestic Violence** - Get ready to delve into a powerful and illuminating exploration of one of societies most pressing and often hidden crisis.
- **The Rise & Fall of Starmer and The Labour Party** - A political fiction that analyses the trajectory of Kier Starmer political career and the fate of the Labour Party.
- **The Emerald Guardians - Hougan Manor** - A ground-breaking dark epic fantasy that is immersive as it is gripping

www.ingramcontent.com/pod-product-compliance
Lightning Source LLC
Chambersburg PA
CBHW062112040426
42337CB00043B/3705